Lecture Notes in Control and Information Sciences

Edited by A. V. Balakrishnan and M. Thoma

Lecture Notes in Control and Information Sciences

Edited by A.V. Balakrishnan and M. Thoma

8

Ruth F. Curtain
Anthony J. Pritchard

Infinite Dimensional Linear Systems Theory

Springer-Verlag
Berlin Heidelberg GmbH 1978

Authors
Dr. Ruth F. Curtain
Control Theory Centre,
University of Warwick
presently at:
Rijksuniversiteit te Groningen
Mathematisch Instituut
Groningen Netherlands

Dr. Anthony J. Pritchard
Director, Control Theory Centre
University of Warwick
Coventry CV4 7AL
United Kingdom

ISBN 978-3-540-08961-2 ISBN 978-3-540-35683-7 (eBook)
DOI 10.1007/978-3-540-35683-7

Originally published by Springer-Verlag Berlin Heidelberg New York in 1978

2061/3020-543210

PREFACE

Over the past five years the major research effort of the Control Theory Centre at the University of Warwick has been in the area of infinite dimensional system theory. The philosophy underlying the research has been to develop a mathematical framework which enables the generalisation of the finite dimensional results to infinite dimensions and which includes both distributed parameter systems and differential delay systems as special cases. So following the lead of Fattorini in [6], we describe the system dynamics in terms of a strongly continuous semigroup on an appropriate Banach space. Using this unifying mathematical approach it is possible to clarify the essential concepts of observability, controllability, the quadratic cost control problem, and the estimation and control problems for stochastic systems. At this stage we feel it is appropriate to present the culmination of this collective effort in a coordinated way in the form of lecture notes.

Of course it has not been possible to cover all of the systems theory concepts, and significant omissions are realization theory and identification. Readers interested in these areas should see for instance [11] and watch out for the forthcoming monograph by Fuhrmann [7]. We hope, however, that these notes will provide an introduction to infinite dimensional system theory, accessible to readers with a knowledge of finite dimensional theory and some functional analysis. The treatment of the material reflects our own personal approach and is by no means the only way or even the most commonly accepted way. While it is aesthetically pleasing that the abstract formulation yields results which mirror those for finite dimensions; because the state space is infinite dimensional this superficial resemblance can be misleading. Consequently we have examined the implications of the abstract theory to specific examples of distributed and delay systems.

Many other researchers have contributed to infinite dimensional systems theory, some using a semigroup approach and others using methods appropriate for special classes of systems. For example Butkovskii [2] and Lions [9] have examined optimal control problems for deterministic distributed parameter systems and Bensoussan [1] estimation and control of stochastic distributed systems. The pioneering work on controllability and observability of hyperbolic and parabolic partial differential equations was developed by Fattorini [5] and Russell[12],whilst Kirillova [8], Manitius [10], Banks [4] and Lee [3] have contributed to the study of differential delay systems. It has not been possible to include all of these special results for particular systems in these notes. What we have tried to do, however, is to illustrate through the examples how many of these special results may be obtained using an abstract semigroup approach and at the end of each chapter included references of other contributions.

The first chapter reviews the types of finite dimensional systems theory results which will be generalized to infinite dimensions in chapters 3-7 and gives several examples of how such problems may arise in distributed and delay systems. To make these notes self-contained, chapter 2 presents the known results on semigroups, which we shall need in later chapters. Chapters 3-7 form the core of the book, namely the extension of the finite dimensional systems theory results outlined in Chapter 1 for time-invariant linear systems. All these results are proved in detail and are illustrated by several examples and would be appropriate for an introductory graduate course in linear systems theory. Chapters 8 & 9 are concerned with extensions of the results of Chapters 3-7 to more complicated systems, namely time dependent systems and distributed systems allowing for boundary control and point observations. The difficulties which arise in trying to extend the results to more general systems are technical mathematical ones rather than conceptual ones. As the technical details are already available in the literature, we have chosen to motivate the approach using simple examples and have omitted proofs which are heavy technical extensions of those in earlier chapters. So although a complete presentation of the results is available in Chapters 8 and 9, many proofs are given in outline only. Again, considerable attention is given to analyzing the implications for distributed and delay systems by means of examples.

These lecture notes have been influenced by the many visitors to the Control Theory Centre and especially by the SRC [1] funded research fellows, S.P. Banks, A. Ichikawa, E.P. Ryan, R. Triggiani, A. Wirth and J. Zabczyk. It is also a pleasure to pay tribute to the former directors of the Centre, Professor L. Markus and Professor P.C. Parks, for their guidance

---

[1] Science Research Council (United Kingdom) which has supported the Control Theory Centre from its inception in 1970.

and encouragement in our research, and to Professor J.L. Douce and Professor J.A. Shercliff of the Engineering Department for their continuing support of the Centre. Finally special thanks to Frances Ryan for transforming a largely illegible manuscript into a respectable typescript.

A.J. Pritchard, Director of Control Theory Centre,
University of Warwick.

Ruth F. Curtain, Control Theory Centre,
University of Warwick.
(presently at: Mathematics Institute,
Rijksuniversiteit Groningen.)

References

[1] Bensoussan, A. Filtrage optimal des systemes lineaires, Dunod 1971.

[2] Butkovskii, A.G. Theory of optimal control of distributed parameter systems, American Elsevier, 1969.

[3] Chyung, D.H. and Lee, E.B. Delayed action control problems, Automatica, 6 (1970), pp.395-400.

[4] Eller, D.H., Aggarwal, J.K. and Banks, H.T. Optimal control of linear time-delay systems, IEEE Trans., AC 14 (1969), pp.678-687.

[5] Fattorini, H.O. On complete controllability of linear systems, J. Diff. Eqns., 3 (1967), pp.391-402.

[6] Fattorini, H.O. Time optimal control of solutions of operational differential equations, SIAM J. Control, 21 (1964) pp.54-59.

[7] Fuhrmann, P.A. Notes on operators and systems, to appear.

[8] Kirillova, F.M. and Chirakova, S.V. Relative controllability of systems with time lag, Dok. Akad. Nauk. USSR, 176 (1967) pp.1260-1263.

[9] Lions, J.L. Optimal control of systems described by partial differential equations, Springer 1971.

[10] Manitius, A. Optimal control of time lag systems with quadratic performance indices, lV IFAC Congress, Warsaw 1969.

[11] Ray, W.H. and Lainiotis, D.G. (Eds), Identification, estimation and control of distributed parameter systems, Marcel-Dekker, 1977.

[12] Russell, D.L. Nonharmonic Fourier series in the control theory of distributed parameter systems, J. Math. Anal. Appl., 18 (1967), pp.542-559.

TABLE OF CONTENTS

CHAPTER 1

INTRODUCTION

Most dynamical systems which describe processes in engineering, physics, and economics are extremely complex and the identification of mathematical models is difficult. Consequently, early investigations of systems were confined mainly to analysing stability behaviour of very simple models using frequency domain methods. In the last fifteen or so years the state space approach has also become very popular and several new systems theory concepts such as controllability, observability, linear quadratic control, estimation and filtering, and realisation have been introduced and analysed [1],[4],[5],[9],[10]. However, these concepts are only well understood for simple systems, namely linear difference equations and linear ordinary differential equations. In the engineering jargon these simple systems are called lumped systems and they can be described by linear maps on finite dimensional linear vector spaces. For systems described by partial differential equations (distributed systems) or by delay equations the appropriate state space is an infinite dimensional function space and there has been some work on generalizing the systems theory concepts to special classes of these systems [2],[6],[7],[8].

Using a semigroup representation, we develop a self contained abstract theory for a wide class of linear systems, both finite and infinite dimensional which includes lumped, delay and distributed systems. Results are obtained which, when interpreted for a particular class of system, yields the known results. Moreover, the abstract approach clarifies the main ideas and mathematical problems so that new results are more easily obtained.

We do not consider all the systems theory concepts here, but first concentrate on controllability, observability and stabilizability which turn out to be more complicated in infinite dimensions. We then consider the quadratic cost control problem and its dual, the filtering problem, and obtain the separation principle for infinite dimensional stochastic systems. To motivate our approach we present a brief survey of the finite dimensional theory concepts and results which we will generalize in Chapters 2 - 7.

Finite dimensional linear systems theory

Here we restrict ourselves to systems which are described by linear ordinary differential equations with a given initial state. Without loss of generality, we suppose that by a suitable choice of state vector the system has been expressed in the canonical form

(1.1) $$\dot{z} = Az + Bu \;; \quad z(0) = z_o$$

where z_o, $z(t) \in R^n$, $u(t) \in R^m$, A and B are $n \times n$ and $n \times m$ real matrices respectively. u is the control term.
(1.1) is a differential equation on the state space R^n and has the unique solution

(1.2) $$z(t) = e^{At}z_o + \int_o^t e^{A(t-s)}Bu(s)\,ds$$

We also suppose that we have an associated observation of (1.1)

(1.3) $$y = Cz$$

where C is a real $k \times n$ matrix, so $y \in R^k$.

The following concepts of stability, controllability and observability for (1.1) and (1.3) are now standard.

Definition 1.1 Exponential stability

The matrix A in (1.1) is exponentially stable if there exists positive constants M, ω such that

$$\|e^{At}\| \le Me^{-\omega t} \quad \text{for all } t \ge 0.$$

This implies that for the uncontrolled system (1.1) (with u = 0), $\|z(t)\| \to 0$ as $t \to \infty$. A necessary and sufficient condition for the exponential stability of A is that the real parts of its eigenvalues are strictly negative.

If one uses a feedback control $u = -Fz$, then (1.1) becomes $\dot{z} = (A-BF)z$ and this type of control can be used to stabilize an unstable system $\dot{z} = Az$.

Definition 1.2 Stabilizability

(1.1) or (A,B) is stabilizable if there exists an $m \times n$ matrix F, such that A-BF is exponentially stable.

Another important systems theory concept is whether or not a preassigned final state can be reached.

Definition 1.3 Controllability

(1.1) or (A,B) is controllable if any initial point z_o can be steered to an arbitrary final point z in some finite time t_1 by some control $u \in L_\infty(0,t_1;R^m)$.

(A,B) is controllable if and only if the following $n \times nm$ matrix has rank n : $[B : AB : A^2B : \dots : A^{n-1}B]$.

It happens that if (A,B) is controllable, then (A,B) is stabilizable. Controllability is also related to observability.

Definition 1.4 Observability

We say that (1.1),(1.3) or (A,C) is observable if $Ce^{At}z_o = 0$ for all $t \geq 0$ implies $z_o = 0$. That is for the controlled system (1.1),(1.3), a knowledge of y(t) and u(t) on a finite time interval $[0,t_1]$ uniquely determines the initial state z_o.

(A,C) is observable if and only if the rank of the following $n \times kn$ matrix is n : $[C' : A'C' : \dots : (A')^{n-1}C']$.

So controllability and observability are dual concepts in the sense that (A,C) is observable if and only if (A',C') is controllable.

If the controller and/or observer is designed so that the system is stable and controllable or observable, then the question of optimality can be considered.

The quadratic control problem (regulator problem)

Consider (1.1) and the cost functional

$$J(u) = z(t_1)'Gz(t_1) + \int_0^{t_1} \{z(t)'Mz(t) + u(t)'Ru(t)\}dt \tag{1.4}$$

when G, M and R are real symmetric $n \times n$, $n \times n$, and $m \times m$ matrices respectively, with $G \geq 0$, $M \geq 0$ and $R > 0$. The regulator problem is to find an optimal control $u^* \in L_2(0,t_1;R^m)$ such that (1.4) is minimized. Under the above assumptions, there exists a unique optimal control

$$u^*(t) = -R^{-1}B'Q(t)z(t) \tag{1.5}$$

where Q(t) is an $n \times n$ real symmetric matrix which is the unique solution of the Riccati equation

$$\begin{cases} \dot{Q}(t) + Q(t)A + A'Q(t) + M = Q(t)BR^{-1}B'Q(t) \\ Q(t_1) = G \end{cases} \tag{1.6}$$

The optimal cost is $J(u^*) = z_o'Q(0)z_o$.

For $G = 0$ and $t_1 = \infty$ we have the infinite time regulator problem and if (A,B) and $(A',M^{\frac{1}{2}})$ are stabilizable, there exists a unique optimal feedback control of the form (1.5), where Q is time invariant and is the unique solution of the algebraic Riccati equation

$$QA + A'Q + M = QBR^{-1}B'Q \tag{1.7}$$

The filtering problem

We consider a noisy signal process and a noisy observation process described by the following stochastic differential equations

$$dz(t) = Az(t)dt + Ddw(t) \;; \qquad z(0) = z_o \tag{1.8}$$

$$dy(t) = Cz(t)dt + Fdv(t) \tag{1.9}$$

where A, D, C and F are real $n \times n$, $n \times m$, $k \times n$, $k \times k$ matrices, z_o is a Gaussian zero mean vector random variable with covariance matrix P_o, and $w(t)$ and $v(t)$ are independent vector-valued Wiener processes of dimensions n and k and incremental covariance matrices W and V respectively. The solution of (1.8) is a zero mean Gaussian stochastic process with continuous sample paths and is given by

$$z(t) = e^{At}z_o + \int_0^t e^{A(t-s)}Ddw(s) \tag{1.10}$$

The filtering problem is to find the best estimate $\hat{z}(t)$ of the signal process $z(t)$ based on the observations $y(s)$, $0 \le s \le t$.

The solution is the well-known Kalman Bucy filter; $\hat{z}(t) = E\{z(t) \mid y(s);\ 0 \le s \le t\}$, which is given by

$$\begin{cases} d\hat{z}(t) = \{A - P(t)C'(FVF')^{-1}C\}\hat{z}(t)dt + P(t)C'(FVF')^{-1}dy(t) \\ \hat{z}(0) = 0 \end{cases} \tag{1.11}$$

where $P(t)$ is the unique solution of the Riccati equation

$$\begin{cases} \dot{P}(t) = AP(t) + P(t)A' + D'WD - P(t)C'(FVF')^{-1}CP(t) \\ P(0) = P_o \end{cases} \tag{1.12}$$

$P(t)$ is the covariance of the error process, i.e.

$$P(t) = E\{[z(t) - \hat{z}(t)]\,[z(t) - \hat{z}(t)]'\} \tag{1.13}$$

If (A',C') and $(A,DW^{\frac{1}{2}})$ are stabilizable, then the filter is stable in the sense that measures induced by $P(t)$ converge as $t_1 \to \infty$ to P, the unique solution of the algebraic Riccati equation

$$PA' + AP + DWD' = PC'(FVF')^{-1}CP \tag{1.14}$$

The Riccati equations (1.12) for filtering and (1.6) for the regulator problem are equivalent if in (1.12) we replace A by A', P(t) by $Q(t_1-t)$, D'WD by M, C by B', FVF' by R and P_o by G. A similar substitution shows that (1.14) and (1.7) are also of the same form. This relationship is known as the duality between the control and the filtering problem.

The smoothing problem and prediction problem are also of interest and are concerned with estimating z(t) based on the observations y(s), $0 \le s \le t_1$, where $t_1 > t$ for the smoothing problem and $t_1 < t$ for the prediction problem. The best optimal predictor $\hat{z}(t|t_1)$ satisfies the stochastic differential equation

$$(1.15)\qquad \begin{aligned} \dot{\hat{z}}(t|t_1) &= A\hat{z}(t|t_1) \\ \hat{z}(t_1|t_1) &= \hat{z}(t_1) \end{aligned}$$

where $\hat{z}(t_1)$ is the best optimal filter up to time t_1. The best linear smoother is also given in terms of the optimal filter $\hat{z}(t)$

$$(1.16)\qquad \begin{cases} d\hat{z}(t|t_1) = A\hat{z}(t|t_1)dt + D'WD\lambda(t)dt + P(t)C'(FVF')^{-1}C\hat{z}(t)dt \\ \hat{z}(t_1|t_1) = \hat{z}(t_1) \end{cases}$$

where

$$(1.17)\qquad \begin{cases} d\lambda(t) = -(A-P(t)C(FVF')^{-1}C)'\lambda(t)-C'(FVF')^{-1}(dy(t)-C\hat{z}(t)dt) \\ \lambda(t_1) = 0 \end{cases}$$

and P(t) is the covariance operator of (1.12).

<u>The stochastic quadratic cost control problem</u>

We consider the stochastic controlled differential equation

$$(1.18)\qquad dz(t) = Az(t)dt + Bu(t)dt + Ddw(t)\ ;\qquad z(0) = z_o$$

with the noisy observation process

$$(1.19)\qquad dy(t) = Cz(t)dt + Fdv(t)$$

where we make the same assumptions on A, D, W, z_o, C, F and V as for the filtering problem. B is a real n × m matrix and u(t) is an admissible stochastic control. By admissible we mean that $u \in L_2(\Omega,p;L_2(0,t_1;R^m))$ and depends only on the past observations, y(s); $0 \le s \le t$. The stochastic control problem is to find the admissible control which minimizes the expected value of the cost J(u) given by (1.4). The solution is usually termed the separation principle, because the optimal control strategy is to use the deterministic feedback law of (1.5), replacing z(t) by its conditional expectation $\hat{z}(t)$, which is obtained using the

Kalman Bucy filter results. More precisely, the optimal control strategy is given by

$$u^*(t) = -R^{-1}B'Q(t)\hat{z}(t) \tag{1.20}$$

$$\begin{cases} d\hat{z}(t) = \{A-P(t)C'(FVF')^{-1} - BR^{-1}B'Q(t)\}\hat{z}(t)dt + \\ \qquad\qquad + P(t)C'(FVF')^{-1}dy(t) \\ \hat{z}(0) = 0 \end{cases} \tag{1.21}$$

where Q(t) and P(t) are the solutions of (1.6) and (1.12) respectively. The optimal cost is then

$$\text{trace}\{GP(t_1)\} + \int_0^{t_1}\text{trace}\{MP(s)\}ds + \int_0^{t_1}\text{trace}\{Q(s)P(s)C'(FVF')^{-1}CP(s)\}ds$$

To motivate the generalisation of the above systems theory to infinite dimensions, we present several simple examples of delay and distributed systems where questions of stability, controllability, and optimality might arise.

Examples of linear infinite dimensional systems

Example 1.1

Suppose we have a thin, narrow, homogeneous, continuous material strip which is fed into a furnace by means of a variable-speed transport mechanism. Then its temperature distribution can be modelled by the diffusion equation

$$z_t(x,t) = \mu z_{xx}(x,t) + v(t)z_x(x,t) + \sigma\{z(x,t)-u(x,t)\}$$

$$z_x(0,t) = 0 = z_x(1,t)$$

where z is the temperature distribution, μ is the coefficient of diffusivity, σ is a constant proportional to the surface conductivity of the material, v is the material-strip velocity, and u(x,t) is the external temperature distribution of the strip. We shall suppose that we can control u and that it is desirable to keep the outlet temperature z(1,t) at some preassigned temperature $\theta(t)$ say. Thus we are led to the controllability problem of whether the desired outlet temperature can be achieved and maintained. In general this will be impossible, and so instead we may seek to minimize the functional

$$J = \int_0^{t_1} \{z(1,t)-\theta(t)\}^2 dt$$

Usually the controls are constrained and we can express this by assuming $|u(t)| \leq 1$ say, or by including a penalty for using too much control in the functional J.

Example 1.2

In steel making plants it is necessary to estimate the temperature distribution of metal slabs based on measurements at certain points on the surface. A possible model for the temperature distribution is

$$\rho C_1 z_t(x,t) = k z_{xx}(x,t) - \alpha[z(x,t) - z_o(x,t)] + \xi(x,t) \; ; \quad 0 < x < 1$$

$$z_x(0,t) = 0 = z_x(1,t)$$

where ρ, C_1, k are the density, heat capacity, and effective thermal conductivity of the metal slab, α is a heat transfer parameter, z_o is the average coolant temperature, and $\xi(x,t)$ is some distributed white noise disturbance. The problem is to estimate the temperature profile $z(x,t)$; $0 \leq x \leq 1$, $t > 0$, based on the noisy measurements

$$y_i(t) = z(x_i,t) + \eta_i(t) \; ; \quad i=1,2,\ldots,k$$

where x_i, $i=1,\ldots,k$ are points on the surface of the slab and $\eta_i(t)$ represents the measurement error.

Example 1.3

The evolution of the population of a country can be described by the following linear hyperbolic partial differential equation

$$\frac{\partial p(t,r)}{\partial t} + \frac{\partial p(t,r)}{\partial r} = -\mu(t,r)p(t,r)$$

$$p(0,r) = p_o(r) \; ; \quad 0 \leq r \leq 1$$

$$p(t,0) = u(t) \; ; \quad 0 \leq t \leq t_1$$

where $p(t,r)$ represents the population density of individuals of age r at time t, $\mu(t,r)$ is the mortality function, $p_o(r)$ is the given initial age distribution and $u(t)$ is the birth rate which we assume is the control variable. The problem is to choose u so as to achieve a desired age profile $q(r)$ at the final time t_1, and mathematically we could interpret this as minimizing

$$J(u) = \int_0^1 \{p(t_1,r) - q(r)\}^2 dr + \int_0^{t_1} \lambda u^2(s) ds$$

where the second term measures the social cost of controlling birthrate.

Example 1.4

Suppose we have a stretched nonuniform string whose motion is described by

$$\rho(x) z_{tt}(x,t) - \Big(\alpha(x) z_x(x,t)\Big)_x = v(x,t)$$

$$z(0,t) = 0 \; ; \quad z(1,t) = u(t)$$

where $z(x,t)$ is the displacement of the string at position x, $\rho(x)$ is the density distribution of the string, $\alpha(x)$ is a scaled tensile parameter, and u is the control at the end of the string and v is a distributed control. We may be concerned with whether we can choose u or v to bring the string to rest. Alternatively, we may wish to minimize the cost functional

$$J(u) = \int_0^{t_1}\int_0^1 [z^2(x,t)+\lambda_1 v^2(x,t)]\,dx\,dt+\lambda_2\int_0^{t_1} u^2(t)\,dt$$

where λ_1, λ_2 are positive constants. Physically this can be interpreted as keeping the string as close to zero over $[0,t_1]\times[0,1]$, while using as little control, as possible.

Example 1.5

In the economic modelling of a trade cycle Kalecki [3] obtained a model for fluctuations of capital stock $K(t)$ in the form

$$\dot{K}(t) = aK(t) + bK(t-h) + cu(t)$$

where a, b, c are constants, and the delay h represents the time lag between the moment of decision to invest and the moment of deliveries of capital equipment. The control problem could be to obtain a desired level of stock K_d at a time t_1, or to maintain it at that level for an interval of time $[t_1,t_1+h]$. Alternatively it may be desired to stabilize the system by a feedback control, or to regulate the system so that the functional

$$J = \int_0^{t_1}\{(K(t)-K_d)^2 + \lambda u^2(t)\}dt$$

is minimized.

Comments

The above examples are only a small typical sample of problems which arise in applications. Many more examples will be found in references [2], [6], [7], [8].

In the next six chapters we will develop an abstract theory for time invariant infinite dimensional systems, which will yield solutions to Examples 1.1, 1.2, Example 1.4 with $u = 0$, and 1.5 when the coefficients are time invariant. However this theory is not applicable to Example 1.3 or to Example 1.4 with $u \neq 0$, where the control is implemented on the boundary of the domain of the system. Control problems with limited control action and estimation problems with limited sensing occur frequently in applications, so in Chapter 8 we show how the theory can be generalized to cover this important class of problems. Finally in

Chapter 9 we generalize all the previous theory to allow for time dependent systems and so all of the above examples fall within the scope of these lecture notes.

While Chapters 2 to 7 are a self-contained, detailed development of infinite dimensional systems theory for time invariant systems, by contrast, the style of Chapters 8 and 9 is expository. The aim here is to motivate the abstract formulation of the extra technical conditions required for time-dependence and limited sensing and control, and only an outline of the proofs is given.

References

[1] Brockett, R.W. Finite dimensional linear systems, Wiley, 1970.

[2] Butkovskii, A.G. Theory of optimal control of distributed parameter systems, American Elsevier, 1969.

[3] Kalecki, A. A macrodynamic theory of business cycles, Econometrica, 3 (1935).

[4] Kalman, R.E., Falb, P.L., Arbib, M.A. Topics in mathematical systems theory, McGraw-Hill, 1969.

[5] Lee, E.B., Markus, L., Foundations of optimal control theory, Wiley, 1967.

[6] Lions, J.L. Optimal control of systems described by partial differential equations, Springer, 1971.

[7] Wang, P.K.C. Bibliography of distributed parameter systems, Int. J. Control, 7 (1968).

[8] Wang, P.K.C. Control of distributed parameter systems; in Advances in control systems, ed. by C.T. Leondes, Academic Press, 1, 1964.

[9] Wolovich, W.A. Linear multivariable systems, Applied Math. Sciences, 11, Springer, 1974.

[10] Wonham, W.M. Linear multivariable control; A geometric approach, Lecture Notes in Economics and Math. Systems, 101, Springer, 1974.

CHAPTER 2

SEMIGROUP THEORY

The examples of infinite dimensional systems we introduced in Chapter 1 were either partial or delay differential equations. In this Chapter our aim is to describe an abstract formulation

$$\dot{z} = Az + Bu \;; \quad z(0) = z_0 \tag{2.1}$$

which will enable us to present a unified treatment of these and finite dimensional systems.

Suppose $z_0 \in Z$ is the state at time zero of a dynamical system defined on a Banach space Z, and the state at time t is z(t). If we assume that the dynamics which govern the evolution from z_0 to z(t) are linear and autonomous, then we can for each time t define a linear operator T_t, such that

$$T_t : Z \to Z \;; \quad T_0 = I \text{ (identity on Z)} \tag{2.2}$$

$$z(t) = T_t z_0 \tag{2.3}$$

Let us also assume that the state of our dynamical system satisfies the Hadamard well-posed conditions, namely

a) it is unique

b) it varies continuously with the initial state.

From the uniqueness, z(t+s) is the same point in Z as the point reached by allowing the dynamics to evolve from z(s) for a time t, from all initial points $z_0 \in Z$, hence

$$z(t+s) = T_{t+s} z_0 = T_t z(s) = T_t T_s z_0$$

$$T_{t+s} = T_t T_s$$

Since we are assuming the state varies continuously with the initial state z_0, we know T_t is a bounded map on Z, and finally we impose some smoothness on the trajectory z(t), and assume that $z(t) \to z_0$ as $t \to 0^+$ for all $z_0 \in Z$, that is

$$\|T_t z_0 - z_0\| \to 0 \quad \text{as} \quad t \to 0^+$$

<u>Definition 2.1 A strongly continuous semigroup</u>

A strongly continuous semigroup is a map T_t from R^+ to $\mathcal{L}(Z)$, which satisfies

$$T_{t+s} = T_t T_s \qquad 0 \le s \le t \tag{2.4}$$

(2.5) $$T_o = I$$

(2.6) $$\|T_t z_o - z_o\| \to 0 \quad \text{as} \quad t \to 0^+ \quad \forall\, z_o \in Z$$

Example 2.2

Let $A \in \mathcal{L}(Z)$, and set

(2.7) $$e^{At} = \sum_{n=o}^{\infty} \frac{(At)^n}{n!}$$

Clearly, the right hand side converges in the uniform topology and it is easy to verify conditions (2.4),(2.5),(2.6), so e^{At} is a strongly continuous semigroup, and in fact is uniformly continuous.

Example 2.3

Let Z be the Banach space of continuous, bounded functions on $[0,\infty)$ with the sup-norm, and consider the translation operator

(2.8) $$(T_t z)(x) = z(x+t) \ ; \quad z \in Z, \quad x \geq 0$$

Clearly, (2.4),(2.5) are satisfied, and for (2.6) we have

$$\|T_t z_o - z_o\| = \sup_{x \geq 0} |z_o(x+t) - z_o(x)|$$

$$\to 0 \text{ as } t \to 0^+$$

Example 2.4

Let $\{\phi_n\}$ n=1,2,... be an orthonormal sequence in a separable Hilbert space, and $\{\lambda_n\}$ n=1,2,... be a sequence of complex numbers, then

(2.9) $$T_t z = \sum_{n=1}^{\infty} e^{\lambda_n t} \phi_n \langle \phi_n, z \rangle$$

is a bounded linear operator if and only if $\{e^{\lambda_n t}\}$ is a bounded sequence, and this is the case if

$$\sup_n \operatorname{Re}\{\lambda_n\} < \infty$$

Under this assumption, we have

$$T_{t+s} z = \sum_{n=1}^{\infty} e^{\lambda_n (t+s)} \phi_n \langle \phi_n, z \rangle$$

and

$$T_t T_s z = \sum_{n=1}^{\infty} e^{\lambda_n t} \phi_n \langle \phi_n, T_s z \rangle$$

$$= \sum_{n=1}^{\infty} e^{\lambda_n t} \phi_n \langle \phi_n, \sum_{m=1}^{\infty} e^{\lambda_m s} \phi_m \langle \phi_m, z \rangle \rangle$$

$$= \sum_{n=1}^{\infty} e^{\lambda_n t} e^{\lambda_n s} \phi_n \langle \phi_n, z \rangle = T_{t+s} z$$

Clearly (2.5) is satisfied, and

$$\begin{aligned} \|T_t z - z\|^2 &= \sum_{n=1}^{\infty} |e^{\lambda_n t} - 1|^2 |\langle \phi_n, z\rangle|^2 \\ &= \sum_{n=1}^{N} |e^{\lambda_n t} - 1|^2 |\langle \phi_n, z\rangle|^2 + \sum_{n>N} |e^{\lambda_n t} - 1|^2 |\langle \phi_n, z\rangle|^2 \\ &\leq \sup_{n=1,..,N} |e^{\lambda_n t} - 1|^2 \sum_{n=1}^{N} |\langle \phi_n, z\rangle|^2 + K \sum_{n>N} |\langle \phi_n, z\rangle|^2 \end{aligned}$$

for some K. But for N sufficiently large and any $\varepsilon > 0$,

$$\sum_{n>N} |\langle \phi_n, z\rangle|^2 < \varepsilon$$

Hence T_t is a strongly continuous semigroup.

Some elementary properties of semigroups are contained in the following theorem.

Theorem 2.5

Let T_t be a strongly continuous semigroup on a Banach space Z, then

(a) $\|T_t\|$ is bounded on every finite subinterval of $[0,\infty)$

(b) $\forall\, z \in Z$, $T_t z$ is strongly continuous

(c) if $\omega_o = \inf_{t>o} \left(\frac{1}{t} \log\|T_t\|\right)$, then $\omega_o = \lim_{t\to\infty} \left(\frac{1}{t} \log\|T_t\|\right) < \infty$

(d) $\forall\, \omega > \omega_o$, $\exists$ a constant M_ω such that $\forall\, t \geq 0$, $\|T_t\| \leq M_\omega e^{\omega t}$

Proof

a) First we show that $\|T_t\|$ is bounded on some neighbourhood of the origin, that is $\exists\, \delta > 0$ and M depending on δ such that

$$\|T_t\| \leq M \quad \text{for } t \in [0,\delta]$$

If this does not hold, then $\exists$ a sequence $\{t_n\}$, $t_n \to 0^+$ such that $\|T_{t_n}\| \geq n$. Hence by the uniform Boundedness Theorem $\exists$ one z such that $\{\|T_{t_n} z\|\}$ is unbounded, but this is a contradiction to the strong continuity at the origin. Now set $t = m\delta + \tau$, with $0 \leq \tau \leq \delta$, then

$$\|T_t\| \leq \|T_\delta\|^m \|T_\tau\| \leq M^{1+m} \leq M\, M^{t/\delta} = Me^{\omega t} \qquad \text{where } \omega = \delta^{-1}\log M.$$

To prove b) we have for fixed $t > 0$, $s \geq 0$,

$$\|T_{t+s} z - T_t z\| \leq \|T_t\|\|T_s z - z\| \leq Me^{\omega t}\|T_s z - z\|$$

Hence

$$\lim_{s\to o^+} \|T_{t+s}z - T_t z\| = 0$$

Also for $t > 0$, $s \geq 0$ sufficiently small

$$\|T_{t-s}z - T_t z\| \leq \|T_{t-s}\| \, \|z - T_s z\|$$

Hence $\lim_{s\to o^-} \|T_{t+s}z - z\| = 0$, and $T_t z$ is continuous.

c) Let $t_o > 0$ be a fixed number, then for every $t \geq t_o$ there exists $n=1,2,\ldots$ such that $nt_o \leq t < (n+1)t_o$. Consequently

$$\frac{\log\|T_t\|}{t} = \frac{\log\|T^n_{t_o} T_{t-nt_o}\|}{t}$$

$$\leq \frac{n \log\|T_{t_o}\|}{t} + \frac{\log M}{t}$$

$$\leq \frac{\log\|T_{t_o}\|}{t_o} \cdot \frac{nt_o}{t} + \frac{\log M}{t}$$

$$\leq \frac{\log\|T_{t_o}\|}{t_o} + \frac{\log M}{t}$$

Thus

$$\overline{\lim_{t\to\infty}} \frac{\log\|T_t\|}{t} \leq \frac{\log\|T_{t_o}\|}{t_o}$$

$$\leq \inf_{t>o} \frac{\log\|T_t\|}{t}$$

$$\leq \underline{\lim}_{t\to\infty} \frac{\log\|T_t\|}{t}$$

d) If $\omega > \omega_o$, $\exists\, t_o$ such that

$$\frac{\log\|T_t\|}{t} < \omega \quad \text{for } t \geq t_o$$

that is $\|T_t\| \leq e^{\omega t}$ for $t \geq t_o$

But $\|T_t\| \leq M_o$ for $0 \leq t \leq t_o$, so if

$$M_\omega = M_o \quad , \ \omega > 0$$

$$M_\omega = e^{-\omega t_o} M_o \ , \quad \omega < 0$$

and we obtain the result.

Example 2.6

It is easy to show that for the semigroups of Examples 2.2, 2.3, 2.4, the bounds for $\|T_t\|$ are $e^{\|A\|t}$, 1, $e^{\sup \mathrm{Re}\lambda_n t}$ respectively.

Since we have only assumed $T_t z$ is continuous, it is not possible in general to differentiate $T_t z$. However, our main aim is to relate $T_t z$ to the solution of an abstract evolution equation, and for this we need the following concept

Definition 2.7 The infinitesimal generator of a semigroup

The infinitesimal generator A of a strongly continuous semigroup on a Banach space Z is defined by

$$Az = \lim_{t \to 0+} \frac{1}{t}(T_t - I)z \tag{2.10}$$

whenever the limit exists; the domain of A, D(A) being the set of elements in Z for which the limit exists.

Example 2.8

The infinitesimal generator of the semigroup of Example 2.2 is $A \in \mathcal{L}(Z)$. For Example 2.3 the infinitesimal generator is $A = \frac{d}{dx}$, with $D(A) = \left\{z, \frac{dz}{dx} \in Z\right\}$. For Example 2.4, the infinitesimal generator is

$$Az = \sum_{n=1}^{\infty} \lambda_n \phi_n \langle \phi_n, z \rangle$$

with

$$D(A) = \left\{ z : \sum_{n=1}^{\infty} |\lambda_n \langle \phi_n, z \rangle|^2 < \infty \right\}$$

Theorem 2.9

Let T_t be a strongly continuous semigroup on a Banach space Z, with infinitesimal generator A, then

a) if $z_o \in D(A)$, $T_t z_o \in D(A)$ $\forall\, t \geq 0$

b) $\frac{d}{dt}(T_t z_o) = AT_t z_o = T_t A z_o$, for $z_o \in D(A)$, $t > 0$

c) $\frac{d^n}{dt^n}(T_t z_o) = A^n T_t z_o = T_t A^n z_o$, $z_o \in D(A^n)$, $t > 0$

d) $T_t z_o - z_o = \int_0^t T_s A z_o ds$, $z_o \in D(A)$

e) A is a closed linear operator, and D(A) is dense in Z

f) $\bigcap_n D(A^n)$ is dense in Z.

Proof

Let $s > 0$ and consider

$$\frac{T_{t+s}z_o - T_t z_o}{s} = T_t \frac{(T_s - I)z_o}{s} = \frac{T_s - I}{s} T_t z_o$$

If $z_o \in D(A)$ the middle limit exists as $s \to 0$, and hence the other limits exist as well. In particular $T_t z_o \in D(A)$, and the strong right derivative of $T_t z_o$ equals $AT_t z_o = T_t A z_o$.

For $t > 0$ and s sufficiently small

$$\frac{T_{t-s}z_o - T_t z_o}{-s} = T_{t-s} \frac{(T_s - I)}{s} z_o$$

Hence the strong left derivative exists and is $T_t A z_o$. Part c) follows by induction on this result.

For d) let Z^* be the dual of Z and take any $z^* \in Z^*$, then

$$<z^*, T_t z_o - z_o> = \int_o^t \frac{d}{du} <z^*, T_u z_o> du$$

where $< , >$ denotes the duality pairing between Z^* and Z. Hence

$$<z^*, T_t z_o - z_o> = \int_o^t <z^*, T_u A z_o> du \qquad \text{for } z_o \in D(A)$$

$$= < z^*, \int_o^t T_u A z_o du >$$

Now

$$\frac{T_s - I}{s} \int_o^t T_u z \, du = \frac{1}{s} \int_o^t T_{s+u} z \, du - \frac{1}{s} \int_o^t T_u z \, du$$

Letting $\rho = s+u$ in the first integral, we have

$$\frac{T_s - I}{s} \int_o^t T_u z \, du = \frac{1}{s} \int_s^{t+s} T_\rho z \, d\rho - \frac{1}{s} \int_o^t T_u z \, du = \frac{1}{s}\left[-\int_o^s T_\rho z d\rho + \int_t^{t+s} T_\rho z \, d\rho \right]$$

$$= \frac{1}{s} \left[\int_o^s (T_{t+u} - T_u) z \, du \right]$$

$$= \frac{1}{s} \int_o^s T_u (T_t - I) z \, du$$

Now as $s \to 0^+$ the right hand side tends to $(T_t - I)z$ since $T_t z$ is strongly continuous. Hence

$$\int_o^t T_u z \, du \in D(A) \tag{2.11}$$

But $\frac{1}{t}\int_0^t T_u z du \to z$ as $t \to 0^+$, hence for any $z \in Z$, $\exists$ a sequence in $D(A)$ which tends to z. This shows $\overline{D(A)} = Z$.

To prove A is closed we let $\{z_n\}$ be a sequence in $D(A)$ converging to z such that Az_n converges to y. Then $||T_s Az_n - T_s y|| \leq Me^{\omega s} ||Az_n - y||$ and so $T_s Az_n \to T_s y$ uniformly on $[0,t]$. Now since $z_n \in D(A)$, we have

$$T_t z_n - z_n = \int_0^t T_s Az_n ds$$

Using the Lebesque dominated convergence theorem

$$T_t z - z = \int_0^t T_s y \; ds$$

Thus $z \in D(A)$ and $Az = y$, which proves A is closed.

For part f) let $C_0^\infty(R^+)$ be the class of all real valued functions on R^+ having continuous derivatives of all orders and of compact support. Then if $\Phi \in C_0^\infty(R^+)$ so does Φ^r, the r-th derivative of Φ, and $\Phi(u)T_u z$ is a continuous vector valued function on R^+ to Z. Let Z_0 be the set of all elements of the form

$$g = \int_0^\infty \Phi(u) T_u z \; du \qquad z \in Z, \; \Phi \in C_0^\infty(R^+) \tag{2.12}$$

We will show that $Z_0 \in D(A^r) \; \forall \; r=1,2,\ldots$ and Z_0 is dense in Z. For s sufficiently small

$$\frac{T_s - I}{s} g = \frac{1}{s}\int_0^\infty \Phi(u)[T_{u+s}z - T_u z] \; du$$

$$= \frac{1}{s}\int_0^\infty \{\Phi(u-s) - \Phi(u)\} T_u z \; du$$

But $\dfrac{\Phi(u-s) - \Phi(u)}{s} \to -\Phi'$ as $s \to 0^+$ uniformly with respect to u.

Thus $Ag = -\int_0^\infty \Phi'(u) T_u z \; du$. Hence $g \in D(A)$. Repeating this argument we see that $g \in D(A^r) \; \forall \; r > 0$, and

$$A^r g = (-1)^r \int_0^\infty \Phi^r(u) T_u z \; du$$

which shows that $Z_0 \subset \bigcap_{r=1}^\infty D(A^r)$

Suppose now the closure of Z_0 is not Z, then $\exists \; z_0 \in Z$ and by the Hahn-Banach theorem a bounded linear functional z_0^* on Z such that

$$\langle z_0^*, g \rangle = 0 \quad \forall \; g \in Z_0 \text{ and } \langle z_0^*, z_0 \rangle = 1$$

Thus $\langle z_o^*, \int_o^\infty \phi(u) T_u z \, du \rangle = \int_o^\infty \phi(u) \langle z_o^*, T_u z \rangle du = 0$

$\forall \phi \in C_o^\infty(R^+)$ and $z \in Z$. But $\langle z_o^*, T_u z_o \rangle$ is continuous with $\langle z_o^*, z_o \rangle = 1$. Hence $\exists \phi \in C_o^\infty(R^+)$ such that $\int_o^\infty \phi(u) \langle z_o^*, T_u z_o \rangle du \neq 0$, and this is a contradiction so $\overline{Z}_o = Z$.

The above theorem shows that semigroups play an important role in determining the solution of an abstract evolution equation

$$\dot{z} = Az, \; z(0) = z_o$$

In particular we know $z(t) = T_t z_o$ is the solution if A generates a strongly continuous semigroup and $z_o \in D(A)$. So it is important to obtain a characterisation of those operators which generate strongly continuous semigroups. This is provided by the Hille-Yosida Theorem.

Theorem 2.10 Hille-Yosida Theorem

A necessary and sufficient condition for a closed linear operator A with domain dense in a Banach space Z to generate a strongly continuous semigroup is that $\exists$ real numbers M, ω, such that $\forall$ real $\lambda > \omega$, $\lambda \in \rho(A)$, the resolvent set of A, and

(2.13) $$\|R(\lambda,A)^r\| \le \frac{M}{(\lambda-\omega)^r} \qquad r = 1,2,\ldots$$

where $R(\lambda,A) = (\lambda I - A)^{-1}$ is the resolvent. In this case

(2.14) $$\|T_t\| \le Me^{\omega t}$$

Proof We need the following Lemma

Lemma 2.11

Let T_t be a strongly continuous semigroup with infinitesimal generator A, and $\|T_t\| \le Me^{\omega t}$. If Re $\lambda > \omega$ then $\lambda \in \rho(A)$, and

$$R(\lambda,A)z = \int_o^\infty e^{-\lambda t} T_t z \, dt$$

Proof

Let $R_\lambda z = \int_o^\infty e^{-\lambda t} T_t z \, dt \qquad z \in Z$, Re $\lambda > \omega$

This operator is well defined, since

$$\|e^{-\lambda t} T_t z\| \le Me^{(\omega-\sigma)t} \|z\| \qquad \text{where } \sigma = \text{Re}\{\lambda\}$$

Moreover the integrand is strongly continuous, hence strongly measurable and so the integral is a well defined Bochner integral. We have

$$\|R_\lambda\| \le M\int_0^\infty e^{-(\sigma-\omega)t}\,dt = \frac{M}{\sigma-\omega} \quad \text{so } R_\lambda \text{ is bounded.}$$

We now show $R_\lambda z \in D(A)$ and $(\lambda I-A)R_\lambda z = z \;\forall\; z \in Z$

$$\frac{T_s-I}{s}\,R_\lambda z = \frac{1}{s}\int_0^\infty e^{-\lambda t}\left[T_{s+t}-T_t\right]z\,dt$$

$$= \frac{e^{\lambda s}-1}{s}\int_s^\infty e^{-\lambda t}T_t z\,dt - \frac{1}{s}\int_0^s e^{-\lambda t}T_t z\,dt$$

Thus $AR_\lambda z = \lim_{s\to 0^+}\left(\frac{T_s-I}{s}\right)R_\lambda z = \lambda R_\lambda z - z, \;\forall\; z \in Z.$

Also $R_\lambda Az = \int_0^\infty e^{-\lambda t}\,T_t Az\,dt = A\int_0^\infty e^{-\lambda t}\,T_t z\,dt = AR_\lambda z\,, \quad z \in D(A)$

Hence $\qquad R_\lambda(\lambda I-A)z = z\,, \quad z \in D(A)$

and $\qquad (\lambda I-A)R_\lambda z = z\,, \quad z \in Z$

so $\qquad R(\lambda,A) = R_\lambda$

Necessity

By the lemma we know $\lambda \in \rho(A)$ if $\operatorname{Re}\lambda > \omega$, and

$$R(\lambda,A)z = \int_0^\infty e^{-\lambda t}\,T_t z\,dt\,, \quad z \in Z, \quad \operatorname{Re}\lambda > \omega$$

Hence $$\frac{d^{(r-1)}R(\lambda,A)z}{d\lambda^{r-1}} = R^{(r-1)}(\lambda,A)z = \int_0^\infty (-t)^{r-1}e^{-\lambda t}\,T_t z\,dt$$

$$r=1,2,\ldots$$

Thus $$\|R^{(r-1)}(\lambda,A)\| \le M\int_0^\infty t^{r-1}e^{-(\sigma-\omega)t}\,dt = M(r-1)!\,(\sigma-\omega)^{-r}$$

But the resolvent is analytic in $\lambda \in \rho(A)$, so

$$R^{(r-1)}(\lambda,A) = (-1)^{r-1}(r-1)!\,(R(\lambda,A))^r$$

Hence $$\|R(\lambda,A)^r\| \le \frac{M}{(\sigma-\omega)^r}$$

Sufficiency

Set $A_\lambda = \lambda^2 R(\lambda,A)-\lambda I$, $\lambda > \omega$, then $A_\lambda \in \mathcal{L}(Z)$, and we may construct the semigroup

$$T_t^\lambda = e^{A_\lambda t} = e^{-\lambda t}\sum_{n=0}^\infty \frac{(\lambda^2 t)^n}{n!}\,(\lambda I-A)^{-n}$$

We will show that the strong limit of T_t^λ exists as $\lambda \to \infty$ and is the desired semigroup T_t. First we show $\|A_\lambda z - Az\| \to 0$ as $\lambda \to \infty$, $z \in D(A)$. If $z \in D(A)$, we have

$$\|\lambda(\lambda I-A)^{-1}z - z\| = \|(\lambda I-A)^{-1}Az\| \leq \frac{M}{\lambda-\omega}\|Az\|$$

Now $$\|\lambda(\lambda I-A)^{-1}\| \leq \frac{\lambda M}{\lambda-\omega} < 2M \quad \text{for large } \lambda$$

Hence we may apply the Banach-Steinhaus theorem to conclude that

$$\lambda(\lambda I-A)^{-1}z \to z \quad \text{as} \quad \lambda \to \infty \quad \text{for \underline{all} } z \in Z.$$

Now $A_\lambda z = \lambda(\lambda I-A)^{-1}Az$, so that $A_\lambda z \to Az$ as $\lambda \to \infty$ for $z \in D(A)$.

Note that $$\|T_t^\lambda\| \leq e^{-\lambda t}\sum_{n=o}^{\infty}\frac{(\lambda^2 t)^n}{n!}\frac{M}{(\lambda-\omega)^n} = M\, e^{\left\{\frac{\lambda\omega}{\lambda-\omega}\right\}t}$$

Now $(\lambda I-A)^{-1}(\mu I-A)^{-1} = (\mu I-A)^{-1}(\lambda I-A)^{-1}$, hence $A_\lambda A_\mu = A_\mu A_\lambda$, and $A_\lambda T_t^\mu = T_t^\lambda A_\mu$, so that if $z \in D(A)$

$$\begin{aligned} T_t^\lambda z - T_t^\mu z &= \int_o^t \frac{d}{ds}(T_{t-s}^\mu T_s^\lambda z)\,ds \\ &= \int_o^t T_{t-s}^\mu (A_\lambda - A_\mu) T_s^\lambda z\, ds \\ &= \int_o^t T_{t-s}^\mu T_s^\lambda (A_\lambda - A_\mu) z\, ds \end{aligned}$$

Thus $$\|T_t^\lambda z - T_t^\mu z\| \leq M^2 e^{\frac{\mu\omega}{\mu-\omega}t}\|(A_\lambda - A_\mu)z\| \int_o^t \exp\frac{-(\lambda-\mu)\omega^2 s}{(\mu-\omega)(\lambda-\omega)}\,ds$$

Choosing $\lambda > \mu$, we have

$$\|T_t^\lambda z - T_t^\mu z\| \leq M^2\, e^{\frac{\mu\omega}{\mu-\omega}t}\|(A_\lambda - A_\mu)z\|\, t$$

But $\|(A_\lambda - A_\mu)z\| \to 0$ as $\lambda, \mu \to \infty$, since $A_\lambda z \to Az$ as $\lambda \to \infty$.

Thus $T_t^\lambda z$ converges to a limit, uniformly on compact intervals, which we will denote by $T_t z$. Now $D(A)$ is dense in Z, so using the Banach-Steinhaus theorem we may extend this convergence to each $z \in Z$. It remains to show that T_t is a strongly continuous semigroup whose generator is A.

We have

$$T_{t+s}z = \lim_{\lambda\to\infty} T_{t+s}^\lambda z = \lim_{\lambda\to\infty} T_t^\lambda T_s^\lambda z = T_t T_s z \quad \forall\, z \in Z$$

Also $T_o = I$, and the strong continuity is a consequence of the uniform convergence on compact intervals.

Now $\|T_t^\lambda A_\lambda z - T_t Az\| \leq \|T_t^\lambda\|\|A_\lambda z - Az\| + \|(T_t^\lambda - T_t)Az\|$

Hence $T_t^\lambda A_\lambda z$ converges strongly to $T_t Az$ as $\lambda \to \infty$, uniformly on compact intervals, for $z \in D(A)$. Thus we may apply the Lebesque dominated convergence theorem to

$$T_t^\lambda z - z = \int_o^t T_s^\lambda A_\lambda z \, ds$$

obtaining

$$T_t z - z = \int_o^t T_s Az \, ds , \qquad z \in D(A)$$

So the generator $\tilde{A}$ of T_t is an extension of A, since

$$\tilde{A}z = \lim_{t \to o^+} \frac{T_t z - z}{t}$$

$$= Az \quad \text{for} \quad z \in D(A)$$

Now if $\lambda > \omega$

$$(\lambda I - A)D(A) = Z$$

and

$$(\lambda I - \tilde{A})D(\tilde{A}) = Z$$

But $AD(A) = \tilde{A}\,D(A)$, hence

$$(\lambda I - \tilde{A})D(A) = (\lambda I - \tilde{A})D(\tilde{A})$$

So that $D(A) = D(\tilde{A})$ and this completes the proof of the theorem.

In Example 2.4 we defined a semigroup on a separable Hilbert space, and derived its generator in Example 2.8. We now illustrate an application of the Hille-Yosida Theorem by proving the converse.

Example 2.12

Let $\{\lambda_n\}$ be a sequence of complex numbers, and $\{\phi_n\}$ an orthonormal sequence in a separable Hilbert space H. Now define an operator on H by

$$Az = \sum_{n=1}^{\infty} \lambda_n \phi_n \langle \phi_n, z \rangle$$

with

$$D(A) = \left\{ z : \sum_{n=1}^{\infty} |\lambda_n \langle \phi_n, z \rangle|^2 < \infty \right\}$$

Then A is a densely defined closed operator, and $(\lambda I - A)$ is invertible if and only if $\inf_n |\lambda - \lambda_n| > 0$. Moreover A generates a strongly continuous semigroup if

$$\sup_n \mathrm{Re}\{\lambda_n\} < \infty$$

Proof

Clearly all sequences $\{z_p\}$ with $\langle\phi_n, z_p\rangle = 0$ for n sufficiently large lie in D(A) and form a dense set in H.

Now let $\{z_p\}$ be a sequence in D(A) with $z_p \to z_o$ and $Az_p \to y_o$ as $p \to \infty$. Since the sequence $\{Az_p\}$ is bounded we have

$$\sum_{n=1}^{\infty} |\lambda_n \langle\phi_n, z_p\rangle|^2 \leq M \quad \text{for } p=1,2,...$$

Thus
$$\sum_{n=1}^{\infty} |\lambda_n \langle\phi_n, z_o\rangle|^2 \leq M$$

and so $Az_o = y_o$, showing that A is closed.

Consider now the equation

$$\text{(2.15)} \qquad \lambda z - Az = y \ , \quad z \in D(A),\ y \in H$$

If we set
$$y = \sum_{n=1}^{\infty} \phi_n \langle\phi_n, y\rangle$$

then (2.15) is equivalent to

$$(\lambda-\lambda_n)\langle\phi_n, z\rangle = \langle\phi_n, y\rangle$$

Hence
$$\langle\phi_n, z\rangle = \frac{1}{\lambda-\lambda_n}\langle\phi_n, y\rangle \quad \text{for } \lambda \neq \lambda_n$$

and
$$\sum_{n=1}^{\infty} \phi_n \langle\phi_n, z\rangle = z \in H \quad \text{if and only if} \quad \inf_n |\lambda-\lambda_n| > 0.$$

Thus $(\lambda I-A)$ is invertible if this condition holds and $\lambda \in \rho(A)$.

From the Hille-Yosida Theorem we know that A generates a semigroup if there exists constants M,ω such that

$$\|R(\lambda,A)^r\| \leq \frac{M}{(\lambda-\omega)^r} \qquad r=1,2,... \qquad \forall \text{ real } \lambda > \omega$$

Now
$$R(\lambda,A)^r y = \sum_{n=1}^{\infty} \frac{1}{(\lambda-\lambda_n)^r} \phi_n \langle\phi_n, y\rangle$$

and so
$$\|R(\lambda,A)^r\| \leq \sup_n \frac{1}{|\lambda-\lambda_n|^r}$$

$$= \left(\sup_n \frac{1}{|\lambda-\lambda_n|}\right)^r$$

So we need to prove that there exists M,ω such that

$$\text{(2.16)} \qquad \left(\sup_n \frac{\lambda-\omega}{|\lambda-\lambda_n|}\right)^k \leq M$$

But if $\mathrm{Re}\{\lambda_n\} \leq \omega$, we have

$$\frac{\lambda-\omega}{|\lambda-\lambda_n|} \leq 1$$

and hence (2.16) is satisfied. Clearly the semigroup generated by A is the one given in Example 2.3.

In general it is difficult to check the conditions of the Hille-Yosida Theorem, and so other more easily verifiable conditions have been developed, one in particular is in terms of the adjoint operator.

Definition 2.13 The adjoint operator

Let A be a closed, densely defined, linear operator with domain D(A) on a Banach space Z. The adjoint A* of A is a transformation whose domain D(A*) consists of all those $z^* \in Z^*$ for which there exists a $g^* \in Z^*$ such that

$$\langle g^*,z\rangle = \langle z^*,Az\rangle \qquad \forall\ z \in D(A)$$

In this case we set $A^*z^* = g^*$.

Theorem 2.14

Let A be a closed, densely defined, linear operator on a Banach space Z, then A generates a semigroup T_t on Z satisfying $\| T_t\| \leq e^{\omega t}$ for all $t \geq 0$ if and only if for all $\lambda > \omega$

(2.17) $$\|(\lambda I-A)z\|_Z \geq (\lambda-\omega)\|z\|_Z , \qquad z \in D(A)$$

(2.18) $$\|(\lambda I-A^*)z^*\|_{Z^*} \geq (\lambda-\omega) \|z^*\|_{Z^*}, \quad z^*\in D(A^*)$$

Proof

Sufficiency

First we show that $(\lambda I-A)$ is one to one onto Z. If this is not the case then for some $z \in D(A)$, we have

$$\lambda z - Az = 0$$

But from (2.17) we see this implies $z = 0$ so we know that $(\lambda I-A)$ is invertible. Its range is a closed subspace of Z since if we set $y_n = \lambda z_n-Az_n$, where $z_n \in D(A)$ and $y_n \to y$ as $n \to \infty$, then

$$\begin{aligned}\|y_n-y_m\|_Z &= \|\lambda(z_n-z_m)-A(z_n-z_m)\| \\ &\geq (\lambda-\omega)\|z_n-z_m\|\end{aligned}$$

Thus z_n is a Cauchy sequence, and so $z_n \to z_o$ as $n \to \infty$.

Moreover, since $(\lambda I-A)$ is closed, $z_o \in D(A)$ and $y = Az_o$. If the range of $(\lambda I-A)$ is not the whole space, then there exists $z^* \in Z^*$,

$z^* \neq 0$, such that

$$\langle z^*, (\lambda I - A)z\rangle = 0 \qquad \forall\, z \in D(A)$$

In which case $\lambda\langle z^*, z\rangle = \langle z^*, Az\rangle$, and so $z^* \in D(A^*)$, and

$$A^* z^* = \lambda z^*$$

But from (2.18)

$$\|(\lambda I - A^*)z^*\|_{Z^*} \geq (\lambda - \omega)\|z^*\|_{Z^*}$$

so $z^* = 0$, thus $\lambda I - A$ is onto Z.

Now from (2.17)

$$\|(\lambda I - A)^{-1}\| \leq \frac{1}{\lambda - \omega}$$

Hence

$$\|(\lambda I - A)^{-r}\| \leq \frac{1}{(\lambda - \omega)^r} \qquad r = 1, 2, \ldots$$

and we may apply the Hille-Yosida Theorem to conclude that A generates a strongly continuous semigroup.

Necessity

If A generates a strongly continuous semigroup T_t with $\|T_t\| \leq e^{\omega t}$, then by the Hille-Yosida Theorem

$$\|R(\lambda, A)\| \leq \frac{1}{\lambda - \omega} \qquad \text{for} \quad \lambda > \omega$$

or equivalently

$$\|\lambda z - Az\| \geq (\lambda - \omega)\|z\| \qquad \text{for} \quad z \in D(A).$$

Moreover, if $z^* \in D(A^*)$

$$\begin{aligned}
\|\lambda z^* - A^* z^*\| &= \sup_{\|z\| \leqslant 1} |\langle (\lambda I - A^*)z^*, z\rangle| \\
&\geq \sup_{\substack{\|z\| \leqslant 1 \\ z \in D(A)}} |\langle z^*, (\lambda I - A)z\rangle| \\
&= \sup_{\|R(\lambda, A)y\| \leqslant 1} |\langle z^*, y\rangle| \\
&\geq \sup_{\frac{\|y\|}{(\lambda - \omega)} \leqslant 1} |\langle z^*, y\rangle| \\
&= (\lambda - \omega)\, \|z^*\|
\end{aligned}$$

For the special case where Z is a Hilbert space we can rewrite conditions (2.17),(2.18) in a simpler form; that is (2.17) is equivalent to

$$\langle \lambda z - Az, \lambda z - Az\rangle \geq (\lambda - \omega)^2 \langle z, z\rangle \qquad \text{for } \lambda > \omega, \quad z \in D(A)$$

or $$2\lambda(\omega\|z\|^2 - \mathrm{Re}\langle Az, z\rangle) + \langle Az, Az\rangle - \omega^2\|z\|^2 \geq 0$$

The above inequality holds with a suitable choice for ω if there exists a β such that

$$\beta\|z\|^2 \geq \mathrm{Re}\{\langle Az,z\rangle\} \qquad z \in D(A)$$

Similarly (2.18) will be satisfied if

$$\beta\|z\|^2 \geq \mathrm{Re}\{\langle A^*z,z\rangle\} \qquad z \in D(A^*)$$

Finally we note that the hypothesis that $\|T_t\| \leq e^{\omega t}$ is not an essential restriction since if we are given a Banach space Z and a semigroup T_t on Z with $\|T_t\| \leq Me^{\omega t}$ it is always possible to introduce an equivalent norm $\|\ \|_*$ on Z such that

$$\|T_t z\|_* \leq e^{\omega t}\|z\|_*$$

In fact if we set

$$\|z\|_* = \sup\ e^{-\omega t}\|T_t z\| \ ; \quad t \geq 0$$

it is easy to check that this norm has the required properties. However it should be noted that if the original space is a Hilbert space, with respect to the new norm $\|\ \|_*$, this property need not be retained.

Example 2.15

Let $\qquad Az = -\dfrac{dz}{d\xi}\ , \qquad Z = L^2[0,1]$

and $\qquad D(A) = \left\{z : z \in H^1[0,1],\ z(0) = 0\right\}$

Then it is easy to show that

$$A^*z = \frac{dz}{d\xi}$$

$$D(A^*) = \left\{z : z \in H^1[0,1],\ z(1) = 0\right\}$$

Moreover

$$\langle Az,z\rangle = -\tfrac{1}{2}z^2(1) \leq \beta\|z\|^2$$

$$\langle A^*z,z\rangle = -\tfrac{1}{2}z^2(0) \leq \beta\|z\|^2$$

where $\beta = 0$. Hence A generates a semigroup T_t on Z and $\|T_t\| \leq 1$.

Example 2.16

Consider the system

$$\ddot{z} + \bar{\alpha}\,\dot{z} + Az = 0\ , \quad z(0) = z_0,\ \dot{z}(0) = z_1\ ,\ \bar{\alpha} \geq 0$$

where A is a positive self adjoint operator on a real Hilbert space H, with domain D(A), so that

$$\langle Az,z\rangle \geq k\|z\|^2 \qquad \forall\, z \in D(A)\ ,\quad k > 0$$

Let $\dot{z} = y$, then

$$\dot{y} = -\bar{\alpha}\, y - Az$$

We may write this formally as a first order system

$$\dot{w} = \mathcal{A}w$$

where $w = \begin{bmatrix} z \\ y \end{bmatrix}$, and

$$\mathcal{A}\begin{bmatrix} z \\ y \end{bmatrix} = \begin{bmatrix} 0 & I \\ -A & -\bar{\alpha} \end{bmatrix}\begin{bmatrix} z \\ y \end{bmatrix}$$

Introducing a Hilbert space $\mathcal{H} = D(A^{\frac{1}{2}}) \times H$ with inner product

$$\langle w,\bar{w}\rangle_{\mathcal{H}} = \langle A^{\frac{1}{2}}z, A^{\frac{1}{2}}\bar{z}\rangle_H + \langle y,\bar{y}\rangle_H$$

where $w = \begin{bmatrix} z \\ y \end{bmatrix}$, $\bar{w} = \begin{bmatrix} \bar{z} \\ \bar{y} \end{bmatrix}$, we have

$$\langle w,\mathcal{A}w\rangle_{\mathcal{H}} = \langle Az,y\rangle + \langle y,-Az-\bar{\alpha}y\rangle$$

$$= -\bar{\alpha}\|y\|^2$$

for $w \in D(\mathcal{A}) = D(A) \times D(A^{\frac{1}{2}})$.

The adjoint of $\mathcal{A}$ with respect to the Hilbert space $\mathcal{H}$ is easily shown to be

$$\mathcal{A}^*\begin{bmatrix} z \\ y \end{bmatrix} = \begin{bmatrix} 0 & -I \\ A & -\bar{\alpha} \end{bmatrix}\begin{bmatrix} z \\ y \end{bmatrix}, \qquad D(\mathcal{A}^*) = D(\mathcal{A})$$

Thus $\langle w,\mathcal{A}^*w\rangle = -\bar{\alpha}\|y\|^2$, and so we may apply Theorem 2.14 to conclude that $\mathcal{A}$ generates a strongly continuous semigroup on $\mathcal{H}$.

2.1 Dual semigroups

First we recall the following proposition from [11].

Proposition 2.17

Let A be a linear operator with D(A) dense in Z, a Banach space.

a) The dual A^* is a weak* closed linear operator, and if in addition A is bounded, then $A^* \in \mathcal{L}(Z^*)$, and $\|A^*\| = \|A\|$.

b) If A is closed then $D(A^*)$ is weak* dense in Z^*, and if Z is reflexive $D(A^*)$ is strongly dense in Z^*.

A straightforward application of this proposition together with the Definitions 2.1 and 2.7 leads to the following theorem.

Theorem 2.18

Let T_t be a strongly continuous semigroup on a Banach space Z, then T_t^* is a linear operator with $\|T_t^*\| = \|T_t\|$, and

a) $T_o^* = I^*$ (identity on Z^*)

b) $T^*_{t+s} = T_t^*T_s^*$, $\quad t,s \geq 0$

c) $\text{weak*} \lim_{t\to o^+} T_t^*z^* = z^* \quad \forall z^* \in Z^*$

In general T_t^* will not be strongly continuous. However we will be mainly interested in reflexive Banach spaces for which the weak and weak* topologies are equivalent, and so T_t^* will be weakly continuous.

Theorem 2.19

If T_t is a weakly continuous semigroup on a Banach space Z then it is also strongly continuous.

Proof

Let $z(t)= T_t z_o$, then z is weakly continuous $\forall\ t \geq 0$. Hence z is strongly measurable, and $\|z(t)\|$ is bounded on compact intervals (see [5]) thus z is Bochner integrable.

Now let $0 \leq \alpha < \eta < \beta < \xi-\varepsilon < \xi$, $\varepsilon > 0$, and set

$$z(\xi) = T_\xi z_o = T_\eta T_{\xi-\eta} z_o = T_\eta z(\xi-\eta)$$

Then
$$(\beta-\alpha)z(\xi) = \int_\alpha^\beta z(\xi)d\eta = \int_\alpha^\beta T_\eta z(\xi-\eta)d\eta$$

So
$$(\beta-\alpha)\{z(\xi\pm\varepsilon)-z(\xi)\} = \int_\alpha^\beta T_\eta\{z(\xi\pm\varepsilon-\eta)-z(\xi-\eta)\}d\eta$$

and
$$(\beta-\alpha)\| z(\xi\pm\varepsilon)-z(\xi)\| \leq \sup \|T_\eta\| \int_{\xi-\beta}^{\xi-\alpha} \|z(s\pm\varepsilon)-z(s)\| ds$$

Now
$$\int_{\xi-\beta}^{\xi-\alpha} \|z(s\pm\varepsilon)-z(s)\| ds \to 0 \quad \text{as} \quad \varepsilon \to 0$$

To see this we note that the result is certainly true for continuous functions z, and for z Bochner integrable $\exists$ a continuous function $\bar{z}$, such that for any $\varepsilon' > 0$

$$\int_{\xi-\beta}^{\xi-\alpha} \|z(s)-\bar{z}(s)\|ds < \varepsilon'$$

Hence
$$\int_{\xi-\beta}^{\xi-\alpha} \|z(s\pm\varepsilon)-z(s)\| ds \leq \int_{\xi-\beta}^{\xi-\alpha} \Big[\|z(s\pm\varepsilon)-\bar{z}(s\pm\varepsilon)\| + \|\bar{z}(s\pm\varepsilon)-\bar{z}(s)\| + \|\bar{z}(s)-z(s)\|\Big] ds$$

This shows that z(t) is strongly continuous for $t > 0$.

Now let t_n be any positive rational number with $t_n < 1$, and consider the countable set S of all finite linear combinations $\Sigma\alpha_n T_{t_n} z_o$ with α_n a rational scalar. If we denote the strong closure of S by $\bar{S}$, then $\bar{S}$ is weakly closed and since $T_{t_n} z_o \to z_o$ as $t_n \to 0$ in the weak topology it follows that $z_o \in \bar{S}$. From the strong continuity of T_t for $t > 0$, we have $T_t T_{t_n} z_o = T_{t+t_n} z_o$, and so

$$T_t T_{t_n} z_o \to T_{t_n} z_o \quad \text{as} \quad t \to 0 \quad .$$

For any $z_m \in S$

$$z_m = \Sigma\, \alpha_n T_{t_n} z_o$$

where the sum is finite, and so

$$T_t z_m \to z_m \quad \text{as} \quad t \to 0 \, .$$

Hence
$$\| T_t z_o - z_o \| \le \| T_t z_m - z_m \| + \| z_m - z_o \| + \| T_t (z_o - z_m) \|$$

$$\le \| T_t z_m - z_m \| + \left[\sup_{t \in [0,1]} \| T_t \| + 1 \right] \| z_m - z_o \|$$

But $\inf_{z_n \in S} \| z_m - z_o \| = 0$ and $T_t z_m \to z_m$ as $t \to 0$, and so $T_t z_o \to z_o$ as $t \to 0$, and this completes the proof.

<u>Theorem 2.20</u>

The dual A^* of the infinitesimal generator A of the strongly continuous semigroup T_t is a closed, densely defined, linear operator if Z is a reflexive Banach space, and

a) if $z^* \in D(A^*)$, then $T_t^* z^* \in D(A^*)$ with

$$A^* T_t^* z^* = T_t^* A^* z^*$$

$$T_t^* z^* - z^* = \int_0^t T_u^* A^* z^* \, du$$

b) an element $z^* \in Z^*$ belongs to $D(A^*)$ if and only if $\dfrac{T_s^* - I^*}{s} z^*$ converges in the weak* topology as $s \to 0^+$, and the weak* limit is $A^* z^*$.

<u>Proof</u>

a) If $z^* \in D(A^*)$, then for each fixed $t \ge 0$, and all $z \in D(A)$

$$\langle T_t^* A^* z^*, z \rangle = \langle z^*, A T_t z \rangle = \langle z^*, T_t A z \rangle = \langle T_t^* z^*, A z \rangle$$

Hence $T_t^* z^* \in D(A^*)$ and $A^* T_t^* z^* = T_t^* A^* z^*$

Moreover $\int_0^t \langle T_u^* A^* z^*, z\rangle du = \int_0^t \langle A^* z^*, T_u z\rangle du$

$$= \langle A^* z^*, \int_0^t T_u z\, du\rangle = \langle z^*, A\int_0^t T_u z\, du\rangle$$

Now we showed in the proof of Theorem 2.9 that

$$A\int_0^t T_u z\, du = T_t z - z \quad \forall\ z \in Z$$

Hence $\int_0^t \langle T_u^* A^* z^*, z\rangle\, du = \langle T_t^* z^* - z^*, z\rangle$ which proves a).

b) Assume $z^* \in Z^*$ is such that $\frac{T_s^* - I^*}{s} z^*$ converges to g^* in the weak* topology as $s \to 0^+$. Then $\forall\ z \in D(A)$

$$\langle g^*, z\rangle = \lim_{s \to 0^+} \left\langle \frac{T_s^* - I^*}{s} z^*, z \right\rangle = \lim_{s \to 0^+} \left\langle z^*, \frac{T_s - I}{s} z \right\rangle$$

$$= \langle z^*, Az\rangle$$

Hence $z^* \in D(A^*)$ and $A^* z^* = g^*$.

Conversely, for any fixed $z^* \in D(A^*)$

$$\frac{1}{s} \langle (T_s^* - I^*) z^*, z\rangle = \frac{1}{s}\int_0^s \langle T_u^* A^* z^*, z\rangle\, du$$

$$= \frac{1}{s}\int_0^s \langle A^* z^*, T_u z\rangle\, du$$

$$= \langle A^* z^*, \frac{1}{s}\int_0^s T_u z\, du \rangle$$

Since $\frac{1}{s}\int_0^s T_u z\, du \to z$ in the strong topology as $s \to 0^+$ we have

$$\lim_{s \to 0^+} \langle \frac{1}{s}(T_s^* - I^*) z^*, z\rangle = \langle A^* z^*, z\rangle \quad \forall\ z \in Z .$$

<u>Remark</u>

The dual operator A^* is the infinitesimal generator of T_t^* .

2.2 Inhomogeneous differential equations

We have seen that if A generates a strongly continuous semigroup T_t, then the solution of

$$\dot{z} = Az \ , \quad z(0) = z_o \ , \quad z_o \ \varepsilon \ D(A)$$

is $$z(t) = T_t z_o$$

Now let us consider the inhomogeneous equation

$$\dot{z} = Az + f \ , \quad z(0) = z_o \tag{2.19}$$

where for the moment we will assume $f \ \varepsilon \ C(0,t_1;Z)$. Suppose that z is a solution on $[0,t_1]$, then

$$\frac{d}{ds}\left[T_{t-s}z(s)\right] = -AT_{t-s}z(s) + T_{t-s}\left[Az(s)+f(s)\right]$$

$$= T_{t-s}f(s)$$

Hence

$$z(t) = T_t z_o + \int_0^t T_{t-s}f(s)\,ds \tag{2.20}$$

It may be thought that (2.20) is always a solution of (2.19) but this is not true in general. However we are able to prove the following partial converse.

Theorem 2.21

If A generates a strongly continuous semigroup T_t on a Banach space Z, and

a) $f \ \varepsilon \ C^1(0,t_1;Z)$

b) $z_o \ \varepsilon \ D(A)$

then (2.20) is continuously differentiable on $[0,t_1]$ and is a solution of (2.19).

Proof

Clearly all we need to show is that $\int_0^t T_{t-s}f(s)ds$ satisfies the differential equation (2.17).

Let $$v(t) = \int_0^t T_{t-s}f(s)ds$$

then $$v(t) = \int_0^t T_{t-s}\left(f(0) + \int_0^s f'(\alpha)d\alpha\right) ds$$

$$= \int_0^t T_{t-s} f(0)ds + \int_0^t \int_\alpha^t T_{t-s} f'(\alpha)ds\, d\alpha$$

Now $$T_{t-\alpha}z - z = A \int_\alpha^t T_{t-s} z\, ds \quad \text{for all} \quad z \in Z$$

Hence $v \in D(A)$ and

$$Av(t) = (T_t - I)f(0) + \int_0^t (T_{t-\alpha} - I)f'(\alpha)d\alpha$$

Now $$v(t) = \int_0^t T_s f(t-s)ds$$

Thus $$\frac{dv}{dt} = T_t f(0) + \int_0^t T_s f'(t-s)ds$$

Therefore

$$\frac{dv}{dt} = Av(t) + f(t)$$

The conditions of Theorem 2.17 are too strong for control applications where in general we do not wish to assume $f \in C^1(0,t_1;Z)$. If we are content with solutions satisfying (2.17) almost everywhere, we can weaken our hypothesis on f.

Lemma 2.22

If A generates a strongly continuous semigroup T_t on a Banach space Z and $T_{t-s}f(s) \in D(A)$ for almost all $t > s \in [0,t_1]$, $f \in L^1(0,t_1;Z)$ and $AT_{t-s}f(s) \in L^1(0,t;Z)$, then (2.20) is the unique solution of (2.19).

Proof

Let $v(t) = \int_0^t T_{t-s}f(s)ds$, then since A is closed, under the above assumptions, $v(t) \in D(A)$ and

$$Av(t) = \int_0^t AT_{t-s}f(s)ds$$

Hence $Av(t)$ is Bochner integrable, and

$$\int_0^\alpha Av(t)dt = \int_0^\alpha \int_0^t AT_{t-s}f(s)ds\, dt$$

$$= \int_0^\alpha \int_s^\alpha AT_{t-s}f(s)dt\, ds \quad \text{by Fubini's theorem}$$

$$= \int_0^{\alpha} [T_{\alpha-s}f(s)-f(s)]ds \quad \text{by Theorem 2.9(d)}$$
$$\text{since } T_{t-s}f(s) \in D(A) \text{ for } t-s > 0$$

$$= v(\alpha) - \int_0^{\alpha} f(s)ds$$

Hence $$v(\alpha) = \int_0^{\alpha} f(s)ds + \int_0^{\alpha} Av(s)ds$$

is differentiable almost everywhere and so satisfies (2.17) almost everywhere. However even this result is too restrictive for most applications so instead we choose to work with the input-output relation (2.20).

Definition 2.23 Mild solution

If $f \in L_p(0,t_1;Z)$, $p \geq 1$, we say that

(2.21) $$z(t) = T_t z_0 + \int_0^t T_{t-s}f(s)ds$$

is a mild solution of (2.19) on $[0,t_1]$.

We note that (2.21) is well defined when the integral is interpreted in the sense of Bochner and we show that

Lemma 2.24

$z(t)$ defined by (2.21) is strongly continuous on $[0,t_1]$.

Proof

Without loss of generality we can assume $z_0 = 0$. For $\delta>0$, consider

$$z(t+\delta)-z(t) = \int_0^t (T_{t+\delta-s}-T_{t-s})f(s)ds + \int_t^{t+\delta} T_{t+\delta-s}f(s)ds$$

Then

$$\|z(t+\delta)-z(t)\| \leq \|(T_\delta-I)z(t)\| + \left(\int_t^{t+\delta} \|T_{t+\delta-s}\|^q\, ds\right)^{\frac{1}{q}} \left(\int_t^{t+\delta} \|f(s)\|^p\, ds\right)^{\frac{1}{p}}$$

$$\to 0 \quad \text{as } \delta \to 0^+ \text{ by (2.6) and Theorem 2.5(b)}$$

Now consider

$$z(t-\delta)-z(t) = \int_0^{t-\delta} (T_{t-\delta-s}-T_{t-s})f(s)ds - \int_{t-\delta}^t T_{t-s}f(s)ds$$

Then

$$\|z(t-\delta)-z(t)\| \leq \int_0^{t-\delta} \|(T_{t-\delta-s}-T_{t-s})f(s)\|ds + \int_{t-\delta}^t \|T_{t-s}f(s)\|ds$$

Now $(T_{t-\delta-s}-T_{t-s})f(s) \to 0$ as $\delta \to 0$ and $\|(T_{t-\delta-s}-T_{t-s})f(s)\|$ is Bochner integrable from Theorem 2.5(a) and since $f \in L^p(0,t_1;Z)$.

So the first term converges to zero as $\delta \to 0$ by the Lebesque dominated convergence theorem. The second term tends to zero by Theorem 2.5(d).

We can show that this mild solution is the same as the concept of weak solution used in the study of partial differential equations.

Definition 2.25

Let Z be a reflexive Banach space, and $f \in L^p[0,t_1;Z]$, then we say that z is a weak solution of

$$(2.22) \qquad \dot{z} = Az + f \;, \qquad z(0) = z_o$$

if a) $t \to z(t)$ is continuous on $[0,t_1]$

b) $$\int_0^{t_1} \langle g(t), z(t)\rangle \, dt + \int_0^{t_1} \langle x(t), f(t)\rangle \, dt + \langle x(0), z_o\rangle = 0$$

for all $g \in C[0,t_1;Z^*]$, where

$$x(t) = -\int_t^{t_1} T^*_{s-t} g(s)ds$$

Proposition 2.26

For every $z_o \in Z$ there exists a unique weak solution of (2.22) and this is the mild solution of (2.22).

Proof

Substituting for $x(t)$ we see that b) is equivalent to

$$\int_0^{t_1} \langle g(t), \left(z(t) - T_t z_o - \int_0^t T_{t-s} f(s)ds\right)\rangle \, dt = 0$$

which shows that the mild solution is a weak solution and vice versa.

To prove uniqueness we note that if $\bar{z}(t)$ is a second weak solution, then

$$\int_0^{t_1} \langle g(t), z(t) - \bar{z}(t)\rangle \, dt = 0 \qquad \forall \;\; g \in C[0,t_1;Z^*]$$

and hence $z(t) = \bar{z}(t)$.

Finally, we note that for a smoother class of g, say $g \in C^1[0,t_1;Z^*]$, we have

$$\dot{x} + A^*x = g \;, \qquad x(t_1) = 0$$

and then b) becomes

$$\int_0^{t_1} <\dot{x}(t)+A^*x(t),z(t)> dt + \int_0^{t_1} <x(t),f(t)> dt + <x(0),z_0> = 0$$

which is the more familiar definition of a weak solution.

2.3 Analytic semigroups

A particularly important class of strongly continuous semigroups are those which can be continued analytically as functions of t into a sector in the complex plane containing $t > 0$.

Definition 2.27 Analytic semigroup

An alalytic semigroup T_t is a strongly continuous semigroup with the additional properties

a) T_t can be continued analytically into the sector

$$S_\omega : |\arg t| < \omega : \omega \in (0,\pi/2) \qquad t \neq 0$$

b) for each $t \in S_\omega$, and all $z \in Z$

$$\frac{d}{dt} T_t z = AT_t z \text{ and } AT_t \in \mathcal{L}(Z)$$

c) for any $0 < \varepsilon < \omega, \exists\, K > 0$ such that

$$\|T_t\| \leq K, \quad \|AT_t\| \leq \frac{K}{|t|}, \quad t \in S_{\omega-\varepsilon}$$

Theorem 2.28

Assume A is a closed densely-defined linear operator on a Banach space Z, with

a) Resolvent of A, $\rho(A)$, is contained in the sector $S_{\frac{1}{2}\pi+\omega}$ for some $\omega \in (0,\frac{1}{2}\pi)$

b) $\exists$ M > 0 independent of λ, such that

(2.23) $$\|R(\lambda,A)\| \leq \frac{M}{|\lambda|}, \quad \text{for } \lambda \in S_{\frac{1}{2}\pi+\omega}$$

then A generates an analytic semigroup.

Proof

We will define T_t via the Dunford integral

(2.24) $$T_t = (2\pi i)^{-1} \int_\Gamma e^{\lambda t} R(\lambda,A)d\lambda$$

where Γ is a contour in $S_{\frac{1}{2}\pi+\omega-\varepsilon}$ running from infinity with arg $\lambda = \frac{1}{2}\pi+\omega-\varepsilon$ to infinity with arg $\lambda = -(\frac{1}{2}\pi+\omega-\varepsilon)$ in such a manner that $|\arg t\lambda| > \frac{1}{2}\pi$ for $\lambda \in \Gamma$, $|\arg t| < \omega$ and $|\lambda| \to \infty$. Then the integral converges absolutely and uniformly and since it can be differentiated, it follows that T_t is analytic in $S_{\omega-\varepsilon}$. In fact using the closedness of A, we have

$$\frac{d}{dt} T_t = \frac{1}{2\pi i} \int_\Gamma e^{\lambda t} \lambda R(\lambda,A)d\lambda$$

$$= \frac{1}{2\pi i} \int_\Gamma e^{\lambda t} (I+AR(\lambda,A))d\lambda$$

$$= \frac{A}{2\pi i} \int_\Gamma e^{\lambda t} R(\lambda,A)d\lambda = AT_t$$

Hence $AT_t = \frac{d}{dt} T_t$, $t \in S_{\omega-\varepsilon}$.

The semigroup property for T_t is proved as follows. We assume T_s is given by a formula like (2.24) but with Γ shifted to the right by a small amount to give a new contour Γ', then

$$T_s T_t = \frac{1}{(2\pi i)^2} \int_{\Gamma'}\int_\Gamma e^{\lambda' s+\lambda t} R(\lambda',A)R(\lambda,A)d\lambda\, d\lambda'$$

Using the resolvent equation

$$R(\lambda',A)R(\lambda,A) = (\lambda-\lambda')^{-1}(R(\lambda',A)-R(\lambda,A))$$

we find

$$T_s T_t = \frac{1}{(2\pi i)^2}\left(\int_{\Gamma'} e^{\lambda' s} R(\lambda',A)d\lambda' \int_\Gamma e^{\lambda t}(\lambda-\lambda')^{-1}d\lambda \right.$$

$$\left. - \int_\Gamma e^{\lambda t} R(\lambda,A)d\lambda \int_{\Gamma'} e^{\lambda' s}(\lambda-\lambda')^{-1}d\lambda \right)$$

But $\int_\Gamma e^{\lambda t}(\lambda-\lambda')^{-1}d\lambda = 0$ and $\int_{\Gamma'} e^{\lambda' s}(\lambda-\lambda')^{-1}d\lambda' = -2\pi i e^{\lambda s}$

Hence $T_s T_t = T_{t+s}$.

Now we change the integration variable λ to $\lambda|t|$ and denote the new contour by $\Gamma' = \Gamma|t|$. Then by the Cauchy Theorem

$$T_t = \frac{1}{2\pi i}\int_{\Gamma} e^{\lambda'(t/|t|)} R((\lambda'/|t|),A)|t|^{-1}\, d\lambda'$$

Hence from (2.23)

$$\|T_t\| \leq \frac{M}{2\pi}\int_{\Gamma} e^{\lambda'(t/|t|)}\ |\lambda|^{-1}|d\lambda'| \ \leq\ K$$

Also
$$AT_t = (2\pi i)^{-1}\int_{\Gamma} e^{\lambda'(t/|t|)} AR((\lambda'/|t|),A)|t|^{-1}\, d\lambda'$$

$$= (2\pi i)^{-1}\int_{\Gamma} e^{\lambda'(t/|t|)}\left(\frac{\lambda'}{|t|}R\left(\frac{\lambda'}{|t|},A\right)-I\right)|t^{-1}|\,d\lambda'$$

Hence

(2.25) $$\|AT_t\| \leq \frac{K}{|t|}$$

To prove the strong continuity of T_t, we compute for $z \in D(A)$,

$$T_t z - z = \frac{1}{2\pi i}\int_{\Gamma} e^{\lambda t}\left\{R(\lambda,A)-\lambda^{-1}\right\} z\, d\lambda$$

$$= \frac{1}{2\pi i}\int_{\Gamma} e^{\lambda t} R(\lambda,A)Az\lambda^{-1}\, d\lambda$$

Hence $T_t z - z \to (2\pi i)^{-1}\int_{\Gamma} R(\lambda,A)Az\lambda^{-1}\, d\lambda = 0$ as $t \to 0^+$.

But T_t is bounded and $D(A)$ is dense in Z, hence

$$T_t z \to z \qquad \text{for} \quad t \in S_{\omega-\varepsilon}$$

For $z \in D(A)$ an easy calculation yields

$$AT_t z = T_t Az = \frac{d}{dt}T_t z$$

Hence the generator of T_t is equal to A on $D(A)$, and a similar argument to that used in Theorem 2.10 shows that in fact A generates T_t.

We have seen in the proof of this theorem that if T_t is an analytic semigroup with generator A, then $z(t) = T_t z_0$ for any $z_0 \in Z$ satisfies

$$\frac{dz}{dt} = Az\,, \qquad t > 0, \quad z(0) = z_0$$

The extra structure of analytic semigroups also enables us to relax the condition imposed for a solution of the inhomogeneous problem.

<u>Theorem 2.29</u>

If A generates an analytic semigroup T_t on a Banach space Z and $f(t)$ is Hölder continuous for $t \geq 0$, with

$$\|f(t)-f(s)\| \le L(t-s)^k \; ; \quad 0 \le s \le t \, , \quad L > 0$$

and $k < 1$. Then for any $z_o \in Z$

$$z(t) = T_t z_o + \int_o^t T_{t-s} f(s)ds$$

satisfies

(2.26) $$\dot{z} = Az + f \, , \quad t > 0; \quad z(0) = z_o$$

<u>Proof</u>

Clearly we only need to show

$$v(t) = \int_o^t T_{t-s} f(s)ds$$

satisfies (2.26). We have

(2.27) $$v(t) = \int_o^t T_{t-s}(f(s)-f(t))ds + \int_o^t T_{t-s} f(t)ds$$

Now $T_{t-s}(f(s)-f(t)) \in D(A)$ and

$$\int_o^t \|AT_{t-s}(f(s)-f(t))\| ds \le \int_o^t \frac{K}{(t-s)} L(s-t)^k ds < \infty$$

Hence since A is closed, $\int_o^t T_{t-s}(f(s)-f(t))ds \in D(A)$

$$A\int_o^t T_{t-s}(f(s)-f(t))ds = \int_o^t AT_{t-s}(f(s)-f(t))ds$$

But by Theorem 2.9(d)

$$\int_o^t T_{t-s} f(t)ds \in D(A)$$

and $$A \int_o^t T_{t-s} f(t)ds = (T_t - I)f(t)$$

So $v(t) \in D(A)$ with

(2.28) $$Av(t) = \int_o^t AT_{t-s}(f(s)-f(t))ds + (T_t - I)f(t)$$

(In fact it can be shown that $v(t) \in D(A)$ for $f \in L^2(0,t_1;Z)$)

For $t, \delta > 0$, we have

$$v(t+\delta) = \int_o^{t+\delta} T_{t+\delta-s} f(s)ds = T_\delta v(t) + \int_t^{t+\delta} T_{t+\delta-s} f(s)ds$$

and so $$\lim_{h \to 0^+} \frac{v(t+h)-v(t)}{h} = Av(t) + f(t),$$ so that

(2.29) $$D^+ v(t) = Av(t) + f(t)$$

Lemma 2.30

Av(t) is continuous for $t \geq 0$

Proof

We prove the continuity on the left for $t > 0$. Clearly the second term in (2.28) satisfies this assertion so we need only consider the first term for which we have

$$A \int_0^{t-h} T_{t-h-s}(f(s)-f(t-h))ds - A \int_0^{t} T_{t-s}(f(s)-f(t))ds$$

$$= A \int_0^{t-h} (T_{t-h-s}-T_{t-s})(f(s)-f(t-h))ds + A \int_0^{t-h} T_{t-s}(f(t)-f(t-h))ds$$

$$+ A \int_{t-h}^{t} T_{t-s}(f(s)-f(t))ds$$

Now in a similar manner to the proof of (2.25) it is possible to show that

$$\|A(T_t-T_s)\| \leq \frac{K(t-s)}{ts}, \quad 0 < s \leq t$$

Using this and the Hölder continuity we obtain the following estimate for the first term on the right

$$KhL \int_0^{t-h} \frac{(t-s-h)^k}{(t-s)(t-s-h)} ds \to 0 \quad \text{as} \quad h \to 0^+$$

Now from Theorem 2.9 the second term is equal to

$$T_t(f(t)-f(t-h)) - T_h(f(t)-f(t-h))$$

which can be estimated by

$$L(Me^{\omega t} + 1)h^k \to 0 \quad \text{as} \quad h \to 0^+$$

Finally for the third term we obtain the estimate

$$\int_{t-h}^{t} \frac{LK}{(t-s)} (t-s)^k \, ds \to 0 \quad \text{as} \quad h \to 0^+$$

A similar construction shows that Av(t) is continuous from the right and so the lemma is proved.

Now (2.29) and lemma 2.30 show that v(t) is differentiable from the left as well and satisfies (2.26).

2.4 Perturbation theory

In applications to control problems, the inhomogeneous term f in (2.19) is often determined by a control input and if this is of feedback type, we have

$$f(t) = Bz(t)$$

and we must study

$$(2.30) \qquad z(t) = T_t z_o + \int_o^t T_{t-s} Bz(s)ds$$

Theorem 2.31

Let A generate a strongly continuous semigroup T_t on a Banach space Z, and let $B \in \mathcal{L}(Z)$, then A+B generates a strongly continuous semigroup S_t, defined by

$$S_t z_o = T_t z_o + \int_o^t T_{t-s} BS_s z_o ds \ , \quad z_o \in Z$$

Moreover, if $\|T_t\| \leq Me^{\omega t}$, then

$$\|S_t\| \leq Me^{(\omega+M\|B\|)t}$$

Proof

First we show that S_t defined by (2.30) is a strongly continuous semigroup. We will seek a solution by the following scheme

$$(2.31) \qquad S_t = \sum_{n=o}^{\infty} S_t^n$$

where

$$(2.32) \qquad S_t^n z_o = \int_o^t T_{t-s} BS_s^{n-1} z_o ds \ , \qquad S_t^o = T_t$$

It is easy to obtain the following estimate by induction

$$\|S_t^n\| \leq M^{n+1} \|B\|^n e^{\omega t} \frac{t^n}{n!}$$

So the series $S_t = \sum_{n=o}^{\infty} S_t^n$ is majorized by

$$Me^{\omega t} \sum_{n=o}^{\infty} \frac{(M\|B\|t)^n}{n!} = Me^{(\omega+M\|B\|)t}$$

Thus $\sum_{n=o}^{\infty} S_t^n$ is absolutely convergent in the uniform topology of $\mathcal{L}(Z)$ on any compact interval. Moreover

$$(2.33) \qquad S_t z_o = \sum_{n=o}^{\infty} S_t^n z_o = S_t^o z_o + \sum_{n=1}^{\infty} S_t^n z_o$$

$$= T_t z_o + \sum_{n=1}^{\infty} \int_o^t T_{t-s} BS_s^{n-1} z_o ds$$

$$= T_t z_o + \int_o^t T_{t-s} BS_s z_o ds$$

So that our construction yields a solution of (2.30) satisfying $S_o = I$.

To prove uniqueness we assume a second solution $\bar{S}_t$, then subtracting the equations for S_t and $\bar{S}_t$ gives

$$(S_t-\bar{S}_t)z_o = \int_o^t T_{t-s}B(S_s-\bar{S}_s)z_o ds$$

Hence $\quad \|(S_t-\bar{S}_t)z_o\| \leq \int_o^t Me^{\omega(t-s)}\|B\|\,\|(S_s-\bar{S}_s)z_o\|\, ds$

Setting $e^{-\omega t}\|(S_t-\bar{S}_t)z_o\| = g(t)$, yields

$$g(t) \leq M\|B\| \int_o^t g(s)ds$$

whence $g(t) = 0$ from Gronwall's lemma.

To prove S_t is strongly continuous, we compute for $h > 0$

$$\|S_{t+h}z_o-S_tz_o\| \leq \|T_{t+h}z_o-T_tz_o\| + \int_o^t \|(T_{t+h-s}-T_{t-s})BS_sz_o\|\, ds + \int_t^{t+h} \|T_{t+h-s}BS_sz_o\|\, ds$$

So using the Lebesque dominated convergence theorem, the strong continuity of T_t, and the bounds for T_t and S_t, we see that S_tz_o is continuous on the right. For the continuity on the left, we have

$$\begin{aligned}\|S_{t-h}z_o-S_tz_o\| &\leq \|T_{t-h}z_o-T_tz_o\| + \Big\|\int_o^{t-h} T_{t-h-s}BS_sz_o ds - \int_o^t T_{t-s}BS_sz_o ds\Big\| \\ &= \|T_{t-h}z_o-T_tz_o\| + \Big\|\int_o^{t-h} T_{t-h-s}BS_sz_o ds - \int_{-h}^{t-h} T_{t-h-s}BS_{s+h}z_o ds\Big\| \\ &\leq \|T_{t-h}z_o-T_tz_o\| + \Big\|\int_o^{t-h} T_{t-h-s}B(S_s-S_{s+h})z_o\, ds\Big\| \\ &\quad + \int_{-h}^{o} \|T_{t-s-h}BS_{s+h}z_o\| ds\end{aligned}$$

Using the right continuity of S_t, the strong continuity of T_t, and the bounds for T_t, S_t and the Lebesque dominated convergence theorem we see that S_tz_o is continuous on the left, and hence S_t is strongly continuous.

In order to prove the semigroup property $S_{t+s} = S_tS_s$, we use (2.33) to obtain

$$\begin{aligned}S_{t+s}z_o-S_tS_sz_o &= T_{t+s}z_o + \int_o^{t+s} T_{t+s-\alpha}ABS_\alpha z_o d\alpha \\ &\quad -\left(T_t + \int_o^t T_{t-\alpha}BS_\alpha d\alpha\right)\left(T_sz_o + \int_o^s T_{s-\beta}BS_\beta z_o d\beta\right) \\ &= \int_o^{t+s} T_{t+s-\alpha}BS_\alpha z_o d\alpha - \int_o^s T_{t+s-\beta}BS_\beta z_o d\beta - \int_o^t T_{t-\alpha}BS_\alpha S_sz_o d\alpha \\ &= \int_s^{t+s} T_{t+s-\alpha}BS_\alpha z_o d\alpha - \int_o^t T_{t-\alpha}BS_\alpha S_sz_o d\alpha \\ &= \int_o^t T_{t-\alpha}B(S_{s+\alpha}-S_sS_\alpha)z_o d\alpha\end{aligned}$$

Hence
$$\| S_{t+s}z_o - S_t S_s z_o \| \le M\|B\| \int_o^t e^{\omega(t-s)} \| S_{s+\alpha} - S_s S_\alpha z_o \| d\alpha$$

If $\quad g(t) = e^{-\omega t}\| S_{t+s}z_o - S_t S_s z_o \|$, then

$$g(t) \le M\|B\| \int_o^t g(s)ds$$

So by Gronwall s lemma,

$$g(t) \le g(0)e^{M\|B\|t}$$

But $\quad g(0) = \| S_s z_o - S_s z_o \| = 0$, so

$$S_{t+s} = S_t S_s$$

By Theorem 2.9 we know that the infinitesimal generator of S_t must be a closed densely defined operator, but although we have motivated the construction of S_t via the operator A+B, we have yet to prove that A+B is its generator. To see that this is the case we show that

$$\int_o^t S_{t-\alpha}(A+B)z_o d\alpha = S_t z_o - z_o, \qquad z_o \in D(A) \tag{2.34}$$

Now from (2.29)

$$\int_o^t S_{t-\alpha}(A+B)z_o d\alpha = \int_o^t T_{t-\alpha}Az_o d\alpha + \int_o^t T_{t-\alpha}Bz_o d\alpha$$
$$+ \int_o^t \int_\alpha^t T_{t-s}BS_{s-\alpha}(A+B)z_o ds d\alpha$$

By Theorem 2.9(d) we have

$$\int_o^t S_{t-\alpha}(A+B)z_o d\alpha = T_t z_o - z_o + \int_o^t T_{t-s}B\left(\int_o^s S_{s-\alpha}(A+B)z_o d\alpha + z_o\right)ds$$

Thus $\int_o^t S_{t-\alpha}(A+B)z_o d\alpha + z_o$ is a solution of (2.30). But we know that $S_t z_o$ is the unique solution of (2.30) so we have (2.34).

Hence
$$\lim_{h\to o+} \frac{S_h z_o - z_o}{h} = \lim_{h\to o+} \left(\int_o^h S_\alpha (A+B)z_o d\alpha\right)\Big/ h, \qquad z_o \in D(A)$$
$$= (A+B)z_o$$

But A+B is closed and densely defined, and so A+B is the generator of S_t.

In the above theorem we assumed that $B \in \mathcal{L}(Z)$. However we will also need to consider perturbation operators $B \in \mathcal{B}^\infty(0,t_1; \mathcal{L}(Z))$, where

$$\mathcal{B}^\infty(0,t_1; \mathcal{L}(Z)) = \left\{ B: B(\cdot)z_o \text{ is strongly measurable and } \operatorname*{ess\,sup}_{0\le t\le t_1} \|B(t)\|_{\mathcal{L}(Z)} < \infty \right\} \tag{2.35}$$

In this case we are examining abstract evolution operators of the form $A+B(t)$ and we would not expect them to generate one-parameter semigroups.

Definition 2.32 Mild evolution operator

Let $\Delta(t_1) = \{(t,s);\ 0 \le s \le t \le t_1\}$, then $U(t,s): \Delta(t_1) \to \mathcal{L}(Z)$ is a mild evolution operator if

a) $U(t,t) = I$, $t \in [0,t_1]$

b) $U(t,r)U(r,s) = U(t,s)$, $0 \le s \le t \le t_1$

c) $U(\cdot,s)$ is strongly continuous on $[s,t_1]$ and $U(t,\cdot)$ is strongly continuous on $[0,t]$

A consequence of c) is that $\operatorname{ess\,sup}_{\Delta(t_1)} \|U(t,s)\| < \infty$.

Clearly if T_t is a strongly continuous semigroup, then T_{t-s} is a mild evolution operator.

Motivated by (2.30) we can construct a mild evolution operator which is associated with the operator $A+B(t)$, by

(2.36) $$U(t,s)z_0 = T_{t-s}z_0 + \int_s^t T_{t-\alpha}B(\alpha)U(\alpha,s)z_0\, d\alpha$$

The construction is carried out by the following scheme

(2.37) $$U_0(t,s) = T_{t-s}$$

(2.38) $$U_n(t,s)z_0 = \int_s^t T_{t-\alpha}B(\alpha)U_{n-1}(\alpha,s)z_0\, d\alpha$$

and

(2.39) $$U(t,s) = \sum_{n=0}^{\infty} U_n(t,s)$$

Using the same method as we used in proving Theorem 2.31, we can establish the following

Theorem 2.33

If T_t is a strongly continuous semigroup on Z and $B \in \mathcal{B}^\infty(0,t_1;\ \mathcal{L}(Z))$, then (2.39) is the unique solution of (2.36) in the class of mild evolution operators on Z.

Unfortunately it is not true that $U(t,s)z$ is differentiable in t and so we cannot hope for solutions in the usual sense of the differential equation

(2.40) $$\dot z = (A+B(t))z\ ; \quad z(0) = z_0 \in D(A)$$

Still, we can regard $U(t,0)z_0$ as the mild solution of (2.40) as it satisfies the integral equation

(2.41) $$z(t) = T_t z_0 + \int_0^t T_{t-\alpha}B(\alpha)z(\alpha)d\alpha$$

Surprisingly we can prove differentiability in the second variable.

Theorem 2.34

Under the assumptions of Theorem 2.33, for $z_o \in D(A)$,

$$\int_s^t U(t,\alpha)(A+B(\alpha))z_o \, d\alpha = U(t,s)z_o - z_o \tag{2.42}$$

$$\frac{\partial}{\partial s} U(t,s)z_o = -U(t,s)(A+B(s))z_o \quad \text{a.e.} \tag{2.43}$$

Proof

Consider the system

$$U_o'(t,s) = T_{t-s}$$

$$U_n'(t,s)z_o = \int_s^t U_{n-1}'(t,\alpha)B(\alpha)T_{\alpha-s}z_o \, d\alpha$$

Then as in Theorem 2.31, we can show that

$$U'(t,s) = \sum_{n=o}^{\infty} U_n'(t,s)$$

is the unique solution of

$$U'(t,s)z_o = T_{t-s}z_o + \int_s^t U'(t,\alpha)B(\alpha)T_{\alpha-s}z_o ds \tag{2.44}$$

But by induction, $U_n'(t,s) = U_n(t,s)$ for each $n \geq 0$, and so

$$U(t,s) = U'(t,s)$$

Hence for $z_o \in D(A)$,

$$U(t,\alpha)Az_o = T_{t-\alpha}Az_o + \int_\alpha^t U(t,\beta)B(\beta)T_{\beta-\alpha}Az_o d\beta$$

and both terms on the right are integrable by Theorem 2.9, so

$$\int_s^t U(t,\alpha)Az_o d\alpha = \int_s^t T_{t-\alpha}Az_o d\alpha + \int_s^t \int_\alpha^t U(t,\beta)B(\beta)T_{\beta-\alpha}Az_o d\beta \, d\alpha$$

$$= \int_s^t T_{t-\alpha}Az_o d\alpha + \int_s^t \int_s^\beta U(t,\beta)B(\beta)T_{\beta-\alpha}Az_o d\alpha \, d\beta$$

by Fubini's theorem

$$= (T_{t-s}-I)z_o + \int_s^t U(t,\beta)B(\beta)(T_{\beta-s}-I)z_o d\beta$$

by Theorem 2.9(d)

So $\int_s^t U(t,\alpha)(A+B(\alpha))z_o d\alpha = U(t,s)z_o - z_o$ by (2.44) and this implies (2.43).

It turns out that this property is important for control and filtering problems so we give operators with the property (2.42) a special name.

Definition 2.35 Quasi-evolution operators

A quasi-evolution operator $U(t,s)$ is a mild evolution operator such that there exists a non-zero $z_o \in Z$ and a closed linear operator $A(s)$ on Z for almost all $s \in [0,t_1]$ satisfying

$$U(t,s)z_o - z_o = \int_s^t U(t,\alpha)A(\alpha)z_o d\alpha \tag{2.45}$$

We denote the set of $z_o \in Z$ for which (2.45) is valid as D_A, and we call $A(t)$ the quasi generator of $U(t,s)$.
Those quasi evolution operators which are also differentiable in the first variable are also important in applications and so we define

Definition 2.36 Almost strong evolution operators

An almost strong evolution operator is a mild evolution operator on Z for which there exists an associated closed linear operator $A(t)$ on Z for almost all $t \in [0,t_1]$ such that

$$U(t,s) : D(A(s)) \to D(A(t)) \text{ for almost all } t>s\in[0,t_1] \tag{2.46}$$

$$\int_s^t A(r)U(r,s)z_o dr = (U(t,s)-I)z_o \tag{2.47}$$

for $z_o \in D(A(s))$.

(2.46) implies that

$$\frac{\partial}{\partial t} U(t,s)z_o = A(t)U(t,s)z_o \text{ a.e. for } z_o \in D(A(s)) \tag{2.47$'$}$$

This of course means that (2.40) will have a unique solution $z(t) = U(t,0)z_o$ which is differentiable almost everywhere. If $U(t,s)$ satisfies (2.46) and (2.47) everywhere it is called a strong evolution operator in the literature, although for our purposes we only use the almost strong concept. We now give sufficient conditions for $A+B(t)$ to generate an almost strong evolution operator.

Lemma 2.37

Suppose T_t is a strongly continuous semigroup on Z and $B \in \mathcal{B}^\infty(0,t_1;\mathcal{L}(Z))$ satisfies

$$\begin{aligned} &T_{t-s}B(s) : Z \to D(A) \quad \text{for almost all } t > s \in [0,t_1] \\ &AT_{t-\cdot}B(\cdot) \in \mathcal{B}^1(0,t;\mathcal{L}(Z)) \end{aligned} \tag{2.48}$$

that is $AT_{t-s}B(s)z_o$ is strongly measurable in s $\forall$ $z_o \varepsilon Z$ and $\int_0^{t_1} \|AT_{t-s}B(s)\|_{\mathcal{L}(Z)}\, ds < \infty$. Then the mild evolution operator U(t,s) generated by A+B(t) is an almost strong evolution operator.

Proof

From (2.36), U(t,s) is defined by

$$U(\alpha,s)z_o = T_{\alpha-s}z_o + \int_s^\alpha T_{\alpha-r}B(r)U(r,s)z_o dr, \quad z_o \varepsilon Z$$

Now by (2.48), $T_{\alpha-r}B(r)U(r,s)z_o \varepsilon D(A)$

and $AT_{\alpha-r}B(r)U(r,s)z_o$ is integrable on (s,α).

Since A is a closed linear operator, we conclude that

$$A\int_s^\alpha T_{\alpha-r}B(r)U(r,s)z_o dr = \int_s^\alpha AT_{\alpha-r}B(r)U(r,s)z_o dr$$

Hence we can integrate, obtaining

$$\int_s^t A\int_s^\alpha T_{\alpha-r}B(r)U(r,s)z_o dr\, d\alpha = \int_s^t \int_r^t AT_{\alpha-r}B(r)U(r,s)z_o\, d\alpha\, dr$$

by Fubini's theorem

$$= \int_s^t (T_{t-r}-I)B(r)U(r,s)z_o\, dr$$

by Theorem 2.9(d)

Hence from (2.36), we have

$$\int_s^t A(U(\alpha,s)-T_{\alpha-s})z_o d\alpha = U(t,s)z_o - T_{t-s}z_o - \int_s^t B(r)U(r,s)z_o dr$$

Thus using Theorem 2.9(d) again,

$$\int_s^t (A+B(\alpha))U(\alpha,s)z_o d\alpha = U(t,s)z_o - z_o$$

For other examples of evolution operators see Chapter 9.

2.5 Abstract evolution equations

In the following chapters we shall meet equations of the form

$$(2.49) \qquad \dot{z} = (A+B(t))z + f(t) \;;\quad z(0)=z_o \varepsilon D(A)$$

where A is the infinitesimal generator of a strongly continuous semigroup T_t, $B \varepsilon \mathcal{B}^\infty(0,t_1;\mathcal{L}(Z))$, and $f \varepsilon L^1(0,t_1;Z)$.

It is natural to define the mild solution of (2.49) to be

$$(2.50) \qquad z(t) = U(t,0)z_o + \int_0^t U(t,s)f(s)ds$$

where $U(t,s)$ is the quasi evolution operator generated by $A+B(t)$.

Then the following result is proved exactly as Lemma 2.22 using property (2.43) for almost strong evolution operators.

Theorem 2.38

If $U(t,s)$ is an almost strong evolution operator and $U(t,s)f(s) \varepsilon D(A)$ for almost all $t > s \varepsilon [0,t_1]$ and $AU(t,\cdot)f(\cdot)$ is Bochner integrable, then (2.50) is the unique solution of (2.49).

From this we can also deduce the useful corollary

Corollary 2.39

If T_t and $B(t)$ satisfy the assumptions of Lemma 2.37, then (2.50) is the unique solution of (2.49) provided that $T_t z_o$ and $T_{t-s}f(s) \varepsilon D(A)$ for almost all $t > s \varepsilon [0,t_1]$, and $AT_{t-s}f(s)$ is Bochner integrable on $(0,t)$.

Proof

Now from the proof of Lemma 2.37, $U(t,s): Z \to D(A)$ and

$$AU(t,s)f(s) = AT_{t-s}f(s) + \int_s^t AT_{t-\alpha}B(\alpha)U(\alpha,s)f(s)d\alpha$$

and this is measurable in s, and

$$\int_0^t \|AT_{t-s}f(s)\|ds < \infty \qquad \text{by assumption.}$$

So
$$\int_0^t \|\int_s^t AT_{t-\alpha}B(\alpha)U(\alpha,s)f(s)d\alpha\|ds \leq \int_0^t\int_s^t \|AT_{t-\alpha}B(\alpha)\| \|U(\alpha,s)\| \|f(s)\| d\alpha\, ds$$
$$\leq \text{const} \int_0^t \|AT_{t-\alpha}B(\alpha)\| d\alpha \int_0^t \|f(s)\| ds$$
$$< \infty \text{ by (2.48) and Definition 2.32(c).}$$

Hence $\int_0^t \|AU(t,s)f(s)\|ds < \infty$ and the assumptions of Theorem 2.38 are satisfied.

2.6 Examples

Example 2.40

A large class of partial differential equations (of the parabolic type) can be associated with analytic semigroups. In this example we consider a special case of Example 2.4 where A is self adjoint on a Hilbert space H and $R(\lambda_o,A)$ is compact for some $\lambda_o \varepsilon \rho(A)$. This implies that $R(\lambda,A)$ is compact for all $\lambda \varepsilon \rho(A)$ (see [10]) and also

a) $\exists$ an infinite sequence $\{\lambda_j\}$ of distinct eigenvalues of A, $|\lambda_j| \to \infty$ as $j \to \infty$, each with finite multiplicity r_j equal to the dimensionality of the corresponding eigenmanifold. Moreover since we are also assuming A generates a strongly continuous semigroup, the λ_j are bounded above and can be ordered $\ldots \lambda_n < \ldots < \lambda_2 < \lambda_1 \leq$ const.

b) $\exists$ a complete orthonormal set $\{\phi_{jk}\}$ of eigenvectors of A.

c) the spectrum consists only of the point spectrum

d) from the unique expansion

$$z = \sum_{j=1}^{\infty} \sum_{k=1}^{r_j} \langle z, \phi_{jk} \rangle \phi_{jk}$$

one gets for $z \in D(A)$

$$Az = \sum_{j=1}^{\infty} \lambda_j \sum_{k=1}^{r_j} \langle z, \phi_{jk} \rangle \phi_{jk}$$

e) for λ not in $P\sigma(A)$ and each $z \in H$

$$R(\lambda, A) z = \sum_{j=1}^{\infty} \frac{1}{\lambda - \lambda_j} \sum_{k=1}^{r_j} \langle z, \phi_{jk} \rangle \phi_{jk}$$

f) the semigroup generated by A is given by

$$T_t z = \sum_{j=1}^{\infty} e^{\lambda_j t} \sum_{k=1}^{r_j} \langle z, \phi_{jk} \rangle \phi_{jk} , \quad z \in H, \ t \geq 0$$

These results may be found in [5] or [10]. Moreover it is easy to obtain the estimate

$$\|R(\lambda, A)\| \leq \frac{M}{|\lambda|}$$

so the semigroup T_t is analytic.

As a special case we consider the partial differential equation of Example 1.2. If we set

$$Az = \frac{k}{\rho c_1} \frac{\partial^2 z}{\partial x^2} - \frac{\alpha}{\rho c_1} z$$

with $\quad D(A) = \left\{ z \in L_2(0,1) : \ \frac{\partial^2 z}{\partial x^2} \in L_2(0,1), \ \frac{\partial z}{\partial x} = 0 \text{ at } x = 0,1 \right\}$

Then A is self adjoint with compact resolvent. The eigenvalues are

$$\rho c_1 \lambda_j = \alpha + (j-1)^2 \pi^2 k \quad \text{and eigenvectors}$$

$$\phi_{j1} = \frac{1}{\sqrt{2}} \cos (j-1) \pi x \qquad j > 1, \quad \phi_{11} = 1$$

Example 2.41

As a special case of Example 2.16, we consider Example 1.5 with $\rho(\xi) = \alpha(\xi) = 1 \ \forall \ \xi \in [0,1]$, then

(2.51)
$$z_{tt} = z_{\xi\xi}$$
$$z(0,t) = z(1,t) = 0$$

If $H = L^2[0,1]$, and $Az = -z_{\xi\xi}$, $z \in D(A)$, where

$$D(A) = H^2(0,1) \cap H_0^1(0,1)$$

then $A^* = A$, and

$$\langle z,Az\rangle_H = \int_0^1 z_\xi^2(\xi)dx \geq \pi^2 \int_0^1 z^2(\xi)d\xi = \pi^2 \|z\|_H^2$$

So we may apply the results of Example 2.16 to conclude that the operator

$$\mathcal{A}w = \begin{bmatrix} 0 & I \\ -A & 0 \end{bmatrix} \begin{bmatrix} w_1 \\ w_2 \end{bmatrix}$$

$$D(\mathcal{A}) = D(A) \times D(A^{\frac{1}{2}})$$

on $\mathcal{H} = D(A^{\frac{1}{2}}) \times H$ generates a strongly continuous semigroup T_t. Here the inner product on $\mathcal{H}$ is for $w,\bar{w} \in H_0^1(0,1) \times L^2(0,1)$ equivalent to

$$\langle w,\bar{w}\rangle = \int_0^1 w_{1\xi}(\xi)\bar{w}_{1\xi}(\xi)d\xi + \int_0^1 w_2(\xi)\bar{w}_2(\xi)d\xi$$

and

$$(2.52) \qquad T_t \begin{bmatrix} w_1 \\ w_2 \end{bmatrix} = \begin{bmatrix} \Sigma \ 2[\langle w_1,\phi_n\rangle \cos n\pi t + \frac{1}{n\pi}\langle w_2,\phi_n\rangle \sin n\pi t]\phi_n \\ \Sigma \ 2[-n\pi\langle w_1,\phi_n\rangle \sin n\pi t + \langle w_2,\phi_n\rangle \cos n\pi t]\phi_n \end{bmatrix}$$

where $\phi_n = \sin n\pi\xi$.

The mild solution of (2.51) is

$$\begin{bmatrix} z \\ z_t \end{bmatrix} = T_t \begin{bmatrix} z_0 \\ z_{0t} \end{bmatrix}$$

for $z_0 \in H_0^1(0,1)$, $z_{0t} \in L^2[0,1]$. If instead $z_0 \in D(A)$, $z_{0t} \in H_0^1[0,1]$, then this solution will be a strong solution.

Example 2.42 Delay equations

We consider the linear system on $[0,t_1]$

$$\dot{x}(t) = A_o x(t) + \sum_{i=1}^{n} A_i \begin{cases} x(t+\theta_i); & t+\theta_i \geq 0 \\ h(t+\theta_i); & t+\theta_i < 0 \end{cases} \tag{2.53}$$

$$+ \int_{-b}^{o} A_{o1}(\theta) \begin{cases} x(t+\theta) & ; t+\theta \geq 0 \\ h(t+\theta) & ; t+\theta < 0 \end{cases} d\theta$$

$$x(0) = h(0)$$

where $-b \leq \theta_n < \theta_{n-1} < \dots < \theta_1 < 0$ and b is a positive number. A_o, A_i; $i=1,2,\dots,n \in \mathcal{L}(H)$, where H is a Hilbert space, and $A_{o1} \in C(-b,0;\mathcal{L}(H))$.

It is possible to define this system on $C(-b,0;H)$, however for control applications it is sometimes useful to define the system on a Hilbert space. So we introduce the space $\mathcal{M}^2(-b,0;H)$ as follows:

Let $\mathcal{L}^2(-b,0;H)$ be the space of measurable, square integrable H valued functions on $[-b,0]$, then $\mathcal{M}^2(-b,0;H)$ is the space of equivalence classes of functions in $\mathcal{L}^2(-b,0;H)$ under the equivalence relation

$$\langle f,g\rangle_{\mathcal{M}^2} = \langle f(0),g(0)\rangle_H + \int_{-b}^{o} \langle f(t),g(t)\rangle_H \, dt$$

and is isometrically isomorphic to the space $H \times L^2(-b,0;H)$.

Detailed studies of Equation (2.53) have been made by a number of authors [1],[2],[4] and we summarize their main conclusions. First we introduce the space $AC^2(-b,0;H)$ as the space of absolutely continuous functions whose derivatives are square integrable, with the inner product

$$\langle f,g\rangle_{AC^2} = \int_{-b}^{o} \langle \frac{df}{dt}, \frac{dg}{dt}\rangle_H \, dt$$

AC^2 is a Hilbert space, and in [4] it has been shown that

$$x(t) = \phi(t,h) \in AC^2(0,t_1;H) \text{ for } h \in \mathcal{M}^2(-b,0;H)$$

Now we introduce $(h \circ x)_t \in \mathcal{M}^2(-b,0;H)$ defined by

$$(h \circ x)_t(\theta) = \begin{cases} x(t+\theta); & t+\theta \geq 0 \\ h(t+\theta); & t+\theta < 0 \end{cases}$$

for all $\theta \in [-b,0]$ and set

$$(T_t h)(\theta) = (h \circ x)_t(\theta) \tag{2.55}$$

where x is the solution of (2.53) satisfying 2.54. Then

a) $T_t \in \mathcal{L}(\mathcal{M}^2(-b,0;H))$

b) $T_o = I$ in $\mathcal{M}^2$

c) T_t is strongly continuous

d) $T_t : AC^2(-b,0;H) \rightarrow AC^2(-b,0;H)$

e) for $t > b$ $T_t : \mathcal{M}^2 \rightarrow AC^2$

f) $T_{t+s} = T_t T_s$

If we set $z(t) = T_t h$, then since T_t is a strongly continuous semi-group, we know that z satisfies an abstract evolution equation on $\mathcal{M}^2$

$$\dot{z} = Az \ ; \ z(0) = h$$

for $h \in D(A)$. From (2.53) it is clear that

$$(Ah)(\theta) = \begin{cases} A_o h(0) + \sum_{i=1}^{n} A_i h(\theta_i) + \int_{-b}^{0} A_{o1}(\theta) h(\theta) d\theta & ; \ \theta = 0 \\ \dfrac{dh}{d\theta} & ; \ \theta \neq 0 \end{cases}$$

and $D(A) = H^1[-b,0;H]$.

Later we shall consider the inhomogeneous equation

$$z(t) = T_t h + \int_0^t T_{t-s} \tilde{f}(s) ds \tag{2.56}$$

where $\tilde{f}$ is degenerate in the sense that

$$(\tilde{f}(s))(\theta) = \begin{cases} f(s) & ; \ \theta = 0 \\ 0 & ; \ \theta \neq 0 \end{cases}$$

$f \in L^2[0,T;H]$, then [4] $z(t)(0)$ is the solution of

$$\dot{x}(t) = A_o x(t) + \sum_{i=1}^{n} A_i \begin{cases} x(t+\theta_i) & t+\theta_i \geq 0 \\ h(t+\theta_i) & t+\theta_i < 0 \end{cases}$$

$$+ \int_{-b}^{0} A_{o1}(\theta) \begin{cases} x(t+\theta) & t+\theta \geq 0 \\ h(t+\theta) & t+\theta < 0 \end{cases} d\theta \ ; \qquad + f(t)$$

$$x(0) = h(0)$$

So the solution of inhomogeneous delay equations may be cast into the abstract form (2.21).

References

[1] Banks, H.T. The representation of solutions of linear functional differential equations, J. Diff. Eqns., 5 (1969) pp.399-410.

[2] Borisovic, J.G. and Turbabin, A.S. On the Cauchy problem for linear non-homogeneous differential equations with retarded arguments, Soviet Math, Dokl., 10 (1969), pp.401-405.

[3] Butzer, P.L. and Berens, H. Semigroups of operators and approximations, Springer Verlag, 1967.

[4] Delfour, M.C. and Mitter, S.K. Hereditary differential systems with constant delays I; General case, J. Diff. Eqns., 12 (1972), pp.213-235.

[5] Dunford, N. and Schwartz, J.T. Linear operators, Interscience 1959, 1963.

[6] Hille, E. and Phillips, R.S. Functional analysis and semigroups, Amer. Math. Soc. Coll. Publ., 31 (1957).

[7] Kato, T. Perturbation theory of linear operators, Springer Verlag, 1966.

[8] Kisynski, J. Applications of semigroups to partial differential equations, Course on control theory and topics in functional analysis, Trieste, 1974.

[9] Ladas, G.E. and Lashmikantham, V. Differential equations in abstract spaces, Academic Press, 1972.

[10] Taylor, A.E. Introduction to functional analysis, John Wiley, 1958.

[11] Yosida, K. Functional analysis, Springer Verlag, 1966.

CHAPTER 3

CONTROLLABILITY, OBSERVABILITY AND STABILITY

In this chapter we consider the controlled system

$$\dot{z} = Az + Bu, \quad z(0) = z_0 \tag{3.1}$$

where A generates a strongly continuous semigroup T_t on a Banach space Z, and B is a bounded operator from a control Banach space U to Z. However if z is a strict solution of (3.1) then $z(t) \in D(A)$ for all $t \in [0,t_1]$ so in the general case where A is unbounded, $D(A) \neq Z$, which means that the system cannot be steered to all of Z. We will, therefore choose to work with the mild solution. (Definition 2.23).

$$z(t) = T_t z_0 + \int_0^t T_{t-s}Bu(s)ds \tag{3.2}$$

and introduce the following concept of exact controllability.

<u>Definition 3.1</u> <u>Exact controllability on $[0,t_1]$</u>

Given any two points $z_0, z_1 \in Z$ we say (3.2) is exactly controllable on $[0,t_1]$ if there exists a control $u \in L^p[0,t_1;U]$ such that

$$z(t_1) = z_1$$

First we prove a negative result

<u>Proposition 3.2</u>

Let Z,U be Banach spaces and $B \in \mathcal{L}(U,Z)$ be such that B is a limit in the uniform topology of operators $\{B_n\}$ which belong to finite dimensional subspaces of $\mathcal{L}(U,Z)$. Then the operator

$$\Lambda u = \int_0^{t_1} T_s Bu(s)ds$$

from $L^1[0,t_1;U]$ into Z is compact.

Proof

In order to prove this proposition we first assume B is of the form

$$Bu = bu^*(u)$$

where $b \in Z$ and $u^* \in U^*$. For some integer N we set

$$t^i = \frac{it_1}{N} \quad i = 0,\dots,N$$

and define an operator $F_N: L^1[0,t_1;U] \to Z$ by

$$F_N u = \sum_{i=1}^{N} T_{t^i} b \int_{t^{i-1}}^{t^i} u^*(u(s))ds$$

Clearly F_N is compact and we show that F_N converges in the uniform topology to an operator F_∞ as $N \to \infty$, where

$$F_\infty u = \int_0^{t_1} T_s bu^*(u(s))ds$$

We have

$$\| F_N u - F_\infty u\|_Z \leq \sum_{i=1} \int_{t^{i-1}}^{t^i} \|T_s b - T_{t^i} b\|_Z \|u^*\| \, \|u(s)\|_U \, ds$$

But T_t is a strongly continuous semigroup on Z so that for $s \in (t^{i-1}, t^i)$ and N sufficiently large

$$\|T_s b - T_{t^i} b\|_Z \leq \varepsilon$$

Thus

$$\|F_N u - F_\infty u\|_Z \leq \varepsilon \|u^*\| \sum_{i=1}^{N} \int_{t^{i-1}}^{t^i} \| u(s)\|_U \, ds$$

$$\leq \varepsilon \|u^*\| \, \|u\|_{L^1[0,t_1;U]}$$

So F_∞ is the uniform limit of a sequence of compact operators and hence F_∞ is compact. We may easily extend this argument to any finite dimensional operator B_n, so the operator Λ_n defined by

$$\Lambda_n u = \int_0^{t_1} T_s B_n u(s)ds$$

is compact. We now show that $\Lambda_n \to \Lambda$ in the uniform topology as $n \to \infty$.

We have

$$\|\Lambda u-\Lambda_n u\|_Z \leq \int_0^{t_1} \|T_s(B-B_n)u(s)\|_Z ds$$

$$\leq \sup_{s\varepsilon[0,t_1]} \|T_s\| \, \|B-B_n\| \int_0^{t_1} \|u(s)\| \, ds$$

But $B_n \to B$ in the uniform topology, thus $\Lambda_n \to \Lambda$ in the uniform topology and so Λ is compact.

We note Λ can be expressed by

$$\Lambda u = \int_0^{t_1} T_{t_1-s} Bu(t_1-s)ds$$

Hence if B is the uniform limit of a sequence of finite dimensional operators (an example is a compact operator on a space with a Schauder basis), (3.2) cannot be exactly controllable. This indicates that the natural extension of the finite dimensional concept of controllability to infinite dimensions may be too strong for many infinite dimensional systems, even when we consider the mild solution (3.2). In this chapter we will introduce a number of different definitions of controllability, but before we do this we prove some theorems which will enable us to obtain necessary and sufficient conditions for controllability and link them naturally with the corresponding concepts of observability.

Theorem 3.3

Let $F \in \mathcal{L}(V,Z)$, $G \in \mathcal{L}(W,Z)$, where V,W,Z are Banach spaces, then if

$$\text{Range}(F) \subset \text{Range}(G)$$

there exists $\gamma > 0$, such that

$$\|F^*z^*\|_{V^*} \leq \gamma\|G^*z^*\|_{W^*}$$

Proof

First we assume that G is a 1-1 mapping, then G^{-1}: $R(G) \to W$ is well defined. Moreover $G^{-1}F$ is a closed transformation from V into W and is therefore bounded. Thus the adjoint of $G^{-1}F$ is bounded, and there exists $\gamma > 0$, such that

(3.3) $$\|(G^{-1}F)^* w^*\|_{V^*} \leq \gamma \|w^*\|_{W^*} \qquad \forall\, w^* \in W^*$$

Now for any $z^* \in Z^*$, we let $w^* = G^* z^*$, then for all $v \in V$

$$\begin{aligned}
\langle (G^{-1}F)^* w^*, v\rangle_{V^*,V} &= \langle (G^{-1}F)^* G^* z^*, v\rangle_{V^*,V} \\
&= \langle G^* z^*, G^{-1}Fv \rangle_{W^*,W} \\
&= \langle z^*, GG^{-1}Fv\rangle_{Z^*,Z} \\
&= \langle z^*, Fv\rangle_{Z^*,Z} \\
&= \langle F^* z^*, v\rangle_{V^*,V}
\end{aligned}$$

Thus (3.3) implies

$$\|F^* z^*\|_{V^*} \leq \gamma \|G^* z^*\|_{W^*}$$

For the general case we define the Banach space $\hat{W} = W/\ker(G)$ with $[w] \in \hat{W}$ being the equivalence class of $w+\tilde{w}$ for which $G(\tilde{w}) = 0$, and

$$\|[w]\|_{\hat{W}} = \inf_{G(\tilde{w})=0} \|w+\tilde{w}\|_W$$

We then define $\hat{G}[w] = Gw$, and so $\hat{G}$ is a 1-1 map on $\hat{W}$, with

$$\text{Range}(F) \subset \text{Range}(\hat{G})$$

From the first part of the proof it follows that

$$\|F^* z^*\|_{V^*} \leq \gamma \|\hat{G}^* z^*\|_{\hat{W}^*}$$

But from the definitions of $\hat{W}$ and $\hat{G}$ it is easy to show

$$\|\hat{G}^* z^*\|_{\hat{W}^*} = \|G^* z^*\|_{W^*}$$

and so the theorem is proved.

Theorem 3.4

If $F \in \mathcal{L}(Z,V)$, $G \in \mathcal{L}(Z,W)$, where V,W,Z are Banach spaces, and there exists $\gamma > 0$, such that

$$\|Fz\|_V \leq \gamma \|Gz\|_W$$

then

$$\text{Range}(F^*) \subset \text{Range}(G^*)$$

Proof

Assume $z^* = F^*v^*$, then our aim is to find w^* such that $z^* = G^*w^*$, or equivalently we are looking for w^* such that

$$(3.5) \qquad \langle v^*, Fz\rangle_{V^*,V} = \langle w^*, Gz\rangle_{W^*,W} \qquad \forall\ z \in Z$$

The identity (3.5) defines a linear functional on Range(G) by

$$f_{w*}(y) = \langle v^*, Fz\rangle_{V^*,V} \quad \text{where} \quad y = Gz$$

Moreover if $\{z_n\}$ is a sequence such that $Gz_n \to 0$ as $n \to \infty$, then by (3.4) $Fz_n \to 0$ as $n \to \infty$ and so $\langle w^*, Gz_n\rangle_{W^*,W} = \langle v^*, Fz_n\rangle_{V^*,V} \to 0$ as $n \to \infty$.

Thus w^* is a continuous linear functional on Range(G) and so by the Hahn-Banach theorem f_{w*} can be extended to the whole of W. Hence w^* is well defined by (3.5).

Corollary 3.5

If V,W,Z are reflexive Banach spaces and $F \in \mathcal{L}(V,Z)$, $G \in \mathcal{L}(W,Z)$ Theorem 3.3 and Theorem 3.4 yield the equivalence of the following

(3.6)
(a) $\text{Range}(F) \subset \text{Range}(G)$

(b) there exists $\gamma > 0$, such that

$$\|F^*z^*\|_{V^*} \leq \gamma\|G^*z^*\|_{W^*}$$

Theorem 3.6

Let $F \in \mathcal{L}(V,Z)$, $G \in \mathcal{L}(W,Z)$, where V,W,Z are Banach spaces, then the following conditions are equivalent

(3.7)
(a) $\ker(G^*) \subset \ker(F^*)$

(b) $\overline{\text{Range}(G)} \supset \overline{\text{Range}(F)}$

Proof

Assume $\ker(G^*) \subset \ker(F^*)$, but $\overline{\text{Range}(G)}$ does not contain $\overline{\text{Range}(F)}$. Then there must exist an element $z \in \overline{\text{Range}(F)}$, but $z \notin \overline{\text{Range}(G)}$, so we can construct a functional $z^* \neq 0$ on Z such that $\langle z^*, z\rangle_{Z^*,Z} \neq 0$ and $z^* = 0$ on Range(G). Thus

$$\langle z^*, Gw\rangle_{Z^*,Z} = 0 \qquad \forall\ w \in W$$

and hence $z^* \in \ker(G^*)$. Now if $z^* \in \ker(F^*)$, we would have

$$\langle z^*, Fv\rangle_{Z^*,Z} = 0 \quad \forall\, v \in V.$$

Since $z \in \overline{\text{Range }(F)}$, there exists a sequence $\{v_n\}$ in V such that $z = \lim_{n\to\infty} Fv_n$. So $\langle z^*, z\rangle_{Z^*,Z} = 0$, contrary to our assumption.

For the converse, we suppose that (3.7)(b) holds and $G^*z^* = 0$. Then

$$\langle z^*, Gv\rangle_{Z^*,Z} = 0 \quad \forall\, v \in V.$$

Hence $z^* = 0$ on $\overline{\text{Range }(G)}$, and so also on Range (F). Thus

$$\langle z^*, Fv\rangle = 0 \quad \forall\, v \in V$$

or $F^*z^* = 0$; that is $z^* \in \ker\, (F^*)$.

In the sequel the spaces V,W,Z will be reflexive Banach spaces and so the major tools in the analysis will be Corollary 3.5 and Theorem 3.6. We will be particularly interested in the map G defined by

$$Gu = \int_0^{t_1} T_{t_1-s}Bu(s)ds$$

where $u \in L^p[0,t_1;U]$ $1 < p < \infty$, T_t is a strongly continuous semigroup on a reflexive Banach space Z, U is also a reflexive Banach space, and $B \in \mathcal{L}(U,Z)$. Then clearly

$$G \in \mathcal{L}(L^p[0,t_1;U],Z)$$

and we can use Corollary 3.5 to obtain the following equivalent condition for exact controllability.

Theorem 3.7

If $u \in L^p[0,t_1;U]$ $1 < p < \infty$ and U,Z are reflexive Banach spaces, then (3.2) is exactly controllable iff there exists $\gamma > 0$, such that

$$\text{(3.8)} \qquad \gamma\|B^*T^*_{(\cdot)}z^*\|_{L^q[0,t_1;U^*]} \geq \|z^*\|_{Z^*}$$

where $\frac{1}{p} + \frac{1}{q} = 1$.

Proof

We apply Corollary 3.5 with $F = I$, the identity on Z, $W = L^p[0,t_1;U]$, and $V = Z$. Then $W^* = L^q[0,t_1;U^*]$ and T_t^* is a strongly continuous semigroup on Z^* (see Theorem 2.20). We need to calculate G^*, and for this we have

$$\langle z^*, Gu\rangle_{Z^*,Z} = \langle z^*, \int_0^{t_1} T_{t_1-s}Bu(s)ds\rangle_{Z^*,Z}$$

$$= \int_0^{t_1} \langle B^* T_{t_1-s}^* z^*, u(s)\rangle_{U^*,U} ds$$

Thus $G^*z^* = B^*T_{t_1-s}^*z^*$, and applying Corollary 3.5 we obtain the equivalence of (3.8) and

$$\text{Range}(G) \supset Z \tag{3.9}$$

But $T_{t_1}z_0$ is a fixed point in Z for any given z_0, and so (3.9) is equivalent to exact controllability on $[0,t_1]$.

Example 3.8

We consider the controlled wave equation of Example 1.5 with $\rho(\xi) = \alpha(\xi) = 1$, then

$$\begin{aligned} z_{tt} &= z_{\xi\xi} + u \\ z(0,t) &= z(1,t) = 0 \end{aligned} \tag{3.10}$$

The analysis of the uncontrolled system has been carried out in Example 2.41, so that we may abstract (3.10) to obtain

$$\dot{w} = \mathcal{A}w + Bu$$

where $B = \begin{bmatrix}0\\I\end{bmatrix}u$, and $\mathcal{A}$ generates a strongly continuous semigroup T_t given by (2.52)

$$T_t\begin{bmatrix}w_1\\w_2\end{bmatrix} = \begin{bmatrix}\Sigma 2[\langle w_1,\phi_n\rangle_H \cos n\pi t + \frac{1}{n\pi}\langle w_2,\phi_n\rangle_H \sin n\pi t]\phi_n \\ \Sigma 2[-n\pi\langle w_1,\phi_n\rangle_H \sin n\pi t + \langle w_2,\phi_n\rangle_H \cos n\pi t]\phi_n\end{bmatrix}$$

on a Hilbert space $\mathcal{H}$, with inner product

$$\langle w,\bar{w}\rangle_{\mathcal{H}} = \int_0^1 w_{1\xi}(\xi)\bar{w}_{1\xi}(\xi)d\xi + \int_0^1 w_2(\xi)\bar{w}_2(\xi)d\xi$$

and $\phi_n = \sin n\pi\xi$, $H = L^2[0,1]$.

It is easy to show that $T_t^* = T_{-t}$, and $B^* = [0,I]$, so that if $u \in L^2[0,t_1;H]$ the system will be exactly controllable iff there exists $\gamma > 0$, such that

$$\gamma \|B^*T^*_{(\cdot)}w\|_{L^2[0,t_1;H]} \geq \|w\|_{\mathcal{H}} \tag{3.11}$$

Calculation of the terms in (3.11) yields

$$\gamma^2 \left\{\Sigma\, n^2\pi^2 \langle w_1,\phi_n\rangle_H^2\left(t_1 - \frac{\sin 2n\pi t_1}{2n\pi}\right) + \langle w_1,\phi_n\rangle_H\langle w_2,\phi_n\rangle_H(1-\cos 2n\pi t_1)\right.$$

$$\left. + \langle w_2,\phi_n\rangle_H^2\left(t_1 + \frac{\sin 2n\pi t_1}{2n\pi}\right)\right\} \geq \|w\|_{\mathcal{H}}^2$$

But $\|w\|_{\mathcal{H}}$ is equivalent to

$$\{\Sigma\, n^2\pi^2\langle w_1,\phi_n\rangle_H^2 + \langle w_2,\phi_n\rangle_H^2\}^{\frac{1}{2}}$$

and so γ in (3.11) can be found if

$$4\left(t_1^2 - \frac{\sin^2 2n\pi t_1}{4n^2\pi^2}\right)n^2\pi^2 \geq (1-\cos 2n\pi t_1)^2 \qquad n = 1,2,\ldots$$

and

$$t_1 > \left|\frac{\sin 2n\pi t_1}{2n\pi}\right|$$

But this reduces to $t_1 > \left|\frac{\sin n\pi t_1}{n\pi}\right|$ and so the system is exactly controllable on $[0,t_1]$ for any $t_1 > 0$.

Example 3.9

Consider the controlled diffusion equation

$$z_t = z_{\xi\xi} + u$$

$$z(0,t) = z(1,t) = 0$$

The semigroup associated with the system is given by

$$T_t z = \Sigma 2e^{-n^2\pi^2 t}\sin n\pi\xi \int_0^1 \sin n\pi y\ z(y)dy$$

on $L^2[0,1]$. If $u \in L^2[0,t_1,L^2[0,1]]$ then $B = I$, and $B^* = I$, so that the condition for exact controllability is the existence of $\gamma > 0$, such that

$$(3.12)\qquad \gamma\left\{\Sigma 2\left(\frac{1-e^{-2n^2\pi^2 t_1}}{2n^2\pi^2}\right)\left(\int_0^1 \sin n\pi y\ z(y)dy\right)^2\right\}^{\frac{1}{2}} \geq \|z\|_{L^2[0,1]}.$$

But $\|z\|_{L^2[0,1]}$ is equivalent to

$$[\Sigma 2(\int_0^1 \sin n\pi y\ z(y)dy)^2]^{\frac{1}{2}}$$

and no such γ exists which satisfies (3.12), and hence the system is never exactly controllable on $[0,t_1]$ for any t_1. We may however ask whether or not the system is exactly controllable to some subspace of $L^2[0,1]$. For example, if in Corollary 3.5 we set F^* to be the injection of Z into V^* where V^* is normed by

$$\|v^*\|^2_{V^*} = \sum \frac{1}{n^2\pi^2}(\int_0^1 \sin n\pi y\ v^*(y)dy)^2$$

then (3.12) is replaced by

$$\gamma^2\left\{\sum\frac{2(1-e^{-2n^2\pi^2 t_1})}{2n^2\pi^2}\left(\int_0^1 \sin n\pi y\ z(y)dy\right)^2\right\} \geq \sum\frac{1}{n^2\pi^2}\left(\int_0^1 \sin n\pi y\ z(y)dy\right)^2$$

But the left hand side is greater than

$$\gamma^2\left(1-e^{-2\pi^2 t_1}\right)\sum\frac{1}{n^2\pi^2}\left(\int_0^1 \sin n\pi y\ z(y)dy\right)^2$$

and so the system is exactly controllable to a subspace V of $L^2[0,1]$ in any time $t_1 > 0$, where

$$\|v\|^2_V = \Sigma\ n^2\pi^2\left(\int_0^1 \sin n\pi y\ v(y)dy\right)^2$$

i.e. $V = H^1_0(0,1)$.

The above example indicates that in those cases where it is not possible to exactly control the system to all points in Z, it may be possible to control the system to points which form a dense set in Z. So we introduce the following

<u>Definition 3.10</u> <u>Approximate controllability</u>

We say that (3.2) is approximately controllable on $[0,t_1]$ if

$$\overline{\text{Range}(G)} = Z.$$

Thus if (3.2) is approximately controllable for any $z_1 \in Z$, and any $\varepsilon > 0$, there exists a control $u \in L^p[0,t_1;U]$ such that

$$\|z(t_1) - z_1\|_Z \leq \varepsilon$$

<u>Theorem 3.11</u>

(3.2) is approximately controllable on $[0,t_1]$ iff

(3.13) $$B^* T_t^* z^* = 0 \quad \text{on } 0 \leq t \leq t_1$$

implies $z^* = 0$.

<u>Proof</u>

We apply Theorem 3.6 with $F = I$, $W = L^p[0,t_1;U]$ $1 < p < \infty$, $V = Z$, then since

$$\overline{\text{Range}(F)} = Z$$

we see that (3.2) is approximately controllable iff

$$\ker(G^*) \subset \ker(I^*)$$

Computing G^* as in Theorem 3.7, we see that the above is equivalent to (3.13), where the equality is taken in $L^q[0,t_1;U]$.

But Z is reflexive and so T_t^* is a strongly continuous semigroup and hence (3.13) may be interpreted in U^*.

<u>Example 3.12</u>

We consider a special case of the semigroup considered in Example 2.12, where $Z = H$ a real separable Hilbert space and A has eigenfunctions ϕ_{nk}

corresponding to eigenvalues $\lambda_n (\lambda_1 > \lambda_2 \ldots)$ of multiplicity r_n. Then

$$T_t z = \sum_{n=1}^{\infty} e^{\lambda_n t} \sum_{k=1}^{r_n} \langle z, \phi_{nk} \rangle_H \phi_{nk}$$

We assume the control system is of the form

$$\dot{z} = Az + \sum_{\rho=1}^{m} b_\rho u_\rho \tag{3.14}$$

where $b_1, \ldots, b_m \in H$, and $u_\rho \in L^p[0,t_1]$ $1 < p < \infty$. Thus if we set $B(u_1, \ldots, u_m) = \sum_{\rho=1}^{m} b_\rho u_\rho$, $u = (u_1, \ldots, u_m) \in U = R^m$, then $u \in L^p[0,t_1;U]$.

Moreover

$$B^* z = (\langle b_1, z \rangle_H, \ldots \langle b_m, z \rangle_H)$$

Hence the mild solution of (3.14) is approximately controllable on $[0,t_1]$ iff

$$\sum_{n=1}^{\infty} e^{\lambda_n t} \sum_{k=1}^{r_n} \langle b_\rho, \phi_{nk} \rangle_H \langle z^*, \phi_{nk} \rangle = 0 \quad \rho = 1 \ldots m \quad t \in [0,t_1] \tag{3.15}$$

implies $z^* = 0$.

Using (3.15) we are able to prove

Proposition 3.13

The mild solution of (3.14) is approximately controllable on $[0,t_1]$ iff

$$\text{rank } B_j = r_j$$

where B_j is the matrix

$$B_j = \begin{bmatrix} \langle b_1, \phi_{j1} \rangle_H & \langle b_2, \phi_{j1} \rangle_H & \cdots & \langle b_m, \phi_{j1} \rangle_H \\ \vdots & & & \vdots \\ \langle b_1, \phi_{jr_j} \rangle_H & \langle b_2, \phi_{jr_j} \rangle_H & \cdots & \langle b_m, \phi_{jr_j} \rangle_H \end{bmatrix}$$

Proof

We need the following lemma.

Lemma 3.14

$$(3.16)\quad \sum_{j=1}^{\infty} e^{\lambda_j t} \alpha_{\rho j} = 0 \;;\; t \in [0,t_1],\ \rho = 1 \ldots m$$

iff

$$\alpha_{\rho j} = 0 \;;\; \rho = 1,\ldots,m,\ j = 1,\ldots,\infty.$$

Proof

Because of the analyticity we may extend (3.16) for all $t \geq 0$. First assume $\lambda_1 < 0$, then

$$\sum_{j=1}^{\infty} |e^{\lambda_j t} \alpha_{\rho j}| \leq \sum_{j=1}^{\infty} |\alpha_{\rho j}| < \infty$$

and we may write $\lambda_j = \lambda_1 + \sigma_j$, with $\sigma_j < 0$, and (3.16) as

$$e^{\lambda_1 t}[\alpha_{\rho 1} + \sum_{j=2}^{\infty} e^{\sigma_j t} \alpha_{\rho j}] = 0 \qquad t \geq 0$$

Hence

$$\alpha_{\rho 1} + \sum_{j=2}^{\infty} e^{\sigma_j t} \alpha_{\rho j} = 0$$

and as $t \to \infty$, we find $\alpha_{\rho 1} = 0$. In a similar manner we can show $\alpha_{ij} = 0$. The general case can be reduced to the case where $\lambda_1 < 0$ as follows:

Assume $\ldots \lambda_2 \leq \lambda_1 \leq c$, and set $\bar{\lambda}_j = \lambda_j - c$, then (3.16) becomes

$$e^{ct} \sum_{j=1}^{\infty} e^{\bar{\lambda}_j t} \alpha_{\rho j} = 0 \qquad t \geq 0$$

or

$$\sum_{j=1}^{\infty} e^{\lambda_j t} \alpha_{\rho j} = 0 \qquad t \geq 0$$

as required.

By the Lemma (3.14) is approximately controllable iff

$$\sum_{k=1}^{r_n} \langle b_\rho, \phi_{nk} \rangle_H \langle z^*, \phi_{nk} \rangle_H = 0 \qquad \rho = 1 \ldots m,\ n = 1 \ldots$$

implies $z^* = 0$. That is iff

$$B_j'v_j = 0, \qquad j = 1,2,\ldots$$

implies $z^* = 0$, where $v_j = [\langle z^*,\phi_{j1}\rangle_H \ldots \langle z^*,\phi_{jr_j}\rangle_H]'$

So if (3.14) is not approximately controllable, there exists a $v_J \neq 0$, such that

$$B_J'v_J = 0$$

and so rank $B_J \neq r_J$.

Conversely if rank $B_J \neq r_J$ for some J, then there exists a $v_J = [v_{J1},\ldots,v_{Jr_J}]' \neq 0$ such that

$$B_J'v_J = 0$$

So we can construct a non-zero $z^* \varepsilon H$ such that

$$\langle z^*,\phi_{jk}\rangle_H = 0 \quad \text{if } j \neq J$$

$$\langle z^*,\phi_{Jk}\rangle_H = v_{Jk} \quad k = 1 \ldots r_J$$

Then

$$\sum_{k=1}^{r_n} \langle b_\rho,\phi_{nk}\rangle_H \langle z^*,\phi_{nk}\rangle_H = 0 \quad n \neq J, \quad \rho = 1 \ldots m$$

$$\sum_{k=1}^{r_J} \langle b_\rho,\phi_{Jk}\rangle_H \langle z^*,\phi_{Jk}\rangle_H = \sum_{k=1}^{r_J} \langle b_\rho,\phi_{Jk}\rangle v_{Jk} \quad \rho = 1 \ldots m$$

$$= B_J'v_J = 0.$$

So if rank $B_J \neq r_J$ (3.14) is not approximately controllable. Thus rank $B_J \neq r_J$ is equivalent to (3.14) being not approximately controllable, and this proves the proposition.

We note that the proposition implies that the number of controls required is at least that of the highest multiplicity of the eigenvalues.

As a special case of this example we let $H = L^2[0,1]$, $Az = \Delta z$, the Laplacian, and

$$D(A) = \{z \,\varepsilon\, H,\ Az \,\varepsilon\, H,\ z = 0 \text{ at } x = 0,1\}$$

Then A is self adjoint with compact resolvent and the eigenvalues and eigenvectors are $\lambda_n = -n^2\pi^2$, and $\phi_{j1} = \sin j\pi x$, $r_j = 1$. So the mild solution will be approximately controllable with a single control if, for example

$$\int_0^1 b_1(\xi)\sin n\pi\xi \, d\xi \neq 0 \qquad \forall\, n = 1,\ldots$$

For finite dimensional systems the concepts of approximate and exact controllability are equivalent, and can be checked via a rank condition involving the operators A,B(see Definition 1.3). For most systems the operators A and B will be given rather than the semigroup T_t, so it is important to attempt to obtain conditions for controllability involving the operators A and B which generalise the rank condition. We can proceed in this direction in two ways; either by differentiation of the semigroup which will lead to domain problems, or use the formula (see Lemma 2.11).

$$R(\lambda,A)z = \int_0^\infty e^{-\lambda t} T_t z \, dt$$

<u>Theorem 3.15</u>

The system (3.2) is approximately controllable in finite time iff the system

$$z(t) = e^{R(\lambda_o,A)t} z_o + \int_0^t e^{R(\lambda_o,A)(t-s)} Bu(s)ds \tag{3.17}$$

is approximately controllable in finite time. Here $R(\lambda_o,A)$ is the resolvent of A and λ_o is any point in the part of resolvent set which contains $\mathrm{Re}\,\lambda > \omega$, where ω is defined by (2.14). By finite time controllability we mean there exists a time t_1 for each z_o,z_1 and it is not fixed apriori.

<u>Proof</u>

Theorem 3.11 can easily be extended to allow for the finite time assumption, and we have to prove the equivalence of the statements

$$B^* T_t^* z^* = 0 \qquad t \geq 0 \text{ implies } z^* = 0 \tag{3.18}$$

and

$$B^* e^{R^*(\lambda_o,A)t} z^* = 0 \qquad t \geq 0 \text{ implies } z^* = 0 \tag{3.19}$$

Moreover, since $R^*(\lambda_o,A)$ is a bounded operator

$$e^{R^*(\lambda_o,A)t} = \sum_{n=o}^{\infty} \frac{t^n}{n!} [R^*(\lambda_o,A)]^n$$

and (3.19) is equivalent to

(3.20) $$B^*[R^*(\lambda_o,A)]^n z^* = 0 \quad n = 0,1\ldots \text{ implies } z^* = 0$$

First suppose $B^*T_t^*z^* = 0 \quad t \geq 0$ for some $z^* \neq 0$. Then since

$$[R^*(\lambda_o,A)]^n z^* = R^n(\lambda_o,A^*)z^* = \frac{1}{(n-1)!}\int_o^{\infty} t^{n-1}e^{-\lambda_o t}T_t^*z^* dt \quad n=1\ldots$$

(see the Hille-Yosida Theorem 2.10) it follows that

$$B^*\left[R^*(\lambda_o,A)\right]^n z^* = 0 \quad n = 0,1,2,\ldots$$

and this contradicts (3.20).

Now assume that $B^*R^n(\lambda_o,A^*)z^* = 0 \quad n = 0,1,2,\ldots$ for some $z^* \neq 0$. Since

$$R(\lambda,A^*)z^* = \sum_{n=o}^{\infty} (\lambda-\lambda_o)^n R^{n+1}(\lambda_o,A^*)z^*$$

we have first for suitably small λ, and then by analytic continuation for all λ with $\text{Re}\,\lambda > \omega$

$$B^*R(\lambda,A^*)z^* = 0$$

But

$$\langle B^*R(\lambda,A^*)z^*,u\rangle_{U^*U} = \int_o^{\infty} e^{-\lambda t}\langle B^*T_t^*z^*,u\rangle_{U^*U}\, dt$$

for all $u \in U$, $z^* \in Z^*$, if $\text{Re}\,\lambda > \omega$. Hence

$$\int_o^{\infty} e^{-\lambda t}\langle B^*T_t^*z^*,u\rangle_{U^*U}\, dt = 0 \qquad \text{Re}\,\lambda > \omega$$

This implies (see Dunford and Schwartz p.626)

$$\langle B^*T_t^*z^*,u\rangle_{U^*U} = 0 \quad t \geq 0$$

or

$$B^*T_t^*z^* = 0$$

which contradicts the assumption.

A sufficient condition for approximate controllability similar to the rank condition can be obtained by differentiating (3.13).

Theorem 3.16

We define $U_\infty = \{u \in U\colon Bu \in D_\infty(A) = \bigcap_n D(A^n)\}$, the largest subspace of U such that $BU_\infty \subset D_\infty(A)$. U_∞ is non empty but need not be dense in U.

(3.2) is approximately controllable on $[0,t_1]$ if

(3.21) $$\overline{sp}\ \{A^n BU_\infty \quad n = 0,1,\ldots,\} = Z$$

Proof

Suppose (3.2) is not approximately controllable, then for some non-zero z^*, and all $u \in U$

$$\langle z^*, T_t BU\rangle_{Z^*Z} = 0$$

and hence

$$\langle z^*, T_t BU_\infty\rangle_{Z^*Z} = 0 \qquad 0 \le t \le t_1$$

Differentiating yields

$$\langle z^*, T_t A^n BU_\infty\rangle_{Z^*Z} = 0 \qquad 0 \le t \le t_1,\ n = 0,1,2,\ldots$$

For t = 0 this yields

$$\langle z^*, A^n BU_\infty\rangle_{Z^*Z} = 0 \qquad n = 0,1,2,\ldots$$

for some nonzero z^* and (3.21) does not hold.

Although this theorem seems to be a natural extension of the rank condition, it may be difficult to check since U_∞ is not easily derived. Moreover the condition (3.21) is sufficient but not necessary, and in fact the converse is in general false. To see this, consider the following example.

Example 3.17

Let $Z = L^2[-\infty,\infty]$, $Az = \dfrac{d^2 z}{d\xi^2}$

$$D(A) = \{z: z, \frac{dz}{d\xi}, \frac{d^2z}{d\xi^2} \in Z\}$$

Then it is easy to show that

$$(T_t z)(\xi) = \frac{1}{\sqrt{4\pi t}} \int_{-\infty}^{\infty} \exp\{-\frac{(\xi-\eta)^2}{4t}\} z(\eta)d\eta$$

Suppose the control system is given by

$$\dot{z} = Az + b_1u_1 + b_2u_2$$

where $u_1, u_2 \in L^2[0,t_1]$, $b_1, b_2 \in Z$. Fattorini[12] and Triggiani[44] have shown that if $b_1(\xi)$ is nonzero, has compact support on $(0,1)$ and $b_1 \in C^\infty(0,1)$ with $b_2(\xi) = b_1(\xi-h)$, $h \neq 0$, then the mild solution is approximately controllable on $[0,t_1]$. But $b_1(\xi)$ and $b_1(\xi-h)$ vanish together with all their derivatives outside $[-h,1]$ for $h > 0$. Hence

$$\overline{sp}\ [A^n b_i \quad i = 1,2 \quad n = 0,1,2,\ldots\ ]$$

is a proper subspace of $L^2[-\infty,\infty]$.

Stronger results of the rank type can be obtained if we specialize the semigroups. For example:

<u>Theorem 3.18</u>

If A is a bounded operator on Z and (3.2) is exactly controllable on $[0,t_1]$, then there exists an integer n, such that

$$sp\ [BU, ABU, \ldots, A^n BU] = Z$$

<u>Proof</u>

From Theorem 3.7 we know there exists a γ such that

$$\gamma \|B^* T^*_{(\cdot)} z^*\|_{L^q[0,t_1,U^*]} \geq \|z^*\|_{Z^*}$$

But $T^*_t = e^{A^* t} = \sum_{n=0}^{\infty} \frac{t^n}{n!}(A^*)^n$, hence

$$\gamma\|B^*T^*_{(\cdot)}z^*\|_{L^q|0,t_1;U^*|} \le \gamma \sum_{n=0}^{\infty}\left(\int_0^{t_1}\left\|\frac{B^*(A^*t)^n}{n!}z^*\right\|^q_{U^*}\right)^{\frac{1}{q}}$$

$$\le \gamma \sum_{n=0}^{\infty}\|B^*(A^*)^n z^*\|_{U^*}\left(\int_0^{t_1}\frac{t^{nq}}{(n!)^q}\,dt\right)^{\frac{1}{q}}$$

$$\le \gamma \sum_{n=0}^{\infty}\|B^*(A^*)^n z^*\|_{U^*}\; t_1^{n+\frac{1}{q}}\Big/ n!\,(nq+1)^{\frac{1}{q}}$$

Thus

$$\gamma \sum_{n=0}^{\infty}\|B^*(A^*)^n z^*\|_{U^*}\; t_1^{n+\frac{1}{q}}\Big/ n!\,(nq+1)^{\frac{1}{q}} \ge \|z^*\|_{Z^*}$$

Since the series $\sum_{n=0}^{\infty} B^*(A^*)^n z^*\; t_1^n/n!$ converges in U^*, there exists N such that

$$\gamma \sum_{n=N+1}^{\infty}\|B^*(A^*)^n z^*\|_{U^*}\; t_1^{n+\frac{1}{q}}\Big/ n!\,(nq+1)^{\frac{1}{q}} \le \tfrac{1}{2}\|z^*\|_{Z^*}$$

Thus

$$\gamma \sum_{n=0}^{N}\|B^*(A^*)^n z^*\|_{U^*}\; t_1^{n+\frac{1}{q}}\Big/ n!\,(nq+1)^{\frac{1}{q}} \ge \tfrac{1}{2}\|z^*\|_{Z^*}$$

Now if $\bar{\gamma} = \max\limits_{n=0,1,\ldots,N} 2\gamma\; t_1^{n+\frac{1}{q}}\Big/ n!\,(nq+1)^{\frac{1}{q}}$, we have

$$\bar{\gamma} \sum_{n=0}^{N}\|B^*(A^*)^n z^*\|_{U^*} \ge \|z^*\|_{Z^*}$$

Using Corollary 3.5 we see that this is equivalent to the statement of the theorem.

In many problems of practical interest the null state plays an important role and so we introduce special definitions for systems which can achieve or approximately achieve the null state.

Definition 3.19 Exactly null controllable on $[0,t_1]$

We say that (3.2) is exactly null controllable on $[0,t_1]$ if

$$\text{Range}\{G\} \supset \text{Range}\{T_{t_1}\}$$

Definition 3.20 Approximately null controllable on $[0,t_1]$

We say that (3.2) is approximately null controllable on $[0,t_1]$ if

$$\overline{\text{Range}\{G\}} \supset \text{Range}\{T_{t_1}\}$$

Criteria for approximate and exact null controllability follow directly from Corollary 3.5 and Theorem 3.6, but instead of expressing these directly we will first introduce four concepts of observability and exploit duality relationships to obtain expressions for controllability. In order to do this we consider the system

$$\begin{aligned} \dot{x} &= \mathcal{A}x \quad , x(0) = x_0 \\ y &= Cx \end{aligned} \tag{3.22}$$

where $\mathcal{A}$ is the infinitesimal generator of a strongly continuous semigroup S_t on a reflexive Banach space X, and $C \in \mathcal{L}(X,Y)$ where Y is also a reflexive Banach space. The mild solution of (3.22) is

$$y = CS_t x_0 \tag{3.23}$$

and if $x_0 \in D(\mathcal{A})$ we may differentiate $x(t) = S_t x_0$ to obtain (3.22). We define a map $\mathcal{C}$, by

$$\mathcal{C} : X \to L^q[0,t_1;Y] : \mathcal{C}x_0 = CS_t x_0$$

Then we say

Definition 3.21 Continuously initially observable on $[0,t_1]$

We say that (3.23) is continuously initially observable on $[0,t_1]$ if there exists $\gamma > 0$, such that

$$\gamma \|\mathcal{C}x\|_{L^q[0,t_1;Y]} \geq \|x\|_X \qquad \forall\, x \in X.$$

Definition 3.22 Initially observable on $[0,t_1]$

We say that (3.23) is initially observable on $[0,t_1]$ if

$$\ker(\mathcal{C}) = \{0\}$$

Definition 3.23 Continuously finally observable on $[0,t_1]$

We say that (3.23) is continuously finally observable on $[0,t_1]$ if there exists $\gamma > 0$, such that

$$\gamma \|\mathcal{C} x\|_{L^q[0,t_1;Y]} \geq \|S_{t_1} x\|_X \qquad \forall\, x \in X$$

Definition 3.24 Finally observable on $[0,t_1]$

We say that (3.23) is finally observable on $[0,t_1]$ if

$$\ker(\mathcal{C}) \subset \ker(S_{t_1})$$

The observation problem is concerned with whether or not it is possible to reconstruct the initial state or state at time t_1 of a system in a unique fashion from the observations. In many problems of optimisation it is only possible to construct an optimal control if the whole state of the system is known. Knowledge of the initial state enables us to obtain the whole state at all times $t \geq 0$, and this is why initial observability is important. Definition 3.22 implies that the initial state is distinguishable, that is

$$y(t) = 0 \quad \text{on } [0,t_1]$$

implies $x_0 = 0$, whereas continuous initial observability implies the existence of a continuous reconstruction operator R_0

$$R_0 : \text{Range}(\mathcal{C}) \to X \text{ , such that } R_0\mathcal{C} = I.$$

In practice it is not possible to construct the initial state until a finite time t_1 has elapsed. For times greater than t_1, the whole state can be determined by the state at time t_1, so that in many control applications the weaker concept of final observability is more useful. Definition 3.24 implies that the states at time t_1 can be distinguished, that is

$$y(t) = 0 \quad \text{on } [0,t_1]$$

implies $x(t_1) = 0$, whereas continuous final observability implies the existence of a reconstruction operator R_{t_1}

$$R_{t_1} : \text{Range}(\mathcal{C}) \to X, \text{ such that } R_{t_1}\mathcal{C} = S_{t_1}$$

Now let us turn to the question of duality. For this we make the dual identifications

$$U = Y^*,\ B = C^*,\ T_t = S_t^*,\ Z = X^*,\ A = \mathcal{A}^*$$

$$\frac{1}{p} + \frac{1}{q} = 1$$

Theorem 3.25

(a) (3.23) is initially observable on $[0,t_1]$ iff (3.2) is approximately controllable on $[0,t_1]$.

(b) (3.23) is continuously initially observable on $[0,t_1]$ iff (3.2) is exactly controllable on $[0,t_1]$.

(c) (3.23) is finally observable on $[0,t_1]$ iff (3.2) is approximately null controllable on $[0,t_1]$.

(d) (3.23) is continuously finally observable on $[0,t_1]$ iff (3.2) is exactly null controllable on $[0,t_1]$.

Proof

We have already proved (a),(b) in Theorem 3.11 and 3.7 respectively. Parts (c),(d) follow from the construction of the dual of G as in Theorem 3.7, and Corollary 3.5 and Theorem 3.6.

Example 3.26

Consider the observation problem on $L^2[0,1]$

$$\begin{aligned} & x_t = x_{\xi\xi} \\ (3.24)\qquad & x(0,t) = x(1,t) = 0,\ x(\xi,0) = x_o(\xi) \\ & y(t) = \int_0^1 b(\xi)x(\xi,t)\,d\xi \end{aligned}$$

The dual problem is the control problem

$$\begin{aligned} & z_t(\xi,t) = z_{\xi\xi}(\xi,t) + b(\xi)u(t) \\ (3.25)\qquad & z(0,t) = z(1,t) = 0,\ z(\xi,0) = z_o(\xi) \end{aligned}$$

Using the results of Example 3.12 we know that the mild solution of (3.25) is approximately controllable iff

$$\int_0^1 b(\xi)\sin n\pi\xi \, d\xi \neq 0 \qquad \forall\, n = 1,2,\ldots$$

Hence by the duality Theorem 3.25 the same conditions ensure that (3.24) is initially observable.

Example 3.27

In Example 3.9 we showed that the controlled diffusion equation

$$\text{(3.26)} \qquad \begin{aligned} z_t &= z_{\xi\xi} + u \\ z(0,t) &= z(1,t) = 0 \end{aligned}$$

is not exactly controllable to all of $z \in L^2[0,1]$, $u \in L^2[0,t_1;Z]$. The dual system is

$$\text{(3.27)} \qquad \begin{aligned} x_t &= x_{\xi\xi} \\ x(0,t) &= x(1,t) = 0 \\ y(t) &= x(t) \end{aligned}$$

So clearly (3.37) is finally observable for any $t_1 \geq 0$, and hence (3.26) is approximately null controllable. To see whether or not (3.27) is continuously finally observable, we need to show there exists γ such that

$$\text{(3.28)} \quad \gamma^2 \sum \frac{2(1-e^{-2n^2\pi^2 t_1})}{2n^2\pi^2}\left(\int_0^1 \sin n\pi y \; z(y)dy\right)^2 \geq \sum 2e^{-2n^2\pi^2 t_1}\left(\int_0^1 \sin n\pi y \; z(y)dy\right)^2$$

It is easy to show that $\gamma^2 = 1/t_1$ satisfies (3.28) and so (3.27) is continuously finally observable for any $t_1 > 0$ and (3.26) is exactly null controllable for any $t_1 > 0$.

One of the most important practical considerations in systems theory is the design of feedback controls so that the controlled system is asymptotically stable.

Definition 3.28 Exponential stabilizability

Let A be the infinitesimal generator of a strongly continuous semigroup T_t on a Banach space Z, and B ε $\mathcal{L}(U,Z)$ where U is a Banach space. If there exists D ε $\mathcal{L}(Z,U)$ such that A+BD generates a strongly continuous semigroup T_t^D with

$$\|T_t^D\| \leq Me^{-\omega t}, \quad \omega > 0$$

then the pair (A,B) is said to be exponentially stabilizable.

There is a very nice and complete theory of stabilizability for finite dimensional Banach spaces in that controllability implies stabilizability. The situation is much more complex in infinite dimensional Banach spaces as we illustrate with the following example.

Example 3.29

Let $Z = \ell^2$, $U = R^1$, and for $z = \{\xi_1, \xi_2, \dots\}$

$$A(\xi_n) = \frac{1}{n}\xi_n$$

$$Bu = \{\beta_1 u, \beta_2 u, \dots\}, \ \beta_n \neq 0.$$

where $\sum_{n=1}^{\infty} n^2\beta_n^2 < \infty$, $\{\beta_1,\beta_2,\dots\} \varepsilon \ \ell^2$. For any feedback control $u = \langle d,z\rangle_{\ell^2}$, $d \ \varepsilon \ \ell^2$ we have

$$Az + Bu = \{\xi_1+\beta_1\langle d,z\rangle_{\ell^2}, \frac{\xi_2}{2}+\beta_2\langle d,z\rangle_{\ell^2},\dots,\}$$

We will show that $0 \ \varepsilon \ \sigma(A+BD)$. Actually this follows since A+BD is a compact operator, however we give below a simple proof by showing that for some $\eta = \{\eta_1,\eta_2,\dots,\} \ \varepsilon \ \ell^2$ there are no solutions of

$$\eta = (A+BD)z.$$

Let us suppose the contrary, then

$$\xi_n = n\eta_n - n\beta_n\langle d,z\rangle_{\ell^2}$$

But $\{n\beta_n\} \ \varepsilon \ \ell^2$, and for some η_n, $\{n\eta_n\} \not\varepsilon \ \ell^2$ and hence no such $\{\xi_n\} \ \varepsilon \ \ell^2$ exists for these η_n. Thus A+BD is not invertible, and so $0 \ \varepsilon \ \sigma(A+BD)$, and from Theorem (2.10)

$$(3.29) \qquad 0 \leq \sup\{\mathrm{Re}\lambda, \ \lambda \ \varepsilon \ \sigma(A+BD)\} \leq \inf\{\omega : \|T_t^D\| \leq M_\omega e^{\omega t}\}$$

where T_t^D is the semigroup generated by A+BD.

Now if $\|T_t^D\| \leq Me^{\omega t}$ then from (3.28) we must have $\omega \geq 0$, and so (A,B) is not stabilizable. Nevertheless we are able to show that the system is approximately controllable in finite time. For this we require (Theorem 3.11)

$$B^* T_t^* z^* = 0 \quad t \geq 0 \text{ implies } z^* = 0$$

But $T_t^* z^* = \{e^{\frac{1}{n}t} \xi_n^*\}$, where $z^* = \{\xi_1^*, \xi_2^*, \ldots,\}$

Therefore $$B^* T_t^* z^* = \sum_{n=1}^{\infty} \beta_n e^{\frac{1}{n}t} \xi_n^* \quad t \geq 0.$$

Using the same argument as in Proposition 3.13 we are able to conclude $\beta_n \xi_n^* = 0$, and hence $\xi_n^* = 0$. Thus the system is approximately controllable, but not stabilizable.

In general we do not have equality in (3.29) Hille-Phillips [18]. Indeed there are strongly continuous semigroups T_t generated by an operator A, with

$$\sup\{\mathrm{Re}\lambda, \ \lambda \in \sigma(A)\} = 0$$

and yet $\|T_t\| = e^t$ (see Zabczyk [53]).

One method we will use to examine stabilizability is via the spectrum of the generator, and we will wish to exclude the above example, so we define

<u>Definition 3.30</u> <u>Spectrum determined growth assumption</u>

A strongly continuous semigroup T_t with generator A is said to satisfy the spectrum determined growth assumption if

$$\sup \mathrm{Re}\, \sigma(A) = \lim_{t\to\infty} \frac{\log\|T_t\|}{t} = \omega_0$$

We note that this is always the case when A is bounded, for $t > t_0$. Triggiani has shown that this is also the case when A generates an analytic semigroup, and Zabczyk has shown that the same is true when T_t is compact for some $t > 0$ (see Triggiani [44]).

An immediate consequence of this definition is that if

$$\sup \mathrm{Re}\, \sigma(A) < -\alpha \text{ for some } \alpha > 0$$

then $$\|T_t\| \leq Me^{-\alpha t} \qquad t \geq 0$$

We will also need to decompose the space Z. Let $\delta > 0$ and consider the portions $\sigma_u(A)$ and $\sigma_s(A)$ of the spectrum of A contained in the closed half plane $\{\lambda: \text{Re } \lambda \geq -\delta\}$ and open half plane $\{\lambda: \text{Re } \lambda < -\delta\}$ respectively.

$$\sigma_u(A) = \sigma(A) \quad \{\lambda: \text{Re } \lambda \geq -\delta\}$$

$$\sigma_s(A) = \sigma(A) \quad \{\lambda: \text{Re } \lambda < -\delta\}$$

Then $\sigma(A) = \sigma_u(A) \cup \sigma_s(A)$ and since A is a generator $\sigma(A)$ is contained in the half plane $\{\lambda: \text{Re } \lambda \leq \omega_o\}$.

<u>Definition 3.31</u> <u>Spectrum decomposition assumption</u>

If the set $\sigma_u(A)$ is bounded and is separated from the set $\sigma_s(A)$ in such a way that a rectifiable, simple, closed curve can be drawn so as to enclose an open set containing $\sigma_u(A)$ in its interior and $\sigma_s(A)$ in its exterior, then A is said to satisfy the spectrum decomposition assumption.

If A satisfies the spectrum decomposition assumption then Kato [2.7] has shown that

(a) the operator A may be decomposed according to the decomposition

$$Z = Z_u + Z_s$$

of the space, meaning

$$PD(A) \subset D(A), \; AZ_s \subset Z_s, \; AZ_u \subset Z_u$$

where P is the projection on Z, $Z_u = PZ$, $Z_s = (I-P)Z$, and

$$P = \frac{1}{2\pi i} \int_\Gamma (\lambda I - A)^{-1} d\lambda \in \mathcal{L}(Z)$$

and Γ is a curve surrounding $\sigma(A_u)$.

(b) $\sigma(A_s) = \sigma_s(A)$, $\sigma(A_u) = \sigma_u(A)$

where A_s and A_u are the restrictions of A on Z_s and Z_u respectively.

(c) A is bounded on Z_u

(d) P and (I-P) commute with A

$$PA \subset AP \; , \quad (I-P)A \subset A(I-P)$$

(e) T_t commutes with P and (I-P)

(e) is not proved in Kato but is a consequence of (d). To see this we note P is bounded and

$$PR(\lambda,A) = R(\lambda,A)P \qquad \lambda \in \rho(A)$$

Hence from

$$R(\lambda,A) = \int_0^\infty e^{-\lambda t} T_t z \, dt$$

we obtain

$$0 = PR(\lambda,A)z - R(\lambda,A)Pz = \int_0^\infty e^{-\lambda t}(PT_t z - T_t Pz)dt$$

Then by the uniqueness of the Laplace Transform we have

$$PT_t = T_t P$$

We now apply this decomposition to the dynamical system

$$\dot{z} = Az + Bu, \; z(0) = z_o. \tag{3.30}$$

From $Pz = z_u, (I-P)z = z_s$, it follows that $P\dot{z} = \dot{z}_u, (I-P)\dot{z} = \dot{z}_s$, and so applying P and (I-P) to (3.29) we have

$$\dot{z}_u = A_u z_u + PBu \qquad z_{ou} = Pz_o$$

$$\dot{z}_s = A_s z_s + (I-P)Bu \qquad z_{os} = (I-P)z_o$$

Also denoting by T_t^u and T_t^s the restrictions to Z_u and Z_s of the strongly continuous semigroup T_t, then

(a) T_t^u, T_t^s are strongly continuous semigroups on Z_u and Z_s generated by A_u and A_s. Actually A_u is bounded on Z_u and T_t^u is a uniformly continuous analytic semigroup

$$T_t^u = e^{A_u t} = \sum_{n=o}^{\infty} A_u^n \, t^n/n!$$

One could also apply P, and (I-P) to the mild solution

$$z(t) = T_t z_o + \int_0^t T_{t-s} Bu(s)ds \tag{3.31}$$

to obtain

$$z_u(t) = T_t^u z_{ou} + \int_0^t T_{t-s}^u PBu(s)ds$$

$$z_s(t) = T_t^s z_{os} + \int_0^t T_{t-s}^s (I-P)Bu(s)ds$$

If we assume that the semigroup T_t^s satisfies the spectrum determined growth assumption, we have

$$\|T_t^s\| \leq Ke^{-\delta t}$$

This decomposition provides the clue for analyzing the stabilizability of (3.31). We note that the projection onto Z_s is naturally stabilizable by taking the zero control. The idea therefore is to stabilize the projection onto Z_u without upsetting the stability properties on Z_s.

Theorem 3.32

(A,B) is exponentially stabilizable on a Banach space Z if

(a) the generator A satisfies the spectrum decomposition assumption,

(b) the semigroup T_t^s satisfies the spectrum determined growth assumption,

(c) the projection onto Z_u is exponentially stabilizable by a feedback control $u = D_u Z_u$, $D_u \in \mathcal{L}(Z_u, U)$.

Proof

We show that (A,B) is stabilizable by means of the control $D = (D_u, O)$: $(Z_u, Z_s) \to U$.

On Z_u we have

$$z_u(t) = e^{(A_u+PBD_u)t} z_{ou}$$

and from the assumption (c) there exists $C, \rho > 0$ such that

$$\|z_u(t)\| \leq Ce^{-\rho t}\|z_{ou}\|$$

Hence for $u = D_u z_u$, we have

$$\|u(t)\| \leq C\|D_u\|e^{-\rho t}\|z_{ou}\|$$

Feeding the control $u = D_u z_u$ onto Z_s, yields

$$\|z_s(t)\| \leq Ke^{-\delta t}\|z_{os}\| + \bar{M}\|z_{ou}\| \int_0^t e^{-\delta(t-s)}e^{-\rho s}ds$$

$$= Ke^{-\delta t}\|z_{os}\| + \bar{M}\|z_{ou}\|\left[\frac{e^{-\delta t}-e^{-\rho t}}{\rho-\delta}\right]$$

where $\bar{M} = KC\|(I-P)B\|\|D_u\|$.

Hence the response of the system (3.31) to $u = Dz$ is

$$\begin{aligned}\|z(t)\| &= \|z_s(t) + z_u(t)\| \\ &\leq Ke^{-\delta t}\|z_{os}\| + \left(\bar{M}\left[\frac{e^{-\delta t}-e^{-\rho t}}{\rho-\delta}\right] + Ce^{-\rho t}\right)\|z_{ou}\| \\ &\leq K\|I-P\|e^{-\delta t}\|z_o\| + \left(\bar{M}\left[\frac{e^{-\delta t}-e^{-\rho t}}{\rho-\delta}\right] + Ce^{-\rho t}\right)\|P\|\,\|z_o\|\end{aligned}$$

and this completes the proof.

Corollary 3.33

If the conditions of Theorem 3.32 hold except that (c) is replaced by

(a) the space Z_u is finite dimensional

(b) the projection onto Z_u is controllable

then again we have (A,B) is exponentially stabilizable.

Example 3.34

Let A be self adjoint with compact resolvent, then there are at most a finite number of non-negative eigenvalues, say J. Hence Z_o is finite dimensional and using Example 3.12 we can easily show that the condition for stabilizability of (A,B) with $B = (b_1,b_2,\ldots,b_n)$, $b_j \in H$ is

$$\operatorname{rank}\begin{bmatrix} \langle b_1,\phi_{j1}\rangle_H,\ldots,\langle b_m,\phi_{j1}\rangle_H \\ \vdots \qquad\qquad \vdots \\ \langle b_1,\phi_{jr_j}\rangle_H,\ldots,\langle b_m,\phi_{jr_j}\rangle_H \end{bmatrix} = r_j \qquad j = 1,\ldots,J.$$

There are not many results which connect controllability with stabilizability without any constraints on the semigroup or its generator. The major general result is the following:

Theorem 3.35

If the mild solution of (3.2) is exactly null controllable in $[0,t_1]$ on a Hilbert space H with controls $u \in L^2[0,t_1;U]$ where U is also a Hilbert space, then (A,B) is exponentially stabilizable.

Proof

The simplest proof of this assumes knowledge of infinite time linear quadratic control problems which we develop in the next chapter. We will anticipate these results here. Since the mild solution is exactly null controllable in $[0,t_1]$ there exists a control $u \in L^2[0,t_1;U]$ such that $z(t_1) = 0$. We now play this control on $[0,t_1]$ and the zero control for $t > t_1$, then $z(t) = 0$ for $t > t_1$. Hence

$$J(u) = \int_0^\infty [\|z(s)\|_H^2 + \|u(s)\|_U^2]ds < \infty$$

We show in the next chapter that this condition is sufficient for the existence of a unique optimal control $u^* \in L^2[0,\infty;U]$ which minimizes $J(u)$. Moreover this control is of the feedback type, being determined via the unique bounded operator solution of an algebraic Riccati equation. Hence implementing this optimal feedback control ensures the existence of a $D \in \mathcal{L}(H,U)$, such that

$$\int_0^\infty (\|T_t^D z_0\|_H^2 + \|DT_t^D z_0\|_U^2)dt \leq K^2\|z_0\|^2 \tag{3.32}$$

where T_t^D is generated by A+BD. Now (3.32) implies

$$\int_0^\infty \|T_t^D z_0\|_H^2 \, dt \leq K^2\|z_0\|^2$$

and the proof is completed by the following lemma.

Lemma 3.36

If T_t is a strongly continuous semigroup on a Hilbert space H, such that

$$\int_0^\infty \|T_t z_0\|_H^2 dt \leq K^2\|z_0\|^2 \qquad \forall\, z_0 \in H$$

then there exists constants $M,\omega > 0$, such that

$$\|T_t\| \leq Me^{-\omega t}$$

Proof

Assume

$$\|T_t\| \le \bar{M}e^{\bar{\omega}t}$$

for some $\bar{M},\bar{\omega} \ge 0$, then since

$$\frac{1 - e^{-2\bar{\omega}t}}{2\bar{\omega}} \|T_t z_o\|^2 = \int_0^t e^{-2\bar{\omega}\alpha} \|T_t z_o\|^2 \, d\alpha$$

$$\le \int_0^t e^{-2\bar{\omega}\alpha} \|T_\alpha\|^2 \|T_{t-\alpha} z_o\|^2 \, d\alpha$$

$$\le \bar{M}^2 \int_0^t \|T_s z_o\|^2 \, ds$$

$$\le \bar{M}^2 K^2 \|z_o\|^2$$

we have $\|T_t z_o\| \le \gamma\|z_o\|$ for some γ independent of t. Thus

$$\|T_t\| \le \gamma$$

and

$$t\|T_t z_o\|^2 = \int_0^t \|T_t z_o\|^2 \, d\alpha \le \int_0^t \|T_\alpha\|^2 \|T_{t-\alpha} z_o\|^2 \, d\alpha$$

$$\le \gamma^2 K^2 \|z_o\|^2$$

Hence

$$\|T_t z_o\| \le \frac{\gamma K}{t^{\frac{1}{2}}} \|z_o\| \qquad \forall \; z_o \in H.$$

But this implies that $\|T_t\| < 1$ for t sufficiently large.

Then

$$\omega_o = \lim_{t\to\infty} \frac{\log\|T_t\|}{t} < 0$$

and so there exists $M,\omega > 0$ such that

$$\|T_t\| \le Me^{-\omega t}$$

Example 3.37

In Example 3.8 we showed that the controlled wave equation was exactly controllable on $[0,t_1]$ for any $t_1 > 0$, and hence it is also exactly null controllable and so stabilizable. In Example 3.25 we showed that the controlled diffusion equation was exactly null controllable and hence stabilizable. Actually this is obvious in this example since for u = 0 the system is stable. However, it is easy to extend the example to consider the case where the uncontrolled system is unstable.

References

[1] Banks, H.T., Jacobs, M.Q. and Langenkop, C.E. Characterisations of the controlled states in W_2^1 of linear hereditary systems, SIAM J. Control, 13 (1975), pp.611-649.

[2] Benchimol, C.D. The stabilizability of infinite dimensional linear time invariant systems, Thesis UCLA, 1977.

[3] Butkovskii, A.G. Theory of optimal control of distributed parameter systems, Elsevier, New York, 1969.

[4] Curtain, R.F. and Pritchard, A.J. A semigroup approach to infinite dimensional systems theory, Proceedings of the IMA Symposium on Recent Theoretical Developments in Control, Leicester, 1976.

[5] Datko, R. Extending a theorem of A.M. Liapunov to Hilbert space, J. Math. Anal. Appl., 32 (1970), pp.610-616.

[6] Datko, R. Uniform asymptotic stability of evolutionary processes in a Banach space, SIAM J. Math. Anal., 3 (1972), pp.428-445.

[7] Delfour, M.C. and Mitter, S.K. Controllability, observability and optimal feedback control of affine hereditary differential systems, SIAM J. Control, 10 (1972), pp.298-328.

[8] Delfour, M.C. and Mitter, S.K. Controllability and observability for infinite dimensional systems, SIAM J. Control, 10 (1972), pp.329-333.

[9] Dolecki, S. and Russell, D. A general theory of observation and control, SIAM J. Control, 15 (1977), pp.185-220.

[10] Fattorini, H.O. On control in finite time of differential equations in Banach space, Comm. Pure App. Maths, XlX (1966), pp.17-34.

[11] Fattorini, H.O. Some remarks on complete controllability, SIAM J. Control, 4 (1966), pp.686-694.

[12] Fattorini, H.O. On complete controllability of linear systems, J. Diff. Eqns., 3 (1967), pp.391-402.

[13] Fattorini, H.O. Controllability of higher order linear systems in mathematical theory of control, Eds. Balakrishnan, A.V. and Neustad, L.W., Academic Press, 1967

[14] Fattorini, H.O. and Russell, D.L. Exact controllability theorems for linear parabolic equations in one space dimension, Archiv. Rat. Mech. Anal., 43 (1971), pp.272-292.

[15] Gabasov , R. and Curakova, S.V. The theory of controllability of linear systems with delay lags, Eng. Cybernetics, 4 (1969), pp.16-27.

[16] Halanay, A. On the controllability of linear difference-differential systems in lecture notes in operations research and mathematical economics, 12, Springer Verlag, 1970.

[17] Helton, J.W. Systems with infinite dimensional state space: the Hilbert space approach, Proc. IEEE, 64 (1976), pp.145-160.

[18] Hille, E. and Phillips, R.S. Functional analysis and semigroups, Publ. Amer. Math. Soc., 1957.

[19] Kirrillova, F.M. and Curakova, S.V. Relative controllability of systems with time lag, Dokl. Akad. Nauk. USSR, 176 (1967), pp.1260-1263.

[20] Kobayashi, T. Initial state determination for distributed parameter systems, SIAM J. Control, 14 (1976), pp.934-944.

[21] Lukes, D.L. Stabilizability and optimal control, Funkial. Ekvac., 2 (1968), pp.39-50.

[22] Manitius, A. Optimal control of hereditary systems, Control Theory and Topics in Functional Analysis Vol III, International Atomic Energy Agency, (1976), pp.43-178.

[23] Manitius, A. and Triggiani, R. Function space controllability for linear retarded systems: a derivation from abstract operator conditions, International Report CRM 605, Centre de Recherches Mathematiques, Universite de Montreal, 1976.

[24] Manitius, A. and Triggiani, R. Sufficient conditions for function space controllability and feedback stabilizability of linear retarded systems, Proc. IEEE Conference on Decision and Control, 1976.

[25] Manitius, A. and Triggiani, R. Controllability, observability and stabilizability of retarded systems, Proc. IEEE Conference on Decision and Control, 1976.

[26] Olbrot, A.W. On controllability of linear systems with time delays in the control, IEEE Trans. Aut. Control, AC 16 (1972), pp.664-666.

[27] Pandolfi, L. On feedback stabilization of functional differential equations, Boll. UHI 4, 11 Supplemento al Fascicolo 3, Giugno, Ser IV Vol XI (1975), pp.626-635.

[28] Popov, V.M. Pointwise degeneracy of linear time invariant delay-differential equations, J. Diff. Eqns., 11 (1972), pp.541-561.

[29] Pritchard, A.J. Stability and control of distributed systems, Proc. IEE, (1969), pp.1433-1438.

[30] Pritchard, A.J. and Triggiani, R. Stabilizability in Banach space, Control Theory Centre Report No.35, University of Warwick, 1974.

[31] Pritchard, A.J. and Zabczyk, J. Stability and stabilizability of infinite dimensional systems, Control Theory Centre Report No.70, University of Warwick, 1977.

[32] Rolewicz, S. On universal time for controllability of time-depending linear control systems, Studia Mathematica, 59 (1976), pp.133-138.

[33] Russek, A. On relations between exact controllability and rank condition, Preprint Inst. Mathematics, Warsaw, 1975.

[34] Russell, D.L. Control theory of hyperbolic equations related to certain questions in harmonic analysis and spectral theory, J. Math. Anal. Appl., 40 (1972), pp.336-368.

[35] Russell, D.L. Linear stabilization of the linear oscillator in Hilbert space, J. Math. Anal. Appl., 25 (1969), pp.663-675.

[36] Russell, D.L. Problems of control and stabilization for partial differential equations, Proc. 6th IFAC Congress, Boston, 1975.

[37] Sakawa, Y. Controllability for partial differential equations of parabolic type, SIAM J. Control, 12 (1974), pp.389-400.

[38] Sakawa, Y. Observability and related problems for partial differential equations of parabolic type, SIAM J. Control, 13 (1975), pp.14-27.

[39] Slemrod, M. A note on complete controllability and stabilizability of linear control systems in Hilbert space. SIAM J. Control, 12 (1974), pp.500-508.

[40] Slemrod, M. The linear stabilization problem in Hilbert space, J. Functional Anal., 11 (1972), pp.334-345.

[41] Triggiani, R. Controllability and observability in Banach spaces with bounded operators, SIAM J. Control, 13 (1975), pp.462-491.

[42] Triggiani, R. On a lack of exact controllability for mild solutions in Banach space, J. Math. Anal. Appl., 50 (1975), pp.438-446.

[43] Triggiani, R. Extension of rank conditions for controllability and observability to Banach spaces and unbounded operators, SIAM J. Control, 14 (1976), pp.313-338.

[44] Triggiani, R. On the stabilization problem in Banach space, J. Math. Anal. Appl., 52 (1975), pp.383-403.

[45] Triggiani, R. On the relationship between first and second order controllable systems in Banach space, Proc. IFIP Conference on Identification and Modelling of Distributed Parameter Systems, Rome, 1976.

[46] Tsujioka, K. Remarks on controllability of second order evolution equations in Hilbert spaces, SIAM J. Control, 8, (1970), pp.90-99.

[47] Wang, P.K.C. On feedback control of distributed parameter systems, Int. J. Control, 3 (1966), pp.255-273.

[48] Wang, P.K.C. Feedback stabilization of distributive systems with applications to plasma stabilization, Instability of Continuous Systems, Ed. H. Leipholz, Springer Verlag, 1971.

[49] Weiss, L. On the controllability of delay-differential systems, SIAM J. Control, 5 (1967), pp.575-587.

[50] Wiberg, D.M. Feedback control of linear distributed systems, Trans. ASME J. Basic Eng., 89 (1967), pp.379-384.

[51] Zabczyk, J. Remarks on the control of discrete time distributed parameter systems, SIAM J. Control, 12 (1974), pp.721-735.

[52] Zabczyk, J. Complete stabilizability implies exact controllability, Seminarul de Ecuatti Functionale, Universitatea din Timosoara, Rumania, 1976.

[53] Zabczyk, J. A note on C_o semigroups, Bull. l'Acad. Pol. de Sc. Serie Math., 23 (1975), pp.895-898.

[54] Zabczyk, J. Remarks on the algebraic Riccati equation in Hilbert space, Appl. Math. Optimisation, 3 (1976), pp.383-403.

[55] Zmood, R.B. The Euclidean space controllability of control systems with delay, SIAM J. Control, 12 (1974), pp.609-623.

CHAPTER 4

QUADRATIC COST CONTROL PROBLEM

4.1 Regulator problem

We suppose that our system is described by the following input-output relationship

(4.1) $$z(t) = T_{t-t_o}z_o + \int_{t_o}^{t} T_{t-s}Bu(s)ds \; ; \quad 0 \leq t_o \leq t \leq t_1 < \infty$$

where H, U are real Hilbert spaces, $B \in \mathcal{L}(U,H)$, $z_o \in H$, and $\{T_t;\ t \geq 0\}$ is a semigroup on H with generator A. From lemma 2.24, $z(t)$ is strongly continuous on $[t_o,t_1]$ for all inputs $u \in L^2(0,t_1;U)$.

The cost functional associated with the system (4.1) is

(4.2) $$J(u;t_o,z_o) = \langle z(t_1),Gz(t_1)\rangle + \int_{t_o}^{t_1}\{\langle z(s),Mz(s)\rangle + \langle u(s),Ru(s)\rangle\}ds$$

where $M,G \in \mathcal{L}(H)$ and $R \in \mathcal{L}(U)$ are self adjoint and nonnegative and

(4.3) $$\langle Ru,u\rangle \geq \alpha \|u\|^2 \qquad \forall\ u \in U \text{ and some } \alpha > 0$$

Our control problem is to find an optimal control $u^* \in L^2(t_o,t_1;U)$ which minimizes $J(u;t_o,z_o)$.

In finite dimensions this is called the "regulator problem", the motivation being to bring the state $z(t_1)$ close to the zero state. Our method of proof is to construct a sequence of feedback controls and to show that they converge to the optimal control.

Consider the following sequence

(4.4) $$u_k(t) = F_k(t)z(t)$$

(4.5) $$\begin{cases} F_k(t) = -R^{-1}B^*Q_{k-1}(t) \; ; \qquad F_o(t) = 0 \\ M_k(t) = M + F_k^*(t)RF_k(t) \\ Q_k(t)h = U_k^*(t_1,t)GU_k(t_1,t)h + \int_t^{t_1} U_k^*(s,t)M_k(s)U_k(s,t)h\,ds \end{cases}$$

where $U_k(t,s)$ is the perturbation of T_t by $BF_k(t)$.

With the choice of control given by (4.4), (4.1) becomes

(4.6) $$z_k(t) = U_k(t,t_o)z_o$$

We also consider the controlled version of (4.6)

(4.7) $$z(t) = U_k(t,t_o)z_o + \int_{t_o}^{t} U_k(t,s)B\bar{u}(s)\,ds$$

for some $\bar{u} \in L^2(0,t_1;U)$.

Now a series of lemmas are established which demonstrate the convergence of the feedback controls (4.4) to the optimal solution of the problem

Lemma 4.1

$$\langle z_k(t), Q_k(t) z_k(t)\rangle = \langle z_k(t_1), G z_k(t_1)\rangle + \int_t^{t_1} \Big\{\langle z_k(s), M_k(s) z_k(s)\rangle - 2\langle z_k(s), Q_k(s) B\bar{u}(s)\rangle\Big\}\, ds$$

where z is given by (4.7).

Proof

This is by direct substitution of (4.7) and (4.5) into the above expression and for simplicity we verify the result in two parts.

(a) Suppose we only consider terms in G :

$$\text{L.H.S.} = \langle U_k(t_1,t_o)z_o, GU_k(t_1,t_o)z_o\rangle + 2\langle U_k(t_1,t_o)z_o, G\int_{t_o}^{t} U_k(t_1,s)B\bar{u}(s)ds\rangle$$
$$+ \langle \int_{t_o}^{t} U_k(t_1,s)B\bar{u}(s)ds,\ G\int_{t_o}^{t} U_k(t_1,s)B\bar{u}(s)ds\rangle$$

since G is self adjoint and using the semigroup property of $U_k(t,s)$ (see Definition 2.32).

Similarly for the other side,

$$\text{R.H.S.} = \langle U_k(t_1,t_o)z_o, GU_k(t_1,t_o)z_o\rangle + 2\langle U_k(t_1,t_o)z_o,\ G\int_{t_o}^{t_1} U_k(t_1,s)B\bar{u}(s)ds\rangle$$
$$+ \langle \int_{t_o}^{t_1} U_k(t_1,s)B\bar{u}(s)ds,\ G\int_{t_o}^{t_1} U_k(t_1,s)B\bar{u}(s)ds\rangle$$
$$- 2\int_t^{t_1} \langle U_k(t_1,t_o)z_o,\ GU_k(t_1,s)B\bar{u}(s)\rangle\, ds$$
$$- 2\int_t^{t_1}\int_{t_o}^{s} \langle U_k(t_1,\alpha)B\bar{u}(\alpha),\ GU_k(t_1,s)B\bar{u}(s)\rangle\, d\alpha\, ds$$
$$= \text{L.H.S.}$$

(b) Suppose we only consider terms in M and R :

$$\text{L.H.S.} = \int_t^{t_1} \langle U_k(s,t_o)z_o, M_k(s)U_k(s,t_o)z_o\rangle\, ds$$
$$+ 2\int_t^{t_1}\int_{t_o}^{t} \langle U_k(s,t_o)z_o, M_k(s)U_k(s,\alpha)B\bar{u}(\alpha)\rangle\, d\alpha\, ds$$

$$+ \int_{t_o}^{t}\int_{t_o}^{t}\int_{t}^{t_1} \langle U_k(\alpha,s)B\bar{u}(s),\ M_k(\alpha)U_k(\alpha,\beta)B\bar{u}(\beta)\rangle \, d\alpha \, d\beta \, ds$$

using the semigroup property of $U_k(t,s)$.

$$\text{R.H.S.} = \int_{t}^{t_1} \langle U_k(s,t_o)z_o,\ M_k(s)U_k(s,t_o)z_o\rangle \, ds$$

$$+ 2\int_{t}^{t_1}\int_{t_o}^{s} \langle U_k(s,t_o)z_o,\ M_k(s)U_k(s,\alpha)B\bar{u}(\alpha)\rangle \, d\alpha \, ds$$

$$+ \int_{t}^{t_1}\int_{t_o}^{s}\int_{t_o}^{s} \langle U_k(s,\alpha)B\bar{u}(\alpha),\ M_k(s)U_k(s,\beta)B\bar{u}(\beta)\rangle \, d\alpha \, d\beta \, ds$$

$$- 2\int_{t}^{t_1}\int_{s}^{t_1} \langle U_k(\alpha,t_o)z_o,\ M_k(\alpha)U_k(\alpha,s)B\bar{u}(s)\rangle \, d\alpha \, ds$$

$$- 2\int_{t}^{t_1}\int_{s}^{t_1}\int_{t_o}^{s} \langle U_k(\alpha,\beta)B\bar{u}(\beta),\ M_k(\alpha)U_k(\alpha,s)B\bar{u}(s)\rangle \, d\beta \, d\alpha \, ds$$

$$= \text{L.H.S.}$$

interchanging the order of integration in the last two terms.

<u>Lemma 4.2</u>

The cost for (4.1) with the feedback control (4.4) is

$$J(u_k;t_o,z_o) = \langle z_o,Q_k(t_o)z_o\rangle$$

For fixed $z_o \in H$ and fixed $t_o < t_1$, $\langle z_o,Q_k(t_o)z_o\rangle$ is monotonically decreasing in k and

$$\langle z_o,Q_k(t_o)z_o\rangle \leq \langle z_o,Q_o(t_o)z_o\rangle \qquad \forall\ z_o \in H.$$

<u>Proof</u>

(a) Let $\bar{u} = 0$ in lemma 4.1, then

$$\langle z(t_o),\ Q_k(t_o)z(t_o)\rangle = \langle z(t_1),\ Gz(t_1)\rangle + \int_{t_o}^{t_1} \langle z(s),\ M_k(s)z(s)\rangle \, ds$$

$$= \langle z(t_1),\ Gz(t_1)\rangle + \int_{t_o}^{t_1} (\langle z(s),\ Mz(s)\rangle + \langle F_k(s)z(s),\ RF_k(s)z(s)\rangle) \, ds$$

$$= \langle z(t_1),\ Gz(t_1)\rangle + \int_{t_o}^{t_1} (\langle z(s),\ Mz(s)\rangle + \langle u_k(s),\ Ru_k(s)\rangle) \, ds$$

$= J(u_k;t_o,z_o)$ from (4.2)

(b) Let $\bar{u}(t) = (-F_k(t) + F_{k+1}(t))z(t)$ in (4.7). Then (4.7) is equivalent to $z_{k+1}(t) = U_{k+1}(t,t_o)z_o$

Substituting for this $\bar{u}(t)$ in lemma 4.1, we obtain

$$<z_o, Q_k(t_o)z_o> = <z(t_1), Gz(t_1)> + \int_{t_o}^{t_1} <z(s), Mz(s)> ds$$

$$+ \int_{t_o}^{t_1} \Big\{<F_k(s)z(s), RF_k(s)z(s)> + 2<z(s), Q_k(s)BF_k(s)z(s)> - 2<z(s), Q_k(s)BF_{k+1}(s)z(s)>\Big\} ds$$

$$= <z(t_1), Gz(t_1)> + \int_{t_o}^{t_1} \{<z(s), Mz(s)> + <u_{k+1}(s), Ru_{k+1}(s)>\} ds$$

$$+ \int_{t_o}^{t_1} \Big\{<F_{k+1}(s)z(s), RF_{k+1}(s)z(s)> + <F_k(s)z(s), RF_k(s)z(s)> - 2<F_{k+1}(s)z(s), RF_k(s)z(s)>\Big\} ds$$

$$= <z(t_o), Q_{k+1}(t_o)z(t_o)> + \int_{t_o}^{t_1} <(F_{k+1}(s) - F_k(s))z(s), R(F_{k+1}(s) - F_k(s))z(s)> ds$$

That is,

$$<z_o, Q_k(t_o)z_o> = <z_o, Q_{k+1}(t_o)z_o> + \int_{t_o}^{t_1} <Ry(s), y(s)> ds$$

where $y(s) = (F_{k+1} - F_k(s))z(s)$

From (4.3) we have the inequality $<z_o, Q_k(t_o)z_o> \geq <z_o, Q_{k+1}(t_o)z_o>$ for all k and $t_o < t_1$.

<u>Lemma 4.3</u>

$Q_k(t)$ of (4.5) converge strongly as $k \to \infty$ to a self adjoint operator $Q(t) \in \mathscr{L}(H)$ for each $t \in [t_o, t_1]$ and $Q(t)$ satisfies the integral equation

$$(4.8) \quad Q(t)h = U^*(t_1,t)GU(t_1,t)h + \int_t^{t_1} U^*(s,t)(M+Q(s)BR^{-1}B^*Q(s))U(s,t)h\, ds$$

where $U(t,s)$ is the perturbed mild evolution operator corresponding to the perturbation of T_t by $-BR^{-1}B^*Q(t)$.

$Q(t)$ is strongly continuous in t on $[t_o, t_1]$.

Proof

From (4.5), $Q_k(t)$ is a self adjoint and nonnegative operator in $\mathcal{L}(H)$ for each t and from lemma 4.2, $Q_k(t)$ is decreasing and uniformly bounded in norm:

$$\begin{aligned} \|Q_k(t)\| &= \sup_{\|z_o\|=1} \langle z_o, Q_k(t) z_o\rangle \\ &\leq \sup_{\|z_o\|=1} \langle z_o, Q_o(t) z_o\rangle \\ &\leq c\ , \quad \text{a constant} \end{aligned}$$

Hence for each t, $Q_k(t)$ converges strongly to a self adjoint nonnegative operator $Q(t) \in \mathcal{L}(H)$ and $Q(t) \leq c$ on $[t_o, t_1]$. From (4.5), $F_k(t)$ and $M_k(t)$ also converge strongly as $k \to \infty$ to $-R^{-1}B^*Q(t)$ and $M+Q(t)BR^{-1}B^*Q(t)$ respectively.

We now proceed to show that $U_k(t,s)$, the perturbation of T_t by $+BF_k(t)$, converges strongly as $k \to \infty$ to $U(t,s)$, the perturbation of T_t by $-BR^{-1}B^*Q(t)$. From Theorem 2.33, we have

$$(U_k(t,s)-U(t,s))h = -\int_s^t T_{t-\rho}B(F_k(\rho)U_k(\rho,s)-R^{-1}B^*Q(\rho)U(\rho,s))h\, d\rho$$

and

$$\begin{aligned} \|(U_k(t,s)-U(t,s))h\| &\leq \int_s^t \|T_{t-\rho}BF_k(\rho)\|\, \|U_k(\rho,s)h-U(\rho,s)h\|\, d\rho \\ &+ \int_s^t \|T_{t-\rho}B\|\, \|(F_k(\rho)-R^{-1}B^*Q(\rho))U(\rho,s)h\|\, d\rho \end{aligned}$$

The second term converges to zero as $k \to \infty$ by the Lebesque dominated convergence theorem and since $F_k(\rho)$ is uniformly bounded in k, using Gronwall's lemma

$$U_k(t,s) \to U(t,s) \quad \text{strongly as} \quad k \to \infty$$

We may now apply the Lebesque dominated convergence theorem to let $k \to \infty$ in the expression for $Q_k(t)$ in (4.5) to prove that $Q(t)$ satisfies (4.8). The strong continuity of $Q(t)$ follows from the strong continuity of $U(t_1,t)$ on $[t_o,t_1]$.

Lemma 4.4

The optimal control which minimizes $J(u;t_o,z_o)$ is the feedback control

$$u(t) = -R^{-1}B^*Q(t)z(t)$$

and the minimum cost is $\langle z_o, Q(t_o)z_o\rangle$.

Proof

Consider an arbitrary admissible control $u \in L^2(t_o,t_1;U)$ so that the controlled system is

$$z(t) = T_{t-t_o} z_o + \int_{t_o}^{t} T_{t-s} Bu(s)\, ds$$

Since $U(t,s)$ is a perturbation of T_t by $-BR^{-1}B^*Q(t)$, we also have

$$z(t) = U(t,t_o)z_o + \int_{t_o}^{t} U(t,s)B\bar{u}(s)\, ds$$

where $\bar{u}(t) = u(t) + R^{-1}B^*Q(t)z(t)$

Applying lemma 4.1, for $t = t_o$, we obtain

$$<z_o, Q(t_o)z_o> = <z(t_1), Gz(t_1)> + \int_{t_o}^{t_1}\Big\{<z(s), Mz(s)>$$

$$+ <R^{-1}B\ Q(s)z(s), B\ Q(s)z(s)> - 2<z(s), Q(s)B\bar{u}(s)>\Big\} ds$$

$$= <z(t_1), Gz(t_1)> + \int_{t_o}^{t_1}\Big\{<z(s), Mz(s)> + <u(s), Ru(s)>\Big\} ds$$

$$- \int_{t_o}^{t_1} <\bar{u}(s), R\bar{u}(s)> ds$$

Now from (4.8)

$$<z_o, Q(t_o)z_o> = <z(t_1), Gz(t_1)> + \int_{t_o}^{t_1}\Big\{<z(s), Mz(s)> + <u^*(s), Ru^*(s)>\Big\} ds$$

and so we have

$$J(u^*;t_o,z_o) = J(u;t_o,z_o) - \int_{t_o}^{t_1} <\bar{u}(s), R\bar{u}(s)> ds \qquad \text{from lemma 4.2}$$

$$\leq J(u;t_o,z_o) \quad \text{by (4.3)}$$

But this inequality holds for arbitrary $\bar{u} \in L^2(t_o,t_1;U)$ and so u^* is optimal.

Lemma 4.5

$Q(t)$ is the unique solution of (4.8) in the class of strongly continuous self adjoint operators in $\mathcal{L}(H)$.

Proof

Let $Q(t)$ be the strong limit of the sequence $Q_k(t)$ of (4.4) and suppose that P(t) is another solution of (4.8). That is

(4.9) $$P(t)h = U_o^*(t_1,t)GU_o(t_1,t)h + \int_t^{t_1} U_o(s,t)(M+P(s)BR^{-1}B^*P(s)) U_o(s,t)h\, ds$$

where $U_o(t,s)$ is the perturbation of T_t by $-BR^{-1}B^*P(t)$

Consider the system

(4.10) $$z(t) = T_{t-t_o}z_o + \int_{t_o}^{t} T_{t-s}Bu(s)\, ds$$

for some $u \in L^2(t_o,t_1;U)$

Using the defining equation for $U_o(t,s)$ from Theorem 2.33, substituting u_o for u in (4.10) we obtain

(4.11) $$z(t) = U_o(t,t_o)z_o + \int_{t_o}^{t} U_o(t,s)B\bar{u}_o(s)\, ds$$

where $\bar{u}_o(t) = u_o(t) + R^{-1}B^*P(t)z(t)$

Now by lemma 4.1, for P(t) given by (4.9) and z(t) by (4.11) we have

(4.12) $$\langle z(t), P(t)z(t)\rangle = \langle z(t_1), Gz(t_1)\rangle + \int_t^{t_1} (\langle z(s), Mz(s)\rangle + \langle B^*P(s)z(s), R^{-1}B^*P(s)z(s)\rangle - 2\langle z(s), P(s)Bu_o(s)\rangle)ds$$

The cost for control $u_o(t)$ is given by

$$J(u_o;t_o,z_o) = \langle z(t_1), Gz(t_1)\rangle + \int_{t_o}^{t_1} (\langle z(s), Mz(s)\rangle + \langle u_o(s), Ru_o(s)\rangle)\, ds$$

$$= \langle z(t_1), Gz(t_1)\rangle + \int_{t_o}^{t_1} \Big\{\langle z(s), Mz(s)\rangle + \langle B^*P(s)z(s), R^{-1}B^*P(s)z(s)\rangle + \langle \bar{u}_o(s), R\bar{u}_o(s)\rangle - 2\langle \bar{u}_o(s), B^*P(s)z(s)\rangle\Big\}ds$$

Hence from (4.12)

(4.13) $$J(u_o;t_o,z_o) = \langle z_o, P(t_o)z_o\rangle + \int_{t_o}^{t_1} \langle \bar{u}_o(s), R\bar{u}_o(s)\rangle ds$$

Since U(t,s) is the perturbation of T_t by $-BR^{-1}B^*Q(t)$, (4.10) is equivalent to

(4.14) $$z(t) = U(t,t_o)z_o + \int_{t_o}^{t} U(t,s)B\bar{u}(s)\, ds$$

where $\bar{u}(t) = u(t)+R^{-1}B^*Q(t)z(t)$.

So arguing as above for $Q(t)$ given by (4.8) and $z(t)$ given by (4.14) we can show that

$$(4.15) \qquad J(u;t_o,z_o) = <z_o, \ Q(t_o)z_o> + \int_{t_o}^{t_1} <\bar{u}(s), \ R\bar{u}(s)> \ ds$$

Now if $u(t) = -R^{-1}B^*P(t)z(t)$ in (4.10), we have

$$\bar{u}(t) = R^{-1}B^*(Q(t)-P(t))z(t) \qquad \text{in } (4.14)$$

$$\text{or } z(t) = U_o(t,t_o)z_o$$

For this particular choice of u, by lemma 4.2 and (4.15), we obtain

$$(4.16) \quad J(u;t_o,z_o) = <z_o, \ Q(t_o)z_o> + \int_{t_o}^{t_1} <R^{-1}B^*(Q(t)-P(t))U_o(t,t_o)z_o,$$

$$B^*(Q(t)-P(t))U_o(t,t_o)z_o> \ dt$$

$$= <z_o, \ P(t_o)z_o>$$

Similarly, choosing $u_o(t) = -R^{-1}B^*Q(t)$ in (4.10), and using lemma 4.2 and (4.13) we obtain

$$(4.17) \quad J(u_o;t_o,z_o) = <z_o, \ P(t_o)z_o> + \int_{t_o}^{t_1} <R^{-1}B^*(P-Q)U(t,t_o)z_o,$$

$$B^*(P-Q)U(t_1,t)z_o> \ dt$$

$$= <z_o, \ Q(t_o)z_o>$$

Adding (4.16) and (4.17), we obtain

$$\int_{t_o}^{t_1} \| R^{-\frac{1}{2}}B^*(P(t)-Q(t))U(t,t_o)z_o \|^2 dt = 0$$

and $\qquad \int_{t_o}^{t_1} \| R^{-\frac{1}{2}}B^*(Q(t)-P(t))U_o(t,t_o)z_o \|^2 dt = 0$

From (4.3), we deduce that

$$B^*Q(t)U_o(t,t_o)z_o = B^*P(t)U_o(t,t_o)z_o$$

$$\text{on } [t_o,t_1]$$

and $\qquad B^*Q(t)U(t,t_o)z_o = B^*Q(t)U(t,t_o)z_o$

which from Theorem 2.33 implies that $U(t,t_o) = U_o(t,t_o)$, and so in fact

$$B^*Q(t)U(t,t_o)z_o = B^*P(t)U(t,t_o)z_o = B^*P(t)U_o(t,t_o)z_o$$

Thus from (4.9) and (4.8),

$$(P(t)-Q(t))h = \int_t^{t_1} U_o^*(s,t)P(s)BR^{-1}B^*P(s)U_o(s,t)h \ ds$$

$$- \int_t^{t_1} U^*(s,t)Q(s)BR^{-1}B^*Q(s)U(s,t)h \ ds$$

$$= 0$$

In fact we can show that $Q(t)$ is the unique solution of a differential Riccati equation analogous to the finite dimensional Riccati equation (1.6).

Lemma 4.6

$Q(t)$ is the unique solution of the following inner product Riccati equation in the class of strongly continuous self adjoint operators in $\mathcal{L}(H)$ with $\langle Q(t)h,k\rangle$ differentiable for $h,k \in D(A)$.

$$(4.18) \quad \frac{d}{dt}\langle Q(t)h,k\rangle + \langle Q(t)h,Ak\rangle + \langle Ah,Q(t)k\rangle + \langle Mh,k\rangle$$
$$= \langle Q(t)BR^{-1}B^*Q(t)h,k\rangle \quad \text{on } [t_o,t_1]$$
$$Q(t_1) = G \quad \text{where } h,k \in D(A).$$

Proof

(a) To show that the unique solution of (4.8) satisfies (4.18) we form the inner product of (4.8) with $h,k \in D(A)$ and differentiate term by term using the following property of the perturbed evolution operator.

$$(4.19) \quad \frac{\partial}{\partial t} U(s,t)h = -U(s,t)(A-BR^{-1}B^*Q(t))h \quad \text{a.e. for } h \in D(A) \text{ and } s>t$$

(see 2.43).

It is routine to verify that the formal differentiation yields (4.18), and so we shall only justify this differentiation for a typical term.

Consider $g(t) = \langle \int_t^{t_1} U^*(s,t)MU(s,t)h\, ds,\ k\rangle$ for $h,k \in D(A)$

then $g(t) = \int_t^{t_1} \langle MU(s,t)h,\ U(s,t)k\rangle\, ds$

and using (4.19)

$$\frac{dg(t)}{dt} = -\langle Mh,k\rangle + \int_t^{t_1} \frac{\partial}{\partial t}\langle MU(s,t)h,\ U(s,t)k\rangle\, ds$$
$$= -\langle Mh,k\rangle - \int_t^{t_1}\langle MU(s,t)(A-BR^{-1}B^*Q(t))h,\ U(s,t)k\rangle\, ds$$
$$- \int_t^{t_1}\langle MU(s,t)h,\ U(t,s)(A-BR^{-1}B^*Q(t))k\rangle\, ds$$

since all terms are integrable. Hence

$$\frac{dq(t)}{dt} = \langle Mh,k\rangle - \langle (A-BR^{-1}B^*Q(t))h, \int_t^{t_1} U^*(s,t)MU(s,t)k\, ds\rangle$$

$$-\langle \int_t^{t_1} U^*(s,t)MU(s,t)h\, ds, (A-BR^{-1}B^*Q(t))k\rangle$$

since $A-BR^{-1}B^*Q(t)$ is a closed operator.

(b) Uniqueness

Let $Q_1(t)$ and $Q_2(t)$ be two solutions of (4.18), then writing $P(t) = Q_1(t)-Q_2(t)$, it is readily verified that

$$(4.20)\quad \frac{d}{dt}\langle P(t)h,k\rangle = -\langle (A-LQ_1(t))h, P(t)k\rangle - \langle P(t)h, (A-LQ_1(t))k\rangle - \langle P(t)LP(t)h,k\rangle$$

and

$$(4.21)\quad \frac{d}{dt}\langle P(t)h,k\rangle = -\langle (A-LQ_2(t))h, P(t)k\rangle - \langle P(t)h,(A-LQ_2(t))k\rangle + \langle P(t)LP(t)h,k\rangle$$

where $L = BR^{-1}B^*$.

If $F(t)h = \int_t^{t_1} U_1^*(s,t)P(s)LP(s)U_1(s,t)h\, ds$, where $U_1(t,s)$ is the perturbation of T_t by $-LQ_1(t)$, then as in (a), for $h,k \in D(A)$, we may differentiate $\langle F(t)h,k\rangle$ to obtain

$$(4.22)\quad \frac{d}{dt}\langle F(t)h,k\rangle = -\langle P(t)LP(t)h,k\rangle - \langle F(t)h, (A-LQ_1(t))k\rangle - \langle (A-LQ_1(t))h, F(t)k\rangle$$

$$F(t_1) = 0$$

Assuming for the moment that (4.22) has a unique solution, we have $F(t) = P(t)$ and

$$\langle P(t)h,h\rangle = \int_t^{t_1} \langle U_1^*(s,t)P(s)LP^*(s)U_1(s,t)h,h\rangle\, ds \geq 0$$

for all $h \in H$. Similarly using (4.21), with Q_2 perturbations, we obtain the inequality

$$\langle P(t)h,h\rangle \leq 0 \text{ for all } h \in H \text{ and hence}$$

$$P(t) = 0$$

(c) Uniqueness of (4.22)

Let $S(t) = T^*_{t-s}F(t)T_{t-s}$ then for $h,k \in D(A)$

$\langle h,S(t)k\rangle$ is differentiable in t and

$$\frac{d}{dt}\langle h,S(t)k\rangle = \langle F(t)AT_{t-s}h,\ T_{t-s}k\rangle + \langle F(t)T_{t-s}h,\ AT_{t-s}k\rangle$$

$$- \langle F(t)T_{t-s}h,\ (A-LQ_1(t))T_{t-s}k\rangle - \langle (A-LQ_1(t))T_{t-s}h,\ F(t)T_{t-s}k\rangle$$

$$= \langle F(t)T_{t-s}h,\ LQ_1(t)T_{t-s}k\rangle + \langle LQ_1(t)T_{t-s}h,\ F(t)T_{t-s}k\rangle$$

So
$$\langle T^*_{t-s}F(t)T_{t-s}h,h\rangle = -\int_t^{t_1}\langle (Q_1(\rho)L^*F(\rho) + F(\rho)LQ_1(\rho))T_{\rho-s}h,\ T_{\rho-s}h\rangle d\rho$$

for all $h \in H$, since $\overline{D(A)} = H$.

Letting $s \to t$, we obtain

$$\langle F(t)h,h\rangle = -\int_t^{t_1}\langle (Q_1(\rho)L^*F(\rho) + F(\rho)LQ_1(\rho)T_{\rho-t}h,\ T_{\rho-t}h\rangle\, d\rho$$

Since F(t) is self adjoint

$$\|F(t)\| = \sup_{\|h\|=1} |\langle F(t)h,h\rangle|$$

$$\leq \sup_{\|h\|=1} \int_t^{t_1} C\|F(\rho)\|\,\|h\|^2\, d\rho, \text{ for some positive constant } C$$

or
$$\|F(t)\| \leq C\int_t^{t_1}\|F(\rho)\|\, d\rho$$

so by Gronwall's inequality, $\|F(t)\| = 0$ and (4.22) has a unique solution.

Corollary 4.7

Q(t) of (4.8) or (4.18) is also uniquely determined by

(4.23) $$Q(t)h = U^*(t_1,t)GT_{t_1-t}h + \int_t^{t_1}U^*(s,t)MT_{s-t}h\, ds \quad \text{or}$$

(4.24) $$Q(t)h = T^*_{t_1-t}GU(t_1,t)h + \int_t^{t_1} T^*_{s-t}MU(s,t)h\,ds$$

(4.25) $$Q(t)h = T^*_{t_1-t}GT_{t_1-t}h + \int_t^{t_1} T^*_{s-t}[M-Q(s)BR^{-1}B^*Q(s)]T_{s-t}h\,ds$$

Proof

(4.23)-(4.25) are established by showing that differentiating $\langle k,Q(t)h\rangle$ with $h,k \in D(A)$ yields (4.18).

4.2 Examples

Example 4.8 Finite dimensional systems

If $T_t = e^{At}$ where A is an $n \times n$ matrix, $H = R^n$, $U = R^m$, then (4.18) holds for all $h,k \in R^n$ and our theory agrees with the finite dimensional regulator problem in §1.

Example 4.9 Parabolic systems

For our system (4.1) we suppose that the semigroup T_t is the analytic semigroup generated by the self adjoint operator A on a Hilbert space H of Example 2.40. Then the Riccati equation (4.18) can be decomposed as follows:

Suppose that it is possible to express Q(t) by

$$Q(t)h = \sum_{i,j=o}^{\infty}\sum q_{ij}(t)\phi_j\langle h,\phi_i\rangle \quad \forall\, h \in H$$

For simplicity we assume that all the eigenvalues of A are unrepeated; then since

$$A\phi_j = \lambda_j\phi_j\,, \quad \text{(4.18) becomes}$$

(4.25) $$\begin{cases} \dot{q}_{ij} + (\lambda_i+\lambda_j)q_{ij} + \langle M\phi_i,\phi_j\rangle - \alpha_{ij} = 0 \\ q_{ij}(t_1) = \langle G\phi_i,\phi_j\rangle \end{cases}$$

where $$\alpha_{ij} = \sum_{k,r=o}^{\infty}\sum q_{ik}q_{jr}\langle R^{-1}B^*\phi_k,B^*\phi_r\rangle$$

Of course we need to justify that such an expansion for Q(t) converges and we do this for the normalised heat equation of Example 1.2.

(4.26) $$\begin{cases} z_t = z_{\xi\xi} + u(t,\xi) \\ z_\xi(0,t) = 0 = z_\xi(1,t)\ ; \quad z(\xi,0) = z_o(\xi) \end{cases}$$

where we seek to minimize

$$J(u) = \int_0^1 z^2(t_1,\xi)d\xi + \int_0^{t_1}(\int_0^1 z^2(t\ ,\xi) + u^2(t,\xi)d\xi)\ dt$$

Then for $\phi_i = \sqrt{2}\cos \pi i\xi$; $i=1,2,\ldots$; $\phi_o = 1$, (4.25) becomes

$$(4.27)\quad \begin{cases} \dot{q}_{ij} - \pi^2(i^2+j^2)q_{ij} + \delta_{ij} - \sum_{k=1}^{\infty} q_{ik}q_{jk} = 0 \\ q_{ij}(t_1) = \delta_{ij} \end{cases}$$

Now $q_{ij}(t)=0$ is a solution to (4.27) and since the solution is unique, we have $q_{ij}(t)\equiv 0$ for $i\neq j$ and

$$\begin{cases} \dot{q}_{ii} - 2\pi^2 i^2 q_{ii} + 1 - q_{ii}^2 = 0 \\ q_{ii}(t_1) = 1 \end{cases}$$

In this case we can solve explicitly for $q_{ii}(t)$, obtaining

$$q_{ii}(t) = \frac{a_i(1-b_i) - b_i(1-a_i)e^{-\alpha_i(t-t_1)}}{(1-b_i) - (1-a_i)e^{-\alpha_i(t-t_1)}}$$

where

$$\alpha_i = 2\sqrt{\pi^4 i^4 + 1}$$

$$a_i = -\pi^2 i^2 - \sqrt{\pi^4 i^4 + 1}$$

$$b_i = -\pi^2 i^2 + \sqrt{\pi^4 i^4 + 1}$$

Hence $|q_{ii}(t)|$ is uniformly bounded in i and t and

$$Q(t)h = \sum_{i=o}^{\infty} q_{ii}(t)\phi_i\langle\cdot,\phi_i\rangle$$

is well defined. Similarly we can expand $u(t)$ and $z(t)$ by

$$u(t) = \sum_{i=0}^{\infty} u_i(t)\phi_i\ , \qquad z(t) = \sum_{i=0}^{\infty} z_i(t)\phi_i\ ,$$

where $\quad u_i(t) = -q_{ii}(t)z_i(t)$

Example 4.10

Consider the controlled wave equation

$$(4.28) \qquad z_{tt} = z_{\xi\xi} + u(t,\xi)$$

$$z(0,t) = z(1,t) = 0 \ , \ z(\xi,0) = z_0(\xi) \ , \ z_t(\xi,0) = z_1(\xi)$$

with the cost functional

$$(4.29) \qquad J(u) = \tfrac{1}{2}\int_0^1 (z_\xi^2(\xi,t_1) + z_t^2(\xi,t_1))d\xi + \int_0^{t_1}\int_0^1 (\tfrac{1}{4}z_t^2(\xi,t) + u^2(\xi,t))\, d\xi\, dt$$

We can express (4.28) as an abstract system on the Hilbert space $\mathcal{H}$ defined in Example 2.41.

$$(4.30) \qquad w(t) = \begin{pmatrix} z(t) \\ z_t(t) \end{pmatrix} = T_t\begin{pmatrix} z_0 \\ z_1 \end{pmatrix} + \int_0^t T_{t-s}\begin{pmatrix} 0 \\ I \end{pmatrix} u(s)\, ds$$

$$(4.31) \qquad J(u) = \tfrac{1}{2}\langle w(t_1), w(t_1)\rangle + \int_0^{t_1} (\tfrac{1}{4}\langle Mw(t), w(t)\rangle + \langle u,u\rangle_H)\, dt$$

where $H = L_2(0,1)$, $M = \begin{pmatrix} 0 & 0 \\ 0 & I \end{pmatrix}$ and the inner product on $\mathcal{H}$ is given by

$$\langle w,\bar{w}\rangle_{\mathcal{H}} = \langle w_\xi^1, \bar{w}_\xi^1\rangle_H + \langle w^2,\bar{w}^2\rangle_H$$

for $w = \begin{pmatrix} w^1 \\ w^2 \end{pmatrix}$, $\bar{w} = \begin{pmatrix} \bar{w}^1 \\ \bar{w}^2 \end{pmatrix}$.

We suppose that Q(t) given by (4.18) can be expressed as

$$Q(t) = \begin{pmatrix} Q_1(t) & Q_2(t) \\ Q_3(t) & Q_4(t) \end{pmatrix}$$

For $h = \begin{pmatrix} h^1 \\ h^2 \end{pmatrix}$ and $k = \begin{pmatrix} k^1 \\ k^2 \end{pmatrix} \in D(\mathcal{A})$, (4.18) reduces to

$$(4.32) \qquad \begin{aligned} &\frac{d}{dt}\langle (Q_1h^1+Q_2h^2)_\xi, k_\xi^1\rangle + \frac{d}{dt}\langle Q_3h^1+Q_4h^2, k^2\rangle \\ &+ \langle h_\xi^2, (Q_1k^1+Q_2k^2)_\xi\rangle + \langle h_{\xi\xi}^1, Q_3k^1+Q_4k^2\rangle \\ &+ \langle k_\xi^2, (Q_1h^1+Q_2h^2)_\xi\rangle + \langle k_{\xi\xi}^1, Q_3h^1+Q_4h^2\rangle \\ &+ \tfrac{1}{4}\langle h^2,k^2\rangle = \langle Q_3h^1+Q_4h^2, Q_3k^1+Q_4k^2\rangle \end{aligned}$$

$$Q_1(t_1) = \tfrac{1}{2}I = Q_4(t_1) \quad ; \quad Q_2(t_1) = 0 = Q_3(t_1)$$

where all the inner products are in H.

We now introduce the following expansions for $Q_i(t)$; i=1,2,3,4.

$$(4.33)\quad \begin{cases} Q_1(t) = \sum\limits_{i,j=1}^{\infty}\sum \alpha_{ij}\phi_i\langle\cdot,\phi_j\rangle_H \\ Q_2(t) = \sum\limits_{i,j=1}^{\infty}\sum \beta_{ij}\phi_i\langle\cdot,\phi_j\rangle_H \\ Q_3(t) = \sum\limits_{i,j=1}^{\infty}\sum \gamma_{ij}\phi_i\langle\cdot,\phi_j\rangle_H \\ Q_4(t) = \sum\limits_{i,j=1}^{\infty}\sum \eta_{ij}\phi_i\langle\cdot\ \phi_j\rangle_H \end{cases}$$

where $\phi_i(\xi) = \sqrt{2}\sin\pi i\xi$.

Since Q(t) is self adjoint in $\mathcal{H}$, we deduce that

$$(4.34)\quad \begin{cases} \alpha_{ij}(t) = \alpha_{ji}(t) \quad ; \quad \eta_{ij}(t) = \eta_{ji}(t) \\ \pi^2k^2\beta_{ki} = \gamma_{ik} \end{cases}$$

Substituting $h^1 = 0 = k^1$ and $h^2 = \phi_m$, $k^2 = \phi_n$ and $Q_i(t)$ given by (4.33) in (4.32), we obtain

$$(4.35)\quad \begin{cases} \dot{\eta}_{nm} + \pi^2n^2\beta_{nm} + \pi^2m^2\beta_{mn} + \tfrac{1}{4}\delta_{mn} = \sum\limits_{i=1}^{\infty}\eta_{im}\eta_{in} \\ \eta_{nm}(t_1) = \tfrac{1}{2}\delta_{nm} \end{cases}$$

Substituting $k^2 = 0 = h^2$ and $h^1 = \phi_r$, $k^1 = \phi_s$ and $Q_i(t)$ given by (4.33) in (4.32), we obtain

$$(4.36)\quad \begin{cases} \pi^2s^2\dot{\alpha}_{sr} - \pi^2r^2\gamma_{rs} - \pi^2s^2\gamma_{sr} = \sum\limits_{i=1}^{\infty}\gamma_{ir}\gamma_{is} \\ \alpha_{sr}(t_1) = \tfrac{1}{2}\delta_{sr} \end{cases}$$

Substituting $h^1 = 0 = k^2$ and $h^2 = \phi_m$, $k^1 = \phi_n$ and $Q_i(t)$ given by (4.33) in (4.32), we obtain

$$(4.37)\quad \begin{cases} \pi^2n^2\dot{\beta}_{nm} + \pi^2m^2\alpha_{mn} - \pi^2n^2\eta_{nm} = \sum\limits_{i=1}^{\infty}\eta_{im}\gamma_{in} \\ \beta_{mn}(t_1) = 0 \end{cases}$$

By inspection, a solution is $\beta_{nm} = \gamma_{mn} = 0$, $\alpha_{mn} = 0$ for $m \neq n$, $\eta_{nm} = 0$ for $m \neq n$ and $\alpha_{mm} = \eta_{mm} = \tfrac{1}{2}$. Since (4.18) has a unique solution it must be

$$Q(t) = \frac{1}{2}\begin{pmatrix} I & 0 \\ 0 & I \end{pmatrix}$$

and so the optimal control is $u(t,\xi) = -z_t(t,\xi)$ and the minimum cost is $\frac{1}{2}\int_0^1 (z_{0\xi}^2(\xi)+z_1^2(\xi))d\xi$.

Example 4.11 Delay equations

We consider the controlled linear delay equation

$$(4.38)\quad \begin{cases} \dot{x}(t) = A_0 x(t) + \sum_{i=1}^{N} A_i \begin{cases} x(t+\theta_i) \ ; & t+\theta_i \geq 0 \\ h(t+\theta_i) \ ; & t+\theta_i < 0 \end{cases} \\ \qquad + \int_{-b}^{0} A_{01}(\theta) \begin{cases} x(t+\theta)d\theta \ ; & t+\theta \geq 0 \\ h(t+\theta)d\theta \ ; & t+\theta < 0 \end{cases} + Bu(t) \\ x(0) = h(0) \end{cases}$$

where $-b \leq \theta_N \leq \theta_{N-1} \leq \cdots \leq \theta_1 < 0$; $b > 0$, A_0, A_i; $i=1,\ldots,N \in \mathcal{L}(R^n)$, $A_{01} \in C(-b,0;\mathcal{L}(R^n))$, as in Example 2.42 and $B \in \mathcal{L}(R^m,R^n)$. We suppose that we wish to choose a control $u \in L^2(0,t_1;R^m)$ so that the following cost functional is minimized

$$(4.39)\qquad J(u) = \langle x(t_1), Gx(t_1)\rangle_{R^n} + \int_0^{t_1} (\langle x(s),Mx(s)\rangle_{R^n} + \langle u(s),Ru(s)\rangle_{R^m})ds$$

where $G,M \in \mathcal{L}(R^n)$ are self adjoint and positive, and $R \in \mathcal{L}(R^m)$ is strictly positive and self adjoint.

As in Example 2.42 we reformulate (4.38) and (4.39) on $\mathcal{M}^2(-b,0;R^n)$

$$(4.40)\qquad \dot{z} = \tilde{A}\, z + \tilde{B}\, u \ ; \qquad z(0) = h$$

$$(4.41)\qquad J(u) = \langle z(t_1),\tilde{G}z(t_1)\rangle_{\mathcal{M}^2} + \int_0^{t_1} (\langle z(s),\tilde{M}z(s)\rangle_{\mathcal{M}^2} + \langle u(s),Ru(s)\rangle_{R^m})ds$$

where $\tilde{B}$, $\tilde{G}$ and $\tilde{M}$ are degenerate maps onto $\mathcal{M}^2$, given by

$$(\tilde{B}\,u)(\theta) = \begin{cases} Bu \ ; & \theta = 0 \\ 0 \ ; & \theta \neq 0 \end{cases} \qquad \text{for } u \in R^m$$

$$(\tilde{M}\,h)(\theta) = \begin{cases} Mh(0) \ ; & \theta = 0 \\ 0 \ ; & \theta \neq 0 \end{cases} \qquad \text{for } h \in \mathcal{M}^2(-b,0;R^n)$$

$$(\tilde{G}\,h)(\theta) = \begin{cases} Gh(0) \ ; & \theta = 0 \\ 0 \ ; & \theta \neq 0 \end{cases} \qquad \text{for } h \in \mathcal{M}^2(-b,0;R^n)$$

and $\widetilde{A}$ is given by

$$\widetilde{A}h(\theta) = \begin{cases} A_o h(0) + \sum_{i=1}^{N} A_i h(\theta_i) + \int_{-b}^{0} A_{o1}(\theta) h(\theta) d\theta \; ; & \theta = 0 \\ \dfrac{dh(\theta)}{d\theta} \; ; & \theta \neq 0 \end{cases}$$

with domain, $D(\widetilde{A}) = \mathcal{M}^2(-b,0;R^n) \cap AC^2(-b,0;R^n)$.
We can decompose the solution $Q(t)$ of (4.18) as follows

$$Q(t) = \begin{pmatrix} Q_{11}(t) & Q_{12}(t) \\ Q_{21}(t) & Q_{22}(t) \end{pmatrix}$$

where

$$Q_{11}(t) \varepsilon \mathcal{L}(R^n), \qquad Q_{22}(t) \varepsilon \mathcal{L}(L_2(-b,0;R^n))$$

$$Q_{21}(t) \varepsilon \mathcal{L}(R^n, L_2(-b,0;R^n)) \quad \text{and} \quad Q_{12}(t) = Q_{21}^*(t)$$

Substituting this into (4.18), we obtain

$$(4.42) \qquad \begin{cases} \dot{Q}_{11}(t) + A_o' Q_{11}(t) + Q_{11}(t) A_o + M = Q_{11}(t) BR^{-1} B^* Q_{11}(t) \\ \qquad\qquad - Q_2(t) - Q_2'(t) \\ Q_{11}(t_1) = G \end{cases}$$

Now define $Q_{21}(t,\theta)$ by

$$Q_{21}(t,\theta)x = (Q_{21}(t)x)(\theta) \quad \text{for } x \,\varepsilon\, R^n$$

and $Q_2(t) \,\varepsilon\, \mathcal{L}(R^n)$ by $Q_2(t)x = Q_{21}(t,0)x$. Substituting these into (4.18) yields the following equation for $Q_{21}(t,\theta)$

$$(4.43) \qquad \begin{cases} \dfrac{\partial}{\partial t} Q_{21}(t,\theta) - \dfrac{\partial}{\partial \theta} Q_{21}(t,\theta) + Q_{21}(t,\theta) A_o + A_{o1}'(\theta) Q_{11}(t) \\ + \sum_{i=1}^{N-1} A_i^* Q_{11}(t) \delta(\theta - \theta_i) - Q_{21}(t,\theta) BR^{-1} B^* Q_{11}(t) + Q_{22}(t,\theta,0) = 0 \\ Q_{21}(t,-b) = A_N^* Q_{11}(t); \quad Q_{21}(t_1,\theta) = 0; \quad Q_{21}(t,0) = 0 \end{cases}$$

$Q_{21}(t,\theta)$ is piecewise absolutely continuous in θ with jumps at θ_i of height $A_i^* Q_{11}(t)$; $i=1,2,\ldots,N-1$.

We define $Q_{22}(t,\theta,\alpha)$ by

$$(Q_{22}(t)h)(\theta) = \int_{-b}^{0} Q_{22}(t,\theta,\alpha)h(\alpha)d\alpha$$

and derive the following equations for $Q_{22}(t,\theta)$

$$-\frac{\partial}{\partial t} Q_{22}(t,\theta,\alpha) + \frac{\partial}{\partial\theta} Q_{22}(t,\theta,\alpha) + \frac{\partial}{\partial\alpha} Q_{22}(t,\theta,\alpha)$$

$$(4.44) \qquad = A'_{01}(\alpha)Q^*_{21}(t,\theta) + Q_{21}(t,\alpha)A'_{01}(\theta) + \sum_{i=1}^{N-1} A'_i Q_{21}(t,\theta)\delta(\alpha-\theta_i)$$
$$+ \sum_{i=1}^{N-1} Q_{21}(t,\alpha)A_i\delta(\theta-\theta_i) - Q_{21}(t,\alpha)BR^{-1}B^*Q^*_{21}(t,\theta)$$

$$Q_{22}(t,-b,\theta) = A'_N Q^*_{21}(t,\theta), \quad Q_{22}(t,\alpha,-b) = Q_{21}(t,\theta)A_N$$

$$Q_{22}(t,0,\theta) = 0 = Q_{22}(t,\alpha,0)$$

$$Q_{22}(t_1,\theta,\alpha) = 0$$

$$Q_{22}(t,\alpha,\theta) = Q_{22}(t,\theta,\alpha)$$

$Q_{22}(t,\alpha,\theta)$ is piecewise continuous in α and θ with jumps of height $A'_i Q^*_{21}(t,\theta)$ at $\alpha=\theta_i$; $i=1,\ldots,N-1$ (resp. $Q_{21}(t,\theta)A_i$ at $\alpha=\theta_i$; $i=1,\ldots,N-1$).

For proofs and explicit solutions of these see [11] and for computational methods for solving these Riccati equations see [12] and [2].

4.3 Tracking problem

Often we do not wish to bring the system to the origin, but rather to a preassigned final state or even to follow a preassigned trajectory as closely as possible. In finite dimensions this is called the "tracking problem" and its mathematical formulation is to minimize the performance index

$$(4.45) \qquad J(u;t_0,z_0) = \langle z(t_1)-r(t_1),\ G(z(t_1)-r(t_1))\rangle$$
$$+ \int_{t_0}^{t_1} (\langle z(\rho)-r(\rho),M(z(\rho)-r(\rho))\rangle + \langle u(\rho),Ru(\rho)\rangle)d\rho$$

over all $u \in L^2(t_0,t_1;U)$, where $r(t)$ is a given continuous H-valued function on $[t_0,t_1]$.

Again our method of proof is to construct a sequence of controls but this time as a combination of feedback and open loop

$$u_k(t) = -F_k(t)z(t) - R^{-1}B^*s_{k-1}(t)$$

where

$$(4.46)\quad \begin{cases} s_k(t) = -U_k^*(t_1,t)Gr(t_1) - \int_t^{t_1} U_k^*(\rho,t)\big[Mr(\rho) \\ \qquad\qquad + (Q_k(\rho)-Q_{k-1}(\rho))BR^{-1}B^*s_{k-1}(\rho)\big]d\rho \\ s_o(t) = 0 \end{cases}$$

and U_k, F_k, Q_k are defined by (4.5) as before.

Since $U_k(t,s)$ is a quasi-evolution operator, as in the proof of Lemma 4.6 we can show that $s_k(t)$ also satisfies the differential equation

$$(4.47)\quad \begin{cases} \frac{d}{dt} <s_k(t),h> = - <s_k(t),(A-BR^{-1}B^*Q_{k-1}(t))h> + <Mr(t),h> \\ \qquad\qquad + <(Q_k(t)-Q_{k-1}(t))BR^{-1}B^*s_{k-1}(t),h> \\ s_k(t_1) = Gr(t_1) \qquad \text{for all } h \in D(A) \end{cases}$$

We now consider the sequence of control problems

$$(4.48)\quad z(t) = T_{t-t_o}z_o + \int_{t_o}^{t} T_{t-s}B(u_k(s)+\bar{u}(s))ds$$

$$= U_k(t,t_o)z_o + \int_{t_o}^{t} U_k(t,\rho)B(\bar{u}(\rho)-R^{-1}B^*s_{k-1}(\rho))d\rho$$

As a consequence of Lemma 4.1, we deduce that

$$(4.49)\quad <z(t),Q_k(t)z(t)> = <z(t_1),Gz(t_1)> + \int_t^{t_1}<z(\rho),M_kz(\rho)>\,d\rho$$

$$-2\int_t^{t_1}<z(\rho),Q_k(\rho)B(\bar{u}(\rho)-R^{-1}B^*s_{k-1}(\rho))>d\rho$$

By direct substitution from (4.47) and (4.48) and interchanging the order of integration as in Lemma 4.1, we can also prove that

$$(4.50)\quad <z(t),s_k(t)> = - <z(t_1),Gr(t_1)>$$

$$- \int_t^{t_1}<z(\rho),Mr(\rho)+(Q_k(\rho)-Q_{k-1}(\rho))BR^{-1}B^*s_{k-1}(\rho)>\,d\rho$$

$$- \int_t^{t_1} <B(\bar{u}(\rho)-R^{-1}B^*s_{k-1}(\rho)),s_k(\rho)>\,d\rho$$

Adding (4.49) and (4.50) with $t=t_o$ and $\bar{u} = 0$, we obtain an expression for the cost of the control u_k.

$$(4.51)\quad J_o(u_k;t_o,z_o) = \langle z_o,Q_k(t_o)z_o\rangle + \langle r(t_1),Gr(t_1)\rangle + \int_{t_o}^{t_1} \langle r(\rho),Mr(\rho)\rangle\, d\rho$$
$$- 2\langle z_o,s_k(t_o)\rangle - 2\int_{t_o}^{t_1} \langle BR^{-1}B^*s_{k-1}(\rho),s_k(\rho)\rangle\, d\rho$$
$$+ \int_{t_o}^{t_1} \langle s_{k-1}(\rho),BR^{-1}B^*s_{k-1}(\rho)\rangle\, d\rho$$

Similarly adding (4.49) and (4.50) with $t= t_o$ and rearranging, we obtain

$$(4.52)\quad J_o(u_k+\bar{u};t_o,z_o) - J_o(u_k;t_o,z_o) =$$
$$\int_{t_o}^{t_1} (\langle \bar{u} + y(\rho),R(\bar{u}+y(\rho))\rangle - \langle y(\rho),Ry(\rho)\rangle)\, d\rho$$

where $\quad y(\rho) = R^{-1}B^*\left[(Q_k(\rho)-Q_{k-1}(\rho))z(\rho) + s_k(\rho) - s_{k-1}(\rho)\right]$

If $\bar{u}(\rho) = -R^{-1}B^*((Q_k(\rho)-Q_{k-1}(\rho))z(\rho)+s_k(\rho)-s_{k-1}(\rho))$, then (4.52) shows that $J_o(u_k;t_o,z_o)$ is decreasing in k. We can show that $J_o(u_k;t_o,z_o)$ converges as $k \to \infty$, from Lemma 4.3 and the following result.

<u>Lemma 4.12</u>

(a) $\quad s_k(t)$ converges strongly as $k \to \infty$ to

$$(4.53)\quad s_\infty(t) = -U^*(t_1,t)Gr(t_1) - \int_t^{t_1} U^*(\rho,t)Mr(\rho)\, d\rho$$

and satisfies the differential equation.

$$(4.54)\quad \begin{cases} \frac{d}{dt} \langle s_\infty(t),h\rangle = -\langle s_\infty(t),(A-BR^{-1}B^*Q(t))h\rangle + \langle Mr(t),h\rangle \\ s_\infty(t_1) = Gr(t_1) \end{cases}$$

(b) $\quad$ If furthermore, T_t^*G and T_t^*M map H to $D(A^*)$ and

$$(4.55)\quad \begin{cases} \int_{t_o}^{t_1} \|A^*T_t^*Gh\|\, dt < \infty \\ \int_{t_o}^{t_1} \|A^*T_t^*Mh\|\, dt < \infty \end{cases} \qquad \text{for all } h \in H$$

then $s_\infty(t)$ is the unique solution of the evolution equation

$$\text{(4.56)}\quad \begin{cases} \dot{s}_\infty(t) = -(A^*-Q(t)BR^{-1}B^*)s_\infty(t) + Mr(t) \\ s_\infty(t_1) = Gr(t_1) \end{cases}$$

Proof

(a) From Lemma 4.3 $Q_k(\rho)$ and $U_k(\rho,t)$ are uniformly bounded in norm in k, and so from (4.46) we deduce that $s_k(t)$ is also uniformly bounded in k and t on $[t_o,t_1]$. We can now apply the Lebesgue dominated convergence theorem to let $k \to \infty$ in (4.46), thus obtaining (4.53). (4.54) is obtained from (4.53) by differentiating $\langle s_\infty(t),h\rangle$ and using the quasi evolution property (2.43) of $U(\rho,t)$.

(b) (4.53) is the mild solution of (4.56) by Definition 2.23. Let $Y(t,\rho) = U^*(t_1-\rho,t_1-t)$ denote the dual mild evolution operator to $U(t,\rho)$. Now by Corollary 4.7, (4.24),

$$T^*_{t-\rho}Q(\rho)h = T^*_{t_1-t}GU(t_1,\rho)h + \int_\rho^t T^*_{\alpha-t}MU(\alpha,\rho)h\, d\alpha$$

Hence since T^*_tG and T^*_tM map H to $D(A^*)$, A^* is closed and (4.55) holds, we see that $T^*_{t-\rho}Q(\rho) : H \to D(A^*)$ and

$$A^*T^*_{t-\rho}Q(\rho)h = A^*T^*_{t_1-t}GU(t,\rho)h + \int_\rho^t A^*T^*_{\alpha-t}MU(\alpha,\rho)h\, d\alpha$$

Moreover (4.55) implies that $A^*T^*_{t-\rho}Q(\rho)h$ is integrable on (t_o,t) and so by Theorem 2.37, $A^*-Q(t)BR^{-1}B^*$ generates an almost strong evolution operator and by Corollary 2.39 that $A^*-Q(t)BR^{-1}B^*$ is almost strong and (4.55) is sufficient for (4.50) to have a unique strong solution.

Now let $k \to \infty$ in (4.52) to obtain

$$J_o(u_\infty+\bar{u};t_o,z_o) - J_o(u_\infty;t_o,z_o) = \int_o^{t_1} \langle\bar{u},R\bar{u}\rangle\, d\rho$$

for all $\bar{u}\in L^2(t_o,t_1;U)$, which shows that

$$u_\infty(t) = -R^{-1}B^*Q(t)z(t)-R^{-1}B^*s_\infty(t)$$

is the minimizing control. The cost for this control is obtained by letting $k \to \infty$ in (4.51), namely

$$\begin{aligned} J_o(u_\infty;t_o,z_o) &= \langle z_o,Q(t_o)z_o\rangle + \langle r(t_1),Gr(t_1)\rangle + \int_{t_o}^{t_1}\langle r(\rho),Mr(\rho)\rangle d\rho \\ &\quad -2\langle z_o,s_\infty(t_o)\rangle - \int_{t_o}^{t_1}\langle s_\infty(\rho),BR^{-1}B^*s_\infty(\rho)\rangle\, d\rho \end{aligned}$$

In fact this result could be obtained more directly by proving the limiting versions of (4.49) and (4.50). However, we have outlined the sequential approach because of its analogy to our proof for the regulator problem and because it is a useful numerical procedure for calculating the optimal control.

Finally we remark that a quadratic cost control problem for the inhomogeneous system

$$w(t) = T_{t-t_o} z_o + \int_{t_o}^{t} T_{t-\rho} Bu(\rho)\, d\rho + \int_{t_o}^{t} T_{t-\rho} g(\rho)\, d\rho$$

where $g \in L^2(t_o,t_1;H)$ can be reduced to the tracking problem considered above, by letting

$$z(t) = w(t)-r(t), \quad r(t) = \int_{t_o}^{t} T_{t-\rho} g(\rho)\, d\rho$$

<u>Example 4.13 Heat equation</u>

Let us consider the system given by (4.26) in Example 4.9, but this time with the cost functional

$$J(u) = \int_0^1 (z(t_1,x)-\sin\pi x)^2 dx + \int_0^{t_1}\int_0^1 (z(t,x)-\sin\pi x)^2 dx + \int_0^{t_1}\int_0^1 u^2(t,x)\, dx\, dt \tag{4.57}$$

We have already found $Q(t)$ and so it remains to solve (4.56) for $s_\infty(t)$. Expressing $s_\infty(t) = \sum_{i=0}^{\infty} s_i(t)\phi_i$, (4.56) becomes

$$\left\{\begin{array}{l} \dot{s}_i(t) = +(\pi^2 i^2 + q_{ii}(t))s_i(t) + \delta_{i1} \\ s_1(t_1) = \delta_{i1} \end{array}\right. \tag{4.58}$$

Hence $s_i(t) = 0$, $s_1(t) = 2e^{t-t_1}-1$

and the optimal control is

$$u_\infty(t) = -\sum_{i=1}^{\infty} q_{ii}(t) z_i(t)\phi_i - s_1(t)\phi_1$$

4.4 The infinite time quadratic cost control problem

We consider (4.1) on the infinite interval

$$(4.1) \qquad z(t) = T_{t-t_o} z_o + \int_{t_o}^{t} T_{t-s} Bu(s) \, ds$$

with the cost functional

$$(4.59) \qquad J_\infty(u;t_o,z_o) = \int_{t_o}^{\infty} (<z(s),Mz(s)> + <u(s),Ru(s)>) ds$$

where we impose the same assumptions on T_t, B, u, M, R and z_o as before and in addition we assume that (A,B) is optimizable; that is, there exists a $K \in \mathcal{L}(H,U)$ such that the feedback control $u_1(t) = -Kz(t)$ yields a finite cost and moreover

$$J_\infty(u_1;t_o,z_o) \leq \alpha \| z_o \|^2$$

for some constant $\alpha > 0$ and all $z_o \in H$. We note that if (A,B) is stabilizable then it is optimizable. Again the problem is to find an optimal control $u^* \in L^2(t_o,\infty;U)$ which minimizes $J_\infty(u;t_o,z_o)$ and the method of proof is similar to that in §4.1. We consider the following sequence of feedback controls

$$(4.60) \qquad u_k(t) = F_k z(t)$$

$$\left\{ \begin{array}{l} F_k = -R^{-1}B^* Q_{k-1}^\infty; \quad F_1 = K \\[2mm] M_k = M + F_k^* R F_k \\[2mm] Q_k^\infty h = \int_0^\infty T_s^k M_k T_s^k h \, ds \end{array} \right.$$

(4.61)

where T_t^k is the perturbation of T_t by BF_k. It is not immediately clear that (4.61) is well-defined and so first we establish this in the following lemmas, which are analogues of Lemmas 4.1 and 4.2.

Lemma 4.13

$$<z(t),Q_k^{t_1}(t)z(t)> = \int_t^{t_1} (<z(s),M_k z(s)> - 2<z(s),Q_k^{t_1}(s)B\bar{u}(s)>) ds$$

where $Q_k^{t_1}(t)$ is given by

$$(4.62) \qquad Q_k^{t_1}(t)h = \int_t^{t_1} T_{s-t}^k M_k T_{s-t}^k h \, ds$$

and

$$z(t) = T_{t-t_o}^k z_o + \int_{t_o}^{t} T_{t-s}^k B\bar{u}(s) \, ds$$

Proof

As for Lemma 4.1, where we have implicitly assumed that $M_k T_t^k$ are well-defined for each k.

Lemma 4.14

$Q_k^{t_1}(t)$ converges strongly as $t_1 \to \infty$ to Q_k^∞ given by (4.61) for each k. The cost of the feedback control (4.60) is given by

$$J(u_k;t_o,z_o) = \langle z_o, Q_k^\infty z_o \rangle$$

and Q_k^∞ is monotonically decreasing in k and bounded above and below.

Proof

The proof is by induction, so first we suppose that k = 1. From (4.62) we have

$$(4.63) \qquad \langle z_o, Q_1^{t_1}(t+\alpha) z_o \rangle = \int_{t+\alpha}^{t_1} \langle T_{s-t-\alpha}^{1*} M_1 T_{s-t-\alpha}^1 z_o, z_o \rangle \, ds$$

$$= \langle z_o, Q_1^{t_1-\alpha}(t) z_o \rangle$$

But $\langle z_o, Q_1^{t_1}(t_o) z_o \rangle$ is increasing in t_1 for fixed t_o and z_o, and

$$\langle z_o, Q_1^{t_1}(t_o) z_o \rangle = \int_{t_o}^{t_1} (\langle z(s), Mz(s) \rangle + \langle u_1(s), Ru_1(s) \rangle) ds$$

$$\leq J(u_1;t_o,z_o) \leq \alpha \|z_o\|^2$$

by the optimizability assumption.

So $Q_1^{t_1}(t_o)$ is an increasing sequence of bounded self adjoint operators which are bounded above, which proves that $Q_1^{t_1}(t_o)$ converges strongly to $Q_1^\infty(t_o)$ as $t_1 \to \infty$. Finally (4.63) shows that $Q_1^\infty(t_o)$ is independent of t_o, and so we have

$$\langle z_o, Q_1^\infty z_o \rangle = J(u_1;t_o,z_o) \leq \alpha \|z_o\|^2$$

Suppose now that $Q_k^{t_1}(t_o)$ converges strongly to Q_k^∞ as $t_1 \to \infty$, and that $\langle z_o, Q_k^\infty z_o \rangle \leq \alpha \|z_o\|^2$ for $k \leq n$.

Consider the feedback control

$$(4.64) \qquad u_{n+1}^{t_1}(t) = -R^{-1} B^* Q_n^{t_1}(t) z(t)$$

If we let $\bar{u}(t) = u_{n+1}^{t_1}(t) - u_n(t)$ in Lemma 4.13, we have

$$<z(t), Q_n^{t_1}(t)z(t)> = \int_t^{t_1} (<z(s),Mz(s)> + <u_n(s),Ru_n(s)> + <u_{n+1}^{t_1}(s),R\bar{u}(s)> + <\bar{u}(s),Ru_{n+1}^{t_1}(s)>)\, ds$$

$$= \int_t^{t_1} <z(s),Mz(s)> + <u_{n+1}^{t_1}(s),Ru_{n+1}^{t_1}(s)>\, ds + \int_t^{t_1} <u_{n+1}^{t_1}(s)-u_n(s),R(u_{n+1}^{t_1}(s)-u_n(s))>\, ds$$

Thus from (4.3) and letting $t = t_o$, we obtain

$$\int_{t_o}^{t_1} <z(s),Mz(s)> + <u_{n+1}^{t_1}(s), Ru_{n+1}^{t_1}(s)>\, ds \le <z_o,Q_n^{t_1}(t_o)z_o> \le <z_o,Q_n^\infty z_o> \le \alpha\|z_o\|^2 \tag{4.65}$$

by our induction assumption.

Now by Fatou's lemma, we have the inequality

$$J_\infty(u_{n+1};t_o,z_o) = \int_{t_o}^\infty <T_{s-t_o}^{n+1} z_o, M_{n+1}T_{s-t_o}^{n+1} z_o>ds$$

$$\le \liminf_{t_1\to\infty}\left(\int_{t_o}^{t_1}(<z(s),Mz(s)> + <u_{n+1}^{t_1}(s),Ru_{n+1}^{t_1}(s)>)ds\right)$$

$$\le <z_o,Q_n^\infty z_o> \le \alpha\|z_o\|^2 \qquad \text{from (4.65).}$$

So from (4.62) we can substitute $t = t_o$ and $t_1 = \infty$ to obtain

$$<Q_{n+1}^\infty(t_o)z_o,z_o> = \int_{t_o}^\infty <T_{s-t_o}^{n+1} z_o, M_{n+1}T_{s-t_o}^{n+1} z_o>\, ds$$

$$\le <z_o,Q_n^\infty z_o> \le \alpha\|z_o\|^2$$

Arguing as for k = 1, we deduce that $Q_{n+1}(t_o)$ is independent of t_o, and hence

$$J_\infty(u_{n+1};t_o,z_o) = <Q_{n+1}^\infty z_o,z_o> \le <z_o,Q_n^\infty z_o> \le \alpha\|z_o\|^2$$

<u>Lemma 4.15</u>

Q_k^∞ converge strongly to Q_∞^∞ as $k\to\infty$ and Q_∞^∞ satisfies

$$Q_\infty^\infty h = \int_0^\infty T_s^{\infty*}(M+Q_\infty^\infty BR^{-1}B^*Q_\infty^\infty)T_s^\infty h\, ds \tag{4.66}$$

where T_t^∞ is the perturbation of T_t by $-BR^{-1}B^*Q_\infty^\infty$.

The optimal control $u^*(t)$ is given by

(4.67) $$u^*(t) = -R^{-1}B^*Q_\infty^\infty z(t)$$

Proof

As in Lemma 4.3, Q_k^∞ converges strongly to Q_∞^∞ using Lemma 4.13 and for finite t_1,

(4.68) $$Q_\infty^{t_1}(t)h = \int_t^{t_1} T_{s-t}^{\infty *}(M+Q_\infty^\infty BR^{-1}B^*Q_\infty^\infty)T_{s-t}^\infty h\, ds$$

Combining these yields (4.66), using the fact that Q_∞^∞ is time invariant, it can be proved that the optimal control law is given by (4.67) as in Lemma 4.4.

In order to show that Q_∞^∞ is the unique solution of an algebraic Riccati equation, as for the finite dimensional case, we need the stronger assumptions that (A,B) and $(A^*,M^{\frac{1}{2}})$ are stabilizable.

Lemma 4.16

Suppose $(A^*,M^{\frac{1}{2}})$ is stabilizable and there exists a self adjoint, positive $Q \in \mathcal{L}(H)$ and $K \in \mathcal{L}(H,U)$, such that

(4.69) $$\langle 2(Q(A-BK) + M + K^*RK)h,h\rangle \leq 0 \qquad \text{for all } h \in D(A)$$

Then $A-BK$ generates an exponentially stable semigroup.

Proof

Since $(A^*,M^{\frac{1}{2}})$ is stabilizable, there exists $S \in \mathcal{L}(H)$ such that $A^*-M^{\frac{1}{2}}S$ generates an exponentially stable semigroup, or equivalently that $A-S^*M^{\frac{1}{2}}$ generates an exponentially stable semigroup T_t^1, say. But

$$A-BK = A-S^*M^{\frac{1}{2}}+(S^*M^{\frac{1}{2}}-BK)$$

and by our perturbation formula (2.31),

(4.70) $$T_t^2 h = T_t^1 h + \int_0^t T_{t-s}^1(S^*M^{\frac{1}{2}}-BK)T_s^2 h\, ds$$

where T_t^2 is the semigroup generated by $A-BK$.

Let $h = T_s^2 k$ in (4.69) to obtain

$$\frac{d}{ds}\left(\tfrac{1}{2}\langle QT_s^2k,\ T_s^2k\rangle\right) + \|M^{\frac{1}{2}}T_s^2k\|^2 + \|R^{\frac{1}{2}}KT_s^2k\|^2 \leq 0$$

for all $s \geq 0$ and $k \in D(A)$.

Since $Q \geq 0$ and R is invertible, we deduce that

$$(4.71)\quad \left\{\begin{aligned} &\int_0^\infty \|M^{\frac{1}{2}}T_s^2k\|^2\, ds < \infty \\ &\int_0^\infty \|KT_s^2k\|^2\, ds < \infty \end{aligned}\right. \qquad \text{for all } h \in H.$$

From (4.70), we have the inequality

$$\|T_t^2h\| \leq \|T_t^1h\| + \int_0^t \|T_{t-s}^1\| (\|S^*M^{\frac{1}{2}}T_s^2h\| + \|BKT_s^2h\|)\, ds$$

$$\leq \|T_t^1h\| + \left(\int_0^t \|T_{t-s}^1\|^2 ds\right)^{\frac{1}{2}} \left(\int_0^t (\|S^*M^{\frac{1}{2}}T_s^2h\| + \|BKT_s^2h\|)^2 ds\right)^{\frac{1}{2}}$$

$$\therefore\ \|T_t^2h\| \leq 2\|T_t^1h\|^2 + \text{const}\left(\int_0^t \|T_{t-s}^1\|^2 ds\right)\left(\int_0^t (\|M^{\frac{1}{2}}T_s^2h\|^2 + \|KT_s^2h\|^2)\, ds\right)$$

Since T_t^1 is exponentially stable and (4.71) holds,

$$\int_0^\infty \|T_t^2h\|^2\, dt < \infty \quad \text{for all } h \in H.$$

By Lemma 3.36, this implies that T_t^2 is an exponentially stable semigroup.

<u>Corollary 4.17</u>

If $(A^*, M^{\frac{1}{2}})$ and (A,B) are stabilizable, then $A - BR^{-1}B^*Q_\infty^\infty$ generates an exponentially stable semigroup.

<u>Theorem 4.18</u>

If $(A^*, M^{\frac{1}{2}})$ and (A,B) are stabilizable, then Q_∞^∞ given by (4.66) is the unique solution of the algebraic Riccati equation

$$(4.72)\qquad \langle Ah, Q_\infty^\infty k\rangle + \langle Q_\infty^\infty h, Ak\rangle + \langle Mh, k\rangle = \langle Q_\infty^\infty BR^{-1}B^*Q_\infty^\infty h, k\rangle$$

for $h,k \in D(A)$.

Proof

(a) Existence

Let Q^∞_∞ be given by (4.66), and consider

$$\langle Q^\infty_\infty h,(A-BR^{-1}B^*Q^\infty_\infty)k\rangle + \langle (A-BR^{-1}B^*Q^\infty_\infty)h,Q^\infty_\infty k\rangle$$

$$= \langle Q^\infty_\infty h,A^\infty k\rangle + \langle A^\infty h,Q^\infty_\infty k\rangle$$

writing $A^\infty = A-BR^{-1}B^*Q^\infty_\infty$

$$= \int_0^\infty (\langle (M+Q^\infty_\infty BR^{-1}B^*Q^\infty_\infty)T^\infty_s h,A^\infty T^\infty_s k\rangle$$

$$+ \langle A^\infty T^\infty_s h,(M+Q^\infty_\infty BR^{-1}B^*Q^\infty_\infty)T^\infty_s k\rangle)\, ds \qquad \text{from (4.66)}$$

$$= \int_0^\infty \frac{d}{ds} \langle T^\infty_s h,(M+Q^\infty_\infty BR^{-1}B^*Q^\infty_\infty)T^\infty_s k\rangle\, ds \qquad \text{for } h,k \in D(A),$$

$$= -\langle h,(M+Q^\infty_\infty BR^{-1}B^*Q^\infty_\infty)k\rangle$$

since, by Corollary 4.17, T^∞_t is exponentially stable with generator A^∞_∞, Q^∞_∞ given by (4.66) is a solution of (4.72).

(b) Uniqueness

Suppose that (4.72) has two solutions P and Q. Then from (4.72) we have

$$2\langle Qh,(A-BR^{-1}B^*Q)h\rangle + \langle h,Mh\rangle + \langle QBR^{-1}B^*Qh,h\rangle = 0$$

and by Lemma 4.16, with $K = R^{-1}B^*Q$, $A-BR^{-1}B^*Q$ generates the exponentially stable semigroup T^Q_t
Writing $K_o = R^{-1}B^*P$, the following identity is readily verified.

(4.73) $$\langle (2P(A-BK_o) + K_o^*RK_o + M)h,h\rangle$$

$$= \langle (2Q(A-BK) + K^*RK + M)h,h\rangle + 2\langle (P-Q)(A-BK)h,h\rangle + 2\langle (K-K_o)^*R(K-K_o)h,h\rangle$$

but P and Q both satisfy (4.72) with h = k and so

(4.74) $$\langle 2(P-Q)(A-BK)h,h\rangle + \langle (K-K_o)^*R(K-K_o)h,h\rangle = 0$$

Since T^Q_t is exponentially stable, for $h \in D(A)$, we have

$$\langle (P-Q)h,h\rangle = -\int_0^\infty \frac{d}{ds} \langle T^Q_s h,(P-Q)T^Q_s h\rangle\, ds$$

$$= -\int_0^{\infty} \langle T_s^Q h, (P-Q)(A-BK)T_s^Q h\rangle \, ds$$

$$= \tfrac{1}{2}\int_0^{\infty} \langle T_s^Q h, (K-K_o)^* R(K-K_o)T_s^Q h\rangle \, ds \qquad \text{by (4.74).}$$

Since $D(A)$ is dense in H, $P \geq Q$ and similarly $Q \geq P$.

Another consequence of our results which has important implications for the filtering problem of §6 is

Lemma 4.19

If (A,B) and $(A^*,M^{\frac{1}{2}})$ are stabilizable and $Q^{t_1}(t)$ denotes the solution of (4.8)(or(4.18)), then $Q^{t_1}(t)$ converges strongly to Q_∞^∞, the unique solution of (4.72) as $t_1 \to \infty$ for all $t \geq 0$.

Proof

(a) Let $Q_o^{t_1}(t_o)$ be the solution of (4.8) for $G = 0$. Then since $\langle Q_o^{t_1}(t_o)z_o, z_o\rangle$ is the optimal cost on $[t_o, t_1]$, we have $Q_o^{t_1}(t_o)$ is monotonically increasing in t_1 and since (A,B) is stabilizable, $Q_o^{t_1}(t_o)$ is bounded above on $[t_o,\infty)$. Hence $Q_o^{t_1}(t_o)$ converges strongly to $P_o(t_o)$ as $t_1 \to \infty$ for each fixed t_o.

From Lemmas 4.13 and 4.14 we recall that

$$Q_k^{t_1}(t_o)h \xrightarrow{t_1 \to \infty} Q_k^\infty h \xrightarrow{k \to \infty} Q_\infty^\infty h \qquad \forall\, h \in H$$

and we can also deduce that

$$(4.75) \qquad Q_k^{t_1}(t_o)h \xrightarrow{k \to \infty} Q_\infty^{t_1} h = \int_0^{t_1} T_s^{*\infty}(M+Q_\infty^\infty BR^{-1}B^*Q_\infty^\infty)T_s^\infty h \, ds$$

where the convergences are in the strong sense.

Since $Q_o^{t_1}(t_o)$ is optimal, we have

$$Q_o^{t_1}(t_o) \leq Q_\infty^{t_1}$$

and letting $t_1 \to \infty$, we obtain

$$P_o(t_o) \leq Q_\infty^\infty \qquad \text{for all } t_o \geq 0$$

But applying Fatou's lemma to (4.75), we have

$$<\int_{t_o}^{\infty} U_p^*(s,t_o)(M+P_o(s)BR^{-1}B^*P_o(s))U_p(s,t_o)h\,ds,h> \leq <P_o(t_o)h,h>$$

where $U_p(s,t)$ is the perturbation of T_t by $-BR^{-1}B^*P_o(t)$.
But the left side is the cost of the feedback control $u = -R^{-1}B^*P_o(t)z(t)$ on $[0,\infty)$ and since Q_∞^∞ is optimal on $[0,\infty)$,

$$Q_\infty^\infty \leq P_o(t_o) \quad \text{for all } t_o \geq 0$$

Hence $$Q_\infty^\infty = P_o(t_o) \quad \text{for all } t_o \geq 0$$

(b) Let $Q^{t_1}(t_o)$ be the solution of (4.8) for $G \neq 0$, then since $Q^{t_1}(t_o)$ is optimal

$$(4.76) \qquad <Q_\infty^{t_1}z_o,z_o> + <T_{t_1}^\infty z_o,GT_{t_1}^\infty z_o> \geq <Q^{t_1}(t_o)z_o,z_o>$$
$$\geq <Q_o^{t_1}(t_o)z_o,z_o>$$

Hence

$$0 \leq <(Q^{t_1}(t_o) - Q_o^{t_1}(t_o))z_o,z_o>$$
$$\leq <(Q_\infty^{t_1} - Q_{t_o}^{t_1}(t_o))z_o,z_o> + <T_t^\infty,z_o\ GT_{t_1}^\infty z_o>$$
$$\to 0 \text{ as } t_1 \to \infty$$

by (4.75) and Corollary 4.17

So $$<(Q^{t_1}(t_o)-Q_o^{t_1}(t_o))z_o,z_o> \to 0 \text{ as } t_1 \to \infty$$

which implies that $Q^{t_1}(t_o) \to Q_o^{t_1}(t_o)$ strongly as $t_1 \to \infty$ using the generalised Schwarz inequality

$$\|B\|^2 \leq <Bh,h><B^2h,Bh> \quad \text{for } B \in \mathcal{L}(H)$$

So from (a), $Q^{t_1}(t_o)$ converges strongly to Q_∞^∞ as $t_1 \to \infty$.

Example 4.20 The Heat Equation

Let us return to the heat equation in Example 4.9. We know that for (4.26) the system operator is self adjoint and generates a stable semigroup. Hence the infinite time problem is well posed and the algebraic Riccati equation has the unique solution

$$Q = \sum_{i=1}^{\infty} (\sqrt{\pi^4 i^4 + 1} - \pi^2 i^2)\phi_i\langle\cdot,\phi_i\rangle$$

The optimal control is given by

$$u(t) = \sum_{i=o}^{\infty} - (\sqrt{\pi^4 i^4 + 1} - \pi^2 i^2) z_i(t)\phi_i$$

where $z(t) = \sum_{i=o}^{\infty} z_i(t)\phi_i$, and the minimum cost is

$$\sum_{i=o}^{\infty} (\sqrt{\pi^4 i^4 + 1} - \pi^2 i^2)(\langle z_o,\phi_i\rangle)^2$$

Example 4.21 Wave equation

In the Example 4.10 we have considered it is obvious that the infinite time problem is well posed since the optimal control and minimum cost are independent of the time interval.

References

[1] Avarado, F.L. and Mukunden, R. An optimization problem in distributed parameter systems, Int. J. Control, 9 (1969) pp.665-677.

[2] Banks, H.T. and Burns, J.A. Hereditary control problems: numerical methods based on averaging approximations, SIAM J. Control, to appear.

[3] Bensoussan, A., Bossavit and Nedelec, Approximations des problemes de controle, Cahiers de l'institut de recherche en informatique et automatique, No.2, 1970.

[4] Butkovskii, A.G. Theory of optimal control of distributed parameter systems, American Elsevier, 1969.

[5] Chyung, D.H. and Lee, E.B. Delayed action control problems, Automatica, 6 (1970), pp.395-400.

[6] Curtain, R.F. and Pritchard, A.J. The infinite dimensional Riccati equation. J. Math. Anal. & Appl., 47 (1974), pp.43-57.

[7] Curtain, R.F. and Pritchard, A.J. The infinite dimensional Riccati equation for systems defined by evolution operators, SIAM J. Control, 14 (1975), pp.951-983.

[8] Curtain, R.F. The infinite dimensional Riccati equation with applications to affine hereditary differential systems, SIAM J. Control, 13 (1975), pp.1130-1143.

[9] Datko, R. A linear control problem in abstract Hilbert space, J. Diff. Eqns., 9 (1971), pp.346-359.

[10] Delfour, M.C. and Mitter, S.K. Controllability, observability and optimal feedback control of hereditary differential systems, SIAM J. Control, 10 (1972), pp.298-328.

[11] Delfour, M.C., McCalla, C. and Mitter, S.K. Stability and infinite time quadratic cost problem for linear hereditary differential systems, SIAM J. Control, 13 (1975), pp.48-88.

[12] Delfour, M.C. Solution numerique de l'equation differentielle de Riccati recontree en theorie de la commande optimale des systemes hereditaires lineaires, Control theory, numerical methods and computer systems modelling, Notes in economics and mathematical systems, 107, Springer Verlag, 1975.

[13] Eller, D.H., Aggarwal, J.K. and Banks, H.T. Optimal control of linear time-delay systems, IEEE Trans. AC 14 (1969), pp.678-687.

[14] Greenberg, S. On quadratic optimization in distributed parameter systems, IEEE Trans., AC 16 (1971), pp.153-159.

[15] Ichikawa, A. Dynamic programming approach to infinite dimensional systems, Control Theory Centre Report No.57, University of Warwick, 1977.

[16] Krasovskii, N.N. On analytical design of optimum regulators in time-delay systems, Prikl. Mat. Mekh., 1 (1962), pp.39-52.

[17] Kushner, H.J. and Barnea, D.I. On the control of a linear functional differential equation with quadratic cost, SIAM J. Control, 8 (1970), pp.257-272.

[18] Lions, J.L. Optimal control of systems described by partial differential equations, Springer, 1971.

[19] Lo, C.T. Optimal linear feedback control for a class of distributed parameter systems, Int, J. Control, 23 (1976), pp.81-88.

[20] Lukes, D.L. and Russell, D.L. The quadratic criterion for distributed systems, SIAM J. Control, 7 (1969), pp.101-121.

[21] Manitius, A. Optimal control of time-lag systems with quadratic performance indices, lV IFAC Congress, Warsaw, 1969.

[22] Narasimha, M. Optimal control of a fluid interface, IEEE Trans., AC 15 (1970), pp.654-658.

[23] Prabhu, S.S. and McCausland, I. Optimal control of linear diffusion processes with quadratic error criteria, Aut. 8 (1972), pp.299-308.

[24] Pritchard, A.J. The linear quadratic problem for systems described by evolution equations, Control Theory Centre Report No. 10, University of Warwick.

|25| Pritchard, A.J. Stability and control of distributed parameter systems governed by wave equations, IFAC Conference on Distributed Parameter Systems, Banff 1971.

[26] Ross, D.W. and Flugge-Lotz, I. An optimal control problem for systems with differential-difference equation dynamics, SIAM J. Control, 7 (1969), pp.609-623.

[27] Russell, D.L. Optimal regulation of linear hyperbolic systems with finite dimensional controls, SIAM J. Control, 4 (1966), pp.276-281.

[28] Wiberg, D.M. Feedback control of linear distributed parameter systems, Trans. ASME, J. Basic Eng., 89 (1967), pp.379-384.

[29] Zabczyk, J. Remarks on the algebraic Riccati equation in Hilbert space, J. App. Math. and Optimization, 2 (1976), pp.251-258.

CHAPTER 5

STOCHASTIC PROCESSES AND STOCHASTIC DIFFERENTIAL EQUATIONS

5.1 Abstract Probability and Estimation Theory [2],[7],[8],[10]

Suppose that $(\Omega,\mathcal{P},p)$ is a complete probability space, X a Banach space and H,K are real separable Hilbert spaces, then we shall use the following standard abstract probability theory.

Definition 5.1

An X-valued random variable is a map $u: \Omega \to X$ which is strongly measurable[1] with respect to p measure. If u is integrable[2] on Ω we define its expectation by

$$E\{u\} = \int_\Omega u \, dp$$

We remark that the random variable u induces a measure p_u on $\mathcal{B}(X)$, the Borel sets of X, by virtue of

$$p_u(A) = p\{\omega: u(\omega) \in A\} \qquad \text{for} \quad A \in \mathcal{B}(X)$$

and $(X, \mathcal{B}(X), p_u)$ is a complete probability space.

Most of our work will be with Hilbert space-valued random variables and for these we introduce the following.

Definition 5.2

The covariance operator of an H-valued random variable $u \in L^2(\Omega,p;H)$ is defined by

$$\mathrm{Cov}\{u\} = E\{(u-E\{u\}) \circ (u-E\{u\})\}$$

where $u \circ v \in \mathcal{L}(H)$ is defined for all $u,v \in H$ by

$$(u \circ v)h = u\langle v,h\rangle \; ; \; h \in H.$$

Then Cov{u} is symmetric, positive and nuclear.

The following identities are readily verified

(5.1) $$E\{\langle u,u\rangle\} = \text{trace Cov}\{u\}$$

---

[1] Strong and weak measurability concepts are identical for separable Hilbert spaces.

[2] The integration used here is in the sense of Bochner.

(5.2) $$E\{\langle Bu,u\rangle\} = \mathrm{trace}(B\,\mathrm{Cov}\{u\}) \quad \text{for } B \in \mathcal{L}(H).$$

A Hilbert space-valued random variable is also uniquely specified by its characteristic functional.

Definition 5.3

If $u \in L^1(\Omega,p;H)$ with induced measure p_u, then its characteristic functional $\chi_u : H \to R$ is defined by

$$\chi_u(h) = E\{\exp(i\langle u,h\rangle)\}$$

$$= \int_H \exp(i\langle k,h\rangle)\,dp_u(k) \qquad \text{for all } h \in H .$$

Of special interest are Gaussian measures or random variables.

Definition 5.4

An H-valued random variable u is Gaussian if $\langle u,e_i\rangle$ is a real Gaussian random variable for all i, where $\{e_i\}_{i=o}^{\infty}$ is a complete orthonormal basis for H.

The corresponding measure is called Gaussian and we have the following characterization theorem from [10].

Theorem 5.5

A measure μ is Gaussian if and only if its characteristic function χ_μ has the form

$$\chi_\mu(h) = \exp\{i\langle\alpha,h\rangle - \tfrac{1}{2}\langle Qh,h\rangle\}$$

where $\alpha \in H$ and Q is a non-negative, self adjoint nuclear operator on H. Of course the associated random variable has expectation α and covariance Q. Another useful property of Gaussian random variables is the following.

Lemma 5.6

If u is an H-valued Gaussian random variable with covariance Q, then

$$E\{\|u\|^4\} \le \mathrm{const.}(\mathrm{trace}\ Q)^2$$

Proof

Let $\{e_i\}$ be a complete orthonormal basis for H, then u can be represented by

$$u = \sum_{i=o}^{\infty} u_i e_i \ ; \qquad u_i = \langle u,e_i\rangle$$

Now

$$E\{\|u\|^2\} = \sum_{i=0}^{\infty} E\{u_i^{\,2}\}$$

$$= \text{trace } Q$$

and

$$E\{\|u\|^4\} = E\{(\sum_{i=0}^{\infty} u_i^{\,2})^2\}$$

$$= \sum_{i,j=0}^{\infty}\sum E\{u_i^{\,2}u_j^{\,2}\}$$

$$\leq \sum_{i,j=0}^{\infty}\sum (E\{u_i^{\,4}\}E\{u_j^{\,4}\})^{\frac{1}{2}}$$

$$\leq 3\sum_{i,j=0}^{\infty}\sum E\{u_i^{\,2}\}E\{u_j^{\,2}\}$$ since u_j and u_i are real Gaussian random variables (Doob[7])

$$= 3(\sum_{i=0}^{\infty} E\{u_i^{\,2}\})^2$$

$$= 3(\text{trace } Q)^2$$

Of the many types of convergence one can introduce for random variables we shall use the following

Definition 5.7

A sequence $\{u_n\}$ of X-valued random variables converges to u

(a) in probability if

$$p\{\|u_n-u\|_X > 0\} \to 0 \text{ as } n \to \infty$$

(b) in mean square if

$$E\{\|u_n-u\|_X^2\} \to 0 \text{ as } n \to \infty$$

(c) with probability one (w.p.l.) if

$$\|u_n-u\|_X \to 0 \text{ as } n \to \infty \text{ except on a set of measure zero}$$

(d) in distribution if for every $f \in C(X)$, the space of bounded real valued continuous functions on X,

$$\int_X f\,d\mu_n \to \int_X f\,d\mu \quad \text{as } n \to \infty$$

where μ_n and μ are the measures induced on $\mathcal{B}(X)$ by u_n and u respectively. We also say that $\mu_n \to \mu$ weakly (in the space of all measures on $\mathcal{B}(X)$)

(a) is the weakest concept and is implied by (b) - (d).

Definition 5.8

X-valued random variables u and v are independent if $\{\omega : u(\omega) \in A\}$ and $\{\omega : u(\omega) \in B\}$ are independent sets in $\mathcal{P}$ for any Borel sets A,B in $\mathcal{B}(X)$. If u and v are in $L^1(\Omega,p;H)$ and are independent, then

$$(5.3) \qquad E\{\langle u,v\rangle\} = \langle E\{u\}, E\{v\}\rangle$$

Definition 5.9

The conditional expectation $E\{h|\mathcal{F}\}$ of an x-valued random variable h relative to a subsigma field $\mathcal{F} \subset \mathcal{P}$ is such that

$$(5.4) \qquad \int_C h(\omega)dp = \int_C E\{h|\mathcal{F}\}(\omega)dp \qquad \forall\, C \in \mathcal{F}$$

$E\{h|\mathcal{F}\}$ is uniquely defined by this relationship and is measurable relative to $\mathcal{F}$.

The following properties of conditional expectations are straight forward generalizations of the finite dimensional case.

(5.5) If $u \in L^1(\Omega,p;X)$ is measurable relative to the sigma field $\mathcal{F} \subset \mathcal{P}$, then $E\{u|\mathcal{F}\} = u$ w.p.1.

(5.6) If $u \in L^1(\Omega,p;X)$ is independent of $\mathcal{F} \subset \mathcal{P}$, then $E\{u|\mathcal{F}\} = E\{u\}$ w.p.1.

(5.7) If $\mathcal{F}_1 \subset \mathcal{F}_2$ and $u \in L^1(\Omega,p;X)$, then $E\{u|\mathcal{F}_1\} = E\{E\{u|\mathcal{F}_2\}|\mathcal{F}_1\}$

(5.8) $E\{E\{u|\mathcal{F}\}\} = E\{u\}$ for $\mathcal{F} \subset \mathcal{P}$.

In §6 we shall be concerned with estimating a Hilbert space valued random variable $h:\Omega \to H$ given a Hilbert space valued random variable $y:\Omega \to K$. The best estimate is of course the conditional expectation of h relative to the sigma field generated by y on $(\Omega,\mathcal{P},p)$ and we shall denote this by $E_y\{h\}$. If p_y denotes the probability measure induced by y on $(K,\mathcal{B}(K))$, then by $L^2(K,p_y;H)$ we mean the Hilbert space of p_y-measurable functions mapping K to H with the norm

$$\|\phi\| = \left(\int_K \|\phi(k)\|_H^2 dp_y(k) \right)^{\frac{1}{2}}$$

$L^2(K,p_y;H)$ is isomorphic to a subspace $\mathcal{H}_y$ of $\mathcal{H} = L^2(\Omega,p;H)$ given by

$$(5.9) \qquad \mathcal{H}_y = \left\{ u(\omega) \in \mathcal{H} : u(\omega) = \lambda(y(\omega)) \text{ and } \lambda : K \to H \text{ is measurable relative to } p_y. \right\}$$

The isomorphism $\tau : L^2(K,p_y;H) \to \mathcal{H}_y$ is thus $\tau\lambda(\cdot) = \lambda(y(\cdot))$ and we write

$$(5.10) \qquad \mathcal{H}_y = \tilde{L}^2(K,p_y;H)$$

If h and y are second order random variables the conditional expectation has the following geometric interpretation.

Lemma 5.10

If $h \in \mathcal{H} = L^2(\Omega,p;H)$ and $y \in L^2(\Omega,p;K)$, then $E_y\{h\}$ is the projection of h on $\mathcal{H}_y$.

Proof

Let χ_C be the characteristic function of C in $\mathcal{B}(K)$, then for $x \in H$ $\chi_C x \in \mathcal{H}_y$ and there exists a measurable map λ_C such that

$$\chi_C x = \lambda_C(y(\omega))$$

From definition 5.9, $E_y\{h\} = \psi(y(\omega))$, for some measurable ψ and so (5.4) implies that

$$\int_\Omega \langle \chi_C x, h(\omega)\rangle_H \, dp(\omega) = \int_\Omega \langle \lambda(y(\omega)), \psi(y(\omega))\rangle_H \, dp(\omega)$$

Hence

$$(5.11) \qquad \int_\Omega \langle \lambda_C(y(\omega)x, h(\omega)\rangle_H \, dp(\omega) = \int_K \langle \lambda(k), \psi(k)\rangle_H \, dp_y(k)$$

Now all $u \in \mathcal{H}_y$ can be expressed by $u = \sum_{i=0}^{\infty} \chi_{C_i} e_i$ where $\{e_i\}$ is a complete orthonormal basis for H and $C_i \in \mathcal{B}(K)$ and so (5.11) shows that $\psi \in \mathcal{H}_y$ is the projection of h on $\mathcal{H}_y$.

We are also interested in linear estimates, as these are easier to calculate.

Definition 5.11

The best linear estimate $\hat{h}$ of $h \in L^2(\Omega,p;H)$ based on $y \in L^2(\Omega,p;K)$ is $\hat{h} = \Lambda y$, where $\Lambda \in \mathcal{L}(K,H)$ is such that $E\{\|x-Gy\|^2\}$ is minimized over all $G \in \mathcal{L}(K,H)$.

We are always assured of the existence of the best global estimate $E_y\{h\}$ provided only $h \in L^1(\Omega,p;H)$, but the best linear estimate need not always exist.

Lemma 5.12

Let $h \in L^2(\Omega,p;H)$ and $y \in L^2(\Omega,p;K)$ have covariances P_1 and P_2 respectively and $P_{12} = E\{h \circ y\}$. Then a necessary and sufficient condition for the best linear estimate $\hat{h} = \Lambda y$ of h based on y to exist is that the following equation has a solution

$$\Lambda P_2 = P_{12}^* \tag{5.12}$$

$\hat{h}$ is unique if and only if (5.12) has a unique solution.

Proof

Sufficiency

Suppose that (5.12) has a solution Λ_o, and define the error term

$$e(\Lambda) = h - \Lambda y \quad \text{for arbitrary } \Lambda \in \mathcal{L}(H)$$

Without loss of generality we can suppose that h and y have zero expectation and then,

$$\begin{aligned} \mathrm{Cov}\{e(\Lambda)\} &= E\{(h-\Lambda y) \circ (h-\Lambda y)\} \\ &= P_1 + \Lambda P_2 \Lambda^* - P_{12}^* \Lambda^* - \Lambda P_{12} \end{aligned}$$

and from (5.1)

$$E\{\|h-\Lambda y\|^2\} = \mathrm{trace}\ \{P_1 + \Lambda P_2 \Lambda^* - 2\Lambda P_{12}\}$$

and

$$E\{\|h-\Lambda_o y\|^2\} = \mathrm{trace}\ \{P_1 - P_{12}^* \Lambda_o^*\}$$

Since P_2 and P_{12} are positive and self-adjoint, from the properties of the trace operation, Λ_o minimizes $E\{\|h-\Lambda y\|^2\}$ and $\hat{h} = \Lambda \circ y$ is the best linear estimate. If Λ_o is unique, $\mathrm{Cov}\{e(\Lambda_o)\} < \mathrm{Cov}\{e(\Lambda)\}$ and trace

$\{e(\Lambda_o)-e(\Lambda)\} < 0$ for all $\Lambda \in \mathcal{L}(H)$.

Necessity

Suppose Λ_o minimizes $E\{\|h-\Lambda y\|^2\}$, then

$$\text{trace } \{\Lambda P_2\Lambda^* - 2\Lambda P_{12}\} \geq \text{trace } \{\Lambda_o P_2 \Lambda_o^* - 2\Lambda_o P_{12}\} \text{ for all } \Lambda \in \mathcal{L}(H).$$

Letting $\Lambda = \Lambda_o + \lambda(\Lambda_o P_2 - P_{12}^*)$, we obtain

$$(5.13)\quad \lambda^2 \text{ trace } \{(\Lambda_o P_2 - P_{12}^*)P_2(\Lambda_o P_2 - P_{12}^*)\} + 2\lambda \text{ trace } \{(\Lambda_o P_2 - P_{12}^*)(P_2\Lambda_o^* - P_{12})\} \geq 0 \quad \text{for all } \lambda,$$

and so

$$\text{trace } \{(\Lambda_o P_2 - P_{12}^*)P_2(\Lambda_o P_2 - P_{12}^*)\} = 0$$

which implies (5.12). If Λ_o is unique we get strict inequality in (5.13), which means $\Lambda P_2 - P_{12}^* = 0$ for just that Λ_o.

Lemma 5.13

If h and y are Gaussian random variables and the best linear estimate of h given y exists, then it equals the best global estimate.

Proof

Let Λ_o be a solution of (5.12), then

$$\begin{aligned} E\{\langle e(\Lambda_o),h_1\rangle_H \langle y,k\rangle_K\} &= E\{\langle h,h_1\rangle_H \langle y,k\rangle_K\} - E\{\langle y,\Lambda_o^* h_1\rangle \langle y,k\rangle_K\} \\ &= \langle h_1,P_{12}k\rangle - \langle \Lambda_o P_2 h_1,k\rangle \\ &= 0 \end{aligned}$$

since Λ_o is a solution of (5.12), and since $\langle e(\Lambda_o),h_1\rangle_H$ and $\langle y,h\rangle_H$ being real Gaussian random variables are independent.
Similarly $\langle e(\Lambda_o),h_1\rangle_H$ and the n vector $\{\langle y,k_1\rangle,\dots, \langle y,k_n\rangle\}$ are independent.
Let $\{k_i\}_{i=o}^{\infty}$ be a complete orthonormal basis for K; $g: K \to H$ continuous and bounded and $f: R^n \to R$ given by

$$f(x_1,\dots, x_n) = \langle h_1, g(\sum_{i=1}^{n} k_i x_i)\rangle_H$$

Then $f(\langle y,k_1\rangle,\dots,\langle y,k_n\rangle)$ is a real random variable which is independent of $\langle e(\Lambda_o), h_1\rangle$ and hence

$$(5.14)\quad E\{\langle e(\Lambda_o),h_1\rangle f(\langle y,k_1\rangle,\ldots,\langle y,k_n\rangle)\} = E\{\langle e(\Lambda_o),h_1\rangle\}E\{f(\langle y,k_1\rangle,\ldots)\} = 0$$

Now $\sum_{i=1}^{n} k_i\langle y,k_i\rangle \to y$ in mean square as $n \to \infty$ and since g and f are continuous, $f(\langle y,k_1\rangle,\ldots,\langle y,k_n\rangle) \to \langle h_1,g(y)\rangle$ in $L^2(\Omega,p;R)$ as $n \to \infty$. So taking limits in (5.14) we obtain

$$(5.15)\qquad E\{\langle e(\Lambda_o),h_1\rangle_H\}E\{\langle h_1,g(y)\rangle_H = 0$$

for all $h_1 \in H$ and taking a basis for H, (5.15) implies that

$$(5.16)\qquad E\{\langle e(\Lambda_o),g(y)\rangle_H\} = 0$$

for all bounded and continuous functions $g: K \to H$. But for arbitrary $v \in L^2(K,p_y;H) = \mathcal{H}_y$, we can approximate v by a continuous and bounded g such that

$$\int_K \|g(k)-v(k)\|_H^2\, dp_y(k) < \varepsilon,$$

or equivalently

$$(5.17)\qquad \int_\Omega \|g(y(\omega)) - v(y(\omega))\|_H^2\, dp(\omega) < \varepsilon$$

Now $\int_\Omega \langle e(\Lambda_o), v(y(\omega))\rangle_H\, d\mu(\omega) = \int_\Omega \langle e(\Lambda_o), v(y(\omega)) - g(y(\omega))\rangle_H\, d\mu(\omega)$ from (5.16)

$$\leq \left(\int_\Omega \|e(\Lambda_o)\|^2_H\, d\mu(\omega)\right)^{\frac{1}{2}} \sqrt{\varepsilon} \text{ by (5.17)}$$

Since ε is arbitrarily small, $\int_\Omega \langle e(\Lambda_o), v(y(\omega))\rangle_H\, d\mu(\omega) \leq 0$ and replacing v by $-v$ we get equality; that is

$$\int_\Omega \langle h, v(y(\omega))\rangle_H\, d\mu(\omega) = \int_\Omega \langle \Lambda_o y(\omega), v(y(\omega))\rangle_H\, d\mu(\omega) = \int_K \langle \Lambda_o k, v(k)\rangle_H\, dp_y(k)$$

which shows that $\Lambda_o y$ is the projection of h on $\mathcal{H}_y$.

5.2 Stochastic processes and stochastic integration [2]-[4],[7],[8],[11]

Definition 5.14

An X-valued stochastic process is a map $u:[t_0,t_1]\times\Omega \to X$ which is measurable in the product measure on $[t_0,t_1]\times\Omega$ using Lebesgue measure on $[t_0,t_1]$.

We remark that this definition is more restrictive than for real stochastic processes where no measurability restrictions are required with respect to t (cf [7]).

Definition 5.15 Continuity of stochastic processes

Let u be an X-valued stochastic process on $[t_0,t_1]$, then

(a) u(t) is continuous in probability if

$$p\{\|u(t+\delta)-u(t)\| > 0\} \to 0 \quad \text{as} \quad \delta \to 0$$

(b) u(t) is continuous with probability one (w.p.1) if

$$\|u(t+\delta)-u(t)\| \to 0 \quad \text{as } \delta \to 0 \text{ w.p.1}$$

(c) u(t) is continuous in mean square if

$$E\{\|u(t+\delta)-u(t)\|^2\} \to 0 \quad \text{as } \delta \to 0$$

(d) u(t) has continuous sample paths if

$$p\left\{\sup_{t_0\le t\le t_1} \|u(t+\delta)-u(t)\|\right\} > 0 \to 0 \quad \text{as } \delta \to 0 .$$

These are obvious generalizations of the definitions for real valued processes (see [7]); (d) => (b) => (a),(c) => (a); but (c) does not imply (b) or (d) or conversely.

In the applications we need to consider estimates of stochastic processes on $[0,t_1]$ and, for these processes, we extend the concept of conditional expectation. If $y:[0,t_1]\times\Omega \to K$ has continuous sample paths, we define y_t to be the restriction of y on $[0,t]$, which is a random variable with values in C(0,t;K). Now define $\mathcal{H}_{y_t}$ by (5.9) for each t and consider the Hilbertian sum $\int^{\oplus} \mathcal{H}_{y_t} dt$ defined by

$$(5.18) \quad \int^{\oplus} \mathcal{H}_{y_t} dt = \left\{h(t,\omega)\in L^2(0,t_1;\mathcal{H}) : h(t)\in\mathcal{H}_{y_t} \text{ for almost all } t\right\}$$

(using the notation in [3]).

Then the conditional expectation of h(t) with respect to $y(s); 0\le s\le t$ is

$E_{Y_t}\{h(t)\}$ and we can prove

Lemma 5.16

$E_{Y_t}\{h(t)\} \varepsilon \int^{\oplus} \mathcal{H}_{Y_t} dt$ except for a null set of $[0, t_1]$.

Proof

Now $\int^{\oplus} \mathcal{H}_{Y_t} dt$ is a sub Hilbert space of $L^2(0, t_1; \mathcal{H})$ and so we can define $\hat{h}$ to be the projection of h on $\int^{\oplus} \mathcal{H}_{Y_t} dt$; that is.

$$(5.19) \qquad \int_0^{t_1} \langle \hat{h}(t), g(t) \rangle_{\mathcal{H}} \, dt = \int_0^{t_1} \langle h(t), g(t) \rangle_{\mathcal{H}} \, dt \text{ for all } g \ \varepsilon \int^{\oplus} \mathcal{H}_{Y_t} dt.$$

For fixed $s_o \ \varepsilon \ (0, t_1)$, and $a \ \varepsilon \ \mathcal{H}_{Y_s}$, define

$$(5.20) \qquad g_o(t) = \begin{cases} 0 \text{ if } t \notin [s_o, s_o+\varepsilon] \\ a \text{ if } t \notin [s_o, s_o+\varepsilon] \end{cases}$$

But $\mathcal{H}_{Y_{s_o}} \subset \mathcal{H}_{Y_t}$ for $t \geq s_o$, and so g_o given by (5.20) $\varepsilon \int^{\oplus} \mathcal{H}_{Y_t} dt$ and substituting in (5.19), we have

$$\int_{s_o}^{s_o+\varepsilon} \langle \hat{h}(t), a \rangle_{\mathcal{H}} \, dt = \int_{s_o}^{s_o+\varepsilon} \langle h(t), a \rangle_{\mathcal{H}} \, dt$$

If s_o is a Lebesgue point, then

$$(5.21) \qquad \langle \hat{h}(s_o), a \rangle_{\mathcal{H}} = \langle h(s_o), a \rangle_{\mathcal{H}} \quad \text{for all } a \ \varepsilon \ \mathcal{H}_{Y_{s_o}}$$

and since the set of non Lebesgue points has measure zero, (5.21) holds for almost all $s_o \ \varepsilon \ (0, t_1)$. But (5.21) implies that

$$\hat{h}(s_o) = E_{Y_{s_o}}\{h(s_o)\}$$

hence

$$\hat{h}(t) = E_{Y_t}\{h(t)\} \text{ for almost all } t \ \varepsilon \ (0, t_1).$$

We remark that if $h \ \varepsilon \int^{\oplus} \mathcal{H}_{Y_t} dt$, from (5.10) and (5.18)

$$h(s) \ \varepsilon \ \mathcal{H}_{Y_t} = L^2(C(0, t; K), P_{Y_t}; H) \text{ for almost all } s \ \varepsilon \ (0, t),$$

where p_{y_t} denotes the probability induced by y_t on $C(O,t;K)$.
Hence

$$(5.22)\qquad \begin{aligned} h &\in L^2(O,t;\ L^2(C(O,t)K),P_{y_t};H)) \\ &\simeq L^2(C(O,t;K),P_{y_t};H)) \end{aligned}$$

We recall the concept of separability for R^n stochastic processes from Doob [7], where we do not impose the measurability property.

<u>Definition 5.17</u>

$\tilde{u}(t)$ is a separable version of an R^n valued stochastic process on $[t_o,t_1]$ if there exists a null set $N \subset \Omega$ and a countable dense subset S of $[t_o,t_1]$ called the separator such that for $\omega \notin N$

$$\tilde{u}(s) = u(s) \text{ for } s \in S$$

$$\tilde{u}(s) = \lim_{s_j \to s} u(s) \text{ for } s \notin S,\ s_j \in S$$

Thus $\forall\ t \in [t_o,t_1]$, $u(t) = \tilde{u}(t)$ for $\omega \notin N_t$, $p\{N_t\} = 1$; which defines $\tilde{u}(t)$ as a version of $u(t)$ on $[t_o,t_1]$.
All R^n-valued stochastic processes $u(t)$ have a separable version $u(t)$. Notice however, that since $\bigcup_t N_t$ need not be a null set, if $u(t)$ is measurable on $(t_o,t_1)\times \Omega$, $\tilde{u}(t)$ need not be.

We now introduce a specialized concept of separability for Hilbert space valued stochastic processes.

<u>Definition 5.18</u>

Let $\{e_i\}_{i=o}^{\infty}$ be a complete orthonormal basis for H, then if u is an H-valued stochastic process, we can write

$$u(t,\omega) = \sum_{i=o}^{\infty} u_i(t,\omega)e_i \quad \text{w.p.1}$$

and associate an ℓ^2 process[1] $u_\infty(t) = \{u_i(t,\omega)\}$ with $u(t)$. We say that $u(t)$ has a separable version if $u_\infty(t)$ has a separable version

---

[1] where by ℓ^2 we mean the set of infinite sequences $\{x_i\}$with $\sum_{i=o}^{\infty} x_i^{\,2} < \infty$.

$u_\infty(t) = \{u_i(t,\omega)\}$, such that $u(t) = \sum_{i=0}^{\infty} u_i(t,\omega)e_i$ satisfies Definition 5.14

We show that a sufficient condition for u(t) to have a separable version is that it be continuous in probability.

<u>Lemma 5.19</u>

If u(t) is an H-valued stochastic process on $[t_o,t_1]$ which is continuous in probability and S is a countable dense subset of $[t_o,t_1]$, then there exists a separable version of u(t) which has S as its separator.

<u>Proof</u>

(a) First we show that there exists a family $\{N_t,\ t \in [t_o,t_1]\}$ of null sets of Ω, such that for all $t \in [t_o,t_1]$:

$$u(t,\omega) = \lim_{\substack{s_k \to t \\ s_k \in S}} u(s_k,\omega),\quad \omega \notin N_t$$

For $t \in [t_o,t_1]$ and a sequence $s_k \to t$, we have $u(t) = \lim u(s_k)$ in probability.
So we can extract a subsequence $u(s_k')$ from $u(s_k)$ such that $u(s_k')$ converges to u(t) w.p.1, i.e. except on a set of measure zero.

(b) From Theorem 5.15, there exists a separable version $\tilde{u}(t)$ of u(t). That is there exists a null set $N \subset \Omega$ and a countable set S_o of $[t_o,t_1]$, so that for $\omega \notin N$, if $s \in S_o$,

$$\tilde{u}(s) = u(s)$$

However, if $\omega \notin N$ and $t \notin S_o$,

$$\tilde{u}(t) = \lim_{s_j \to t,\ s_j \in S_o} u(s_j), \text{ where the limit is in } \ell^2$$

Hence for all $t \in [t_o,t_1]$, $\tilde{u}(t) = u(t)$ for $\omega \notin N_t$, $p(N_t) = 1$, where N_t may be identified with those in (a).

Now define a stochastic process on ℓ^2, y(t) by

$$y(s) = u(s) \text{ if } s \in S$$

$$y(s) = \tilde{u}(s) \text{ if } s \notin S$$

By definition, y(t) is a version of u(t), and we proceed to show that it is separable with separator S.

Define the null set, $N_1 = N \cup (\bigcup_{S_o} N_s)$

For $\omega \notin N_1$, and $t \notin S_o$, we have

$$y(t,\omega) = \lim_{\substack{s_j \to t \\ s_j \in S_o}} y(s_j,\omega) \quad \text{in } \ell^2$$

and for each $t \in S_o$, from (a),

$$u(t,\omega) = \lim_{\substack{s'_k \to t \\ s'_k \in S}} u(s'_k,\omega) \quad \text{in } H$$

This implies that for $t \in S_o$,

$$y(t,\omega) = \lim_{\substack{s'_k \to t \\ s'_k \in S}} y(s'_k,\omega) \text{ in } \ell^2$$

Thus for $\omega \notin N_1$ and $t \notin S$, one can find a subsequence s'_k in S converging to t such that

$$y(t,\omega) = \lim_{s'_k \to t} y(s_k,\omega) \text{ in } \ell^2$$

All of the processes we meet in this text will be at least continuous in probability, which is a very weak concept from an applications point of view. A more desirable property is for a process to have continuous sample paths and so we develop a useful sufficient condition for Hilbert space valued stochastic processes.

Lemma 5.20

Let u(t) be an H-valued stochastic process on $[t_o,t_1]$ such that

$$E\{\|u(t+\delta) - u(t)\|^{\alpha}\} \le c\,\delta^{1+\beta} \text{ for each } t \in [t_o,t_1], \tag{5.23}$$

for some constants c, α, $\beta > 0$. Then u(t) has a separable version with continuous sample paths.

Proof

(a) u(t) is separable.

$$p\{\|u(t+\delta) - u(t)\| > \varepsilon\} = p\{\|u(t+\delta) - u(t)\|^{\frac{1}{2}\alpha} > \varepsilon^{\frac{1}{2}\alpha}\}$$

$$\le \frac{1}{\varepsilon^{\alpha}} E\{\|u(t+\delta) - u(t)\|^{\alpha}\}$$

(5.24) by Tchebychev's inequality [7].

$$\le \frac{C}{\varepsilon^{\alpha}} \delta^{1+\beta} \text{ by (5.23)}$$

$$\to 0 \text{ as } \delta \to 0$$

and so u(t) is continuous in probability.

Without loss of generality we can choose $[t_o, t_1] = [0,1]$. Now $S = \left\{\frac{k}{2^n};\ k = 0,1,\dots,2^n;\ n = 0,1,2,\dots\right\}$ is dense in $[0,1]$, and so by Lemma 5.19, there is a separable version $\tilde{u}(t)$ of u(t) with separator S.

(b) $\tilde{u}(t)$ is a well-defined H-valued random variable for each $t \in [0,1]$. For positive integer m, denote

$$z_m = \sup_{0<k<2^m} \{\|u((k+1)2^{-m}) - u(k2^{-m})\|\}$$

Then from (5.24), we have

$$p\{z_m > 2^{-m\gamma}\} \le \sum_{0\le k<2^m} p\{\|u((k+1)2^{-m}) - u(k2^{-m})\| > 2^{-\gamma m}\}$$

$$\le 2^m \frac{C}{(2^{-m\gamma})^{\alpha}} (2^{-m})^{1+\beta} \text{ from (5.23)}$$

$$= C\ 2^{m(\alpha\gamma-\beta)}$$

So for $\gamma > \beta/2$, we have

(5.25) $$\sum_{m=o}^{\infty} z_m < \infty \quad \text{w.p.1.}$$

Let n be a fixed positive integer and suppose that $s \in S$ is such that

$$|s - k2^{-n}| < 2^{-n}$$

then

$$s = k2^{-n} \pm \sum_{m=1}^{n'} \tau_m 2^{-m} \qquad \text{where } n' \geq n \text{ and } \tau_m = 0 \text{ or } 1.$$

By repeated application of the triangle inequality, we deduce that for $s \in S$ with $|s-k2^{-n}| < 2^{-n}$

$$\text{(5.26)} \qquad \| u(s) - u(k2^{-n})\| \leq \sum_{m=n+1}^{n'} z_m \leq \sum_{m>n}^{\infty} z_m$$

and so for $s \in [k2^{-n} - 2^{-n}, k2^{-n} + 2^{-n}] \cap S = I_{n_k} \cap S$

$$\text{(5.27)} \qquad \sqrt{\sum_{i=0}^{\infty} |u_i(s)|^2} \leq \|u(k2^{-n})\| + \sum_{m>n} z_m$$

where $\tilde{u}(s) = \sum_{i=0}^{\infty} u_i(s)e_i$ is the separable version of u.

Let $t \in I_{n_k}$, then there exists a sequence $\{s_j\} \in S$ $s_j \to t$, and for all $\omega \notin N$, a null set,

$$\text{(5.28)} \qquad \tilde{u}(t,\omega) = \lim_{s_j \to t} u(s_j,\omega) \text{ in } \ell^2$$

$$(\text{or } \tilde{u}(s,\omega) = u(s,\omega) \text{ if } s \in S)$$

Since $t \in I_{n_k}$, for j sufficiently large, $s_j \in I_{n_k}$ and from (5.27), we have

$$\|u(s_j,\omega)\| \leq \text{constant}$$

So we can extract a weakly convergent subsequence with limit $u^*(t,\omega)$ in H (for fixed t,ω). But from (5.28), $\langle u(s_j,\omega),e_i\rangle \to u_i(t,\omega)$ for each i, and so

$$\tilde{u}(t,\omega) = u^*(t,\omega)$$

and thus $\tilde{u}(t,\omega) \in H$ for all $t \in I_{n_k}$ and $\omega \notin N$.

Taking n=1=k, that is $I_{nk} = [0,1]$, we have shown that for each $t \in [0,1]$, $u(t,\cdot)$ defines a H-valued random variable.

(c) $\tilde{u} : [0,1] \times \Omega \to H$ is measurable.

Define the sequence $\{v_n\}$ by

$$v_n(t,\omega) = u(k2^{-n},\omega) \quad \text{if} \quad t \in [k2^{-n},(k+1)2^{-n}].$$

Then for $s \in [k2^{-n},(k+1)2^{-n}] \cap S$

$$\|\tilde{u}(s,\omega)-v_n(s,\omega)\| = \|u(s,\omega)-u(k2^{-n},\omega)\|$$

$$\leq 2 \sum_{m>n} z_m(\omega)$$

from (5.26), since $|s-k2^{-n}| < 2^{-n}$. So $v_n \to \tilde{u}$, except on a null set of $[0,1]\times\Omega$.

(d) $\tilde{u}(t)$ has continuous sample paths.

Let s, t be such that $|s-t| < 2^{-n+1}$, then there exists k such that $s,t \in I_{nk}$. Now if $s_j \in I_{nk} \cap S$, from (5.26) we have

$$\|u(s_j)-u(k2^{-n})\| \leq \sum_{m>n}^{\infty} z_m$$

But for arbitrary $s \in I_{nk}$, $\tilde{u}(s)$ is the weak limit of $u(s_j)$ for some sequence $s_j \in I_{nk} \cap S$ and so for $s,t \in I_{nk}$,

$$\|\tilde{u}(t)-\tilde{u}(s)\| \leq \|\tilde{u}(t)-u(k2^{-n})\| + \|\tilde{u}(s)-u(k2^{-n})\|$$

$$\leq 2 \sum_{m>n} z_m$$

So

$$\sup_{|t-s|<2^{-n+1}} \|\tilde{u}(t)-\tilde{u}(s)\| \leq 2 \sum_{m>n} z_m$$

$$\to 0 \quad \text{w.p.1}$$

as $n \to \infty$ and so $\tilde{u}(t)$ has continuous sample paths.

A special class of stochastic processes which occur frequently in the applications are martingales.

Definition 5.21

Let $m(\cdot,\cdot)$ be an X-valued stochastic process on $[t_0,t_1]$ such that $m(t,\cdot) \in L^1(\Omega,p;X)$ for almost all $t \in [t_0,t_1]$. Suppose that $\{\mathcal{F}_t\}$ is an increasing family of sigma fields, $\mathcal{F}_s \subset \mathcal{F}_t \subset \mathcal{P}$ for $s < t$ and $m(t,\cdot)$ is measurable relative to $\mathcal{F}_t$ for almost all $t \in [t_0,t_1]$. Then $\{m(t,\cdot),\mathcal{F}_t,[t_0,t_1]\}$ is a martingale if

$$E\{m(t,\cdot)\mid \mathcal{F}_s\} = m(s,\cdot) \quad \text{w.p.1 for } s \in [t_0,t_1].$$

A particular example of a martingale is a Wiener process, which is used for modelling white noise disturbances in Engineering systems. The following is one of several equivalent definitions (cf [2]).

Definition 5.22 Wiener Process

$w(t)$ is an H-valued Wiener process on $[0,t_1]$ if it is an H-valued process on $[0,t_1]$, such that

$$w(t) - w(s) \in L^2(\Omega,p;H) \text{ for all } s,t \in [0,t_1] \text{ and}$$

i) $E\{w(t)-w(s)\} = 0$

ii) $\text{Cov}\,\{w(t)-w(s)\} = (t-s)W$ where $W \in \mathcal{L}(H)$ and is positive and nuclear.

iii) $w(s_4) - w(s_3)$ and $w(s_2) - w(s_1)$ are independent whenever $0 \le s_1 \le s_2 \le s_3 \le s_4 \le t$.

iv) $w(t)$ has continuous sample paths on $[0,t_1]$.

If we choose $\mathcal{F}_t$ to be the sigma field generated by $\{w(s);\ 0 \le s \le t\}$, then $w(t) - w(s)$ is independent of $\mathcal{F}_s$ for all $t > s$ from property (iii) and so

$$\begin{aligned} E\{w(t)-w(s) \mid \mathcal{F}_s\} &= E\{w(t)-w(s)\} \\ &= 0 \quad \text{by (i)} \end{aligned}$$

Hence $E\{w(t) \mid \mathcal{F}_s\} = w(s)$ w.p.1 and $\{w(t), \mathcal{F}_t\}$ is a martingale on $[0,\infty)$.

A particularly useful representation for a Wiener process is the following expansion.

Lemma 5.23

If $w(t)$ is an H-valued Wiener process, then there exists a complete orthonormal basis $\{e_i\}_{i=0}^{\infty}$ for H, such that

$$w(t) = \sum_{i=0}^{\infty} \beta_i(t) e_i \quad \text{w.p.1}$$

where $\beta_i(t)$ are mutually independent real Wiener processes with incremental covariance λ_i and $\sum_{i=0}^{\infty} \lambda_i < \infty$

Proof

Since W is nuclear and positive, we can form an orthonormal basis for H by augmenting its eigenvectors to give $\{e_i\}_{i=o}^{\infty}$:

$$We_i = \lambda_i e_i \; ; \; \lambda_i \geq 0.$$

We can always write

$$w(t) = \sum_{i=o}^{\infty} \beta_i(t) e_i$$

where $\beta_i(t) = \langle w(t), e_i \rangle$ is a real stochastic process.

From (i), we have $E\{\beta_i(t)-\beta_i(s)\} = 0$

and from (ii), we have $E\{(\beta_i(t)-\beta_i(s))^2\} = \langle We_i, e_i \rangle = \lambda_i$

(5.29) $$E\{(\beta_i(t)-\beta_i(s))(\beta_j(t)-\beta_j(s))\} = 0 \quad \text{for } i \neq j$$

From (iii), β_i has independent increments and from (iv) it has continuous sample paths and hence $\beta_i(t)$ is a real Wiener process.

$\beta_i(t)$ and $\beta_j(t)$ are independent on nonoverlapping intervals from (iii) and since they are Gaussian processes their independence on the same interval $[s,t]$ follows from the orthogonality condition (5.29)

Corollary 5.24

(a) $w(t)$ is Gaussian for all $t \in [0,t_1]$.

(b) $$E\{\|w(t)-w(s)\|^2\} = \sum_{i=o}^{\infty} \lambda_i (t-s)$$

$$= (t-s) \text{ trace } W$$

(c) $E\{\|w(t)-w(s)\|^4\} \leq 3(t-s)^2 (\text{trace } W)^2$

We remark that an alternative definition is to replace (iv) of Definition 5.23 by assuming that $w(t)$ is Gaussian for all $t \in [0,t_1]$. Then one can prove that $w(t)$ must have a separable version with continuous sample paths using (c) of the above corollary and Lemma 5.20.

We now develop a theory of stochastic integration for the Hilbert space-valued Wiener process, restricting ourself to the case of nonrandom integrands[1] in the space

---

[1] For random integrands see [4].

$$\mathcal{B}^2(t_o,t_1;\ \mathcal{L}(K,H)) = \left\{\Phi:[t_o,t_1] \to \mathcal{L}(K,H),\ \text{such that } \Phi(t) \text{ is strongly measurable and } \int_{t_o}^{t_1} \|\Phi(t)\|^2\, dt < \infty \right\}$$

We define the integral with respect to a Hilbert space-valued Wiener process using the representation of w(t) in Lemma 5.23.

Definition 5.25

$$\int_{t_o}^{t} \Phi(s)dw(s) = \sum_{i=o}^{\infty} \int_{t_o}^{t} \Phi(s)e_i d\beta_i(s);\ 0 \leq t_o \leq t \leq t_1;$$

where $w(s) = \sum_{i=o}^{\infty} \beta_i(s)e_i$, $\Phi \in \mathcal{B}^2(t_o,t_1;\ \mathcal{L}(K,H))$ and the limit is in $L^2(\Omega,p;H)$.

In order to justify Definition 5.25 we must first define integrals of the form $\int_{t_o}^{t} f(s)d\beta(s)$, where β is a real Wiener process of incremental covariance λ and $f \in L^2(t_o,t_1;H)$.

Lemma 5.26

Let $f \in L^2(t_o,t_1;H)$ be a step function, such that

$$f(s) = f_i \text{ on } [s_i,s_{i+1});\ t_o = s_o < s_1 < \ldots < s_k = t,$$

then if we define

$$\int_{t_o}^{t} f(s)d\beta(s) = \sum_{i=o}^{k-1} f_i(\beta(s_{i+1})-\beta(s_i)),$$

the following holds

(a) $E\{\int_{t_o}^{t} f(s)d\beta(s)\} = 0$

(b) $E\{<\int_{t_o}^{t} f(s)d\beta(s),\ \int_{t_o}^{t} f(s)d\beta(s)>\} = \lambda\int_{o}^{t} <f(s),f(s)>\, ds$

Proof

(a) $$E\{\int_{t_o}^{t} f(s)d\beta(s)\} = \sum_{i=o}^{k-1} f_i E\{\beta(s_{i+1})-\beta(s_i)\}$$

$$= 0 \text{ by property (i)}$$

(b) $$E\{<\int_{t_o}^{t} f(s)d\beta(s), \int_{t_o}^{t} f(s)d\beta(s)>\} = \sum_{i,j=o}^{k-1}\sum E\{<f_i(\beta(s_{i+1})-\beta(s_i)), f_i(\beta(s_{i+1})- (s_i)>\}$$

$$= \sum_{i=1}^{k-1} <f_i,f_i>\lambda(s_{i+1}-s_i)$$

by properties (ii) and (iii)

$$= \lambda\int_{t_o}^{t} <f(s),f(s)> ds$$

Since the step functions are dense in $L^2(t_o,t;H)$, we can extend this integral to arbitrary $f \varepsilon L^2(t_o,t;H)$ by defining

$$\int_{t_o}^{t} f(s)d\beta(s) = \lim_{n\to\infty} \int_{t_o}^{t} f_n(s)d\beta(s)$$

where the limit is in $L^2(\Omega,p;H)$ and f_n is a sequence of step functions converging to f in $L^2(t_o,t;H)$.

As a consequence of Lemma 5.26, $\int_{t_o}^{t} f(s)d\beta(s)$ is a well defined H-valued random variable satisfying

(5.30) $$E\{\int_{t_o}^{t} f(s)d\beta(s)\} = 0$$

(5.31) $$E\{<\int_{t_o}^{t} f(s)d\beta(s), \int_{t_o}^{t} f(s)d\beta(s)>\} = \lambda\int_{t_o}^{t} <f(s),f(s)> ds.$$

If $g \varepsilon L^2(t_o,t;H)$ and α is another Wiener process independent of β, then by approximating f and g by step functions and taking the appropriate limits we easily obtain the properties

(5.32) $$E\{<\int_{t_o}^{s_1} f(s)d\beta(s), \int_{t_o}^{s_2} g(s)d\alpha(s)>\} = 0$$

$$(5.33) \qquad E\{<\int_{t_o}^{s_1} f(s)d\beta(s), \int_{t_o}^{s_2} g(s)d\beta(s)>\} = \lambda\int_{t_o}^{\min(s_1,s_2)} <f(s),g(s)> ds$$

$$(5.34) \quad E\{<\int_{t_o}^{s_1} f(s)d\beta(s),e_1><\int_{t_o}^{s_2} g(s)d\beta(s),e_2>\} = \lambda \int_{t_o}^{\min(s_1,s_2)} <f(s),e_1><g(s),e_2>ds$$

where e_1, $e_2 \in H$.

We now establish analogous properties for the integral of Definition 5.25.

Lemma 5.27

$$\int_{t_o}^{t_1} \Phi(s)dw(s) \in L^2((t_o,t_1)\times \Omega;H) \text{ and}$$

(a) $$E\{\int_{t_o}^{t} \Phi(s)dw(s)\} = 0$$

(b) $$E\{ \int_{t_o}^{t} \|\Phi(s)dw(s)\|^2\} = \text{trace } \{\int_{t_o}^{t} \Phi(s)W\Phi^*(s)ds\}$$

$$\leq \text{trace } W \int_{t_o}^{t} \|\Phi(s)\|^2 ds$$

(c) $$E\{\int_{t_o}^{s_1} \Phi_1(s)dw(s) \circ \int_{t_o}^{s_2} \Phi_2(s)dw(s)\} = E\{\int_{t_o}^{\min(s_1,s_2)} \Phi_1(s)W\Phi_1^*(s)ds\}$$

(d) $$E\{\int_{s_1}^{s_2} \Phi_1(s)dw_1(s) \circ \int_{s_3}^{s_4} \Phi_2(s)dw_2(s)\} = 0$$

where Φ, Φ_1, $\Phi_2 \in \mathcal{B}_2(t_o,t_1; \mathcal{L}(K,H))$, w_1, w_2 are independent K-valued Wiener processes and s_1, s_2, s_3, s_4, $t \in [t_o,t_1]$.

Proof

(a) $$E\{\sum_{i=o}^{N}\int_{t_o}^{t} \Phi(s)e_i d\beta_i(s)\} = \sum_{i=o}^{N} E\{\int_{t_o}^{t} \Phi(s)e_i d\beta_i(s)\}$$

$$= 0 \text{ by } (5.30)$$

(b) $$E\{\| \sum_{i=o}^{N} \int_{t_o}^{t} \Phi(s)e_i d\beta_i(s)\|^2\} = \sum_{i,j=o}^{N} E\{<\int_{t_o}^{t} \Phi(s)e_i d\beta_i(s), \int_{t_o}^{t} \Phi(s)e_j d\beta_j(s)>\}$$

$$= \sum_{i=o}^{N} \lambda_i \int_{t_o}^{t} <\Phi(s)e_i, \Phi(s)e_i> ds$$

from (5.30), (5.31).

$$\to \int_{t_o}^{t} \text{trace } \{\Phi(s)W\Phi^*(s)\} \, ds \text{ as } N \to \infty$$

since W is nuclear

$$\leq \text{trace } W \int_{t_o}^{t} \|\Phi(s)\|^2 \, ds.$$

This establishes $\int_{t_o}^{t} \Phi(s)dw(s) \in L^2((t_o,t_1)\times\Omega;H)$ and (b).

(c) Write $u = \int_{t_o}^{s_1} \Phi_1(s)dw(s)$, $v = \int_{t_o}^{s_2} \Phi_2(s)dw(s)$

then $$E\{<e_k, (u \circ v)e_r>\} = \sum_{i,j=o}^{\infty} E\{<e_k, \int_{t_o}^{s_1} \Phi_1(s)e_i d\beta_i(s)> \cdot < \int_{t_o}^{s_2} \Phi_2(s)e_j d\beta_j(s), e_r>\}$$

$$= \sum_{i=o}^{\infty} E\{<e_k, \int_{t_o}^{s_1} \Phi_1(s)e_i d\beta_i(s)> \cdot < \int_{t_o}^{s_2} \Phi_2(s) d\beta_i(s), e_r>\}$$

since β_i and β_j are independent

$$= \sum_{i=o}^{\infty} \int_{t_o}^{\min(s_1,s_2)} \lambda_i <e_k, \Phi_1(s)e_i><e_r, \Phi_2(s)e_i> ds$$

by (5.34) and since β_i has independent increments.

Hence $$E\{u \circ v\} = \int_{t_o}^{\min(s_1,s_2)} \sum_{i=o}^{\infty} \lambda_i \Phi_1(s)e_i \circ \Phi_2(s)e_i \, ds$$

$$= \int_{t_o}^{\min(s_1,s_2)} \Phi_1(s)\left(\sum_{i=o}^{\infty} \lambda_i e_i \circ e_i\right)\Phi_2^*(s)\, ds$$

$$= \int_{t_o}^{\min(s_1,s_2)} \Phi_1(s) W \Phi_2^*(s)\, ds$$

where interchanging E, $\int$ and infinite summations can be justified as in (b).

(d) This follows from the independence of w_1 and w_2 using (5.34).

<u>Lemma 5.28</u> <u>The indefinite integral</u>

$y(t) = \int_{t_o}^{t} \Phi(s)dw(s)$ is an H-valued stochastic process with the following properties

(a) $\{y(t), \mathcal{F}_t;\ t \geq t_o\}$ is a martingale, where $\mathcal{F}_t$ is the sigma field generated by $\{\langle w(s), e_i\rangle;\ t_o \leq s \leq t;\ \ i = 0,1,2,\ldots\}$.

(b) $y(t)$ has a separable version which has continuous sample paths.

(c) $E\{y(t) = 0\}$ and $\text{Cov}\{y(t)-y(s)\} = \int_{s}^{t} \Phi(s)W\Phi^*(s)ds$.

<u>Proof</u>

From Lemma 5.27, $y(t)$ is a well-defined random variable for all $t \in [t_o,t_1]$ and

$$E\{\|y(t)\|^2\} \leq \text{trace } W \int_{t_o}^{t} \|\Phi(s)\|^2\, ds$$

$$< \infty$$

(a) Since $\Phi \in \mathcal{B}^2(t_o,t_1;\ \mathcal{L}(K,H))$, there exists a sequence $\{\Phi_n\} \in \mathcal{B}^2(t_o,t_1;\ \mathcal{L}(K,H))$ such that $\int_{t_o}^{t_1}\|\Phi-\Phi_n\|^2\, ds \to 0$ as $n \to \infty$ and Φ_n are step functions in t.

Then using an obvious notation,

$$y_n(t) = \int_{t_o}^{t} \Phi_n(s)dw(s)$$

$$= \sum_{j=o}^{k_n} \Phi_{n_j}\,(w(t_j+1)-w(t_j))$$

So $y_n(t)$ is measurable relative to $\mathcal{F}_t$ and $y(t)$ is also measurable relative to $\mathcal{F}_t$, since

$$E\{\|y(t)-y_n(t)\|^2\} \le \text{trace } W \int_{t_o}^{t} \|\Phi-\Phi_n\|^2 \, ds \text{ by Lemma 5.27(b)}$$

$$\to 0 \text{ as } n \to \infty$$

$\{y_n(t), \mathcal{F}_t, [t_o,t_1]\}$ is an H-martingale, since for $t > s$

$$y_n(t) = y_n(s) + \sum_{s \le t_{j-1} \le t}^{k_n} \Phi_{n_j}(w(t_{j+1})-w(t_j))$$

and $$E\{y_n(t) \mid \mathcal{F}_s\} = E\{y_n(s) \mid \mathcal{F}_s\} + \sum_{s \le t_{j-1} \le t}^{k_n} \Phi_{n_j} E\{w(t_{j+1})-w(t_j) \mid \mathcal{F}_s\}$$

$$= y_n(s) + \sum_{s \le t_{j-1} \le t}^{k_n} \Phi_{n_j} E\{w(t_{j+1})-w(t_j)\}$$

$$= y_n(s) \text{ w.p.1.}$$

since $w(t)$ has independent increments (Definition 5.22(iii)).

Now from [11], $\{y(t), \mathcal{F}_t, [t_o,t_1]\}$ is a martingale if and only if

$$\int_F y(t)dp = \int_F y(s)dp \text{ for } s < t \text{ and } \forall\, F \in \mathcal{F}_s$$

But $$\int_F y_n(t)dp = \int_F y_n(s)dp \quad \text{w.p.1.}$$

and $\int_F (y_n(t)-y(t))dp \to 0$ in probability as $n \to \infty$, since convergence in mean square implies convergence in probability.

Hence $\{y(t), \mathcal{F}_t, [t_o,t_1]\}$ is a martingale.

(b) We note that we can always take $\|y(t)-y_n(t)\|$ to be a real separable semi-martingale, since it is only determined up to a null set. From [7], we have

$$p\{\sup_{t_o \le t \le t_1} \|y(t)-y_n(t)\| > \tfrac{1}{\varepsilon}\} \le \varepsilon^2 E\{\|y_n(t_1)-y(t_1)\|^2\}$$

$$\le \varepsilon^2 \text{trace } W \int_{t_o}^{t_1} \|\Phi-\Phi_n\|^2 ds \text{ from Lemma 5.27(b)}$$

Choose a subsequence Φ_{n_k}, such that $\sum_{k=1}^{\infty} k^2 \int_{t_o}^{t_1} \|\Phi-\Phi_{n_k}\|^2 ds$ converges.
Then we have

$$\sum_{k=1}^{\infty} p\{ \sup_{t_o \le t \le t_1} \|y(t)-y_{n_k}(t)\| \ge \frac{1}{k}\} < \infty$$

and by the Borel-Cantelli lemma, there exists an $M > 0$ such that

$$\sup_{t_o \le t \le t_1} \|y(t)-y_{n_k}(t)\| \le \frac{1}{k} \quad \text{w.p.1.} \quad \forall\, k \ge M$$

Now $y_{n_k}(t)$ has a separable version with continuous sample paths since $w(t)$ has. Hence $y(t)$ has a separable version with continuous sample paths.

(c) These are a consequence of Lemma 5.27 (a) and (c).
We remark that the indefinite integral $y(t) = \int_{t_o}^{t} \Phi(s)dw(s)$ satisfies properties (i), (ii) and (iv) of Definition 5.22, the only difference being its covariance function. It is often called the Levy-Wiener process.

We also use double integrals of a mixed type, namely

$$\int_{t_o}^{t_1}\int_{t_o}^{t_1} \Phi(t,s)dt\, dw(s) \quad \text{or} \quad \int_{t_o}^{t_1}\int_{t_o}^{t_1} \Phi(t,s)dw(s)dt$$

which are both well-defined for $\Phi \in \mathcal{B}^2((t_o,t_1)\times(t_o,t_1); \mathcal{L}(K,H))$.
For these we can prove a stochastic Fubini type theorem.

Lemma 5.29

Let $w(t)$ be a K-valued Wiener process and $\Phi(t,s) \in \mathcal{B}^2((t_o,t_1)\times(t_o,t_1); \mathcal{L}(K,H))$,

then

$$y_1 = \int_{t_o}^{t_1}\int_{t_o}^{t_1} \Phi(t,s)dw(s)dt \quad \text{and} \quad y_2 = \int_{t_o}^{t_1}\int_{t_o}^{t_1} \Phi(t,s)dt\, dw(s)$$

are both in $L^2(\Omega,p;H)$ and are equal w.p.1.

Proof

If $\Phi_n(t,s)$ are step functions in s, then the result is obvious. For $\Phi \in \mathcal{B}^2$, we approximate it by a sequence of step functions in s, $\Phi_n(t,s)$, such that $\int_{t_o}^{t_1}\int_{t_o}^{t_1} \|\Phi(t,s) - \Phi_n(t,s)\|^2 ds\, dt \to 0$ for almost all t.

Then

$$E\{\|y_1-y_2\|^2\} \leq 2\, E\{\|\int_{t_o}^{t_1}\int_{t_o}^{t_1} (\Phi(t,s)-\Phi_n(t,s))dw(s)dt\|^2\}$$
$$+ 2E\{\|\int_{t_o}^{t_1} (\int_{t_o}^{t_1} \Phi_n(t,s)-\Phi(t,s)dt)dw(s)\|^2\}$$

$$\leq 2(t_1-t_o)\int_{t_o}^{t_1} E\{\|\int_{t_o}^{t_1} (\Phi(t,s)-\Phi_n(t,s))dw(s)\|^2\}dt$$
$$+ 2 \text{ trace } W \int_{t_o}^{t_1} \|\int_{t_o}^{t_1} (\Phi_n(t,s)-\Phi(t,s))dt\|^2 ds$$

by the Schwarz inequality and Lemma 5.27(b)

$$\leq 4(t_1-t_o) \text{ trace } W \int_{t_o}^{t_1}\int_{t_o}^{t_1} \|\Phi_n(t,s)-\Phi(t,s)\|^2 ds\, dt$$

by the Schwarz inequality and Lemma 5.27(b)

$\to 0$ as $n \to \infty$.

5.3 Stochastic evolution equations [4],[5]

The stochastic analogue of (2.19) is

(5.35) $$dz(t) = Az(t)dt + D(t)dw(t) + g(t)dt;\; z(t_o) = z_o,$$

where by (5.35) we mean the integral equation

(5.36) $$z(t) = z_o + \int_{t_o}^{t} (Az(s)+g(s))ds + \int_{t_o}^{t} D(s)dw(s)$$

A is the infinitesimal generator of a strongly continuous semigroup T_t, $D \in \mathcal{B}^2(t_o,t_1;\mathcal{L}(K,H))$, $g \in L^1(t_o,t_1;H)$ w.p.1., z_o is an H-valued random variable, and w is a K-valued Wiener process. We are interested in obtaining sufficient conditions for (5.36) to have the solution

(5.37) $$z(t) = T_{t-t_o}z_o + \int_{t_o}^{t} T_{t-s}D(s)dw(s) + \int_{t_o}^{t} T_{t-s}g(s)ds$$

From Lemma 5.27, $z(t)$ is a well-defined stochastic process and analogously to Definition 2.23, we call (5.37) the mild solution of (5.35). For our definition of strong solution we take

Definition 5.30

$z(t)$ is a strong solution of (5.35) if $z(t) \in D(A)$ w.p.1., $z(t)$ satisfies (5.36) almost everywhere on $[t_o,t_1]\times \Omega$ and $z(t)$ has continuous sample paths.
$z(t)$ is unique if whenever $z_1(t)$ is another solution,

$$p\{ \sup_{t_o \le t \le t_1} \|z(t)-z_1(t)\| \neq 0\} = 0.$$

In chapter 6, we shall meet more general stochastic evolution equations of the type

$$(5.38) \qquad dz(t) = (A+F(t))z(t)dt + D(t)dw(t) + g(t)dt; \; z(t_o) = z_o$$

where $F \in \mathcal{B}^{\infty}(t_o,t_1; \mathcal{L}(H))$.
We define the strong solution of (5.38) analogously to Definition 5.30 and its mild solution by

$$(5.39) \qquad z(t) = U(t,t_o)z_o + \int_{t_o}^{t} U(t,s)g(s)ds + \int_{t_o}^{t} U(t,s)D(s)dw(s),$$

where $U(t,s)$ is the quasi evolution operator generated by $A + F(t)$.
In general (5.37) will not be a strong solution of (5.35) and in fact will not even have continuous sample paths. However it is always a H-valued stochastic process and it is continuous in a mean square sense (see Definition 5.30(c)).

Lemma 5.31

$y(t) = \int_{t_o}^{t} U(t,s)D(s)dw(s)$ is continuous in mean square.

Proof

(a) $\int_{t_o}^{t} U(t,s)D(s)e_i d\beta_i(s) = y_i(s)$ is continuous in mean square.

Let $\delta > 0$, then

$$E\{\|y_i(t+\delta)-y_i(t)\|^2\} = E\{\|\int_{t_o}^{t} (U(t+\delta,t)-I)U(t,s)D(s)e_i d\beta_i(s) + \int_{t}^{t+\delta} U(t+\delta,s)D(s)e_i d\beta_i(s)\|^2\}$$

$$\leq 2E\{\|(U(t+\delta,t)-I)y_i(t)\|^2\} + 2\lambda_i M^2\int_{t}^{t+\delta} \|D(s)\|^2 ds$$

by Lemma 5.27(b)

$\to 0$ as $\delta \to 0$ since $U(t,s)$ is strongly continuous.

$$E\{\|y_i(t)-y_i(t-\delta)\|^2\} = E\{\|\int_{t_o}^{t-\delta} (U(t,s)-U(t-\delta,s))D(s)e_i d\beta_i(s) + \int_{t-\delta}^{t} U(t,s)D(s)e_i d\beta_i(s)\|^2\}$$

$$\leq 2\lambda_i\int_{t_o}^{t-\delta} \|(U(t,s)-U(t-\delta,s))D(s)e_i\|^2 ds + \lambda_i\int_{t-\delta}^{t} M^2\|D(s)\|^2\, ds$$

by Lemma 5.27(b)

$\to 0$ as $\delta \to 0$ since $U(t,s)$ is strongly continuous and using the Lebesgue dominated convergence theorem.

(b) Let $X = C(t_o,t_1;\, L^2(\Omega,p;H))$. Then we show that

$\sum_{i=o}^{N} \int_{t_o}^{t} U(t,s)D(s)e_i d\beta_i(s)$ converges to $\int_{t_o}^{t} U(t,s)D(s)dw(s)$ in X.

$$E\{\|\int_{t_o}^{t} U(t,s)D(s)dw(s) - \sum_{i=o}^{N} \int_{t_o}^{t} U(t,s)D(s)e_i d\beta_i(s)\|^2\}$$

$$= \sum_{N+1}^{\infty} E\|\int_{t_o}^{t} U(t,s)D(s)e_i d\beta_i(s)\|^2 \text{ by Definition 5.25}$$

and since β_i and β_j are independent and (5.32)

$$\leq \sum_{N+1}^{\infty} M^2\int_{t_o}^{t_1} \|D(s)\|^2\, ds \text{ by Lemma 5.27(b)}$$

$\to 0$ as $N \to \infty$ uniformly in t.

So $$\int_{t_o}^{t} U(t,s)D(s)dw(s) \in C(t_o,t_1;L^2(\Omega,p;H)).$$

Before proving existence theorems for (5.35), we need the following technical lemmas.

Lemma 5.32

Let A be a closed densely-defined linear operator on H, $\Phi \in \mathcal{B}^2(t_o,t_1;\mathcal{L}(K,H))$ and w(t) a K-valued Wiener process with decomposition $w(t) = \sum_{i=o}^{\infty} \beta_i(t)e_i$. If $D(s)e_i \in D(A)$ for all i and

$$\sum_{i=o}^{\infty} \lambda_i \int_{t_o}^{t_1} \|AD(s)e_i\|^2 \, ds < \infty, \tag{5.40}$$

then $\int_{t_o}^{t_1} D(s)dw(s) \in D(A)$ w.p.1, has finite expectation

and $$A\int_{t_o}^{t_1} D(s)dw(s) = \sum_{i=o}^{\infty} \int_{t_o}^{t_1} AD(s)e_i d\beta_i(s) \triangleq \int_{t_o}^{t_1} A\Phi(s)dw(s).$$

Proof

(a) First we show that for each i,

$$A\int_{t_o}^{t_1} D(s)e_i d\beta_i(s) = \int_{t_o}^{t_1} AD(s)e_i d\beta_i(s) \text{ w.p.1}$$

If D(s) is a step function in time, the above assertion is true. Now fix i and consider $f(s) = D(s)e_i$. Suppose that $f_n(s)$ are step functions in s, such that

$$\int_{t_o}^{t_1} \|f(s) - f_n(s)\|^2 \, ds + \int_{t_o}^{t_1} \|Af(s) - Af_n(s)\|^2 \, ds \to 0 \text{ as } n \to \infty.$$

(Such a sequence exists since the step functions are dense in $L^2(t_o,t_1;\, D(A))$ where $D(A)$ has the graph norm.)

Let $y_n = \int_{t_o}^{t_1} f_n(s)d\beta_i(s)$ and let $\mathcal{H} = L^2(\Omega,p;H)$ be the underlying space, then we have the following:

$$y_n \to \int_{t_o}^{t_1} f(s)d\beta_i(s) \text{ as } n \to \infty \text{ in } \mathcal{H}.$$

$$A\,y_n \to \int_{t_o}^{t_1} Af(s)d\beta_i(s) \text{ as } n \to \infty \text{ by Lemma 5.27(b) and (5.40)}$$

Since A is closed, $\int_{t_o}^{t_1} f(s)d\beta_i(s) \in D(A)$ and

$$A\int_{t_o}^{t_1} f(s)d\beta_i(s) = \int_{t_o}^{t_1} Af(s)d\beta_i(s) \text{ w.p.1.}$$

(b) From (a), we have

$$A\sum_{i=o}^{N}\int_{t_o}^{t_1} D(s)e_i d\beta_i(s) = \sum_{i=o}^{N}\int_{t_o}^{t_1} AD(s)e_i d\beta_i(s) \text{ w.p.1.}$$

and $$E\{\|\sum_{i=o}^{N}\int_{t_o}^{t_1} AD(s)e_i d\beta_i(s)\|^2\} \leq \sum_{i=o}^{N}\lambda_i\int_{t_o}^{t_1}\|AD(s)e_i\|^2\,ds$$

by Lemma 5.27(b).

So by assumption (5.40), $\sum_{i=o}^{\infty}\int_{t_o}^{t_1} AD(s)e_i d\beta_i(s) \in \mathcal{H}$.

Since A is closed, $\sum_{i=o}^{\infty}\int_{t_o}^{t_1} D(s)e_i d\beta_i(s) \in D(A)$ and

$$A\sum_{i=o}^{\infty}\int_{t_o}^{t_1} D(s)e_i d\beta_i(s) = \sum_{i=o}^{\infty}\int_{t_o}^{t_1} AD(s)e_i d\beta_i(s) \text{ w.p.1.}$$

Corollary 5.33

If $A \in \mathcal{L}(H)$, then

$$A\int_{t_o}^{t_1} D(s)dw(s) = \int_{t_o}^{t_1} AD(s)dw(s) \text{ w.p.1.}$$

Corollary 5.34

Under the assumptions of the above theorem, $A\int_{t_o}^{t} D(s)dw(s)$ has continuous sample paths.

Proof

From Lemma 5.28(a), $\sum_{i=o}^{N}\int_{t_o}^{t} AD(s)e_i d\beta_i(s)$ is an H-valued martingale and by Lemma 5.32 it converges in mean square to $\int_{t_o}^{t} AD(s)dw(s)$.

So as in (a) of the proof of Lemma 5.28, $\int_{t_o}^{t} AD(s)dw(s)$ is also a martingale.

As in (c) of the proof of Lemma 5.28 we can deduce that

$$\sup_{t_o \le t \le t_1} \left\| \int_{t_o}^{t} AD(s)dw(s) - \sum_{i=o}^{n_k} \int_{t_o}^{t} AD(s)e_i d\beta_i(s) \right\| \le \frac{1}{k} \text{ w.p.1.}$$

for all $k \ge M$.

But $\sum_{i=o}^{n_k} \int_{t_o}^{t} AD(s)e_i d\beta_i(s)$ has continuous sample paths by Lemma 5.28 and hence $\int_{t_o}^{t} AD(s)dw(s)$ has continuous sample paths.

We now prove our main existence theorem.

Theorem 5.35

If $T_{t-s}D(s)e_i$, $T_{t-s}g(s)$ and $T_{t-t_o}z_o \in D(A)$ w.p.1 for all i, $t_o \le s \le t \le t_1$ and

(5.41) $$\int_{t_o}^{t} \|AT_{t-s}g(s)\| \, ds < \infty \text{ w.p.1.}$$

(5.42) $$\sum_{i=o}^{\infty} \lambda_i \int_{t_o}^{t} \|AT_{t-s}D(s)e_i\|^2 \, ds < \infty$$

then z(t) given by (5.39) is the unique strong solution of (5.37).

Proof

Uniqueness

By the linearity this follows from the uniqueness of solutions of $\dot{z} = Az$; $z(t_o) = z_o$.

Existence

By Lemma 5.31 (5.39) is continuous in mean square and by Lemma 5.14,

$\int_{t_o}^{t} T_{t-s}D(s)dw(s) \in D(A)$ w.p.l. for each t. Since A is closed, $\int_{t_o}^{t} T_{t-s}g(s)\,ds \in D(A)$ w.p.l and so $z(t) \in D(A)$ w.p.l. From Lemma 5.32 we also have

$$A\int_{t_o}^{t} T_{t-s}D(s)dw(s) = \int_{t_o}^{t} AT_{t-s}D(s)dw(s) \text{ w.p.l.} \tag{5.43}$$

and by Lemma 5.29, under (5.42), we have

$$\begin{aligned}
\sum_{i=o}^{N}\int_{t_o}^{t}\int_{t_o}^{s} AT_{s-\alpha}D(\alpha)e_i d\beta_i(\alpha)ds &= \sum_{i=o}^{N}\int_{t_o}^{t}\int_{\alpha}^{t} AT_{s-\alpha}D(\alpha)e_i ds d\beta_i(\alpha) \text{ w.p.l.}\\
&= \sum_{i=o}^{N}\int_{t_o}^{t} (T_{t-\alpha}D(\alpha)e_i - D(\alpha)e_i)d\beta_i(\alpha)\\
&\qquad \text{by Theorem 2.9(b)}\\
&= \sum_{i=o}^{N}\int_{t_o}^{t} T_{t-\alpha}D(\alpha)e_i d\beta_i(\alpha)\\
&\qquad - \int_{t_o}^{t} D(\alpha)e_i d\beta_i(\alpha)\\
&\to \int_{t_o}^{t} T_{t-\alpha}D(\alpha)dw(\alpha) - \int_{t_o}^{t} D(\alpha)dw(\alpha)
\end{aligned}$$

as $N \to \infty$ by Definition 5.32.

So $\sum_{i=o}^{N}\int_{t_o}^{s} AT_{s-\alpha}D(\alpha)e_i d\beta_i(\alpha) \to \int_{t_o}^{s} AT_{s-\alpha}D(\alpha)dw(\alpha)$ as $N \to \infty$.

Hence it is integrable and

$$\int_{t_o}^{t}\int_{t_o}^{s} AT_{s-\alpha}D(\alpha)dw(\alpha)ds = \int_{t_o}^{t} T_{t-\alpha}D(\alpha)dw(\alpha) - \int_{t_o}^{t} D(\alpha)dw(\alpha) \text{ w.p.l.}$$

By the usual Fubini theorem

$$\int_{t_o}^{t}\int_{t_o}^{s} AT_{s-\alpha}g(\alpha)d\alpha\, ds = \int_{t_o}^{t} T_{t-\alpha}g(\alpha)d\alpha - \int_{t_o}^{t} g(\alpha)d\alpha \text{ w.p.l.}$$

and using (5.43) we have shown that

$$z_o + \int_{t_o}^{t} Az(s)ds = z(t) - \int_{t_o}^{t} D(\alpha)dw(\alpha) - \int_{t_o}^{t} g(\alpha)d\alpha \text{ w.p.1.}$$

and z(t) given by (5.37) satisfies (5.36) w.p.1.

Now by Lemma 5.28, $\int_{t_o}^{t} D(\alpha)dw(\alpha)$ has continuous sample paths and since $Az(s)$ is integrable in s w.p.1., $\int_{t_o}^{t} Az(s)ds$ has continuous sample paths.

Hence z(t) has continuous sample paths.

Corollary 5.36

If $A(t) = A + F(t)$ generates an almost strong evolution operator U(t,s) and $U(t,s)g(s)$, $U(t,s)D(s)e_i$, $U(t,t_o)z_o \in D(A)$ w.p.1. for all $t_o \le s \le t \le t_1$, and

(5.44)
$$\int_{t_o}^{t} \|A(t)U(t,s)g(s)\| \, ds < \infty \text{ w.p.1.}$$

(5.45)
$$\sum_{i=o}^{\infty} \lambda_i \int_{t_o}^{t} \|A(t)U(t,s)D(s)e_i\|^2 \, ds < \infty$$

then z(t) given by (5.39) is the unique strong solution of (5.38).

Proof

An obvious generalization of that for Theorem 5.35, using property (2.43) of almost strong evolution operators.

The following sufficient conditions for strong solutions of (5.38) are more readily verifiable.

Corollary 5.37

Consider (5.38), where A, D, w, g, z_o are as in Theorem 5.35 and conditions (5.41) and (5.42) are satisfied and in addition $F \in \mathcal{B}^{\infty}(t_o,t_1; \mathcal{L}(H))$ satisfies

(5.46)
$$T_{t-s}F(s) : H \to D(A) \quad \text{and}$$

(5.47)
$$AT_{t-s}F(s) \in \mathcal{B}^2(t_o,t_1; \mathcal{L}(H))$$

Then (5.38) has the unique strong solution (5.39).

Proof

From Lemma 2.37, $A + F(t)$ generates an almost strong evolution operator $U(t,s)$ and so by Corollary 5.4, all we need to establish is that (5.44) and (5.45) are satisfied.

Now as in Lemma 2.37, (5.46) and (5.47) imply that

$$AU(t,s)h = AT_{t-s}h + \int_s^t AT_{t-\rho}F(\rho)U(\rho,s)h\,d\rho$$

and from the assumptions of Theorem 5.35 on z_o and g, it follows that $U(t,t_o)z_o$ and $U(t,s)g(s) \varepsilon\ D(A)$ with

$$\int_{t_o}^t \|AU(t,s)g(s)\|\,ds < \infty \quad \text{w.p.1.}$$

Similarly $U(t,s)D(s)e_i \varepsilon\ D(A)$ for all i and

$$\begin{aligned}\int_{t_o}^t \|AU(t,s)D(s)e_i\|^2\,ds &\leq 2\int_{t_o}^t \|AT_{t-s}D(s)e_i\|^2\,ds \\ &\quad + 2\int_{t_o}^t \left\|\int_s^t AT_{t-\rho}F(\rho)U(\rho,s)D(s)e_i\,d\rho\right\|^2 ds \\ &\leq 2\int_{t_o}^t \|AT_{t-\rho}D(\rho)e_i\|^2 ds \\ &\quad + 2\int_{t_o}^t \left(\int_s^t \|AT_{t-\rho}F(\rho)\|^2 d\rho \int_s^t \|U(\rho,s)D(s)\|^2 d\rho\right) ds\end{aligned}$$

using the Schwarz inequality

So (5.45) follows from (5.42) and (5.47), since $\sum_{i=o}^{\infty} \lambda_i < \infty$.

5.4 Examples ([4],[5],[12])

Example 5.38 Finite dimensional equations

If $H = R^n$, $K = R^m$, then all the assumptions of Theorem 5.35 and Corollary 5.36 are satisfied and (5.35) and (5.38) have unique strong solutions.

Example 5.39 Heat equation

Suppose we have a stochastic version of Example 1.2.

(5.48) $$dz(t) = Az(t)dt + dw(t) \; ; \; z(0) = z_o$$

where $Ah = \frac{\partial^2 h}{\partial \xi^2}$ for $h \in D(A)$,

$$D(A) = \{u \in H = L^2(0,1) : u_\xi, u_{\xi\xi} \in H \; ; \; u_\xi(0) = 0 = u_\xi(1)\}$$

and $w(t)$ is an H-valued Wiener process

$$w(t)(\xi) = \sum_{i=o}^{\infty} \beta_i(t)\sqrt{2}\cos i\pi\xi + \beta_o(t)$$

and $\beta_i(t)$ are real Wiener processes, independent, with incremental covariance λ_i, and such that $\sum_{i=o}^{\infty} \lambda_i < \infty$.

z_o is a second order Gaussian H-valued random variable with expectation $\bar{z}_o \in H$ and covariance operator $P_o \in \mathcal{L}(H)$. By definition 5.2, P_o must be nuclear and we suppose that it is given by

$$P_o\sqrt{2}\cos i\pi\xi = \alpha_i\sqrt{2}\cos i\pi\xi \quad ; \; i \geq 1$$

and $$\sum_{i=o}^{\infty} \alpha_i < \infty .$$

A generates the analytic semigroup T_t, given by

$$(T_t h)(\xi) = \sum_{n=1}^{\infty} 2e^{-n^2\pi^2 t}\cos n\pi\xi \int_0^1 \cos n\pi y h(y)dy + \int_0^1 h(y)dy$$

So $T_t : H \to D(A)$ and for

$$z(t) = T_t z_o + \int_0^t T_{t-s}dw(s)$$

to be the strong solution of (5.48) we must verify that

$$\sum_{n=o}^{\infty} \lambda_n \int_0^t \|AT_{t-s}\cos n\pi(\cdot)\|^2 \, ds < \infty$$

Now $AT_{t-s}\cos n\pi(\cdot) = -\pi^2 n^2 e^{-n^2\pi^2(t-s)}\cos n\pi(\cdot)$ and so we require $\sum_{n=1}^{\infty} n^2\lambda_n < \infty$, an extra restriction on the variance of the noise disturbance.

Example 5.40 Hyperbolic system

Consider the formal stochastic evolution equation

$$(5.49)\qquad \begin{cases} z_{tt} = z_{\xi\xi} + \eta(t,\xi) \\ z(0,t) = 0 = z(1,t) \;;\; z(0,\xi) = z_o(\xi), z_t(0,\xi) = z_1(\xi) \end{cases}$$

where $\eta(t,\xi)$ represents some distributed noise disturbance. Then following the approach in Example 4.10, we use the integral model

$$(5.50)\qquad \begin{pmatrix} z \\ z_t \end{pmatrix} = T_t \begin{pmatrix} z_o \\ z_{ot} \end{pmatrix} + \int_o^t T_{t-s} \begin{pmatrix} 0 \\ I \end{pmatrix} dw(s)$$

where from Example 2.41, T_t is the semigroup on $\mathcal{H}$ generated by

$$\mathcal{A} = \begin{bmatrix} 0 & I \\ \frac{\partial^2}{\partial \xi^2} & 0 \end{bmatrix}$$

and for the noise process $w(t)$, we take

$$w(t)(\xi) = \sum_{i=1}^{\infty} \beta_i(t)\sqrt{2}\sin \pi i \xi$$

where $\beta_i(t)$ are mutually independent processes with incremental covariance λ_i and $\sum_{i=1}^{\infty} \lambda_i < \infty$.

Using the representation of T_t from Example 2.41, we calculate that

$$\mathcal{A} T_{t-s} \begin{pmatrix} 0 \\ e_i \end{pmatrix} = \begin{pmatrix} \cos \pi i(t-s) e_i \\ -i\pi \sin \pi i(t-s) e_i \end{pmatrix} .$$

Thus $$\sum_{i=1}^{\infty} \lambda_i \int_{t_o}^{t} \left\| \mathcal{A} T_{t-s} \begin{pmatrix} 0 \\ e_i \end{pmatrix} \right\|^2 ds = \sum_{i=1}^{\infty} \lambda_i \pi^2 i^2 (t-t_o)$$

So from Theorem 5.35, we see that for (5.50) to be a strong solution of a stochastic evolution equation on $\mathcal{H}$ we require that the initial state z_o, z_1 be in $H^2[0,1] \cap H_o^1[0,1] \times H_o^1[0,1]$ and $\sum_{i=1}^{\infty} \lambda_i i^2 < \infty$; a restriction on the distributed noise disturbance.

Example 5.41 Delay equation

Consider the stochastic version of Example 2.42

$$d\xi(t) = A_o\xi(t)dt + \sum_{i=i}^{N} A_i \begin{Bmatrix} \xi(t+\theta_i);t+\theta_i \geq 0 \\ h(t+\theta_i);t+\theta_i < 0 \end{Bmatrix} dt$$

(5.51) $$+ \int_{-b}^{o} A_{o1}(\theta) \begin{Bmatrix} \xi(t+\theta);t+\theta \geq 0 \\ h(t+\theta);t+\theta < 0 \end{Bmatrix} d\theta\ dt + Ddw(t)$$

$$\xi(0) = h(0)$$

where A_o, A_i, A_{01} satisfy the assumptions of Example 2.42 and $h \in L^1(\Omega,p;L^2(-b,0;R^n))$, $h(0) \in L^2(\Omega,p;R^n)$ and $D \in \mathcal{L}(R^n)$ where for simplicity we take $H = R^n$. Then $w(t)$ is an n dimensional Wiener process with matrix incremental variance, W, say. The corresponding $\mathcal{M}^2$version of (5.51) is

(5.52) $$\begin{cases} dz(t) = \tilde{A}z(t)dt + \tilde{D}dw(t) \\ z(0) = \tilde{h} \end{cases}$$

where $\tilde{D} : R^n \to \mathcal{M}^2(-b,0;R^n)$ is given by

(5.53) $$(\tilde{D}u)(\theta) = \begin{cases} Du \ ; \ \theta = 0 \\ 0 \ ; \ \theta \neq 0 \end{cases}$$

and $\tilde{h} = (h(0),h(\cdot)) \in L^2(\Omega,p;\mathcal{M}^2)$.

We need the following representation of T_t

(5.54) $$(T_t h)(\theta) = \begin{Bmatrix} \Phi^o(t+\theta)h(0);t+\theta \geq 0 \\ 0 \qquad \theta < 0 \end{Bmatrix} + \begin{Bmatrix} \Phi^1(t+\theta)h(\theta);t+\theta \geq 0 \\ h(t+\theta) \qquad ;t+\theta < 0 \end{Bmatrix}$$

where $\Phi^o(t) \in \mathcal{L}(R^n)$ is the unique solution of

$$\frac{d\Phi^o(t)}{dt} = A_o\Phi^o(t) + \sum_{i=1}^{N} A_i \begin{Bmatrix} \Phi^o(t+\theta_i);t+\theta_i \geq 0 \\ 0 \qquad ;t+\theta_i < 0 \end{Bmatrix}$$

$$+ \int_{-b}^{o} A_{o1}(\theta) \begin{Bmatrix} \Phi^o(t+\theta);t+\theta \geq 0 \\ 0 \qquad ;t+\theta < 0 \end{Bmatrix} d\theta$$

$$\Phi^0(0) = I$$

and $\Phi^1(t) \in \mathcal{L}(L^2(-b,0;R^n))$, but we do not need its representation. The mild solution of (5.52) is

$$z(t) = T_t h + \int_0^t T_{t-s}\tilde{D}dw(s) \tag{5.56}$$

and from (5.53) and (5.54) we have

$$z(t)(0) = \Phi^0(t)h(\theta) + \int_0^{t+\theta} \Phi^0(t+s)\tilde{D}dw(s) \tag{5.57}$$

Now for $z(t) \in D(\tilde{A})$, we need $z(t)(\theta)$ to be differentiable in θ, but since the Wiener process is not differentiable, this will never happen. So it is futile to seek strong solutions of (5.52) in the sense of Definition 5.30. Instead we show that $z(t)$ given by (5.56) has continuous sample paths in $\mathcal{M}^2$ (and hence $z(t)(0)$ has continuous sample paths in R^n) and that $z(t)(0)$ satisfies (5.51) w.p.1 (i.e. the integrated version). So (5.51) has a solution and it must be unique (according to Definition 5.30) because the deterministic equation with $D = 0$ and nonrandom initial state has unique solutions. Since T_t is strongly continuous, $T_t h$ has continuous sample paths and that $z(t)$ has continuous sample paths follows from the following lemma.

Lemma 5.42

$g(t) = \int_0^t T_{t-s}\tilde{D}\, dw(s)$ has continuous sample paths in $\mathcal{M}^2$.

Proof

Suppose $\delta > 0$

(a) $\|\Phi^0(t+\delta)y - \Phi^0(t)y\|_{R^n} \leq \text{const.}\delta\|y\|_{R^n} \quad \forall\, y \in R^n$, since from (5.55) we see that $\sup_{0\leq t\leq t_1} \|\Phi^0(t)\| \leq c$, and

$$\Phi^0(t+\delta)y - \Phi^0(t)y = \int_t^{t+\delta}\left(A_0\Phi^0(s) + \sum_{i=1}^N A_i \begin{cases}\Phi^0(s+\theta_i); & s+\theta_i \geq 0\\ 0 & ; s+\theta_i < 0\end{cases}\right.$$

$$\left. + \int_{-b}^0 A_{01}(\theta)\begin{cases}\Phi^0(s+\theta); & s+\theta \geq 0\\ 0 & ; s+\theta < 0\end{cases} d\theta\right) y\, ds$$

(b) $$g(t+\delta) - g(t) = \int_0^t (T_{t+\delta-s} - T_{t-s})\tilde{D}dw(s) + \int_t^{t+\delta} T_{t+\delta-s}\tilde{D}dw(s)$$

$$\mathrm{Cov}\,\{g(t+\delta)-g(t)\} = \int_0^t (T_{t+\delta-s}-T_{t-s})\tilde{D}W\tilde{D}^*(T_{t+\delta-s}-T_{t-s})^*ds + \int_t^{t+\delta} T_{t+\delta-s}\tilde{D}W\tilde{D}^*T^*_{t+\delta-s}ds$$

by Lemma 5.27(c).

Now

$$\mathrm{trace}\,\{\mathrm{Cov}\{g(t+\delta)-g(t)\}\} \leq \mathrm{const.} \int_0^t \|(T_{t+\delta-s}-T_{t-s})\tilde{D}\|^2\,ds + \mathrm{const.}\int_t^{t+\delta} \|T_{t+\delta-s}\|^2_{\mathcal{M}^2}\,ds$$

$$\leq \mathrm{const.}\int_0^t \|(T_{t+\delta-s}-T_{t-s})\tilde{D}\|^2\,ds + \mathrm{const.}\delta$$

From (5.53) and (5.54), we have

$$\|(T_{t+\delta-s}-T_{t-s})\tilde{D}y\|^2_{\mathcal{M}^2} = \|(\Phi^0(t+\delta-s)-\Phi^0(t-s))Dy\|^2_{R^n} + \int_{t+\delta-s}^{0} \|(\Phi^0(t+\delta-s)-\Phi^0(t-s))Dy\|^2_{R^n}d\theta + \int_{t-s}^{t+\delta-s} \|\Phi^0(t-s)Dy\|^2_{R^n}d\theta$$

$$\leq \mathrm{const.}\delta^2\|y\|^2 + \mathrm{const.}\delta^2\|y\|^2 + \mathrm{const.}\delta\|y\|^2$$

from (a)

Hence trace $\{\mathrm{Cov}\{g(t+\delta)-g(t)\}\} \leq \mathrm{const.}\delta$, and since $g(t)$ is Gaussian, by Lemma 5.6

$$E\{\|g(t+\delta)-g(t)\|^2\} \leq \mathrm{const.}\delta^2$$

and by Lemma 5.9, $g(t)$ has a version with continuous sample paths. (The proof for $\delta < 0$ is similar).

References

[1] Balakrishnan, A.V. Applied functional analysis, Springer Verlag, 1976.

[2] Bensoussan, A. Filtrage optimal des systemes lineaires, Dunod, 1971.

[3] Bensoussan, A. and Viot, M. Optimal control of stochastic linear distributed parameter systems, SIAM J. Control, 13 (1975), pp.904-926.

[4] Curtain, R.F. and Falb, P.L. Stochastic differential equations in Hilbert space, J. Diff. Eqns., 10 (1971), pp.412-430.

[5] Curtain, R.F. Stochastic evolution equations with general white noise disturbance, J. Math. Anal. Appl., 60 (1977), pp.570-595.

[6] Dawson, D.A. Stochastic evolution equations and related measure processes, J. Multivariate Analysis, 5 (1975), pp.1-52.

[7] Doob, L. Stochastic processes, John Wiley, 1972.

[8] Dunford, N. and Schwartz, J.T. Linear operators, Part I:general theory, Inter Science, New York, 1958.

[9] Haussmann, U.G. Asymptotic stability of the linear Ito equation in infinite dimensions, J. Diff. Eqns., to appear.

[10] Parthasarathy, K.R. Probability measures on metric spaces, Academic Press, 1967.

[11] Scalora, F.S. Abstract Martingale convergence theorems, Pacific J. Math., 11 (1961), pp.347-374.

[12] Vinter, R.B. A representation of solutions to stochastic delay equations, Imperial College Dept. Computing and Control Report, 1975.

CHAPTER 6

THE STATE ESTIMATION PROBLEM

To avoid problems of existence and uniqueness of stochastic evolution equations we consider an integral abstract signal process

(6.1) $$x(t) = S_t x_o + \int_o^t S_{t-s} D \, dw(s) \; ; \; 0 \leq t \leq t_1,$$

and for the observation

(6.2) $$y(t) = \int_o^t Cx(s)ds + Fv(t)$$

where S_t is a strongly continuous semigroup with generator A on a separable Hilbert space H; w(t) is a Wiener process on a separable Hilbert space K and has incremental covariance operator W; $D \in \mathcal{L}(K,H)$; $x_o \in L^2(\Omega,p;H)$ and is Gaussian with zero mean and covariance operator P_o. v(t) is a vector valued Wiener process on R^k [1] and has incremental covariance matrix V. $V,V^{-1},F,F^{-1} \in \mathcal{L}(R^k)$, $C \in \mathcal{L}(H,K)$ and x_o,w,v are mutually independent. (x(t) and y(t) both have continuous sample paths).

The state estimation problem is to find the best estimate of the state x(t) at time t, based on the observation process $y_{t_o} = \{y(s); 0 \leq s \leq t_o\}$; that is, $E^{y_{t_o}}\{x(t)\}$ using the notation of §5.2. If $t=t_o$, this is called the filtering problem, if $t < t_o$ it is the smoothing problem and for $t > t_o$, the prediction problem.

6.1 The filtering problem

Our approach is to find the best linear estimate and then to prove that it is the best global estimate, because of the Gaussian property

---

[1] Our assumption of a finite dimensional observation space is necessary because V is nuclear and V^{-1} exists only if K is finite dimensional. However this is not always the practical situation.

of the processes. So initially we restrict ourselves to linear estimates of the form

$$(6.3)\qquad \hat{x}(t|t_o) = \int_o^{t_o} K(t,s)\,dy(s)$$

where $K(t,\cdot) \in \mathcal{B}^2(0,t_1;\ \mathcal{L}(R^k,H))$ and we seek $K(t,\cdot)$ which minimizes $E\{\langle h,x(t)-\hat{x}(t|t_o)\rangle^2\}$ for all $h \in H$. We shall call this our primal linear estimation problem and we proceed to obtain an explicit characterization for $\hat{x}(t|t_o)$, the best primal linear estimate.

Lemma 6.1

If $\Lambda(t,s) = E\{x(t) \circ x(s)\}$, where $x(t)$ is given by (6.1), then

$$(6.4)\qquad \Lambda(t,s)h = S_t P_o S_s^* h + \int_o^{\min(t,s)} S_{t-r} DWD^* S_{s-r}^* h\,dr\ ;\ h \in H.$$

Proof

Apply Lemma 5.27.

The following lemma plays a fundamental role.

Lemma 6.2 Orthogonal projection Lemma

$\hat{x}(t|t_o)$ given by (6.3) is the best primal linear estimate if and only if $E\{\tilde{x}(t|t_o) \circ (y(\sigma)-y(\tau))\} = 0$[1] for σ,τ such that $0 \le \tau \le \sigma \le t_o \le t_1$. ($\tilde{x}(t|t_o) = x(t)-\hat{x}(t|t_o)$ is the error process).

Proof

For fixed $h \in H$, define the Hilbert space $X(h)$ by

$$X(h) = \left\{ \begin{array}{l} \langle u,h\rangle\ :\ u \in L^2(\Omega,p;H) \text{ with the inner product} \\ [\langle u,h\rangle,\langle v,h\rangle] = E\{\langle u,h\rangle\langle v,h\rangle\} \end{array} \right\}$$

Note that $E\{u \circ u\} = 0$ if $[\langle u,h\rangle^2] = 0$ for all $h \in H$ and $E\{\langle u,h\rangle\langle v,h\rangle\} = 0\ \forall\ h$ if $E\{u \circ v\} = 0$.

[1] $u \circ v$ for $u \in H$, $v \in K$ is defined by $(u \circ v)k = u\langle v,k\rangle_K\ \forall\ k \in K$.

For fixed $[t,t_o]$, we define the subspace $X(h;t,t_o)$ by

$$X(h;t,t_o) = \left\{ \begin{array}{l} \langle x(t,t_o),h\rangle \text{ when } x(t,t_o) = \int_0^{t_o} B(t,s)dy(s) \\ \text{and } B(t,\cdot)\in \mathcal{B}^2(0,t_o;\mathcal{L}(R^k,H)) \end{array} \right\}$$

So $\langle\tilde{x}(t|t_o),h\rangle \in X(h;t_o,t)$ and we seek to minimise $\tilde{x}(t|t_o)$ in the $X(h)$ norm for all $h \in H$. By the orthogonal projection lemma for Hilbert spaces, this is equivalent to requiring that

$$\langle x(t,t_o),h\rangle \perp X(h;t_o,t) \text{ in } X(h)$$

i.e. $E\{\langle h,x(t|t_o)\rangle\langle h,x(t,t_o)\rangle\} = 0 \;\forall\; \langle h,x(t,t_o)\rangle \in X(h;t,t_o)$.

So it remains to establish that

$$\text{(6.5)} \qquad E\{\tilde{x}(t|t_o)\circ x(t,t_o)\} = 0 \quad \text{iff}$$

$$\text{(6.6)} \qquad E\{\tilde{x}(t|t_o)\circ(y(\sigma)-y(\tau))\} = 0 \text{ for } 0 \le \tau \le \sigma \le t_o.$$

Suppose that (6.6) holds. Then (6.5) holds whenever

$$x(t,t_o) = \int_0^{t_o} B_o(t,s)dy(s)$$

where $B_o(t,s)$ is a step function in s, since

$$E\{\tilde{x}(t|t_o)\circ \sum_i B_i(t)(y(t_{i+1})-y(t_i))\} = \sum_i E\{\tilde{x}(t|t_o)\circ(y(t_{i+1})-y(t_i))\}B_i^*$$

We extend this to general $B \in \mathcal{B}^2(0,t_o;\mathcal{L}(R^k,H))$, by approximating it by a sequence of step functions $\{B_n(t,\cdot)\}$ such that

$$\int_0^{t_o} \|B(t,s) - B_n(t,s)\|^2 ds \to 0 \text{ as } n \to \infty$$

and using Lemma 5.27(b).

Suppose that (6.5) holds and choose $B(t,s) = \begin{cases} B(t); & 0 \le \tau \le s \le \sigma \le t_o \\ 0 & \text{elsewhere} \end{cases}$

for $B(t) \in \mathcal{L}(R^k,H)$. Then we have

$$E\{\tilde{x}(t|t_o)\circ x(t,t_o)\} = E\{\tilde{x}(t|t_o)\circ(y(\sigma)-y(\tau))\}B^*(t) = 0,$$

and in particular for $B(t) = E\{\tilde{x}(t|t_o) \circ (y(\sigma)-y(\tau))\}$. So (6.6) holds.

Corollary 6.3

$E\{\tilde{x}(t|t_o) \circ \hat{x}(s)\} = 0$ for $s < t_o$

In finite dimensions it has proved particularly useful to introduce an innovations process, which in the linear case is essentially a Wiener process on the information field generated by the observation process [15]. The appropriate innovations process for (6.1),(6.2) is given by

$$\rho(t,\omega) = y(t,\omega) - \int_0^t C\hat{x}(s,\omega)ds. \tag{6.7}$$

This contains the same information as the observation process in the following sense:

Lemma 6.4

For all $M \in Y = \mathcal{B}^2(0,t;\ \mathcal{L}(R^k,H))$, there exists a unique $N \in Y$ such that

$$\int_0^t N(s)d\rho(s,\omega) = \int_0^t M(s)dy(s,\omega)$$

and conversely.

Proof

For any $N \in Y$, from (6.6) we have

$$\begin{aligned}\int_0^t N(s)d\rho(s,\omega) &= \int_0^t N(s)dy(s,\omega) - \int_0^t N(s)C\hat{x}(s,\omega)ds\\ &= \int_0^t N(s)dy(s,\omega) - \int_0^t N(s)C\int_0^s K(s,\alpha)dy(\alpha,\omega)ds \\ &= \int_0^t N(s)dy(s,\omega) - \int_0^t\int_\alpha^t N(s)CK(s,\alpha)ds\ dy(\alpha,\omega)\end{aligned} \tag{6.8}$$

by Lemma 5.29 and using Fubini's theorem.

For given $M \in Y$, consider the following operator integral equation for $N \in Y$:

$$(6.9) \qquad M(\alpha)b = N(\alpha)b - \int_\alpha^t N(s)CK(s,\alpha)b\,ds, \quad b \in R^k$$

Now
$$M^*(\alpha)h = N^*(\alpha)h - \int_\alpha^t K^*(s,\alpha)C^*N^*(s)h\,ds; \; h \in H$$

is a Volterra integral equation for $N^* \in \mathcal{B}^2(0,t;\mathcal{L}(H,R^k))$ and it has a unique solution since

$$\int_0^t \int_\alpha^t \|K^*(s,\alpha)C^*\|^2 ds\,d\alpha < \infty.$$

Hence (6.9) has a unique solution $N \in Y$ for a given $M \in Y$, and from (6.8)

$$\int_0^t N(s)d\rho(s,\omega) = \int_0^t M(s)dy(s,\omega) \quad .$$

The converse is proved similarly.

We now have an alternative way of expressing our best linear primal estimates, which will be particularly useful in solving the smoothing and prediction problems.

<u>Corollary 6.5</u>

The best primal linear estimate may also be represented by

$$\hat{x}(t|t_0) = \int_0^{t_0} G(t,s)d\rho(s,\omega)$$

for some $G(t,\cdot) \in \mathcal{B}^2(0,t_0;\mathcal{L}(R^k,H))$.

<u>Corollary 6.6</u>

$\hat{x}(t|t_0)$ is a solution to the primal linear estimation problem if and only if

$$E\{\tilde{x}(t|t_0)\circ(\rho(\sigma)-\rho(\tau))\} = 0 \; ; \quad 0 \leq \tau \leq \sigma \leq t_0.$$

Now we specialize our attention to the filtering problem which means finding a $K(t,\cdot) \in \mathcal{B}^2(0,t;\mathcal{L}(R^k,H))$ satisfying Lemma 6.2. We shall see that this $K(t,\cdot)$ is the solution of a Generalized Wiener Hopf equation.

Lemma 6.7

Under the assumptions of our problem the following integral equation has a unique solution $K(t,\cdot) \in \mathcal{B}^2(0,t;\ \mathcal{L}(R^k,H))$ for $t \in [0,t_1]$

$$(6.10)\quad \int_0^t K(t,s)C\Lambda(s,\sigma)C^* b\, ds + K(t,\sigma)FVF^* b = \Lambda(t,\sigma)C^* b,\ b \in R^k.$$

Proof

Let $t \in [0,t_1]$ be fixed and define $M \in \mathcal{L}(H,L^2(0,t;R^k))$, $N \in \mathcal{L}(L^2(0,t;R^k))$ by

$$(Mf)(\sigma) = C\Lambda(\sigma,t)f(\sigma)$$

$$(Nf)(\sigma) = FVF^* f(\sigma) + \int_0^t C\Lambda(\sigma,s)C^* f(s)ds.$$

Since $(FVF^*)^{-1}$ exists and since $\Lambda(\sigma,s)$ is symmetric, N is strictly positive, self adjoint and N^{-1} exists. Define $K(t,\cdot) = (N^{-1}M)^*$ and $k(\sigma) = K(t,\sigma)^* h$ for $h \in H$.

Then $(Nk)(\sigma) = Mh(\sigma)$ and

$$FVF^* k(\sigma) + \int_0^t C\Lambda(\sigma,s)C^* k(s)ds = C\Lambda(\sigma,t)h.$$

Substituting $k(s) = K^*(t,\sigma)h$, we obtain $K(t,\cdot) \in \mathcal{B}^2(0,t;\ \mathcal{L}(R^k,H))$ which satisfies (6.10). The uniqueness of $K(t,\cdot)$ follows from the linearity of (6.10).

We now establish the connection of this Wiener Hopf equation to the primal linear filtering problem.

Lemma 6.8

There is a solution $\hat{x}(t) = \int_0^t K(t,s)dy(s)$ to the primal linear filtering problem if and only if (6.10) has a solution.

Proof

Necessity

Suppose that there is a solution to the filtering problem given by

$$\hat{x}(t) = \int_0^t K(t,s)dy(s)$$

and introduce the process

(6.11) $$\eta(\sigma) = \int_0^\sigma Cx(s)ds = y(\sigma) - y(0) - \int_0^\sigma F\ dv(s).$$

Then from Lemmas 5.27, 6.1 and the independence of x_0, v and w, we have

(6.12) $$\begin{aligned}\frac{d}{d\sigma}(E\{\tilde{x}(t) \circ \eta(\sigma)\}) &= E\{\tilde{x}(t) \circ Cx(\sigma)\} \\ &= \bar{\Lambda}(t,\sigma)C^* - \int_0^t K(t,s)C\Lambda(s,\sigma)C^* ds\end{aligned}$$

But from Lemma 6.4,

$$\begin{aligned}E\{\tilde{x}(t) \circ \eta(\sigma)\} &= -E\{\tilde{x}(t) \circ \int_0^\sigma Fdv(s)\} \\ &= \int_0^\sigma K(t,s)FVF^* ds \quad \text{by Lemma 5.27 and}\end{aligned}$$

since z_0, v and w are independent.

Hence $$\frac{d}{d\sigma}(E\{\tilde{x}(t) \circ \eta(\sigma)\}) = K(t,\sigma)FVF^*.$$

Equating this to (6.10) shows that $K(t,\cdot)$ is a solution to (6.10).

Sufficiency

Suppose now that $K_0(t,\cdot)$ is the solution to (6.10). Then from Lemma 6.4 it suffices to show that $\hat{x}(t) = \int_0^t K_0(t,s)dy(s)$ satisfies

(6.13) $$E\{\tilde{x}(s) \circ (y(\sigma)-y(\tau))\} = 0 \quad \text{for } 0 \le \tau \le \sigma \le t.$$

From the linearity, we may assume $\tau = 0$ without loss of generality.

Now $$\begin{aligned}E\{\tilde{x}(t) \circ x(\sigma)\} &= E\{\tilde{x}(t) \circ \eta(\sigma)\} + E\{\tilde{x}(t) \circ \int_0^\sigma Fdv(s)\} \text{ from (6.11)} \\ &= \int_0^\sigma [\Lambda(t,\sigma)C^* - \int_0^t K_0(t,s)C\Lambda(s,\alpha)C^* ds]d\alpha \\ &\qquad - \int_0^\sigma K_0(t,s)FVF^* ds\end{aligned}$$

by (6.12) and Lemma 5.27 and the independence of x_0,v and w,

$$= 0$$

since $K_o(t,s)$ is the solution to (6.10). So (6.13) is established.

We now obtain equations for the best primal linear filter by exploiting the results on the Riccati equation obtained in §4.

Theorem 6.9

$K(t,s) = Y(t,s)P(s)C^*(FVF^*)^{-1}$ is the unique solution to (6.10) where $P(t)$ is the unique solution of the Riccati equation

$$(6.14)\quad \begin{cases} \frac{d}{dt}\langle P(t)h,k\rangle - \langle P(t)h,A^*k\rangle - \langle A^*h,P(t)k\rangle - \langle DWD^*h,k\rangle \\ \qquad\qquad + \langle P(t)C^*(FVF^*)^{-1}CP(t)h,k\rangle = 0 \\ P(0) = P_o, \quad h,\ k \in D(A^*) \end{cases}$$

and $Y(t,s)$ is the perturbation evolution operator of S_t by $-P(t)C^*(FVF^*)^{-1}C$.

Proof

(a) First we establish the existence and uniqueness for (6.14). Writing $Q(s) = P(t_1-s)$ and $t = t_1-s$, we obtain

$$\frac{d}{ds}\langle Q(s)h,k\rangle + \langle Q(s)h,A^*k\rangle + \langle A^*h,Q(s)k\rangle + \langle DWD^*h,k\rangle$$
$$= \langle Q(s)C^*(FVF^*)^{-1}CQ(s)h,k\rangle$$
$$Q(t_1) = P_o$$

and this has a unique solution $Q(s)$ which is self adjoint and positive and strongly continuous in t by Lemma 4.6.

So $P(t)$ and $Y(t,s)$ are well-defined and from Corollary 4.7,(4.24), $P(t)$ is also given by

$$(6.15)\qquad P(t)h = Y(t,0)P_oS_t^*h + \int_o^t Y(t,s)DWD^*S_{t-s}^*h\,ds,\ h \in H.$$

(If $U^*(t,s)$ is the perturbation of S_t^* by $-Q^*(t)BR^{-1}B^*$ in (4.24), we see that $Y(t,s) = U^*(t_1-s,t_1-t)$).

(b) We now show that $K(t,s)$ satisfies (6.10). Writing $C^*(FVF^*)^{-1}C = M$, we have

$$\int_0^t Y(t,s)P(s)M\Lambda(s,\sigma)C^*h\,ds = Y(t,\sigma)\int_0^\sigma Y(\sigma,s)P(s)M\int_0^s S_{s-\tau}DWD^*S^*_{s-\tau}d\tau C^*h\,ds$$

$$+ \int_\sigma^t Y(t,s)P(s)MS_{s-\sigma}\int_0^\sigma S_{\sigma-\tau}DWD^*S^*_{\sigma-\tau}d\tau C^*h\,ds$$

$$+ \int_0^t Y(t,s)P(s)MS_sP_oS^*_\sigma C^*h\,ds \text{ by Lemma 6.1}$$

$$= Y(t,\sigma)\int_0^\sigma\int_\tau^\sigma Y(\sigma,s)P(s)MS_{s-\tau}DWD^*S^*_{\sigma-\tau}C^*h\,ds\,d\tau$$

$$+ (S_{t-\sigma}-Y(t,\sigma))\int_0^\sigma S_{\sigma-\tau}DWD^*S^*_{\sigma-\tau}C^*h\,d\tau$$

$$+ \int_0^t Y(t,s)P(s)MS_sP_oS^*_\sigma C^*h\,ds$$

changing the order of integration and since $Y(t,s)$ is a perturbation of S_t by $-P(t)M$ (see(2.44))

$$= Y(t,\sigma)\int_0^\sigma (S_{\sigma-\tau}-Y(\sigma,\tau))DWD^*S^*_{\sigma-\tau}C^*h\,d\tau$$

$$+ (S_{t-\sigma}-Y(t,\sigma))\int_0^\sigma S_{\sigma-\tau}DWD^*S^*_{\sigma-\tau}C^*h\,d\tau$$

$$+ \int_0^t Y(t,s)P(s)MS_sP_oS^*_\sigma C^*h\,ds$$

using the perturbation argument again

$$= -\int_0^\sigma Y(t,\tau)DWD^*S^*_{\sigma-\tau}C^*h\,d\tau$$

$$+ \int_0^\sigma S_{t-\tau}DWD^*S^*_{\sigma-\tau}C^*h\,d\tau$$

$$+ \int_0^t Y(t,s)P(s)MS_sP_oS^*_\sigma C^*h\,ds$$

$$= -Y(t,\sigma)P(\sigma)C^*h + Y(t,0)P_oS^*_\sigma C^*h$$

$$+ \int_0^t Y(t,s)P(s)MS_sP_oS^*_\sigma C^*h\,ds$$

$$+ \Lambda(t,\sigma)C^*h - S_tP_oS^*_\sigma C^*h$$

by (6.5) and Lemma 6.1.

$$= -Y(t,\sigma)P(\sigma)C^*h + \Lambda(t,\sigma)C^*h$$

since $Y(t,s)$ is the perturbation of S_t by $-P(s)M$. So $K(t,s)$ satisfies (6.10).

We can now prove that our original filtering problem has a unique solution, by showing that the best primal linear filter is exactly the best global filter.

Theorem 6.10

$$E_{Y_t}\{x(t)\} = \hat{x}(t) = \int_0^t Y(t,s)P(s)C^*(FVF^*)^{-1}dy(s)$$

where $P(s)$ is the unique solution of (6.14) and $Y(t,s)$ is the perturbation of S_t by $-P(t)C^*(FVF^*)^{-1}C$.

Proof

From Theorem 6.9 and Lemmas 6.8 and 5.13 since $x(t)$ is Gaussian, we only need to show that $\hat{x}(t)$ is the best linear filter according to Definition 5.11.
For fixed t, let $X = L^2(0,t;R^k)$. Then the best linear estimate of $x(t)$ from $y(s)$; $0 \le s \le t$ is $x_1(t) = Jy(\cdot)$, where $J \in \mathcal{L}(X,H)$ minimizes $E\{\|x(t)-Gy\|_H^2\}$.
So by the orthogonal projections lemma, $\hat{x}(t)$ is the best linear filter if

$$E\{\langle x(t)-\hat{x}(t),Gy\rangle_H\} = 0 \quad \forall\, G \in \mathcal{L}(X,H).$$

So we must show that $E\{\langle\tilde{x}(t),Gy\rangle_H\} = 0 \quad \forall\, G \in \mathcal{L}(X,H)$.
Since H is separable, we may take

$$\tilde{x}(t) = \sum_{i=0}^{\infty} \langle\tilde{x}(t),e_i\rangle e_i$$

for some orthonormal basis $\{e_i\}$ of H. Similarly, for $G \in \mathcal{L}(X,H)$

$$Gy = \sum_{i=0}^{\infty} \langle Gy,e_i\rangle_H e_i = \sum_{i=0}^{\infty} \langle y,G^*e_i\rangle_X e_i$$

Hence $$E\{\langle\tilde{x}(t),Gy\rangle_H\} = \sum_{i=0}^{\infty} E\{\langle y,G^*e_i\rangle_X \langle\tilde{x}(t),e_i\rangle_H\}$$
$$= 0$$

iff $\langle\tilde{x}(t),e_i\rangle_H$ and $\langle y,G^*e_i\rangle_X$ are orthogonal $\forall\, i$.

This is so if $\langle\tilde{x}(t),e_i\rangle_H$ and $\int_0^t \langle y(s),f(s)\rangle_X\, ds$ are orthogonal $\forall\, f \in X$.

Suppose f is a step function, then

$$\int_0^t \langle f(s),y(s)\rangle_X ds = \Sigma\, f_j'(y(t_{j+1})-y(t_j)),\quad f_j \in R^k.$$

But

$$E\{\langle e_i,\tilde{x}(t)\rangle_H f_j'(y(t_{j+1})-y(t_j))\} = \langle e_i, E\{\tilde{x}(t)\circ(y(t_{j+1})-y(t_j))\}f_j\rangle_H$$

$$= 0 \text{ by Lemma 6.4 since } t \geq t_{j+1}.$$

The step functions are dense in $L^2(0,t;R^k)$ and so for all $f \in X$ $\langle\tilde{x}(t),e_i\rangle$ and $\int_0^t \langle y(s),f(s)\rangle ds$ are orthogonal. We can also express the optimal filter in terms of the innovations process.

Corollary 6.11

The global optimal filter is also given by

$$\hat{x}(t) = \int_0^t S_{t-s}P(s)C^*(FVF^*)^{-1}d\rho(s,\omega).$$

Proof

From Corollary 6.5 there exists a $G(t,\cdot) \in \mathcal{B}^2(0,t;\mathcal{L}(R^k,H))$ such that

$$\hat{x}(t) = \int_0^t G(t,s)d\rho(s,\omega).$$

It is readily verified that $G(t,s) = S_{t-s}P(s)C^*(FVF^*)^{-1}$ is the solution, using the fact that $Y(t,s)$ is the perturbation of S_t given by

$$Y(t,s)h = S_{t-s}h - \int_s^t S_{t-\alpha}P(\alpha)C^*(FVF^*)^{-1}CY(\alpha,s)h\, d\alpha,\quad h \in H.$$

(see Theorem 2.27).

$P(t)$ has the physical interpretation as being the covariance operator function for the error process.

Lemma 6.12

(a) $P(t) = E\{\tilde{x}(t)\circ\tilde{x}(t)\}$ and

(b) $E\{\|\tilde{x}(t)\|^2\} = \text{trace}\,\{P(t)\}$.

Proof

(a) By Lemma 6.4,

$$Q(t) = E\{\tilde{x}(t) \circ \tilde{x}(t)\} = E\{\tilde{x}(t) \circ x(t)\}$$

$$= \Lambda(t,t) - E\{\int_0^t K(t,s)dy(s) \circ x(s)\} \text{ by Lemma 6.1 and Theorem 6.1.}$$

$$= \Lambda(t,t) - E\{\int_0^t K(t,s)Cx(s)ds \circ x(t)\} \text{ since } v \text{ is independent of } x_o \text{ and } w.$$

$$= \Lambda(t,t) - \int_0^t K(t,s)C\Lambda(s,t)ds \text{ by Lemma 6.1.}$$

So since K(t,s) satisfies (6.10)(Theorem 6.9),

$$Q(t)C^* = K(t,t)FVF^*C^*$$

$$= P(t)C^* \quad \text{by Theorem 6.9.}$$

So $Y(t,s)$ is also the perturbation of S_t by $-Q(t)C^*(FVF^*)^{-1}C$.

Now for $s > t$, $\Lambda(s,t)$ is obtained from (6.4)

$$\Lambda(s,t)h = S_s P_o S_t^* h + \int_0^t S_{s-\rho} DWD^* S_{t-\rho}^* h \, d\rho$$

and since $Y(s,\rho)$ is the perturbation of S_s by $-Q(t)C^*(FVF^*)^{-1}C$, from (2.44)

$$S_{s-\rho}h = Y(s,\rho)h + \int_0^s Y(s,\alpha)Q(\alpha)C^*(FVF^*)^{-1}CS_{\alpha-\rho}h \, d\alpha$$

Substituting this expression for $S_{s-\rho}$ and S_s in (a) and then these versions of $\Lambda(t,t)$ and $\Lambda(s,t)$ into our expression for $Q(t)$ yields

$$Q(t)h = Y(t,0)P_o S_t^* h + \int_0^t Y(t,s)DWD^* S_{t-s}^* h \, ds$$

So $Q(t)$ satisfies (6.15), but since (6.15) has the unique solution $P(t)$, $P(t) = Q(t)$.

(b) This follows from the definition of the tensor product operator $\circ$.

6.2 Stability of the filter

Of practical importance is whether or not the filter is stable in some sense as $t \to \infty$. A partial answer to this question is obtained from Lemma 4.19 using the duality between the control and filtering problems introduced in the proof of Theorem 6.9.

Corollary 6.13

If $(A, DW^{\frac{1}{2}})$ and (A^*, C^*) are stabilizable, then as $t \to \infty$, $P(t)$ converges strongly to P_∞, the unique solution of the algebraic Riccati equation

$$(6.16)\qquad \begin{aligned} &\langle P_\infty h, A^* k\rangle + \langle A^* h, P_\infty k\rangle + \langle DWD^* h, k\rangle \\ &\qquad = \langle P_\infty C^* (FVF^*)^{-1} C P_\infty h, k\rangle \quad \text{for } h,k \in D(A^*). \end{aligned}$$

In fact we shall have a stronger result which shows that not only does our filter $\hat{x}(t)$ produce desirable asymptotic properties for the error process, but it is also insensitive to modelling errors in the initial state x_0. To make this more precise we introduce the following definitions.

For an arbitrary H-valued random variable we define the following

$$(6.17)\qquad f(\eta,t) = S_t \eta + \int_0^t S_{t-\alpha} D dw(\alpha)$$

$$(6.18)\qquad y(\eta,t) = \int_0^t C f(\eta,s) ds + Fv(t)$$

$$(6.19)\qquad \tilde{K}y(\eta,t) = \int_0^t Y(t,s) P(s) C^* (FVF^*)^{-1} dy(\eta,s).$$

We call the map $\tilde{K}$ the 'Kalman' filter and note that if $\eta = x_0$ is Gaussian and second order with zero mean, (6.19) coincides with $\hat{x}(t)$ of Theorem 6.10. However for general η, (6.19) will not be Gaussian or second order. Using (2.36), the following representation for the error process $e(\eta,t)$ is obtained.

$$(6.20)\qquad \begin{aligned} e(\eta,t) &= f(\eta,t) - \tilde{K}y(\eta,t) \\ &= Y(t,0)\eta + \int_0^t Y(t,\alpha) D dw(\alpha) + \int_0^t Y(t,\alpha) P(\alpha) C^* (FVF^*)^{-1} F dv(\alpha). \end{aligned}$$

Definition 6.14 Stability of the 'Kalman' Filter

For any H-valued random variable η, let $\mu_t(\eta)$ be the measure induced on $\mathcal{B}(H)$, the Borel sets of H, by $e(\eta,t)$. Then the 'Kalman' filter is stable if there exists a measure μ on $\mathcal{B}(H)$ such that $\mu_t(\eta)$ converges to μ in the weak topology on H as $t \to \infty$. In order to prove our stability result we need the following preliminary results.

Lemma 6.15

Let X be a topological space and $\{\mu_t; 0 \le t < \infty\}$ a family of measures on $\mathcal{B}(X)$ with $\sup_{0 \le t < \infty} \mu_t(X) < \infty$. Suppose there exists an increasing sequence Σ_m in $\mathcal{B}(X)$ such that

(a) Σ_m is compact, separable and metrizable for each m

(b) $\mu_t(X \setminus \Sigma_m) \to 0$ weakly as $m \to \infty$ uniformly in m on $[0,\infty)$.

Then μ_t is weakly sequentially precompact.

Proof

This is proved in [28] for X a complete separable metric space, but the proof carries over provided the Σ_m's are separable and metrizable.

Lemma 6.16

If $(A, DW^{\frac{1}{2}})$ and (A^*, C^*) are stabilizable and $Y(t,s)$ is the perturbation of S_t by $-P(t)C^*(FVF^*)^{-1}C$, then $\|Y(t,0)\| \to 0$ as $t \to \infty$.

Proof

Since C has finite dimensional range, $C^*(FVF^*)^{-1}C$ can be represented by

$$C^*(FVF^*)^{-1}Ch = \sum_{i=1}^{k} \langle c_i, h \rangle b_i \quad \text{for all } h \in H$$

for some integer k and some set $\{b_1, \ldots, b_k, c_1, \ldots, c_k\}$ in H.

Hence

$$\|P(t)C^*(FVF^*)^{-1}C - P_\infty C^*(FVF^*)^{-1}C\|$$

$$\le \sum_{k=1}^{\infty} \|(P(t) - P_\infty)c_i\| \, \|b_i\| \tag{6.21}$$

$$\to 0 \text{ as } t \to \infty \text{ by Corollary 6.5.}$$

Let S_t^∞ denote the semigroup generated by $A-P_\infty C^*(FVF^*)^{-1}C$ then by the perturbation property (2.36), we have

$$Y(t+\delta,t)h = S_\delta^\infty h - \int_t^{t+\delta} S_{t+\delta-s}^\infty (P(s)-P_\infty)C^*(FVF^*)^{-1}C\, Y(s,t)h\, ds$$

$$= S_\delta^\infty h - \int_0^\delta S_{\delta-s}^\infty (P(s+t)-P_\infty)C^*(FVF^*)^{-1}C\, Y(t+s,t)h\, ds$$

Writing $g(s) = \|Y(t+s,t)\|$, we have

$$g(\delta) \leq \|S_\delta^\infty\| + c_1 \int_0^\delta \|S_{\delta-s}^\infty\| g(s)ds$$

for some $c_1 > 0$ by (6.21)

$$\leq c_2 e^{-\omega\delta} + c_2 \int_0^\delta e^{-\omega(\delta-s)} g(s)ds$$

for some $c_2 > 0$, $\omega > 0$ since S_t^∞ is exponentially stable by the dual of Corollary 4.17.

By Gronwall's inequality Lemma, we obtain

$$g(\delta) \leq c_2(e^{-\omega\delta} + \int_0^\delta e^{-\omega(\delta-s)} e^{-\omega\delta} \exp(\int_s^\delta e^{-\omega(\delta-\alpha)} d\alpha) ds$$

So $g(\delta) \leq \text{const}\ e^{-\omega\delta}$ and $\|Y(t+\delta,t)\| \leq ce^{-\omega\delta}$ for all $t > 0$, $\delta > 0$, which proves the lemma.

We can now establish the stability of the 'Kalman' filter in the sense of Definition 6.14.

Theorem 6.17

If $(A,DW^{\frac{1}{2}})$ and (A^*,C^*) are stabilizable, then the 'Kalman' filter is stable.

Proof

Decompose $e(\eta,t) = a(t) + e(x_o,t)$, where $a(t) = Y(t,0)(\eta-x_o)$ and x_o is a zero mean Gaussian random variable with covariance P_o and is independent of w and v.

First we establish that

(6.22) $\quad P\{\|a(t)\| \leq m\} \to 1$ as $m \to \infty$ uniformly in t on $[0,\infty)$.

Introducing $\Sigma_m = \{h \in H: \|h\| \leq m\}$, we have that $H = \bigcup_{m=1}^{\infty} \Sigma_m$.

Since the measure induced by $\eta - x_o$ on $\mathcal{B}(H)$ is sigma additive, we have

$$P\{\|x_o - \eta\| \leq m\} \to 1 \text{ as } m \to \infty.$$

Hence

$$P\{\|a(t)\| \leq m\} \geq P\{\|Y(t,0)\| \, \|x_o - \eta\| \leq m\}$$

$$\to 1 \text{ as } m \to \infty \text{ uniformly in } t \text{ by}$$

Lemma 6.16.

We now prove that

$$(6.23) \qquad P\{\|e(x_o,t)\| \leq m\} \to 1 \text{ as } m \to \infty \text{ uniformly in } t \text{ on } [0,\infty).$$

Since $E\{e(x_o,t)\} = 0$, by Tchebychev's inequality, we have

$$P\{\|e(x_o,t)\| \geq \tfrac{1}{m}\} \leq \tfrac{1}{m^2} E\{\|e(x_o,t)\|\}$$

$$\leq \tfrac{1}{m^2} E\{\|e(x_o,t)\|^2\}$$

$$= \tfrac{1}{m^2} \operatorname{trace}\{P(t)\} \text{ by Lemma 6.12.}$$

So (6.23) holds if we establish that trace $\{P(t)\}$ is uniformly bounded in norm on $[0,\infty)$. Exploiting the duality between the control and filtering problems, from (4.76) we deduce that

$$\langle P(t)h,h\rangle \leq \langle S_t^{\infty *}h, P_o S_t^{\infty *}h\rangle + \int_0^t \langle S_s^{\infty *}h, DWD^* S_s^{\infty *}h\rangle \, ds$$

$$+ \int_0^t \langle S_s^{\infty *}h, P_\infty C^* (FVF^*)^{-1} C P_\infty S_s^{\infty *}h\rangle \, ds$$

and since P_o, W and $(FVF^*)^{-1}$ are trace class, we have

$$\operatorname{trace}\{P(t)\} \leq \|S_t^\infty\|^2 \operatorname{trace}\{P_o\} +$$

$$\left(\|D\|^2 \operatorname{trace}\{W\} + \|CP_\infty\|^2 \operatorname{trace}\{(FVF^*)^{-1}\}\right) \int_0^t \|S_s^\infty\|^2 \, ds$$

Hence trace $\{P(t)\}$ is uniformly bounded in norm, since S_s^∞ is exponentially stable.

Combining (6.22) and (6.23), we deduce that

(6.24) $\quad P\{\|e(\eta,t)\| \le m\} \to 1$ as $m \to \infty$ uniformly in t on $[0,\infty)$.

The family $\{\Sigma_m; m=1,\ldots,\}$ satisfies condition (a) of Lemma 6.15 with respect to the weak topology on H by standard results on weak topologies |28|. If μ_t is the measure induced on $\mathcal{B}(H)$ by $e(\eta,t)$, then from (6.24), $\mu_t(\Sigma_m) \to 1$ as $m \to \infty$ uniformly in t on $[0,\infty)$ and so by Lemma 6.15, $\{\mu_t;\ t \ge 0\}$ is weakly sequentially compact.

Let $\{t_j\}$ be any sequence increasing to infinity, then there exists a subsequence which we also write as $\{t_j\}$ such that $\mu_{t_j} \to \bar{\mu}$ weakly, where $\bar{\mu}$ is some measure on $\mathcal{B}(H)$.

Since $\eta \to \exp i\langle\eta,h\rangle$ is a weakly continuous bounded functional on H for each fixed $h \in H$, we have

(6.25) $$\chi_{\mu_{t_j}}(h) \to \chi_{\bar{\mu}}(h) \text{ as } j \to \infty$$

where χ_μ is the characteristic functional of the measure μ. (See Definition 5.3).

From Lemma 6.12, $e(x_o,t)$ is a zero mean Gaussian random variable with covariance operator $P(t)$, and hence from Theorem 5.5

$$\chi_{e(x_o,t)}(h) = \exp(-\tfrac{1}{2}\langle P(t)h,h\rangle)$$

and by Corollary 6.13, we have

(6.26) $\quad E\{\exp i\langle e(x_o,t),h\rangle\} \to \exp(-\tfrac{1}{2}\langle P_\infty h,h\rangle)$ as $t \to \infty$.

Now
$$\begin{aligned}\chi_{\mu_t}(h) &= E\{\exp i\langle a(t)+e(x_o,t),h\rangle\}\\ &= E\{\exp i\langle e(x_o,t),h\rangle\} + E\{(\exp(i\langle a(t),h\rangle)-1)\\ &\qquad\qquad \exp i\langle e(x_o,t),h\rangle\}\\ &\to \exp -\tfrac{1}{2}\langle P_\infty h,h\rangle \text{ as } t \to \infty\end{aligned}$$

from (6.26) and the second term converges to zero, since $a(t) \to 0$ almost surely as $t \to \infty$ as a consequence of Lemma 6.16.

Combining the result with (6.25), we obtain

$$\chi_{\mu_{t_j}}(h) \to \chi_{\bar{\mu}}(h) = \exp(-\tfrac{1}{2}\langle P_\infty h,h\rangle) \quad \text{as } j \to \infty.$$

This is true for all convergent subsequences μ_{t_j} and since the characteristic function uniquely determines the measure $\bar{\mu}$, all subsequences converge to a unique measure $\bar{\mu}$, which is zero mean and Gaussian with covariance P_∞ from Theorem 5.5.

6.3 Smoothing and prediction estimators

We now consider the smoothing and prediction problems, both of which depend on the Kalman filter and the following rather surprising result.

Theorem 6.18

The innovations process is a k-dimensional Wiener process with incremental covariance FVF^* relative to the sigma field $\mathcal{Y}_s$ generated by the observation process $\{y(s);\ 0 \le s \le t\}$.

Proof

From Theorem 6.10, $\hat{x}(t) = E_{Y_t}\{x(t)\}$ and so

$$\rho_i(t,\omega) = y_i(t,\omega) - \int_0^t E_{Y_s}\{(Cx(s))_i\}ds$$

Now

$$E_{Y_s}\{y_i(t)-y_i(s)\} = E_{Y_s}\{\int_s^t (Cx(\alpha))_i d\alpha\} + E_{Y_s}\{\int_s^t Fdv(\alpha)\}$$

$$= E_{Y_s}\{\int_s^t E_{Y_\alpha}\{(Cx(\alpha))_i\}d\alpha\}$$

since by property (5.7) of conditional expectations

$$E_{Y_s}\{\int_s^t F_{ij}\, dv_j(\alpha)\} = E_{Y_s}\{E_{r_s}\{\int_s^t F_{ij}dv(\alpha)\}\}$$

$$\text{where } r(s) = (z_0,w(s),v(s))'$$

and $E_{r_s}\{\int_s^t F_{ij}dv_j(\alpha)\} = 0$ by the independent increment property of v_j.

Hence

$$E_{Y_s}\{y_i(t)-y_i(s) - \int_s^t E_{Y_\alpha}\{(Cx(\alpha))_i\}d\alpha\} = 0 \quad \text{w.p.1.}$$

and $\{\rho_i(t,\omega),\mathcal{Y}_t\}$ is a real martingale process; $i = 1,.,k$.
Consider the local semi martingale $\beta_i(t)$; $i = 1,.,k$, given by

$$\beta_i(t) = \int_0^t (F^{-1}Cx(\alpha))_i d\alpha + v_i(t) \qquad \text{or} \tag{6.27}$$

$$\beta_i(t) = \int_0^t E_{Y_\alpha}\{(F^{-1}Cx(\alpha))_i\}d\alpha + (F^{-1}\rho(t))_i \tag{6.28}$$

Then $\beta_i(t)$ is a local semi martingale relative to $\mathcal{Y}_t$ and $\mathcal{F}_t$, where $\mathcal{F}_t$ is the sigma field generated by $\{v_i(s),(F^{-1}Cx(s))_i;\ i=1,.,k;\ 0 \le s \le t\}$.
Applying the differentiation rule for local semi martingales [18], we obtain

$$\beta_i^2(t) = 2\int_0^t \beta_i(s)d\beta_i(s) + \langle v_i,v_i\rangle_t \qquad \text{from (6.27) and}$$

$$\beta_i^2(t) = 2\int_0^t \beta_i(s)d\beta_i(s) + \langle (F^{-1}\rho)_i,(F^{-1}\rho)_i\rangle_t \text{from (6.28).}$$

Hence $\langle (F^{-1}\rho)_i,(F^{-1}\rho)_i\rangle_t = \langle v_i,v_i\rangle_t$, where $\langle ,\rangle_t$ is the increasing process associated with a scalar continuous martingale ([18]).
Now using the product rule on $\beta_i(t)\beta_j(t)$, we obtain

$$\beta_i(t)\beta_j(t) = \int_0^t \beta_i(t)d\beta_j(t) + \int_0^t \beta_j(t)d\beta_i(t) + \langle v_i,v_j\rangle_t \text{ from (6.27)}$$

$$\beta_i(t)\beta_j(t) = \int_0^t \beta_i(t)d\beta_j(t) + \int_0^t \beta_j(t)d\beta_i(t) + \langle (F^{-1}\rho)_i,(F^{-1}\rho)_j\rangle_t$$
from (6.28).

Hence $\langle (F^{-1}\rho)_i,(F^{-1}\rho)_j\rangle_t = \langle v_i,v_j\rangle_t = 0$ since v_i and v_j are independent.

From the uniqueness of the increasing process for a Wiener process, we see that $F^{-1}\rho(t)$ is a k-valued Wiener process relative to $\mathcal{Y}_t$ and has the same incremental matrix as $v(t)$. That is $\rho(t)$ is a k-valued Wiener process relative to $\mathcal{Y}_t$ with incremental covariance matrix $(FVF^*)^{-1}$.

Using this representation for the innovations process we obtain the optimal predictor and smoother as stochastic integrals with respect to a Wiener process.

<u>Theorem 6.19</u> <u>Optimal predictor</u>

The optimal predictor is given by

$$\hat{x}(t|t_o) = S_{t-t_o}\hat{x}(t_o) \quad \text{for } t > t_o.$$

<u>Proof</u>

As in Theorem 6.10 we can show that the best primal linear predictor is in fact the best global predictor, so from Corollary 6.5 we seek

$$\hat{x}(t|t_o) = \int_o^{t_o} G(t,s)d\rho(s,\omega)$$

for some $G(t,\cdot) \in \mathcal{B}^2(0,t_o;\mathcal{L}(R^k,H))$.

Now $$E\{x(t) \circ \rho(s)\} = E\{\hat{x}(t|t_o) \circ \rho(s)\} \text{ for } 0 \leq s \leq t_o < t \leq t_1$$
by Corollary 6.6

$$= E\{\int_o^{t_o} G(t,s)d\rho(s,\omega) \circ \int_o^s d\rho(\alpha)\}$$

$$= \int_o^s G(t,\alpha)FVF^* d\alpha$$ by Theorem 6.18 and Lemma Lemma 5.27.

Hence
$$G(t,s)FVF^* = \frac{\partial}{\partial s} E\{x(t) \circ \rho(s)\} \quad \text{for } 0 \leq s \leq t_o \leq t.$$

But $$E\{x(t) \circ \rho(s)\} = E\{x(t) \circ (\int_o^s C\tilde{x}(\alpha)d\alpha + \int_o^s Fdv(\alpha))\}$$ from (6.7)

$$= E\{x(t) \circ \int_o^s C\tilde{x}(\alpha)d\alpha\}$$ since x_o, w and v are independent.

So
$$\frac{\partial}{\partial s} E\{x(t) \circ \rho(s)\} = E\{x(t) \circ \tilde{x}(s)\}C^*$$

$$= S_{t-s}E\{x(s) \circ \tilde{x}(s)\}C^* - E\{\int_s^t S_{t-\alpha}Ddw(\alpha) \circ \tilde{x}(s)\}C^*$$

$$= S_{t-s}E\{\tilde{x}(s) \circ \tilde{x}(s)\}C^*$$

since w has independent increments and is independent of x_o, v and by Lemma 6.4.

Hence by Lemma 6.12 we have

$$G(t,s)FVF^* = S_{t-s}P(s) \quad \text{for } s \leq t_o \leq t \text{ and}$$

$$\hat{x}(t|t_o) = \int_o^{t_o} S_{t-s}P(s)(FVF^*)^{-1}d\rho(s,\omega)$$

$$= S_{t-t_o}\hat{x}(t_o) \qquad \text{by Corollary 6.11.}$$

Theorem 6.20 Optimal smoother

The optimal smoother is given by

$$\hat{x}(t|t_o) = \hat{x}(t) + P(t)\lambda(t)$$

where P(t) is the unique solution of (6.14) and $\lambda(t)$ is given by

$$\lambda(t) = \int_t^{t_o} Y^*(s,t)C^*(FVF^*)^{-1}d\rho(s,\omega)$$

where Y(t,s) is the perturbation of S_t by $-P(t)C^*(FVF^*)^{-1}C$.

Proof

As for the predictor, we need only show that $\hat{x}(t|t_o)$ is the best primal linear smoother and from Corollary 6.4 we have

$$\hat{x}(t|t_o) = \int_o^{t_o} G(t,s)d\rho(s,\omega)$$

for some $G \in \mathcal{B}^2(0,t_o; \mathcal{L}(R^k,H))$.

Now arguing as in Theorem 6.19 for $s \leq t_o$ we have

$$G(t,s) = \frac{\partial}{\partial s} E\{x(t)\circ\rho(s)\}(FVF^*)^{-1}$$

$$= E\{x(t)\circ\tilde{x}(s)\}(FVF^*)^{-1}$$

(6.29) $$= E\{\tilde{x}(t)\circ\tilde{x}(s)\}C^*(FVF^*)^{-1} \quad \text{for } s > t$$

by Corollary 6.3.

We now calculate $P(t,s) = E\{\tilde{x}(t) \circ \tilde{x}(s)\}$ for $s > t$:

$$x(s) = S_{s-t}x(t) + \int_t^s S_{s-\alpha}Ddw(\alpha)$$

and

$$\tilde{x}(s) = x(s) - \int_0^s Y(s,\alpha)P(\alpha)C^*(FVF^*)^{-1}dy(\alpha)$$

$$= x(s) - \int_0^s Y(s,\alpha)P(\alpha)C^*(FVF^*)^{-1}(Cx(\alpha)d\alpha - Fdv(\alpha))$$

So

$$\hat{x}(s) = Y(s,t)\hat{x}(t) + \int_t^s Y(s,\alpha)P(\alpha)C^*(FVF^*)^{-1}(Cx(\alpha)d\alpha - Fdv(\alpha))$$

But from (2.44)

$$S_{s-t}h = Y(s,t)h + \int_t^s Y(s,\alpha)P(\alpha)C^*(FVF^*)^{-1}CS_{\alpha-t}h\, d\alpha$$

and hence

$$x(s) - \hat{x}(s) = Y(s,t)\tilde{x}(t) + \int_t^s S_{s-\alpha}Ddw(\alpha) - \int_t^s Fdv(\alpha)$$

and so

$$E\{\tilde{x}(t) \circ \tilde{x}(s)\} = E\{\tilde{x}(t) \circ \tilde{x}(t)\}Y^*(s,t)$$

since

$$E\{\tilde{x}(t) \circ \int_t^s S_{s-\alpha}Ddw(\alpha)\} = 0$$

and

$$E\{\tilde{x}(t) \circ \int_t^s Fdv(\alpha)\} = 0$$

from the independence of x_o, v and w and the independent increment property of w and v.

Thus $P(t,s) = P(t)Y^*(s,t)$ for $s > t$ using Lemma 6.12 and from (6.29).

$$G(t,s) = P(t)Y^*(s,t)C^*(FVF^*)^{-1} \qquad \text{for } s > t$$

and

$$G(t,s) = S_{t-s}P(s)C^*(FVF^*)^{-1}$$ for $s < t$ is proved in Theorem 6.19.

So

$$\hat{x}(t|t_o) = \int_0^{t_o} G(t,s)d\rho(s,\omega)$$

$$= \int_0^t S_{t-s}P(s)C^*(FVF^*)^{-1}d\rho(s,\omega) + \int_t^{t_o} P(t)Y^*(s,t)C^*(FVF^*)^{-1}d\rho(s,\omega)$$

$$= \hat{x}(t) + P(t)\lambda(t) \quad \text{by Corollary 6.11.}$$

6.4 Differential forms for the estimators

In the finite dimensional case the optimal estimators are normally expressed as the solutions of stochastic differential equations rather than integral equations. Because of the complications arising from unbounded operators, we can only express the infinite dimensional estimators in differential form under more restrictive assumptions on the noise processes.

Theorem 6.21

The optimal predictor is the strong solution of the stochastic evolution equation

$$(6.30) \qquad d\hat{x}(t|t_o) = A\hat{x}(t|t_o)dt \;;\; \hat{x}(t|t_o) = \hat{x}(t_o)$$

for $S_t\hat{x}(t_o) \in D(A)$ w.p.1.

Under the additional assumptions

$$(6.31) \qquad S_tP_o \text{ and } S_tDW : H \to D(A) \text{ for } t > 0 \text{ and all } i$$

$$(6.32) \qquad \sum_{i=o}^{\infty} \lambda_i^2 \int_o^{t_1} \|AS_tDe_i\|^2 \, dt < \infty$$

$$(6.33) \qquad \sum_{i=o}^{\infty} \int_o^{t_1} \mu_i^2 \|AS_tf_i\|^2 \, dt < \infty$$

(where $(\lambda_i,e_i),(\mu_i,f_i)$ are the eigenvalues and eigenvectors of the operators W and P_o respectively), the optimal filter $\hat{x}(t)$ is the unique solution of the stochastic evolution equation

$$(6.34) \qquad \begin{cases} d\hat{x}(t) = A\hat{x}(t)dt + P(t)C^*(FVF^*)^{-1}d\rho(t) \\ \hat{x}(0) = 0 \end{cases}$$

and the optimal smoother is the unique solution of

$$(6.35) \qquad \begin{cases} d\hat{x}(t|t_o) = A\hat{x}(t|t_o)dt + DWD^*\lambda(t)dt \\ \hat{x}(t|t_o) = \hat{x}(t_o) \end{cases}$$

where $\lambda(t)$ is given in Theorem 6.20.

Proof

That $\hat{x}(t|t_o)$ of Theorem 6.19 is the unique solution of (6.30) follows from Theorem 5.35. By Theorem 6.18, $\rho(t)$ is a k-dimensional Wiener process with incremental covariance FVF^*, so by Theorem 5.35,(6.34) has a unique solution provided that

$$S_{t-s}P(s)C^*(FVF^*)^{-1} : R^k \to D(A) \qquad \text{and}$$

$$(6.36) \qquad \int_{t_o}^{t} \| AS_{t-s}P(s)C^*(FVF^*)^{-1}b\|^2\, ds < \infty \quad \text{for all } b \in R^k.$$

Now from the adjoint of (6.15),

$$P(t)h = S_tP_oY^*(t,0)h + \int_o^t S_{t-s}DWD^*Y^*(t,s)h\, ds$$

By assumption (6.31),

$$S_tP_oY^*(t,0)h \in D(A)$$

and since A is closed, (6.32) implies that

$$\int_o^t S_{t-s}DWD^*Y^*(t,s)h\, ds \in D(A).$$

Thus

$$S_{t-s}P(s) : H \to D(A) \text{ for } t > s, \text{ and moreover}$$

$$(6.37) \qquad AS_{t-s}P(s)h = AS_tP_oY(s,0)h + \int_o^s AS_{s-\rho}DWD^*Y^*(s,\rho)h\, d\rho$$

provided we can now show that $\int_o^t \|AS_{t-\rho}DWf(\rho)\|\, d\rho < \infty$ for all $f \in L^\infty(0,t;H)$.

Let $f(\rho) = \sum_{i=o}^{\infty} \alpha_i(\rho)e_i$ where $\{e_i\}$ is a complete orthonormal basis for H formed by augmenting the eigenvectors of W.

Then $Wf(\rho) = \sum_{i=o}^{\infty} \lambda_i\alpha_i(\rho)e_i$ and

$$\int_o^t \|AS_{t-\rho}DWf(\rho)\|^2 d\rho \leq \int_o^{t_1} \|\sum_{i=o}^{\infty} \lambda_i\alpha_i(\rho)AS_{t-\rho}De_i\|^2 d\rho$$

$$\leq \int_o^{t_1} (\sum_{i=o}^{\infty} |\alpha_i(\rho)|^2)(\sum_{i=o}^{\infty} \lambda_i^2\|AS_{t-\rho}De_i\|^2 d\rho$$

$$\leq \|f\|_\infty \int_o^{t_1} \sum_{i=o}^{\infty} \lambda_i^2 \|AS_{t-\rho}De_i\|^2 d\rho$$

$$< \infty \quad \text{by (6.32).}$$

Hence (6.37) is established and so $S_{t-s}P(s)C^*(FVF^*)^{-1}: R^k \to D(A)$. Moreover

$$\int_o^s AS_{t-\rho}DWD^*Y^*(s,\rho)h\, d\rho \;\varepsilon\; L^\infty(O,t;H).$$

Using a similar argument to the above, we can also show that (6.33) implies that

$$\int_o^{t_1} \|AS_\rho P_o f(\rho)\|^2 d\rho < \infty \text{ for all } f \;\varepsilon\; L^\infty(O,t;H).$$

Hence (6.36) is established and (6.34) has a unique solution, which is clearly the optimal filter $\hat{x}(t)$ given by Corollary 6.11.

We remark that (6.35) is a degenerate stochastic evolution equation with no 'dw(t)' term, with initial state $\hat{x}(t_o) \;\varepsilon\; D(A)$ w.p.1 from the foregoing. Moreover, (6.31) implies that $S_{t-s}DWD^*\lambda(s) \;\varepsilon\; D(A)$ w.p.1 and so by Theorem 5.35, to show that (6.35) has a unique solution, we need only to establish that

$$\text{(6.38)} \qquad \int_o^t \|AS_{t-s}DWD^*\lambda(s)\| ds < \infty \qquad \text{w.p.1.}$$

Now by Lemma 5.31, $\lambda(t)$ of Theorem 6.20 is in $C(O,t_1;L_2(\Omega,H))$ and so we may expand

$$\text{(6.39)} \qquad D^*\lambda(t) = \sum_{i=o}^{\infty} \alpha_i(t)e_i$$

and

$$\|AS_{t-\rho}DWD^*\lambda(\rho)\|^2 = \|\sum_{i=o}^{\infty} AS_{t-\rho}D\lambda_i\alpha_i(\rho)e_i\|^2$$

$$\leq \left(\sum_{i=o}^{\infty} \|\alpha_i(\rho)\|^2\right)\left(\sum_{i=o}^{\infty} \lambda_i^2\|AS_{t-\rho}De_i\|^2\right)$$

$$= \|D^*\lambda(\rho)\|^2 \left(\sum_{i=o}^{\infty} \lambda_i^2\|AS_{t-\rho}De_i\|^2\right)$$

from (6.39).

Consequently,

$$E\{\int_0^t \|AS_{t-\rho}DWD^*\lambda(\rho)\|^2 d\rho \le \|D\|^2 \sup_{0\le\rho\le t_1} E\{\|\lambda(\rho)\|^2\}\int_0^t \sum_{i=0}^{\infty} \lambda_i^2 \|AS_{t-\rho}De_i\|^2 d\rho$$

$$< \infty$$

by (6.32) and since $\lambda \in C(0,t_1;L^2(\Omega,H))$. This establishes (6.38) and the existence and uniqueness of the solution of (6.35).

6.5 Examples

Example 6.22 Finite dimensional filtering

If we take $H = R^n$, $U = R^m$, then we deduce the finite dimensional Kalman Bucy filter and the usual smoothing and prediction equations. It is interesting to note that the stability result of Theorem 6.17 is the sharpest known for the finite dimensional filter above (c.f. [15]).

Example 6.23 Filtering for the heat equation

We consider the filtering problem for the heat equation of Example 5.39 and suppose that we can observe the process

$$dy(t) = Cx(t)dt + dv(t) \tag{6.39}$$

where v is a scalar Wiener process of unit incremental covariance and the observation map C is defined by

$$Ch = \int_0^1 b(\xi)h(\xi)d\xi \quad \text{for some fixed } b \in L^2(0,1). \tag{6.40}$$

The solution of the Riccati equation (6.14) can be expressed as

$$P(t)h = \sum_{i,j=0}^{\infty}\sum p_{ij}(t)\phi_j\langle h,\phi_i\rangle \qquad \forall\, h \in H \tag{6.41}$$

where $\phi_i(\xi) = \sqrt{2}\cos \pi i\xi$; $i \ge 1$; $\phi_0(\xi) = 1$.

Then (6.14) can be reduced to the infinite system

$$\begin{cases} \dot{p}_{ij}(t) + \pi^2(i^2+j^2)p_{ij}(t) - \lambda_i\delta_{ij} + \sum_{m,n=0}^{\infty}\sum p_{im}(t)p_{jn}(t)\alpha_{mn} = 0 \\ p_{ij}(0) = \delta_{ij}\alpha_i \quad ; \quad i,j = 1,2,\ldots \end{cases} \tag{6.42}$$

where

$$\alpha_{mn} = \left(\int_0^1 b(\xi)\sqrt{2}\cos \pi m\xi \, d\xi\right)\left(\int_0^1 b(\xi)\sqrt{2}\cos n\pi\xi \, d\xi\right); \quad m,n=1,2,\ldots$$

$$\alpha_{mo} = \left(\int_0^1 b(\xi)d\xi\right)\left(\int_0^1 b(\xi)\sqrt{2}\cos m\pi\xi \, d\xi\right); \quad \alpha_{oo} = \left(\int_0^1 b(\xi)d\xi\right)^2$$

Unfortunately, $p_{ij}(t) = 0$ for $i \neq j$ is not a solution of (6.41) in this case and numerical methods for solving (6.42) must be used. (One of these is to truncate the series after N terms and solve for

$$P^N_{ij}(t) \;;\; i,j = 1,\ldots,N).$$

The filter $\hat{x}(t)$ is then given by

$$\hat{x}(t) = \int_0^t Y(t,s)P(s)C^* dy(s)$$

and it is stable since $A = A^*$ generates a stable semigroup.(Example 3.37)

We now examine conditions for $\hat{x}(t)$ to be expressible in differential form. From Example 5.38 we know that $S_t : L^2(0,1) \to D(A), t > 0$, and that

$$AS_{t-s}\phi_i = -\pi^2 i^2 e^{-i^2\pi^2(t-s)}\phi_i$$

So (6.32) holds provided $\sum_{i=1}^{\infty} \lambda_i^2 i^2 < \infty$ and (6.33) holds if $\sum_{i=1}^{\infty} \alpha_i^2 i^2 < \infty$.

Under this additional restriction on the disturbances, $\hat{x}(t)$ is the unique solution of

$$(6.43) \quad \begin{cases} d\hat{x}_i(t) = -\pi^2 i^2 \hat{x}_i(t)dt - \left(2 \sum_{i=o}^{\infty} \sum_{j=o}^{\infty} \sum_{r=o}^{\infty} p_{ij}(t)\hat{x}_r(t)\alpha_{rj}\right)dt \\ \qquad\qquad + 2 \sum_{j=o}^{\infty} p_{ij}(t)\int_0^1 \cos \pi j\xi b(\xi)d\xi \cos \pi i\xi \, dy(t) \\ \hat{x}_i(0) = 0 \end{cases}$$

where $\hat{x}(t) = \sum_{i=1}^{\infty} \hat{x}_i(t)\sqrt{2}\cos \pi i\xi + \hat{x}_o(t)$.

Similarly one can obtain the smoothing estimate as the solution of a stochastic differential equation.

Example 6.24 Wave equation

Consider the noisy wave equation modelled by (5.50) in Example 5.40, and the observation process

$$y(t) = \int_0^t (C\ 0)\begin{pmatrix} x \\ x_s \end{pmatrix} ds + dv(t) \tag{6.44}$$

where C is defined by (6.40), that is

$$y(t) = \int_0^t \int_0^1 x(\xi,s)b(\xi)d\xi\ ds + v(t)$$

Then there exists a unique optimal filter given by Theorem 6.10. It is again possible to obtain a decomposition for P(t) in (6.14) analogously to the decomposition for Q(t) in Example 4.10. From Theorem 6.17, we see that the filter is stable if

$$\left(\mathcal{A}, \begin{pmatrix} 0 \\ W^{\frac{1}{2}} \end{pmatrix}\right) \text{ and } \left(\mathcal{A}^*, \begin{pmatrix} C^* \\ 0 \end{pmatrix}\right)$$

are stabilizable and this is the case by Example 3.37.

From our calculations in Example 5.40, we see that sufficient conditions for the estimators to be strong solutions of differential stochastic evolution equations are that

$$\sum_{i=1}^{\infty} \lambda_i^2 i^2 < \infty$$

for the covariance parameters of the distributed noise $w(\tau)$ and similar conditions on the noise parameters of

$$P_0 = \mathrm{Cov}\begin{pmatrix} x_0 \\ x_1 \end{pmatrix}.$$

Example 6.25 Filtering for delay equations

Consider the stochastic delay system, that is, the $\mathcal{M}^2$ version (5.54) of Example 5.41 and for the observation process take

$$y(t) = \int_0^t Cx(s)ds + v(t) \tag{6.45}$$

where v(t) is a k dimensional Wiener process with unit incremental covariance, x(t) is given by (6.19) and C is given by

$$\text{(6.46)} \qquad Ch = \int_{-b}^{0} k(\theta)h(\theta)d\theta \qquad \text{for } h \in \mathcal{M}^2$$

where $k \in L^2(-b,0; \mathcal{L}(R^n,R^k))$.

We remark that as we require C to be bounded from $\mathcal{M}^2$ to R^k we cannot allow for delayed observations, although we can approximate them by suitably choosing k. As in Example 4.11, by introducing the decomposition

$$P(s) = \begin{pmatrix} P_1(s) & P_3^*(s) \\ P_3(s) & P_2(s) \end{pmatrix}$$

where $P_1(s) \in \mathcal{L}(R^n)$, $P_3 \in \mathcal{L}(R^n,\mathcal{M}^2)$, $P_2 \in \mathcal{L}(\mathcal{M}^2)$, we can obtain partial differential equations for the matrix functions $P_1(s)$, $P_2(t,\theta,\alpha)$ and $P_3(t,\theta)$, where

$$(P_2(t)h)(\theta) = \int_{-b}^{0} P_2(t,\theta,\alpha)h(\alpha)d\alpha$$

and

$$P_3(t,\theta)b = (P_3(t)b)(\theta) \qquad \text{for } b \in R^n.$$

So the $\mathcal{M}^2$ filtering problem has a unique solution and we now examine the implication for filtering for the delay equation of Example 5.39, whose solution is $\xi(t) = x(t)(0)$. The observation process is then

$$y(t) = \int_0^t \int_{-b}^{0} k(\theta) \begin{Bmatrix} \xi(t+\theta); t+\theta \geq 0 \\ h(t+\theta); t+\theta < 0 \end{Bmatrix} d\theta\, dt$$

an 'averaged' delayed observation which can approximate observations at $\xi(t+\theta_i); -b \leq \theta_i \leq 0$ by suitably shaping k.

From Corollary 6.11,

$$\hat{x}(t) = \int_0^t S_{t-s}P(s)C^*(FVF^*)^{-1}d\rho(s,\omega),$$

where ρ is a Wiener process, and if $\hat{x}(t)$ has continuous sample paths in $\mathcal{M}^2$, $\hat{x}(t)(0) = \hat{\xi}(t)$ is the best estimate of $x(t)(0) = \xi(t)$.

Now from the adjoint of (6.15)

$$S_{t-s}P(s)h = S_tP_oY^*(s,0)h + \int_o^s S_{t-\alpha}\tilde{D}W\tilde{D}^*Y^*(s,\alpha)h\,d\alpha$$

and so

$$\hat{x}(t) = \int_o^t S_{t-s}P_oY^*(s,0)C^*(FVF^*)^{-1}d\rho(s) + \int_o^t S_{t-\alpha}\int_\alpha^t \tilde{D}W\tilde{D}^*Y^*(s,\alpha)C^*(FVF^*)^{-1}\,d\rho(s)\,d\alpha$$

changing the order of integration by Lemma 5.29.

If P_o= Cov {h} has the special property $(P_oh)(\theta) = 0$ for $\theta \neq 0$, then Lemma 5.32 shows that $\hat{x}(t)$ has continuous sample paths in $\mathcal{M}^2$. This means we must assume that the initial state h(·) is known on [-b,0) and only nonrandom at time zero, which is not realistic. A more realistic assumption is to suppose that h(·), though random, is sufficiently regular in t, namely $h \in L^2(\Omega,p;\ D(A))$. This implies that $P_o: \mathcal{M}^2 \to D(A)$ and and under this assumption $\hat{x}(t)$ has continuous sample paths, by virtue of the following lemma.

__Lemma 6.26__

$\phi(t) = \int_o^t S_{t-s}P_oY^*(s,0)C^*(FVF^*)^{-1}d\rho(s)$ has continuous sample paths in $\mathcal{M}^2$ if $P_o : H \to D(A)$.

__Proof__

(a) If $h \in D(A)$, then we have

$$(S_\delta - I)h = \int_o^\delta AS_sh\,ds = \int_o^\delta S_sAh\,ds$$

and $\|(S_\delta - I)h\| \leq \text{const}\ \delta\|Ah\|$.

(b) Without loss of generality, we can take $FVF^* = I$ on R^k and writing $G(s) = P_oY^*(s,0)C^*CY(s,0)P_o$, arguing as in Lemma 5.25, we have

$$(6.47)\quad \text{Cov}\{\phi(t+\delta)-\phi(t)\} = \int_o^t (S_\delta - I)S_{t-s}G(s)S_{t-s}^*(S_\delta - I)^*ds + \int_t^{t+\delta} S_{t+\delta-s}G(s)S_{t+\delta-s}^*\,ds$$

By the properties of trace, we have

$$\text{trace}\{(S_\delta - I)S_{t-s}P_o Y^*(s,0)C^*CY(s,0)P_o T^*_{t-s}(S_\delta - I)^*\}$$

$$= \text{trace}\{\ CY(s,0)P_o\ S^*_{t-s}(S_\delta - I)^*(S_\delta - I)S_{t-s}P_o Y^*(s,0)C^*\}$$

$$= \sum_{i=1}^{k} \|S_{t-s}(S_\delta - I)P_o Y^*(s,0)C^* f_i\|^2 \text{ where } f_i \text{ is a basis for } R^k.$$

$$\leq \text{const.} \sum_{i=1}^{k} \delta^2 \|P_o Y^*(s,0)C^* f_i\|^2 \quad \text{by (a)}.$$

So taking the trace of (6.47) and substituting this inequality we have $\text{trace}\{\text{Cov}\{\phi(t+\delta)-\phi(t)\}\} \leq \text{const.}\delta^2$.

The rest of the argument follows Lemma 5.32.

6.6 Extensions

It is also of interest to solve the estimation problem for the forced system

$$(6.48) \qquad x(t) = S_t x_o + \int_o^t S_{t-s} D dw(s) + \int_o^t S_{t-s} g(s) ds$$

where $g \in L^2(0,t_1;H)$.

Our approach this time is to initially find the optimal filter in the class

$$(6.49) \qquad \hat{x}(t|t_o) = \beta(t|t_o) + \int_o^{t_o} K(t,s) dy(s)$$

where $K(t,\cdot) \in \mathcal{B}^2(0,t_1;\ \mathcal{L}(R^k,H))$ and $\beta \in L^2(0,t_1;H)$ is nonrandom. For an unbiased estimate, we require

$$(6.50) \qquad \beta(t) = E\{x(t)\} - E\{\int_o^t K(t,s) dy(s)\}$$

Lemma 6.1 remains true replacing $x(t)$ by $x(t)-E\{x(t)\}$ and Lemma 6.4 still holds. Now we introduce the second innovations process

$$(6.51) \qquad \rho_o(t,\omega) = y(t,\omega) - \int_o^t C(\hat{x}(s,\omega)-\beta(s)) ds.$$

It is easily shown that Lemma 6.4 holds replacing ρ by ρ_o and we can prove the existence of a linear optimal filter.

Analogously to Lemma 6.4 we can show that (6.10) has a solution if and only if there is an optimal filter, and then the existence of an optimal filter follows from Lemma 6.7.

Suppose $\hat{x}(t) = \beta(t) = \int_o^t K_o(t,s)dy(s)$ is optimal, and introduce the process

$$(6.52)\qquad \eta(s) = \int_o^\sigma C(x(s)-E\{x(s)\}ds = y(\sigma)-y(0) - \int_o^\sigma Fdv(s) - \int_o^\sigma CE\{x(s)\}ds$$

Then

$$\frac{d}{d\sigma} E\{\tilde{x}(t)\circ\eta(\sigma)\} = E\{(x(t)-\beta(t)-\int_o^t K_o(t,s)dy(s))\circ(x(\sigma)-E\{x(\sigma)\})\}C^*$$

a.e. since $\sigma < t$

$$= \Lambda(t,\sigma)C^* - E\{\int_o^t K_o(t,s)dy(s)\circ(x(\sigma)-E\{x(\sigma)\})\}C^*$$

from (6.50) and Lemma 6.1 since $\Lambda(t,\sigma) = E\{(x(t)-E\{x(t)\})\circ(x(\sigma)-E\{x(\sigma)\})\}$.

Hence

$$(6.53)\qquad \frac{d}{d\sigma} E\{\tilde{x}(t)\circ\eta(\sigma)\} = \Lambda(t,\sigma)C^* - \int_o^t K_o(t,s)C\Lambda(s,\sigma)C^*\,ds$$

from Lemmas 5.27, 6.1 and the independence of x_o, v and w.

But from Lemma 6.4

$$E\{\tilde{x}(t)\circ\eta(\sigma)\} = -E\{\tilde{x}(t)\circ\int_o^\sigma Fdv(s)\} - E\{\tilde{x}(t)\circ\int_o^\sigma CE\{x(s)\}ds\}$$

$$(6.54)\qquad = -E\{\tilde{x}(t)\circ\int_o^\sigma Fdv(s)\} \text{ since } E\{\tilde{x}(t)\} = 0$$

$$= \int_o^\sigma K_o(t,s)FVF^*ds$$

by Lemma 5.27 and since x_o, v and w are mutually independent.

Equating (6.53) and the derivative of (6.54) shows that $K_o(t,s)$ is a solution to (6.10).

Conversely suppose that K(t,s) is the solution of (6.10), then we show that $\hat{x}(t) = \beta(t) + \int_o^t K(t,s)dy(s)$ satisfies Lemma 6.4. Taking $\tau = 0$ as before, from (6.52) we have

$$E\{\tilde{x}(t)\circ(x(\sigma)-x(0))\} = E\{\tilde{x}(t)\circ\eta(\sigma)\} + E\{\tilde{x}(t)\circ\int_0^\sigma F dv(s)\}$$

since $E\{\tilde{x}(t)\} = 0$

$$= \int_0^\sigma (\Lambda(t,\alpha)C^* - \int_0^t K(t,s)C^*\Lambda(s,\alpha)C^* ds)d\alpha$$

$$- \int_0^\sigma K(t,s)FVF^* ds$$

from (6.10) and Lemma 5.27 and the independence of x_0, v and w.

$$= 0 \quad \text{since } K(t,s) \text{ satisfies (6.10).}$$

So we have shown the existence of an optimal linear filter and from Theorem 6.9, K(t,s) is specified in terms of $\rho(t)$, the unique solution of the Riccati equation (6.14).

Moreover

$$\beta(t) = E\{x(t)\} - E\{\int_0^t K(t,s)dy(s)\}$$

$$= \int_0^t S_{t-s}g(s)ds - E\{\int_0^t K(t,s)Cx(s)ds\} \quad \text{from (6.48)}$$

$$= \int_0^t S_{t-s}g(s)ds - \int_0^t K(t,s)C\int_0^s S_{s-\alpha}g(\alpha)d\alpha\, ds \text{ from (6.48)}$$

$$= \int_0^t (S_{t-\alpha}g(\alpha) - \int_\alpha^t Y(t,s)P(s)C^*(FVF^*)^{-1}CS_{s-\alpha}g(\alpha)ds)d\alpha$$

interchanging the order of integration

$$= \int_0^t Y(t,\alpha)g(\alpha)d\alpha \quad \text{since Y is the perturbation of } S_t \text{ by } -P(S)C^*(FVF^*)^{-1}C.$$

That this estimate is in fact the best global estimate follows as before and also its representation in terms of the innovations process

$$(6.55) \qquad \hat{x}(t) = \int_0^t S_{t-\alpha}g(\alpha)d\alpha + \int_0^t S_{t-\alpha}P(\alpha)C^*(FVF^*)^{-1}d\rho(\alpha)$$

which is again a k dimensional Wiener process with incremental covariance FVF^*. This representation can again be used to obtain the optimal prediction and the optimal smoother.

(6.56) $$\hat{x}(t) = E\{x(t)\} + S_{t-t_o}\hat{x}(t_o) \quad \text{for } t > t_o$$

(6.57) $$\hat{x}(t|t_o) = \hat{x}(t) + P(t)\int_t^{t_o} Y^*(s,t)C^*(FVF^*)^{-1}d\rho(s) \quad \text{for } t < t_o$$

Notice that the extra inhomogeneous term $\int_0^t S_{t-s}g(s)ds$ has not affected the random part of the estimates (6.55)-(6.57) but only the expected value. So under the same assumptions as Theorem 6.19, the random parts of the estimates can be expressed as solutions of the stochastic differential equations (6.30),(6.34),(6.35). For details see [14].

References

[1] Angel, E. and Jain, A. Filtering of multidimensional diffusion processes, 6th Asilomar Conf. on Circuits and Systems, Nov. 1972.

[2] Angel, E. and Jain, A. A dimensionality reducing model for distributed filtering, IEEE Trans. Automatic Control, AC 18 (1973), pp.59-62.

[3] Atre, S.R. and Lamba, S.S. Optimal estimation in distributed processes using innovations approach, IEEE Trans. Automatic Control, AC 17 (1972), pp.710-712.

[4] Atre, S.R. and Lamba, S.S. Derivation of an optimal estimator for distributed parameter systems via maximum principle, IEEE Trans. Automatic Control, AC 17 (1972), pp.388-390.

[5] Atre, S.R. Kalman filtering for systems corrupted by boundary and interior disturbances, IEEE Trans. Automatic Control, AC 17 (1972), pp.712-713.

[6] Bagchi, A. A Martingale approach to continuous time linear smoothers, SIAM J. Appl. Math., 28 (1975), pp.276-281.

[7] Balakrishnan, A.V. Applied functional analysis, Springer Verlag, Berlin, 1976.

[8] Bensoussan, A. Filtrage optimal des systemes lineaires, Dunod 1971.

[9] Coddington, E.A. and Levinson, N. Theory of ordinary differential equations, McGraw Hill, 1955.

[10] Curtain, R.F. Infinite dimensional filtering, SIAM J. Control, 13 (1975), pp.89-104.

[11] Curtain, R.F. A survey of infinite dimensional filtering, SIAM Review, 17 (1975), pp.395-411.

[12] Curtain, R.F. A Kalman-Bucy filtering theory for affine differential equations, Int. Symp. on Control Theory, Numerical Methods and Computer Systems Modelling, June 1974. (Springer Verlag, Lecture Notes in Economics and Math. Systems, 107, 1974.)

[13] Curtain, R.F. Infinite dimensional estimation theory for linear systems, Control Theory Centre Report No.38, University of Warwick.

[14] Curtain, R.F. Estimation theory for abstract evolution equations excited by general white noise processes, SIAM J. Control, 14 (1976), pp.1124-1150.

[15] Davis, M.H.A. Linear estimation and stochastic control, Chapman and Hall, 1977.

[16] Delfour, M.C. Numerical solution of the operator Riccati equation for the filtering of linear stochastic hereditary diff differential systems, Optimization Techniques, Proc. 7th IFIP Conference, Nice, 1975. Lecture Notes in Computer Science 41, Springer Verlag, 1976.

[17] Dunford, N. and Schwartz, J. Linear operators Part I, Interscience, 1957.

[18] Doleans-Dade, C. and Meyer, P.A. Integrales stochastiques par rapport aux Martingales locales, Seminaire de Probabilities IV, Lecture Notes in Mathematics 124,

[19] Falb, P. Infinite dimensional filtering, Information and Control, (1967), pp.102-137.

[20] Hwang, M., Seinfeld, J.H. and Gavalas, G.R. Optimal least squares filtering and interpolation in distributed parameter systems, J. Math. Anal. Appl., 39 (1972), pp.49-74.

[21] Kwong, R. and Willsky, A. Optimal filtering and filter stability of linear stochastic delay systems, IEEE Trans., AC 22 (1977), pp.196-201.

[22] Kushner, H.J. Filtering for linear distributed parameter systems, SIAM J. Control, 8 (1970), pp.346-359.

[23] Kwakernaak, H. Optimal filtering in linear systems with time delays, IEEE Trans. AC 12 (1967), pp.169-173.

[24] Lamont, G.B. and Kumar, K.S.P. State estimation in distributed parameter systems via least squares and invariant embedding, J. Math. Anal. Appl., 38 (1972), pp.588-606.

[25] Meditch, J.S. Least squares filtering and smoothing for linear parameter systems, Automatica (1971), pp.315-322.

[26] Mitter, S.K. and Vinter, R.B. Filtering for linear stochastic hereditary differential systems, Int. Symp. on Control Theory, Numerical Methods and Computer Systems Modelling, 1974. (Lecture Notes in Economics and Math. Systems, 107, Springer Verlag, 1974.)

[27] Omatu, S., Tomita, Y. and Soeda, T. Fixed-point smoothing in Hilbert space, to appear in J. Information and Control.

[28] Parthasarathy, K.R. Probability measures on metric spaces, Academic Press, 1967.

[29] Phillipson, C.A. and Mitter, S.K. State identification of a class of linear distributed systems, Proc. 4th IFAC Congress, Warsaw, 1969.

[30] Sakawa, Y. Optimal filtering in linear distributed-parameter systems, Internat. J. Control, (1972), pp.115-127.

[31] Thau, F.E. On optimal filtering for a class of linear distributed parameter systems, J. Basic Eng., (1969), pp.173-178.

[32] Tzafestas, S.G. and Nightingale, J. Optimal filtering, smoothing and prediction in linear distributed parameter systems, Proc. IEE (1968), pp.1207-1212.

[33] Tzafestas, S.G. and Nightingale, J. Concerning optimal filtering of linear distributed parameter systems, Ibid., (1968), pp.1737-1742.

[34] Tzafestas, S.G. and Nightingale, J. Maximum likelihood approach to the optimal filtering of distributed parameter systems, Ibid., (1969), pp.1085-1093.

[35] Tzafestas, S.G. On optimum distributed parameter filtering and fixed interval smoothing for coloured noise, IEEE Trans. Automatic Control, AC 17 (1972), pp.448-458.

[36] Tzafestas, S.G. Bayesian approach to distributed parameter filtering and smoothing, Internat. J. Control, 15 (1972), pp.273-295.

[37] Tzafestas, S.G. On the distributed parameter least squares state estimation theory, Internat. J. Systems Sci., 4 (1973), pp.833-858.

[38] Vinter, R.B. Filter stability for stochastic evolution equations, SIAM J. Control, 15 (1977), pp.465-487.

[39] Vinter, R.B. On the evolution of the state of linear differential delay equations in M^2: Properties of the generator, Technical Report Electronic Systems Lab. MIT 1974.

CHAPTER 7

THE SEPARATION PRINCIPLE FOR STOCHASTIC OPTIMAL CONTROL

The separation principle is the main result for the linear stochastic control problem for incompletely observed systems with quadratic cost. In essence it states that the problem can be separated into the filtering problem of §6 and the deterministic quadratic cost control problem of §4, the optimal control strategy being a deterministic feedback of the best estimate of the state.

We consider a general stochastic tracking problem for the abstract signal and observation models

$$(7.1) \quad z(t) = T_t z_o + \int_o^t T_{t-s}Bu(s)ds + \int_o^t T_{t-s}Ddw(s) + \int_o^t T_{t-s}g(s)ds$$

$$(7.2) \quad y(t) = \int_o^t Cz(s)ds + Fv(t)$$

where the cost functional to be minimized is

$$(7.3) \quad J(u) = E\Big\{ \langle z(t_1)-r(t_1),\ G(z(t_1)-r(t_1))\rangle + \int_o^{t_1} (\langle z(s)-r(s), M(z(s)-r(s))\rangle + \langle u(s), Ru(s)\rangle)ds \Big\}$$

(Ω,p), H, K, T_t, D, C, F, w, v, z_o and g are defined as in §6 and t_1, U, B, G, M, R, r as in §4. Our control problem is to minimize (7.3) over a certain admissible subset $\mathcal{U}_{ad}$ of controls from $L^2(0,t_1;\mathcal{U})$, where we write $\mathcal{U} = L^2(\Omega,p;U)$.

7.1 Admissible controls

From physical considerations we would seek controls which depend only on the observation process[1] y_t, say $u \in \int^{\oplus} \mathcal{U}_{y_t} dt$.

[1] We recall that the notation y_t means the restriction of $y(\cdot,\omega)$ on $(0,t)$ and is a random variable with values in $C(0,t;\,R^k)$ and $\int^{\oplus} \mathcal{U}_{y_t} dt$ is defined as for (5.18).

Now for an arbitrary $u \in L^2(0,t_1;\mathcal{U})$, $\mathcal{U}_{y_t}$ depends on the particular control chosen and even if we restrict u to $\int^{\oplus} \mathcal{U}_{y_t} dt$, $\mathcal{U}_{y_t}$ is not the same as $\mathcal{U}_{\eta_t}$, where $\eta(t)$ is the observation process under zero control.

$$(7.4) \qquad \xi(t) = T_t z_o + \int_o^t T_{t-s} D dw(s) + \int_o^t T_{t-s} g(s) ds$$

$$(7.5) \qquad \eta(t) = \int_o^t C\xi(s) ds + Fv(t)$$

This is best illustrated by means of the following scalar counter-example:

$$z(t) = \int_o^t u(s) ds + g(t), \qquad (\text{where } T_t \equiv I)$$

$$y(t) = \int_o^t z(s)\, ds + v(t)$$

Let us choose g so that $\eta(t) = \int_o^t g(s) ds + v(t) \equiv 0$, and take the random control $u_o(t) = \xi$, a random variable.

Then

$$y(t) = \int_o^t \left(\int_o^s \xi d\alpha\right) ds + \int_o^t g(s) ds + v(t)$$

$$= \tfrac{1}{2} t^2 \xi$$

$$= \tfrac{1}{2} t^2 u_o(t)$$

Hence $u_o \in \int^{\oplus} \mathcal{U}_{y_t} dt$, but $\mathcal{U}_{\eta_t}$ is nonrandom and is not equal to $\mathcal{U}_{y_t}$.

To avoid this problem of the dependence of $\mathcal{U}_{y_t}$ on the control strategy, we choose our admissible control set

$$(7.6) \qquad \mathcal{U}_{ad} = \int^{\oplus} \mathcal{U}_{\eta_t} dt \;\cap\; \int^{\oplus} \mathcal{U}_{y_t} dt$$

For these admissible controls, $u \in \mathcal{U}_{ad}$, we now show that $\mathcal{U}_{y_t} = \mathcal{U}_{\eta_t}$ and so is independent of the particular control law chosen.

Lemma 7.1

If y is defined by (7.1),(7.2) for some $u \in \int^{\oplus} \mathcal{U}_{y_t} dt$, then for all $t \in [0,t_1]$, $\mathcal{U}_{\eta_t} \subset \mathcal{U}_{y_t}$.

Proof

Define z_1 and y_1 by

$$z_1(t) = \int_0^t T_{t-s} Du(s)ds$$

$$y_1(t) = \int_0^t Cz_1(s)ds$$

Then

$$z(t) = z_1(t) + \xi(t)$$

$$y(t) = y_1(t) + \eta(t)$$

and the mapping χ_t: $u_t \rightarrow y_{1t}$ is linear and continuous from $L^2(0,t;U)$ to $C(0,t;R^k)$. Hence

(7.7) $$y_t(\omega) = \chi_t u_t(\omega) + \eta_t(\omega)$$

But from (5.22), since $u_t \in \int^{\oplus} \mathcal{U}_{y_t} dt$, there exists

$$\lambda_t \in L^2(C(0,t;R^k), P_{y_t}, L^2(0,t;U))$$ [1]

such that

$$u_t(\omega) = \lambda_t(y_t(\omega))$$

Hence

$$\eta_t(\omega) = y_t(\omega) - \chi_t \lambda_t(y_t(\omega))$$

and the result follows from the composition rule for measurable maps. Similarly, we obtain the following corollaries.

Corollary 7.2

If $u \in \int^{\oplus} \mathcal{U}_{\eta_t} dt$ and y is the corresponding solution of (7.1),(7.2), then for any $t \in [0,t_1]$, $\mathcal{U}_{y_t} \subset \mathcal{U}_{\eta_t}$.

---

[1] Where P_{y_t} denotes the probability on $C(0,t;R^k)$ induced by the random variable y_t .

Corollary 7.3

If $u \in \mathcal{U}_{ad}$ and y is the corresponding solution of (7.1)(7.2), then for any $t \in [0,t_1]$, $\mathcal{U}_{y_t} = \mathcal{U}_{\eta_t}$.

We can also prove that $\mathcal{U}_{ad}$ contains the delayed controls which depend on the observation process up to time $t-\varepsilon$ and that $\int^{\oplus} \mathcal{U}_{y_t} dt$ is dense in $\mathcal{U}_{ad}$.

Lemma 7.4

Let y be the observation process corresponding to $u \in L^2(0,t_1;\mathcal{U})$ and $\varepsilon > 0$, then if $u \in \int^{\oplus} \mathcal{U}_{y_{t-\varepsilon}} dt$, then $u \in \mathcal{U}_{ad}$. (We suppose $\mathcal{U}_{y_{t-\varepsilon}} = u$ for $0 \leq t \leq \varepsilon$).

Proof

For $t \in [0,\varepsilon]$, $u_t \in L^2(0,t;U)$ and $z_t(\omega) = \chi_t u_t(\omega) + \eta_t(\omega)$

where χ_t is defined as in the proof of Lemma 7.1.

Hence $\mathcal{U}_{y_t} = \mathcal{U}_{\eta_t}$ for all $t \in [0,\varepsilon]$.

We now proceed to prove by induction that if for any $a \geq \varepsilon$

$$\mathcal{U}_{y_t} = \mathcal{U}_{\eta_t} \quad \text{on } [0,a], \text{ then}$$

$$\mathcal{U}_{y_t} = \mathcal{U}_{\eta_t} \quad \text{on } [0,a+\varepsilon]$$

Now $u(s) \in \mathcal{U}_{y_{s-\varepsilon}}$ a.e. on $[a,a+\varepsilon]$, and by our induction assumption, $\mathcal{U}_{y_{s-\varepsilon}} = \mathcal{U}_{\eta_{s-\varepsilon}} \subset \mathcal{U}_{\eta_s}$ everywhere on $[a,a+\varepsilon]$. By (5.22) this means that for fixed $t \in [a,a+\varepsilon]$, there exists

$$\pi_t \in L^2(C(0,t;R^k), P_{y_t}, L^2(0,t;U))$$

such that

$$u_t(\omega) = \pi_t(\eta_t(\omega))$$

and

$$y_t(\omega) = \chi_t \pi_t(\eta_t(\omega)) + \eta_t(\omega)$$

from (7.7).

This implies that $\mathcal{U}_{y_t} \subset \mathcal{U}_{\eta_t}$ on $[a,a+\varepsilon]$ and as the reverse inclusion is obvious, we have

$$\mathcal{U}_{y_t} = \mathcal{U}_{\eta_t} \quad \text{everywhere on } [0,a+\varepsilon].$$

Hence $u(s) \in \mathcal{U}_{y_{s-\varepsilon}} = \mathcal{U}_{\eta_{s-\varepsilon}} \subset \mathcal{U}_{\eta_s}$ on $[a,a+\varepsilon]$

i.e. $u \in \int^{\oplus} \mathcal{U}_{\eta_t} dt \cap \int^{\oplus} \mathcal{U}_{y_t} dt$ as required.

<u>Corollary 7.5</u>

$\mathcal{U}_{ad}$ is dense in $\int^{\oplus} \mathcal{U}_{\eta_t} dt$.

<u>Proof</u>

For $u \in \mathcal{U}_{ad}$, define

$$u_n(t) = \begin{cases} u(t - \frac{1}{n}) & \text{if } t \in (\frac{1}{n},t_1] \\ 0 & \text{if } t \in [0,\frac{1}{n}) \end{cases}$$

Then $u_n \to u$ in $L^2(0,t_1;U)$ as $n \to \infty$ and from the proof of Lemma 7.2,

$$u_n \in \int^{\oplus} \mathcal{U}_{\eta_t} dt.$$

We remark that our class of admissible controls is an open loop class and so for $u \in \mathcal{U}_{ad}$, (7.1)(7.2) is always well-defined. As in the deterministic case (§4) feedback laws are preferable from physical considerations. However, if one specifies a feedback control law $u(t,\omega) = \Psi(t,y_t(\omega))$, in general there is no guarantee that (7.1)(7.2) has a unique solution or even that $u \in \mathcal{U}_{ad}$. This can be overcome by introducing a small delay, say, $u(t,\omega) = \Psi(t-\varepsilon,y_{t-\varepsilon}(\omega))$ and appealing to Lemma 7.2 or alternatively one can impose Lipschitz conditions on Ψ.

<u>Lemma 7.6</u>

If $u \in L^2(0,t_1;U)$ is defined by

$$u(t,\omega) = \Psi(t,y_t(\omega))$$

where $\Psi : (0,t_1) \times C(0,t_1;R^k) \to U$ satisfies

$$\Psi(t,f) = \Psi(t,g) \quad \text{if } f(s) = g(s) \text{ for } s \leq t. \tag{7.8}$$

(7.9) $$\|\Psi(t,f) - \Psi(t,g)\| \leq c \sup_{0\leq s\leq t} \|f(s) - g(s)\|_{R^k}$$

for any $f, g \in C(0,t_1;R^k)$,

then (7.1), (7.2) corresponding to this u have a unique solution and $u \in \mathcal{U}_{ad}$.

Proof

Let $$y^o(t) = Fv(t) + \int_0^t CT_s z_o ds + \int_0^t C \int_0^s T_{s-\alpha} Ddw(\alpha) ds + \int_0^t C \int_0^s T_{s-\alpha} g(\alpha) d\alpha\, ds$$

and $$y^n(t) = \int_0^t C \int_0^s T_{s-\alpha} B\Psi(\alpha, y_\alpha^{n-1}) d\alpha\, ds$$

Then from (7.9), we obtain the estimates

$$\sup_{0\leq s\leq t} \|y^{n+1}(s) - y^n(s)\|_{R^k} \leq \text{const.} \int_0^t \sup_{0\leq \tau\leq s} \|y^n(\tau) - y^{n-1}(\tau)\|_{R^k} ds \quad \text{a.e.}$$

and for some sufficiently large k

$$\sup_{0\leq s\leq t} \| y^{(n+1)k}(s) - y^{nk}(s)\|_{R^k} \leq \gamma \sup_{0\leq s\leq t} \|y^{nk}(s) - y^{(n-1)k}(s)\|_{R^k}$$

where $0 < \gamma < 1$.

So by the contraction mapping theorem, $x_t^n \triangleq y_t^{nk}$ converges to y_t in $L^2(\Omega,P;C(0,t;R^k))$, and (7.1),(7.2) has a unique solution corresponding to $u(t,\omega) = \Psi(t,y_t(\omega))$. Furthermore, by construction, $x_t^n = \lambda_t^n(\eta_t)$ for some $\lambda_t^n \in L^2(C(0,t;R^k), P_{y_t}, C(0,t;R^k))$ and so $x_t^n \in L^2(C(0,t;R^k), P_{y_t}, C(0,t;R^k))$ for each n and so does y_t since L^2 is closed. So $\int^\oplus \mathcal{U}_{y_t} dt = \int^\oplus \mathcal{U}_{\eta_t} dt$ and $u = \Psi(t,y_t)$ is admissible.

Corollary 7.7

$u(t) = \bar{u}(t) + \int_0^t K(t,s)dy(s) \in \mathcal{U}_{ad}$ for all $K(t,\cdot) \in \mathcal{B}^\infty(0,t; (R^k,H))$ and deterministic $\bar{u} \in L^2(0,t;U)$.

7.2 Optimal control for complete observations

First we solve the problem of minimizing (7.3), when we can observe the state $z(t)$ exactly. In fact we need to consider the more general signal-observation process

$$(7.10)\qquad z(t) = T_t z_o + \int_o^t T_{t-s}Bu(s)ds + \int_o^t T_{t-s}S(s)d\beta(s) + \int_o^t T_{t-s}g(s)ds$$

where $S \in \mathcal{B}^\infty(0,t_1;\mathcal{L}(R^k,H))$ and β is a R^k-valued Wiener process with incremental covariance matrix V_o and all other terms as previously specified.

Theorem 7.8

Consider the problem of minimizing (7.3) over all $u \in \mathcal{U}_{ad}$ when $z(t)$ is given by (7.10). Under the aforesaid assumptions, there exists a unique minimizing control $u_* \in \int^\oplus \mathcal{U}_{\beta_t} dt$ where

$$(7.11)\qquad u_*(t) = -R^{-1}B^*(Q(t)z_*(t) + s(t))$$

$$(7.12)\qquad z_*(t) = U_\infty(t,0)z_o + \int_o^t U_\infty(t,s)S(s)d\beta(s) + \int_o^t U_\infty(t,s)g(s)ds$$
$$- \int_o^t U_\infty(t,s)BR^{-1}B^*s(s)ds$$

$$(7.13)\qquad s(t) = -U_\infty^*(t_1,t)Gr(t_1) - \int_t^{t_1} U_\infty^*(s,t)(Mr(s)-Q(s)g(s))ds$$

$Q(t)$ is the unique solution of (4.18) and U_∞ is the perturbation of T_t by $-BR^{-1}B^*Q(t)$.

Proof

(a) **Existence**

$\mathcal{U}_{t_1} = L^2(0,t_1;\mathcal{U})$ and $\mathcal{H}_{t_1} = L^2(0,t_1;\mathcal{H})$ are Hilbert spaces ($\mathcal{H} = L^2(\Omega,p;H)$). If we denote the inner products in $\mathcal{U}_{t_1}$ and $\mathcal{H}_{t_1}$ by $\langle\langle\cdot,\cdot\rangle\rangle$ and in $\mathcal{H}$ by $(\cdot,\cdot)$, then (7.3) may be rewritten

$$(7.14)\qquad J(u) = (\bar{z}(t_1)+\Phi_1(u), G(\bar{z}(t_1)+\Phi_1(u)))$$
$$+ \langle\langle\bar{z}+\Phi u, M(\bar{z}+\Phi u)\rangle\rangle + \langle\langle u,Ru\rangle\rangle$$

where $$\bar{z}(t) = T_t z_o + \int_o^t T_{t-s}S(s)d\beta(s) + \int_o^t T_{t-s}g(s)ds - r(t)$$

and $$(\Phi u)(t) = \int_o^t T_{t-s}Bu(s)ds$$

$$\Phi_1 u = (\Phi u)(t_1)$$

We note that $\Phi \in \mathcal{L}(\mathcal{U}_{t_1}, \mathcal{H}_{t_1})$, $\Phi_1 \in \mathcal{L}(\mathcal{U}_{t_1}, H)$, z_o is independent of u and $\int^{\oplus} \mathcal{U}_{\beta_t} dt$ is a closed convex subspace of $\mathcal{U}$. Now J is strictly convex and lower-semi continuous in u and so there exists a unique minimizing element $u_* \in \int^{\oplus} \mathcal{U}_{\beta_t} dt$ given by

$$Ru_* + \Phi_1^* G(\bar{z}(t_1) + \Phi_1 u_*) + \Phi^* M(\bar{z} + \Phi u_*) = 0$$

If we write $x_* = \bar{z} + \Phi u_*$ we obtain

$$u_* = -R^{-1} B^* (T^*_{t_1 - t} G E_{\beta_t} \{x_*(t_1) + \int_t^{t_1} T^*_{s-t} M E_{\beta_t} \{x_*(s)\} ds\})$$

interpreting the adjoints of Φ and Φ_1 in the spaces $\mathcal{L}(\mathcal{U}_{t_1}, \mathcal{H}_{t_1})$ and $\mathcal{L}(\mathcal{U}_{t_1}, H)$ respectively.

Introducing the adjoint state, p(t), by

$$(7.15) \qquad p(t) = \int_t^{t_1} T^*_{s-t} M z_*(s) ds + T^*_{t_1 - t} G z_*(t_1)$$

and writing $p(t) = E_{\beta_t}\{p(t)\}$, we have

$$(7.16) \qquad u_*(t) = -R^{-1} B^* (p(t) + f(t))$$

where $f(t) = -T^*_{t_1 - t} G r(t_1) - \int_t^{t_1} T^*_{s-t} M r(s) ds$

From (7.10) we obtain for $s > t$

$$(7.17) \qquad z_*(s) = T_{s-t} z_*(t) - \int_t^s T_{s-\alpha} B R^{-1} B^* p(\alpha) d\alpha + \int_t^s T_{s-\alpha} S(\alpha) d\beta(\alpha) + \int_t^s T_{s-\alpha} g_o(\alpha) d\alpha$$

where $\qquad g_o(\alpha) = g(\alpha) - BR^{-1} B^* f(\alpha)$

(b) Feedback synthesis

We show that

$$\hat{p}(t) + f(t) = Q(t)z_*(t) + s(t) \tag{7.18}$$

Defining $\tilde{p}(s) = E_{\beta_t}\{p(s)\}$ for $s \geq t$ (fixed), then from (7.15) and (7.17) we have

$$\hat{p}(t) = \tilde{p}(t) = \int_t^{t_1} T^*_{s-t}M(T_{s-t}z_*(t) - \int_t^s T_{s-\alpha}BR^{-1}B^*\tilde{p}(\alpha)d\alpha + \int_t^s T_{s-\alpha}g_o(\alpha)d\alpha)ds$$

$$+ T^*_{t_1-t}G\Big(T_{t_1-t}z_*(t) - \int_t^{t_1} T_{t_1-\alpha}BR^{-1}B^*\tilde{p}(\alpha)d\alpha + \int_t^{t_1} T_{t_1-\alpha} g_o(\alpha)d\alpha\Big)$$

where we have used

$$E_{\beta_t}\{\int_t^s T_{s-\alpha}S(\alpha)d\beta(\alpha)\} = E\{\int_t^s T_{s-\alpha}S(\alpha)d\beta(\alpha)\}$$

$$= 0 \qquad \text{by Lemma 6.4(a).}$$

Now
$$\tilde{p}(t) = (\int_t^{t_1} T^*_{s-t}MT_{s-t}ds + T^*_{t_1-t}GT_{t_1-t})z_*(t)$$

$$-\Big[\int_t^{t_1} T^*_{s-t}M\int_\alpha^{t_1} T_{s-\alpha}BR^{-1}B^*(p(\alpha)+f(\alpha))ds\,d\alpha$$

$$+ T^*_{t_1-t}G\int_t^{t_1} T_{t_1-\alpha}BR^{-1}B^*(p(\alpha)+f(\alpha))d\alpha\Big]$$

$$+\Big[\int_t^{t_1} T^*_{s-t}M\int_\alpha^{t_1} T_{s-\alpha}g(\alpha)ds\,d\alpha + T^*_{t_1-t}G\int_t^{t_1} T_{t_1-\alpha}g(\alpha)d\alpha\Big]$$

using Fubini's theorem and rearranging terms

$$= (Q(t) + \int_t^{t_1} T^*_{s-t}Q(s)BR^{-1}B^*Q(s)T_{s-t}ds)z_*(t)$$

$$-\int_t^{t_1} T^*_{\alpha-t}(Q(\alpha)+\int_\alpha^{t_1} T^*_{s-\alpha}Q(s)BR^{-1}B^*Q(s)T_{s-\alpha}ds)BR^{-1}B^*(p(\alpha)+f(\alpha))\,d\alpha$$

$$+\int_t^{t_1} T^*_{\alpha-t}(Q(\alpha)+\int_\alpha^{t_1} T^*_{s-\alpha}Q(s)BR^{-1}B^*Q(s)T_{s-\alpha}ds)g(\alpha)d\alpha$$

by Corollary 4.7, (4.25)

$$= Q(t)z_*(t) + \int_t^{t_1} T^*_{s-t}Q(s)BR^{-1}B^*(-p(s)-f(s)+Q(s)T_{s-t}z_*(t)$$

$$- Q(s)\int_t^s T_{s-\alpha}BR^{-1}B^*(p(\alpha)+f(\alpha))d\alpha + Q(s)\int_t^s T_{s-\alpha}g(\alpha)d\alpha)ds$$

$$+ \int_t^{t_1} T^*_{\alpha-t}Q(\alpha)g(\alpha)d\alpha$$

using Fubini's theorem and regrouping terms.

Hence using (7.17) again,

$$\tilde{p}(t)+f(t)-Q(t)z_*(t) = -\int_t^{t_1} T^*_{s-t}Q(s)BR^{-1}B^*(\tilde{p}(s)+f(s)-Q(s)\tilde{z}_*(s))\, ds$$

$$-T^*_{t_1-t}Gr(t_1) + \int_t^{t_1} T^*_{s-t}(Q(s)g(s)-Mr(s))\, ds$$

where $\tilde{z}_*(s) = E_{\beta_t}\{z_*(s)\}$, $s \geq t$ and $z_*(t) = \tilde{z}_*(t)$.

Writing $\gamma(s) = \tilde{p}(s) + f(s) - Q(s)\tilde{z}_*(s)$, we have

$$\gamma(t) = -\int_t^{t_1} T^*_{s-t}Q(s)BR^{-1}B^*\gamma(s)ds - T^*_{t_1-t}Gr(t_1) - \int_t^{t_1} T^*_{s-t}(Q(s)g(s)$$
$$-Mr(s))ds$$

But since $U_\infty{}^*(s,t)$ is the perturbation of T^*_t by $-Q(s)BR^{-1}B^*$, we have

$$\gamma(t) = \int_+^{t_1} U^*_\infty(s,t)(Q(s)g(s)-Mr(s))ds - U^*_\infty(t_1,t)Gr(t_1)$$

which from (7.13) proves (7.18), and thus establishes the feedback control law (7.11).

(c) <u>State equation</u>

Substituting for u_* in (7.10), we obtain

$$z_*(t) = T_tz_o - \int_o^t T_{t-s}BR^{-1}B^*Q(s)z_*(s)ds - \int_o^t T_{t-s}BR^{-1}B^*s(s)ds$$

$$+ \int_o^t T_{t-s}S(s)d\beta(s) + \int_o^t T_{t-s}g(s)ds$$

$$= U_\infty(t,0)z_o+\int_o^t U_\infty(t,s)S(s)d\beta(s) +\int_o^t U_\infty(t,s)g(s)ds -\int_o^t U_\infty(t,\beta)BR^{-1}B^*s(\beta)d\beta$$

from the definition of $U_\infty(t,s)$ as the perturbation of T_t by $-BR^{-1}B^*Q(s)$. This establishes (7.12) and that $u_* \in \int^\oplus \mathcal{U}_{\beta_t}dt$.

7.3 Separation principle for incomplete observations

Returning to our original problem we introduce the following decomposition of the state and signal process.

(7.20) $$z(t) = \xi(t) + z_u(t)$$

(7.21) $$y(t) = \eta(t) + y_u(t)$$

where ξ,η are defined by (7.4), (7.5) and

(7.22) $$z_u(t) = \int_0^t T_{t-s}Bu(s)ds$$

(7.23) $$y_u(t) = \int_0^t Cz_u(s)ds$$

We also define

(7.24) $$\hat{z}(t) = E_{\rho_t}\{z(t)\} = \hat{\xi}(t) + z_u(t)$$

(7.25) $$e(t) = z(t) - \hat{z}(t)$$

where we recall from §6 Corollary 6.8

(7.26) $$\hat{\xi}(t) = E_{\eta_t}\{\xi(t)\} = E_{\rho_t}\{\xi(t)\}$$

$\rho(t,\omega)$ being the innovations process for (7.4)(7.5), namely

(7.27) $$\rho(t) = \eta(t) - \int_0^t C\hat{\xi}(s)ds$$

Hence $$E\{\langle M(z(t)-r(t)),\ z(t)-r(t)\rangle\}$$

$$= E\{\langle M(\hat{z}(t)+e(t)-r(t)),\ \hat{z}(t)+e(t)-r(t)\rangle\} \quad \text{from (7.25)}$$

$$= E\{\langle M(\hat{z}(t)-r(t)),\ \hat{z}(t)-r(t)\rangle + \langle Me(t),e(t)\rangle\}$$
$$+ 2E\{\langle Me(t),\hat{\xi}(t)+z_u(t)-r(t)\rangle\} \quad \text{from (7.20)}$$

$$E\{\langle Me(t),\hat{\xi}(t)+z_u(t)-r(t)\rangle\}$$

$$= E\{\langle Me(t),z_u(t)-r(t)\rangle\} \quad \text{by Corollary 6.3 and (7.25)}$$

$$= E\{\langle E_{\eta_t}\{e(t)\},\ M(z_u(t)-r(t))\rangle\} \quad \text{since } u \in \int^{\oplus} \mathcal{U}_{\eta_t} dt$$

$$= 0 \quad \text{by (7.26)}$$

So the problem of minimizing (7.3) is equivalent to minimizing

$$(7.28)\qquad J_o(u) = E\{\int_o^{t_1} (<M(\hat{z}(t)-r(t)),\hat{z}(t)-r(t)> + <Ru,u>)\,dt + <G(\hat{z}(t_1)-r(t_1)),(\hat{z}(t_1)-r(t_1))>\}$$

where from (7.24) and (6.57), $\hat{z}(t)$ is given by

$$(7.29)\qquad \hat{z}(t) = \int_o^t T_{t-s}Bu(s)ds + \int_o^t T_{t-s}P(s)C^*(FVF^*)^{-1}d\rho(s,\omega) + \int_o^t T_{t-s}g(s)ds$$

where $P(t)$ is the unique solution of (6.14). From Theorem 6.18 $\rho(t)$ is a k dimensional Wiener process with incremental covariance matrix FVF^* and so Theorem 7.8 guarantees the existence of a unique minimizing control $u_* \in \int^{\oplus}\mathcal{U}_{\rho_t}dt$, such that

$$(7.30)\qquad u_*(t) = -R^{-1}B^*(Q(t)z_*(t)+s(t))$$

$$(7.31)\qquad \hat{z}_*(t) = \int_o^t U_\infty(t,s)P(s)C^*(FVF^*)^{-1}d\rho(s) + \int_o^t U_\infty(t,s)g(s)ds$$

We now show that this control is in our admissible class and obtain the separation principle.

<u>Theorem 7.9</u>

There exists a unique control $u_* \in \mathcal{U}_{ad}$ which minimizes (7.3), subject to (7.1)(7.2) and is given by

$$(7.32)\qquad u_*(t) = -R^{-1}B^*(Q(t)\hat{z}_*(t) + s(t))$$

$$(7.33)\qquad \hat{z}_*(t) = \int_o^t U_o(t,s)g(s)ds + \int_o^t U_o(t,s)P(s)C^*(FVF^*)^{-1}dy(s)$$

$$(7.34)\qquad s(t) = -U_\infty^*(t_1,t)Gr(t_1) + \int_t^{t_1} U_\infty^*(s,t)(Q(s)g(s)-Mr(s))ds$$

where P and Q are the unique solutions of (6.14) and (4.18) respectively and U_o is the perturbation of T_t by $-BR^{-1}B^*Q(t) - P(t)C^*(FVF^*)^{-1}C$.

Proof

The innovations process $\rho(t)$ is given by

$$\rho(t) = \eta(t) - \int_0^t C\hat{\xi}(s)ds$$
$$= y_*(t) - \int_0^t C\hat{z}_*(s)ds \qquad \text{from } (7.5),(7.20)$$

corresponding to the optimal control u_*. Substituting for this in (7.31), we obtain

$$\hat{z}_*(t) = \int_0^t U_\infty(t,s)P(s)C^*(FVF^*)^{-1}(dy(s)-C\hat{z}_*(s))ds + \int_0^t U_\infty(t,s)g(s)ds$$
$$= \int_0^t U_0(t,s)P(s)C^*(FVF^*)^{-1}dy(s) + \int_0^t U_0(t,s)g(s)ds$$

from the definition of $U_\infty(t,s)$ and $U_0(t,s)$ as perturbations of T_t by $-BR^{-1}B^*Q(t)$ and $-BR^{-1}B^*Q(t) - P(t)C^*(FVF^*)^{-1}C$ respectively.
So $\hat{z}_*(t) \in \int^{\oplus} \mathcal{H}_{y_t} dt$ and from (7.30), $u_*(t) \in \int^{\oplus} \mathcal{U}_{y_t} dt$. From Theorem 7.8, $u_* \in \int^{\oplus} \mathcal{U}_{\rho_t} dt$ and from Lemma 6.4, $\mathcal{U}_{\rho_t} = \mathcal{U}_{\eta_t}$ and so $u_*(t)$ defined by (7.30) is admissible.

So the optimal strategy is completely specified by the unique solutions of the two Riccati equations (4.18) and (6.14) and is implemented by first estimating the initial state via (7.33) and then obtaining the feedback control law via (7.32) whence the name separation principle for Theorem 7.9.

One can obtain explicit expressions for the optimal cost in terms of Q,P and the other known parameters. The special case, where $g = 0 = r$ gives some insight into the dependence of the cost on the noise effects through P and the cost of the deterministic control law through Q.

Lemma 7.10

If $g = 0 = r$, the optimal cost is given by

$$J(u_*) = \text{trace}\{GP(t_1)\} + \int_0^{t_1} \text{trace}\{MP(s)\}ds$$
$$+ \int_0^{t_1} \text{trace}\{Q(s)P(s)C^*(FVF^*)^{-1}CP(s)\}ds$$

Proof

Now $$J(u_*) = J_o(u_*) + E\{<Ge(t_1),e(t_1)> + \int_o^{t_1} <Me(s),e(s)>ds\}$$
$$= J_o(u_*) + \text{trace}\ \{GP(t_1)\} + \int_o^{t_1} \text{trace}\ \{MP(s)\}ds$$

since $P(t) = \text{Cov}\ \{e(t)\}$ from Lemma 6.12, and by (5.2).

But

$$J_o(u_*) = E\{<G\hat{z}_*(t_1),\hat{z}_*(t_1)>\} + \int_o^{t_1} E\{<(M+Q(s)BR^{-1}B^*Q(s))\hat{z}_*(s),\hat{z}_*(s)>\}ds$$

from (7.32)

$$= \int_o^{t_1} \text{trace}\ \{GU_\infty(t_1,s)P(s)C^*(FVF^*)^{-1}CP(s)U_\infty^*(t_1,s)\}ds$$
$$+ \int_o^{t_1} \text{trace}\{\int_o^{t} (M+Q(t)BR^{-1}B^*Q(t)U_\infty(t,s)P(s)C^*(FVF^*)^{-1}CP(s) U_\infty^*(t,s)ds\}dt$$

using (7.31) and Lemma 5.27(c) for ρ, and noting that trace $\{VJV^*\}$ = trace $\{JV^*V\}$ for nuclear J, we have that

$$J_o(u_*) = \int_o^{t_1} \text{trace}\ \{U_\infty^*(t_1,s)GU_\infty(t,s)P(s)C^*(FVF^*)^{-1}CP(s)\ ds$$
$$+ \int_o^{t_1} \text{trace}\ \{\int_s^{t} U_\infty^*(t,s)(M+Q(t)BR^{-1}B^*Q(t))U_\infty(t,s)dt\ P(s)C^*(FVF^*)^{-1}CP(s)\}ds$$

interchanging the order of integration and reordering the traces

$$= \int_o^{t_1} \text{trace}\{Q(s)P(s)C^*(FVF^*)^{-1}CP(s)\}ds$$

As a final remark we note that since $u_* \in \mathcal{U}_{ad}$, from Corollary 7.3, $\mathcal{U}_{y_t} = \mathcal{U}_{\eta_t}$ and similarly Lemma 6.4 implies that $\mathcal{U}_{\eta_t} = \mathcal{U}_{\rho_t}$. So although we originally defined $\hat{z}_*(t) = E_{\rho_t}\{z(t)\}$ it is also defined by $\hat{z}_*(t) = E_{y_t}\{z(t)\}$.

7.4 Examples

Example 7.11 Finite dimensional case

If we restrict H, K and U to be finite dimensional spaces, then we obtain the standard finite dimensional result [10].

Example 7.12 Heat equation

Consider the controlled noisy heat equation

$$\text{(7.35)}\qquad \begin{aligned} dz(t) &= z_{xx}dt + dw(t) + u(t)dt\ ; \qquad z(0) = z_o \\ z_x(t,0) &= 0 = z_x(t,1) \end{aligned}$$

with the observation process

$$\text{(7.36)}\qquad dy(t) = Cz(t)dt + dv(t)$$

where $H = K = U = L^2(0,1)$ and A, w, P_o are defined as in Example 5.39, and C, v as in Example 6.23.

For our cost functional we take

$$\text{(7.37)}\qquad J(u) = E\left\{\int_0^1 z^2(t_1,x)dx + \int_0^{t_1}\int_0^1 (z^2(t,x) + u^2(t,x))dxdt\right\}$$

Then the assumptions of Theorem 7.9 are satisfied and the unique optimal control is given by

$$\text{(7.38)}\qquad \begin{aligned} u_*(t) &= -\ Q(t)\ \hat{z}_*(t) \\ \hat{z}_*(t) &= \int_0^t U_o(t,s)P(s)C^*\ dy(s) \end{aligned}$$

where P and Q are the unique solutions of (6.42) and (4.27) respectively.

Example 7.13 Wave equation

Under the assumptions of Example 6.24, consider the controlled noisy wave equation

$$\text{(7.39)}\qquad \begin{aligned} dz_{tt} &= z_{xx}dt + dw(t) + u(t,x)dt \\ z(t,0) &= 0 = z(t,1) \\ z(0,x) &= z_o(x);\quad z_t(0,x) = z_1(x) \end{aligned}$$

with the observation process of Example 6.24

$$y(t) = \int_0^t\int_0^1 z(s,x)b(x)dx\ ds + v(t)$$

and for our cost functional take

$$J(u) = E\left\{\tfrac{1}{2}\int_0^1 z_x^2(t_1,x)+z_t^2(t_1,x)dx + \int_0^{t_1}\int_0^1 (\tfrac{1}{2}z_t^2(t,x)+u^2(t,x))dx\ dt\right\}$$

Then the assumptions of Theorem 7.9 are satisfied for the following abstract system on $\mathcal{H} = H_o^1(0,1) \times L^2(0,1)$

$$(7.40) \qquad \begin{pmatrix} z \\ z_t \end{pmatrix} = S_t \begin{pmatrix} z_o \\ z_1 \end{pmatrix} + \int_0^t S_{t-s} \begin{pmatrix} 0 \\ I \end{pmatrix} u(s)\,ds + \int_0^t S_{t-s} \begin{pmatrix} 0 \\ I \end{pmatrix} dw(s)$$

$$(7.41) \qquad dy_t = (C \quad 0) \begin{pmatrix} z \\ z_t \end{pmatrix} dt + dv(t)$$

$$(7.42) \qquad J(u) = E\left\{ \tfrac{1}{2}\langle \xi(t_1), \xi(t_1)\rangle + \int_0^{t_1} (\langle M\xi(t), \xi(t)\rangle + \langle u,u\rangle)\,dt \right\}$$

where $M = \begin{pmatrix} 0 & 0 \\ 0 & I \end{pmatrix}$, and $\xi(t) = \begin{pmatrix} z(t) \\ z_t(t) \end{pmatrix}$.

Example 7.14 Delay equation

Consider the controlled stochastic delay equation

$$(7.43) \qquad \begin{cases} d\xi(t) = A_o\xi(t)dt + \sum_{i=1}^{N} A_i \begin{Bmatrix} \xi(t+\theta_i); & t+\theta_i \geq 0 \\ h(t+\theta_i); & t+\theta_i < 0 \end{Bmatrix} dt \\ \qquad + \int_{-b}^{0} A_{o1}(\theta) \begin{Bmatrix} \xi(t+\theta); & t+\theta \geq 0 \\ h(t+\theta); & t+\theta < 0 \end{Bmatrix} d\theta\, dt \\ \qquad + Bu(t)dt + Ddw(t) \\ \xi(0) = h(0) \end{cases}$$

where the assumptions are as in Examples 4.11 and 5.41. We take the observation process of Example 6.25, namely

$$(7.44) \qquad dy(t) = \int_{-b}^{0} k(\theta) \begin{Bmatrix} \xi(t+\theta); & t+\theta \geq 0 \\ h(t+\theta); & t+\theta < 0 \end{Bmatrix} d\theta\, dt + dv(t)$$

and the cost functional

$$(7.45) \quad J(u) = E\left\{ \langle \xi(t_1), G\xi(t_1)\rangle_{R^n} + \int_0^{t_1} \langle \xi(s), M\xi(s)\rangle_{R^n}\, ds \right.$$
$$\left. + \int_0^{t_1} \langle u(s), Ru(s)\rangle_{R^n}\, ds \right\}$$

Then for the integral $\mathcal{M}^2$ version of (7.43) (cf (5.54)), and the $\mathcal{M}^2$ versions of (7.44) and (7.45) (cf (6.45) and (4.31)), the assumptions of Theorem 7.9 are satisfied and the $\mathcal{M}^2$ problem has a unique control given by

$$(7.42)\qquad \begin{cases} u_*(t) = -R^{-1}\tilde{B}^*Q(t)z_*(t) \\ \hat{z}_*(t) = \int_0^t U_o(t,s)P(s)C^*\, dy(s) \end{cases}$$

From (7.31),

$$\hat{z}_*(t) = \int_0^t U_\infty(t,s)P(s)C^*\, d\rho(s)$$

$$= \int_0^t T_{t-s}P(s)C^*\, d\rho(s) - \int_0^t\int_0^t T_{t-\alpha}\tilde{B}R^{-1}\tilde{B}^*Q(\alpha)U_\infty(\alpha,s)P(s)C^*\, d\alpha\, d\rho(s)$$

since U_∞ is the perturbation of T_t by $-\tilde{B}R^{-1}B^*Q(t)$

$$= \int_0^t T_{t-s}P(s)C^*\, d\rho(s) - \int_0^t T_{t-s}\int_0^\alpha T_{s-\alpha}\tilde{B}R^{-1}\tilde{B}^*Q(\alpha)U_\infty(\alpha,s)P(s)C^*\, d\rho(s)\, d\alpha$$

changing the order of integration by Lemma 5.29.

Now the second term has continuous sample paths by Lemma 5.28 and from our results of Example 6.24, the first term has continuous sample paths provided either $P_o: \mathcal{M}^2 \to D(A)$ or $(Ph)(\theta) = 0$ for $\theta \neq 0$. So under either of these assumptions, $\hat{z}_*(t)(0)$ and $u_*(t)(0)$ solve the stochastic control problem for the original system (7.43)-(7.45).

References

[1] Balakrishnan, A.V. Stochastic control: A function space approach, SIAM J. Control, 10 (1972), pp.285-297.

[2] Balakrishnan, A.V. Applied functional analysis, Springer Verlag, 1976.

[3] Bensoussan, A. On the separation principle for distributed parameter systems, IFAC Conference on Distributed Parameter Systems, Banff, Canada, 1971.

[4] Bensoussan, A. and Viot, M. Optimal control of stochastic linear distributed parameter systems, SIAM J. Control, 13 (1975), pp.904-926.

[5] Brooks, R.A. Linear stochastic control: An extended separation principle, J. Math. Anal. Appl., 38 (1972), pp. 569-587.

[6] Curtain, R.F. and Ichikawa, A. The separation principle for stoch-

astic evolution equations, SIAM J. Control, 15 (1977), p.367.

[7] Kushner, H.J. On the optimal control of a system governed by a linear parabolic equation with white noise inputs, SIAM J. Control, 6 (1968), pp.596-614.

[8] Lindquist, A. A theorem on duality between estimation and control for linear stochastic systems with time delay, J. Math. Anal. Appl., 37 (1972), pp.516-536.

[9] Lindquist, A. On feedback control of linear stochastic systems, SIAM J. Control, 11 (1973), pp.323-343.

[10] Wonham, W.M. On the separation principle of stochastic control, SIAM J. Control, 6 (1968), pp.312-326.

CHAPTER 8

UNBOUNDED CONTROL AND SENSING IN DISTRIBUTED SYSTEMS

8.1 Motivation

We recall that in Chapter 3 our basic model (3.2) for the control system was

$$z(t) = T_t z_o + \int_o^t T_{t-s} Bu(s)\, ds \tag{8.1}$$

where T_t is a strongly continuous semigroup on a Banach space Z, $u \in L^p[0,t_1;U]$, U a Banach space, and $B \in \mathcal{L}(U,Z)$. The model for the observation process (3.12) is

$$y(t) = CS_t x_o \tag{8.2}$$

where S_t is a strongly continuous semigroup on a Banach space X, and $C \in \mathcal{L}(X,Y)$, Y a Banach space also.

However, the assumptions that B, C are bounded operators is very restrictive and does not allow us to consider many examples of practical importance. In fact most systems described by partial differential equations have severe limitations on the control and observation processes; sensing and control is usually restricted to subsets within Ω, or of the boundary Γ, and this gives rise to unbounded B, and C in (8.1) and (8.2). In this chapter we will show how the theories of the previous chapters may be extended to a class of unbounded observation and control operators which arise in sensing and control on subsets of Ω. To motivate the abstract theory we consider some examples to see how unbounded operators arise in distributed parameter systems.

Example 8.1

Consider the observation process

$$\begin{aligned} x_t &= x_{\xi\xi} \\ x(0,t) &= x(1,t) = 0,\quad x(\xi,0) = x_o(\xi) \\ y(t) &= x(\xi_1,t) \qquad 0 < \xi_1 < 1 \end{aligned} \tag{8.3}$$

Supposing that x is the temperature of a bar, the observation map then corresponds to measuring the temperature at the point ξ_1.

If we let $X = L^2[0,1]$ the solution of (8.3) is given by (8.2) where the semigroup S_t is defined by

$$(8.4) \qquad (S_t x)(\xi) = \sum_{n=1}^{\infty} 2\, e^{-n^2\pi^2 t} \sin n\pi\xi \int_0^1 \sin n\pi\rho \; x(\rho)\, d\rho$$

and the operator C is defined by

$$(Cx)(t) = x(\xi_1, t)$$

We note that C is not defined on all of X, but only on a dense subset of $L^2[0,1]$ (for example $C(0,1)$); moreover C is not closed. These are typical characteristics of observation operators, that is they are densely defined but not closed.

From the duality results of Chapter 3 we would expect to be able to express the control operator $B = C^*$ for some observation operator C. Now since C is densely defined, C^* will be closed but may have trivial domain. In fact, this is the case for many control operators, for example the following:

<u>Example 8.2</u>

The controlled system is

$$(8.5) \qquad \begin{aligned} z_t &= z_{\xi\xi} \\ z(0,t) = z(1,t)&, \; z(\xi,0) = z_0(\xi) \\ -[z_\xi]_{\xi_1} &= u \qquad 0 < \xi_1 < 1 \end{aligned}$$

where $[\;]_\xi$ denotes the change from ξ^- to ξ^+. This system is motivated by the thermal conduction for a bar with its ends kept at zero temperature, but with heat injection of magnitude $u(t)$ at the point ξ. Then heat balance considerations for the case where the thermometric conductivity is set equal to unity yield

$$\int_{\xi-}^{\xi+} \theta_t(\xi,t)\,d\xi = [\theta_\xi(\xi,t)]_{\xi-}^{\xi+} \quad \text{for } \xi \neq \xi_1$$

and

$$\int_{\xi-}^{\xi+} \theta_t(\xi,t)\,d\xi = [\theta_\xi(\xi,t)]_{\xi-}^{\xi+} + u(t) \text{ for } \xi = \xi_1$$

Thus $\Theta_t = \Theta_{\xi\xi}$ for $\xi \neq \xi_1$ and $-[\Theta_\xi]_{\xi_1} = u$. So if we identify Θ with z, equation (8.5) describes this process. However, the equations are not in the usual form for which we can write down a mild solution, and it is not obvious how the operator B should be chosen. In fact we need to examine more closely the concept of a mild solution and its relationship with the formal partial differential equation (8.4). To do this we first define a weak solution of (8.5), for which we make use of the following Green's formula for $Z = L^2[0,1]$.

$$(8.6) \qquad \langle \phi_{\xi\xi}, \psi \rangle_Z - \langle \phi, \psi_{\xi\xi} \rangle_Z = \phi(\xi_1)[\psi_\xi]_{\xi_1} - \phi_\xi(\xi_1)[\psi]_{\xi_1}$$

for $\phi \in C_0^\infty[0,1]$, $\psi \in C^\infty\Big[[0,\xi_1)\Big] \cup C^\infty\Big[(\xi_1,1]\Big]$ with $\psi(0) = \psi(1) = 0$.

Proceeding formally, if we take the inner product of (8.5) with a given function $x(\xi,t)$ and integrate by parts with respect to t on $[0,t_1]$ we obtain

$$\int_0^{t_1}\int_0^1 (x_t(\xi,t)+x_{\xi\xi}(\xi,t))z(\xi,t)d\xi\, dt + \int_0^{t_1} x(\xi_1,t)u(t)dt + \int_0^1 x(\xi,0)z_0(\xi)d\xi = 0$$

for $x(\xi,t_1) = 0$, and $[z]_{\xi_1} = 0$.

Now we define $x(\xi,t)$ by

$$x_t + x_{\xi\xi} = f$$

with

$$x(\xi,t_1) = 0, \; x(0,t) = x(1,t) = 0$$

Then a weak solution of (8.5) is defined as a function $z \in C[0,t_1;Z]$ which satisfies

$$(8.7) \quad \int_0^{t_1}\int_0^1 f(\xi,t)z(\xi,t)d\xi dt + \int_0^{t_1} x(\xi_1,t)u(t)dt + \int_0^1 x(\xi,0)z_0(\xi)d\xi = 0$$

for a certain class of f.

We note that for smooth f, we have

$$x(t) = -\int_t^{t_1} S_{s-t}f(s)ds$$

where S_t is given by (8.4). Moreover, the second term in (8.7) may be rewritten as

$$(8.8) \qquad \int_0^{t_1} x(\xi_1,t)u(t)dt = \int_0^{t_1}\int_0^1 \delta(\xi-\xi_1)x(\xi,t)u(t)dt$$

where δ is the Dirac delta function. So (8.8) suggests that we should consider the differential equation

$$\bar{z}_t = \bar{z}_{\xi\xi} + \delta(\xi-\xi_1)u \tag{8.9}$$

$$\bar{z}(0,t) = \bar{z}(1,t) = 0, \ \bar{z}(\xi,0) = z_o(\xi)$$

Multiplying (8.9) by $x(\xi,t)$, taking the inner product and integrating with respect to t on $[0,t_1]$ leads formally to exactly the same expression (8.7). This indicates that the weak solutions of (8.9) and (8.5) are related and motivates the choice of

$$B = \delta(\xi-\xi_1) \tag{8.10}$$

In this case we have $Bu \notin L^2[0,1]$ for any $u \neq 0$, so it is not clear what is meant by (8.9). However, we are now in a position to write down a mild solution of (8.9) as

$$\bar{z}(t) = T_t z_o + \int_0^t T_{t-s}\delta u(s)ds \tag{8.11}$$

where $T_t = S_t^* = S_t$.

If we substitute (8.11) in (8.7) we obtain at least formally

$$\int_0^{t_1} \langle f(t),\bar{z}(t)\rangle dt = \int_0^{t_1} \langle S_t f(t), z_o\rangle dt + \int_0^{t_1}\int_0^t \langle S_{t-s} f(t), \delta u(s)\rangle ds\ dt$$

$$= -\langle x(0), z_o\rangle - \int_0^{t_1} \langle x(s), \delta u(s)\rangle\ ds$$

Hence the mild solution (8.11) is a weak solution of (8.5). Of course we have yet to make the arguments rigorous but at least they indicate the way to proceed. That is

(1) to establish the operator B via a Green's formula

(2) to provide a framework for the problem so that (8.1) makes sense

(3) to check to see whether this framework justifies the formal manipulations carried out in establishing that the mild solution is a weak solution.

Now that we have indicated the nature of the operators B and C we will again use these examples to illustrate the appropriate framework for formulating the problems. It is easy to verify the following properties of the observation operator C

(8.12)

(a) $H^{o}(0,1) \supset D(C) \supset H^{\frac{1}{2}+\varepsilon}(0,1)$ for some small $\varepsilon > 0$.

(b) $C \in \mathscr{L}(H^{\frac{1}{2}+\varepsilon}(0,1), R)$

(c) $S_t \in \mathscr{L}(H^{o}(0,1), H^{\frac{1}{2}+\varepsilon}(0,1))\ t > 0$

(d) $\|S_t x\|_{H^{\frac{1}{2}+\varepsilon}} \leq \frac{M}{t^{\frac{1}{4}+\frac{1}{2}\varepsilon}} \|x\|_{H^{o}}$

So if we set $\mathscr{C}x_o = CS_t x_o$ we see that $\mathscr{C} \in \mathscr{L}(X;L^q[0,t_1;R])$ for $q < 4$. So the observation process determined by the operator $\mathscr{C}$ as given in Chapter 3 is well defined.

We will seek conditions of the type (8.12)(a),(b),(c),(d) for the general case. It may seem that such conditions are rather strong if we only require that $\mathscr{C} \in \mathscr{L}(X;\ L^q[0,t_1;R])$. However these conditions are necessary to develop a complete duality theory analagous to that in Chapter 3.

The dual conditions to (8.12)(a),(b),(c),(d) are the following.

(a) $(H^{+\frac{1}{2}+\varepsilon}(0,1))^* \supset R(B) \supset Z$

(b) $B \in \mathscr{L}(R, (H^{+\frac{1}{2}+\varepsilon}(0,1))^*)$

(c) $T_t \in \mathscr{L}((H^{+\frac{1}{2}+\varepsilon}(0,1))^*, H^{o}(0,1))\ t > 0$

(d) $\|T_t z\|_{H^{o}} \leq \frac{M}{t^{\frac{1}{4}+\frac{1}{2}\varepsilon}} \|z\|_{(H^{+\frac{1}{2}+\varepsilon})^*}$

It is easy to show that if $u \in L^p[0,t_1;R]$, $p > 4/3$ and

$$z(t) = T_t z_o + \int_0^t T_{t-s} Bu(s)\,ds$$

with $B = \delta(\xi-\xi_1)$, then $z \in C[0,t_1;H^{o}]$.

In fact we shall show later that the two problems in Examples 8.1 and 8.2 are dual to each other in the sense that if any observability result holds for Example 8.1, then the corresponding controllability result holds for Example 8.2.

8.2 General conditions

We now generalise the conditions (8.12)(a),(b),(c),(d) appropriately for the general system (8.2). To do this, we assume the existence of a Banach space $\underset{\sim}{W}$ which is dense in X with respect to the norm in X, and such that

(8.17)

(a) $X \supset D(C) \supset \underset{\sim}{W}$

(b) $C \in \mathcal{L}(\underset{\sim}{W}, Y)$

(c) $S_t \in \mathcal{L}(X, \underset{\sim}{W}) \quad t > 0$

(d) $\|S_t x\|_{\underset{\sim}{W}} \leq g(t)\|x\|_X$ for all $x \in X$, where $g \in L^q[0,t_1]$, $q \geq 1$.

Clearly

(8.15) $$\|CS_t x\|_Y \leq \|C\|_{\mathcal{L}(\underset{\sim}{W},Y)}\|S_t x\|_{\underset{\sim}{W}} \leq g(t)\|C\|_{\mathcal{L}(\underset{\sim}{W},Y)}\|x\|_X$$

Hence $\mathcal{C} \in \mathcal{L}(X; L^q[0,t_1;Y])$.

We remark that property (c) is similar to the assumption that S_t is an analytic semigroup for which $S_t: X \to D(\mathcal{A})$, $t > 0$. However, we are not able to use $\underset{\sim}{W} = D(\mathcal{A})$ with the graph norm, since

$$\|\mathcal{A} S_t\| \leq \frac{M}{t} \quad \text{for some } M > 0$$

and (d) will not hold.

The assumptions (8.14) have the following important consequences for filtering theory:

If $f \in L^p[0,t_1;X]$ with $\frac{1}{p} + \frac{1}{q} = 1$, then $S_{t-s}f(s) \in \underset{\sim}{W}$ for almost all $s < t$; furthermore it is Bochner integrable with respect to W, and

(8.16) $$C\int_0^t S_{t-s}f(s)ds = \int_0^t CS_{t-s}f(s)ds,$$

despite the fact that C is usually not closed.

The various Definitions (3.21) to (3.24) for observability were given in terms of the operator $\mathcal{C}$ and these still make sense for the case of C being unbounded. However, before we can extend Theorem 3.7 we need to examine a class of control problems in which B is unbounded. For this we assume the existence of a Banach space $\widetilde{W}$, with Z dense in $\widetilde{W}$, such that

(a) $\widetilde{W} \supset R(B) \supset Z$

(b) $B \in \mathcal{L}(U, \widetilde{W})$

(c) $T_t \in \mathcal{L}(\widetilde{W}, Z) \quad t > 0$

(d) $\|T_t w\|_Z \leq g(t)\|w\|_{\widetilde{W}}$ for all $w \in \widetilde{W}$, with $g \in L^q[0,t_1,Z]$.

Proposition 8.3

Suppose that (8.17) holds, $z_o \in Z$ and $u \in L^p[0,t_1;U]$ where $\frac{1}{p} + \frac{1}{q} = 1$. Then

$$z(t) = T_t z_o + \int_0^t T_{t-s} Bu(s)ds \tag{8.18}$$

is well defined and furthermore $z \in C[0,t_1,Z]$.

Proof

Firstly, z is well defined since

$$\left\| \int_0^t T_{t-s} Bu(s)ds \right\|_Z \leq \int_0^t g(t-s)\|B\|_{\mathcal{L}(U,\tilde{W})}\|u(s)\|_U\, ds$$

$$\leq \|B\|_{\mathcal{L}(U,\tilde{W})}\|g\|_{L^q[0,t_1]}\|u\|_{L^p[0,t_1;U]}$$

by the Schwarz inequality.

To prove the continuity we compute for $h > 0$

$$z(t+h) - z(t) = (T_{t+h}-T_t)z_o + \int_0^t (T_{t+h-s}-T_{t-s})Bu(s)ds$$

$$+ \int_t^{t+h} T_{t+h-s}Bu(s)ds$$

Hence

$$\|z(t+h) - z(t)\|_Z \leq \|(T_h-I)z(t)\| + \|B\|_{\mathcal{L}(U,\tilde{W})}\|g\|_{L^q[0,h]}\|u\|_{L^p[t,t+h;U]}$$

Using the strong continuity of T_t we conclude the continuity on the right.

Also

$$z(t) - z(t-h) = (T_\varepsilon-T_{\varepsilon-h})z(t-\varepsilon) + \int_{t-\varepsilon}^{t-h} T_{t-h-s}Bu(s)ds$$

$$+ \int_{t-\varepsilon}^{t} T_{t-s}Bu(s)ds$$

for $t > 0$, $t > \varepsilon > h > 0$.

Thus

$$\|z(t) - z(t-h)\|_Z \leq \|(T_\varepsilon-T_{\varepsilon-h})z(t-\varepsilon)\|_Z$$

$$+ \|B\|_{\mathcal{L}(U,\tilde{W})}\|g\|_{L^q[0,\varepsilon-h]}\|u\|_{L^p[t-\varepsilon,t-h;U]}$$

$$+ \|B\|_{\mathcal{L}(U,\widetilde{W})}\|g\|_{L^q[0,\varepsilon]}\|u\|_{L^p[t-\varepsilon,t;U]}$$

From which we conclude the continuity on the left.

So the controlled system with unbounded B is well defined under assumption (8.17) and the controllability Definitions (3.1),(3.10),(3.19), (3.20) still make sense. To see the duality between the control and observation problems we assume that X is reflexive and $Z = X^*$. Now $C \in \mathcal{L}(\underset{\sim}{W},Y)$, so if we set $\underset{\sim}{W}^* = \widetilde{W}$, $Y^* = U$ and $B = C^*$, we find $B \in \mathcal{L}(U,\widetilde{W})$. Finally we set $T_t = S_t^*$, and then the conditions (8.14) on C and S_t imply the conditions (8.17) on B and T_t. Moreover

$$\langle f,\mathcal{C}x\rangle_{L^p[0,t_1;U],L^q[0,t_1,Y]} = \int_0^{t_1} \langle f(t),CS_tx\rangle_{U,Y}\,dt$$

for $f \in L^p[0,t_1;U]$ with $\frac{1}{p}+\frac{1}{q} = 1.$

$$= \int_0^{t_1} \langle C^*f(t),S_tx\rangle_{\widetilde{W},\underset{\sim}{W}}\,dt$$

$$= \int_0^{t_1}\langle T_tBf(t),x\rangle_{Z,X}\,dt$$

$$= \langle \mathcal{C}^*f,x\rangle_{Z,X}$$

where $\mathcal{C}^*f = \int_0^{t_1} T_tBf(t)dt.$

For $f(t) = u(t_1-t)$, $\mathcal{C}^*f = \int_0^{t_1} T_{t_1-t}Bu(t)dt$, which is related to the control problem (8.18)

$$z(t) = T_tz_o + \int_0^t T_{t-s}Bu(s)ds$$

and this construction enables us to extend Theorem 3.25 to the case where B and C are unbounded operators.

Although it is usually easy to interpret the operator C, it is not obvious how we should interpret the control problem for which $B = C^*$. As indicated in Example 8.2, we will do this via a Green's formula and show that (8.18) is a weak solution of a controlled abstract differential equation. First we prove the following lemma.

<u>Lemma 8.4</u>

For $f \in C[0,t_1;X]$ and $x(t) = -\int_t^T S_{s-t}f(s)ds$, z(t) satisfies (8.18) iff it satisfies

$$(8.19)\quad \int_0^{t_1} \langle f(t),z(t)\rangle_{X,Z}dt + \int_0^{t_1} \langle Cx(t),u(t)\rangle_{Y,U}dt + \langle x(0),z_o\rangle_{X,Z} = 0$$

Proof

Substitution of (8.18) into the left hand side of (8.19) yields

$$\int_0^{t_1} \langle f(t),T_t z_o + \int_0^t T_{t-s}Bu(s)ds\rangle_{X,Z}dt + \int_0^{t_1} \langle -C\int_t^T S_{s-t}f(s)ds,u(t)\rangle_{Y,U}dt$$

$$- \langle\int_0^{t_1} S_s f(s)ds,z_o\rangle_{X,Z}$$

$$= \int_0^{t_1} \langle f(t),(T_t-S_t^*)z_o\rangle_{X,Z}dt + \int_0^{t_1}\int_0^t \langle f(t),T_{t-s}Bu(s)\rangle_{X,Z}ds\, dt$$

$$- \int_0^{t_1}\int_0^s \langle CS_{s-t}f(s),u(t)\rangle_{Y,U}dt\, ds$$

using (8.16).

Now $T_t = S_t^*$, $B = C^*$ so the above expression is zero, and Z defined by (8.18) satisfies (8.19).

Conversely, substituting for x(t) in (8.19) gives

$$\int_0^{t_1} \langle f(t),z(t) - T_t z_o - \int_0^t T_{t-s}Bu(s)ds\rangle_{X,Z}dt = 0$$

for all $f \in C[0,t_1;X]$, and so

$$z(t) = T_t z_o + \int_0^t T_{t-s}Bu(s)ds$$

We remark that if f is smooth, namely $f \in C^1[0,t_1;X]$, then

$$\dot{x} + \mathcal{A}x = f \;,\; x(t_1) = 0$$

and so z defined by (8.18) satisfies

$$\int_0^{t_1} \langle\dot{x}(t)+\mathcal{A}x(t),z(t)\rangle_{X,Z}dt + \int_0^{t_1} \langle Cx(t),u(t)\rangle_{Y,U}dt + \langle x(0),z_o\rangle_{X,Z} = 0$$

This suggests that z is a weak solution of a controlled abstract differential equation. To see how we can derive this equation we assume that A, the infinitesimal generator of T_t, and $\mathcal{A}$, the generator of T_t^*, are defined on appropriate function-spaces on an open bounded set Ω, with boundary conditions on Γ, the boundary of Ω. If Y is a Banach space of functions on a subset Ω_1 of $\bar{\Omega}$ we denote by $\tilde{A}$ the same formal operator as

A, but now defined on the restriction of the function space to Ω/Ω_1, with the same boundary conditions on Γ/Ω_1. Then we assume the existence of a Green's formula

$$(8.20) \qquad \langle\phi,\tilde{A}\psi\rangle_{X,Z} = \langle \mathcal{A}\phi,\psi\rangle_{X,Z} + \langle C\phi,D\psi\rangle_{Y,U} + \langle G\phi,E\psi\rangle_{Y,U}$$

for $\phi \in D(\mathcal{A})$, $\psi \in D(\tilde{A})$.

We will show that (8.18) is a weak solution of the differential equation

$$(8.21) \qquad \begin{aligned} \dot{z} &= \tilde{A}z \\ Dz = u, \quad Ez &= 0, \quad z(0) = z_o \end{aligned}$$

where our definition of a weak solution is motivated by Lemma 8.4.

<u>Definition 8.5</u>

A weak solution of (8.21) is a function $z \in C[0,t_1;Z]$ such that

$$(8.22) \quad \int_o^{t_1} \langle f(t),z(t)\rangle_{X,Z}dt + \int_o^{t_1} \langle Cx(t),u(t)\rangle_{Y,U} + \langle x(0),z_o\rangle = 0$$

where

$$\dot{x} + \mathcal{A}x = f$$

$$x(t_1) = 0, \; f \in C^1[0,t_1;X]$$

To see that this is a reasonable definition we apply the Green's formula (8.20) with $\phi = x$, $\psi = z$ to obtain

$$\begin{aligned} 0 &= \int_o^{t_1} \langle x(t),\dot{z}(t)-\tilde{A}z(t)\rangle_{X,Z}dt \\ &= \langle x(t_1),z(t_1)\rangle_{X,Z} - \langle x(0),z_o\rangle_{X,Z} - \int_o^{t_1} \langle\dot{x}(t)+\mathcal{A}x(t),z(t)\rangle_{X,Z}dt \\ &\qquad - \int_o^{t_1} \langle Cx(t),u(t)\rangle_{Y,U} - \int_o^{t_1} \langle Gx(t),Ez(t)\rangle_{Y,U}dt \end{aligned}$$

since $\tilde{A}$ satisfies (8.21).

But $x(t_1) = 0$, $Ez = 0$ and $\dot{x} + \mathcal{A}x = f$, and so we obtain (8.22).

With this definition of a weak solution, Lemma (8.4) yields the following theorem.

Theorem 8.6

Under the assumptions (8.17) and (8.20)

$$z(t) = T_t z_o + \int_o^t T_{t-s} Bu(s)ds$$

is a weak solution of (8.21).

Example 8.7

To apply these abstract results to Examples 8.1 and 8.2 we specify the spaces and operators as follows

$$\Omega = (0,1), \; X = L^2(\Omega), \; D(\mathcal{A}) = H^2(\Omega) \cap H^1_o(\Omega)$$

$$\mathcal{A}x = x_{\xi\xi}, \; Cx = x(\xi_1,t)$$

We have the Green's formula (8.20)

$$(8.20) \qquad \int_o^1 \phi\psi_{\xi\xi} = \int_o^1 \phi_{\xi\xi}\psi - C\phi[\psi_\xi]_{\xi_1} + \phi_\xi(\xi_1)[\psi]_{\xi_1}$$

So $D\psi = -[\psi_\xi]_{\xi_1}$, $E\psi = [\psi]_{\xi_1}$ and $D(\tilde{A}) = H^2(\Omega\backslash\{\xi_1\}) \cap H^1_o(\Omega\backslash\{\xi_1\})$

Hence the dual system is the diffusion equation of Example 8.2 with $z(0,t) = z(1,t) = 0$, $z(\xi,t)$ continuous at ξ_1 but has a discontinuity of z_ξ at ξ_1 such that $-[z_\xi]_{\xi_1} = u$.

Note that $H^2(\Omega\backslash\{\xi_1\}) \not\subset C^1(\Omega)$ since the open set $\Omega\backslash\{\xi_1\}$ is not locally on one side of its boundary.

Example 8.8

Consider now the following observed system on $L^2(0,1)$

$$x_t = x_{\xi\xi}$$

$$x(0,t) = x_\xi(1,t) = 0, \; x(\xi,0) = x_o(\xi)$$

Then $$D(\mathcal{A}) = H^2(\Omega) \cap \{x \in H^o(\Omega), \; x(0) = x_\xi(1) = 0\}$$

$$Cx = x(1)$$

and $$D(\tilde{A}) = H^2(\Omega) \cap \{z \in H^o(\Omega), \; z(0) = 0\}$$

The condition $z_\xi(1) = 0$ is not necessarily satisfied since $\Omega_1 = \{1\}$.

Then $Dz = z_\xi(1)$, and the dual controlled system is

$$z_t = z_{\xi\xi}$$

$$z(0,t) = 0,\ z_\xi(1,t) = u,\ z(\xi,0) = z_o(\xi).$$

8.3 Perturbation results

As in Chapter 3, we shall consider feedback controls $u = Fz$ for the system (8.2) where B is an unbounded operator satisfying the assumptions (8.17), but now we may also include the case where F is unbounded. Our assumptions on the feedback operator F are similar to those for the observation operator C, namely:

There exists a Banach space $\bar{W}$ dense in Z such that

(8.23)

(a) $Z \supset D(F) \supset \bar{W}$

(b) $F \in \mathcal{L}(\bar{W},U)$

(c) $T_t \in \mathcal{L}(Z,\bar{W}) \quad t > 0$

(d) $\|T_t z\|_{\bar{W}} \leq \bar{g}(t)\|z\|_Z$ for all $z \in Z$, and $\bar{g} \in L^p[0,t_1]$

We have the following

Theorem 8.9

Let F satisfy the assumptions (8.23), and B the assumptions (8.17), with $\frac{1}{p} + \frac{1}{q} = 1$, then the controlled system

$$z(t) = T_t z_o + \int_0^t T_{t-s} Bu(s)ds$$

with $u(t) = Fz(t)$ has a unique solution

$$z(t) = V_t z_o$$

where V_t is the strongly continuous semigroup, which is the unique solution of

(8.24)
$$V_t z_o = T_t z_o + \int_0^t T_{t-s} BFV_s z_o\, ds$$

Proof

First we show that for $u \in L^p[0,t_1;U]$, $Fz \in L^p[0,t_1;U]$. Indeed

$$Fz(t) = FT_t z_o + \int_0^t FT_{t-s} Bu(s)ds$$

Thus

$$\|Fz(t)\|_U \le \|F\|_{\mathcal{L}(\bar{W},U)}\bar{g}(t)\|z_o\|_Z$$

$$+ \int_0^t \|F\|_{\mathcal{L}(\bar{W},U)}\bar{g}(\tfrac{1}{2}(t-s))g(\tfrac{1}{2}(t-s))\|B\|_{\mathcal{L}(U,\tilde{W})}\|u(s)\|_U\, ds$$

Clearly the first term on the right hand side is in $L^p[0,t_1]$. For the second term we have $g\bar{g} \in L^1[0,t_1]$ since $\frac{1}{p} + \frac{1}{q} = 1$. Thus the second term is a convolution of an L^1 function with an L^p function and so is in $L^p[0,t_1]$.

We will construct the semigroup V_t by means of the iterative scheme

$$(8.25)\qquad \begin{aligned} V_o(t) &= T_t \\ V_n(t)z &= \int_0^t T_{t-s}BFV_{n-1}(s)z\, ds \\ FV_n(t)z &= \int_0^t FT_{t-s}BFV_{n-1}(s)z\, ds \end{aligned}$$

We need the following lemma

Lemma 8.10

Consider the integral equation

$$(8.26)\qquad f(t) = h(t) + \int_0^t g(t-s)f(s)ds$$

where $h \in L^p[0,t_1]$, $g \in L^1[0,t_1]$ and are positive. Then (8.26) has a unique solution $f \in L^p[0,t_1]$.

Proof

Set $\int_0^t e^{-\omega s}g(t)ds = M_\omega$ for $\omega > 0$, and note that for ω sufficiently large we may choose $M_\omega < 1$.

We have

$$\int_0^t g(t-s)h(s)ds \le e^{\omega t}\int_0^t e^{-\omega(t-s)}g(t-s)h(s)ds$$

Thus

$$\begin{aligned}\|g * h\|_{L^p[0,t_1]} &\le e^{\omega t_1}\|e^{-\omega\cdot}g(\cdot) * h(\cdot)\|_{L^p[0,t_1]} \\ &\le e^{\omega t_1}\|e^{-\omega\cdot}g(\cdot)\|_{L^1[0,t_1]}\|h\|_{L^p[0,t_1]}\end{aligned}$$

$$\leq e^{\omega t_1} M_\omega \|h\|_{L^p[0,t_1]}$$

So the Volterra operator G is well defined, where G is given by

$$(Gh)(t) = \int_0^t g(t-s)h(s)ds$$

The iterates G^n are given by

$$(G^n h)(t) = \int_0^t g_n(t-s)h(s)ds$$

where

$$g_n(t) = \int_0^t g(t-s)g_{n-1}(s)ds$$

$$g_1(t) = g(t)$$

Now by induction we prove that

$$\int_0^{t_1} e^{-\omega t} g_n(t)dt \leq M_\omega^n$$

Supposing the result is valid for n-1, we have

$$\int_0^{t_1} e^{-\omega t} g_n(t)dt = \int_0^{t_1} e^{-\omega t} \int_0^t g(t-s)g_{n-1}(s)ds\, dt$$

$$= \int_0^{t_1} \int_s^{t_1} e^{-\omega t} g(t-s)g_{n-1}(s)dt\, ds$$

Setting $t = \rho + s$ we obtain

$$\int_0^{t_1} e^{-\omega t} g_n(t)dt \leq \int_0^{t_1} \int_0^{t_1} e^{-\omega(\rho+s)} g(\rho)g_{n-1}(s)d\rho\, ds$$

$$= M_\omega^n$$

Thus $$\|(G^n h)(\cdot)\|_{L^p} \leq e^{\omega t_1} M_\omega^n \|h\|_{L^p}$$

By choosing ω so that $M_\omega < 1$, we see that the series $h(\cdot) + \sum_{n=1}^{\infty} G^n h(\cdot)$ converges in $L^p[0,t_1]$, from which it follows that

$$f(t) = h(t) + \sum_{n=1}^{\infty} (G^n h)(t)$$

is the unique solution of (8.26).

Corollary 8.11 Generalized Gronwall's Inequality

Suppose

$$f(t) \leq h(t) + \int_0^t g(t-s)f(s)ds$$

with $h \in L^p[0,t_1]$, $g \in L^1[0,t_1]$ both positive, then

$$f(t) \leq h(t) + \sum_{n=1}^{\infty} (G^n h)(t)$$

and in particular if $h = 0$, then $f = 0$.

Returning to the proof of Theorem 8.9, we use Lemma 8.10 to show that in U, $FV_o(t) + \sum_{n=1}^{\infty} FV_n(t)$ is majorized by $\bar{g}(t) + \sum_{n=1}^{\infty} (G^n\bar{g})(t)$ and hence the series converges and the limit $(FV(t))_\infty$ satisfies

$$(8.27) \qquad (FV(t))_\infty z = FT_t z + \int_0^t FT_{t-s}B(FV(s))_\infty z \, ds$$

in $L^p[0,t_1;U]$.

Moreover we have

$$\|FV_n z\|_{L^p[0,t_1;U]} \leq e^{\omega t_1} M_\omega^n \|\bar{g}\|_{L^p[0,t_1]} \|z\|_Z$$

Hence

$$\|V_n(t)z\|_Z \leq e^{\omega t_1} M_\omega^{n-1} \|\bar{g}\|_{L^p[0,t_1]} \|g\|_{L^q[0,t_1]} \|z\|_Z$$

So $\Sigma V_n(t)z$ converges and the limit $V_\infty(t)z$ must satisfy

$$V_\infty(t)z = T_t z + \int_0^t T_{t-s}B(FV(s))_\infty z \, ds$$

So $FV_\infty(t)$ satisfies (8.27) and we have

$$FV_\infty(t) = (FV(t))_\infty$$

That is $V_\infty(t) = V_t$ is the unique solution of (8.24).

The strong continuity of V_t can be proved via the construction or we may prove it directly as follows.

Let $h > 0$, then we have

$$(V_{t+h}-V_t)z = T_{t+h}z - T_tz + (T_h-I)\int_0^t T_{t-s}BFV_sz\,ds$$
$$+ \int_t^{t+h} T_{t+h-s}BFV_sz\,ds$$

From which the continuity on the right follows using the strong continuity of T_t and the fact that $T_{t-s}BFV_sz \in L^1[0,t_1;Z]$. For the continuity on the left we have for $t > h > 0$.

$$(V_t-V_{t-h})z = T_tz - T_{t-h}z + \int_0^{t-h} T_{t-s-h}BF(V_s-V_{s+h})z\,ds$$
$$+ \int_{-h}^{0} T_{t-s-h}BFV_{s+h}z\,ds$$

So the continutiy on the left follows from the strong continuity of T_t, the continuity on the right of V_t and the fact that

$$T_{t-s}BFV_sz \in L^1[0,t_1;Z]$$

For the semigroup property we can easily show

$$F(V_{t+s}-V_tV_s)z = \int_0^t FT_{t-\sigma}BF(V_{s+\sigma}-V_\sigma V_s)z\,d\sigma$$

Then using the generalized Gronwall's lemma we have

$$F(V_{t+s}-V_tV_s)z = 0 \text{ in } L^p[0,t_1;Z]$$

We also have

$$(V_{t+s}-V_tV_s)z = \int_0^t T_{t-\sigma}BF(V_{s+\sigma}-V_\sigma V_s)z\,d\sigma$$

Hence $V_{t+s} = V_tV_s$.

The Theorem shows that we are able to construct a semigroup V_t from a feedback perturbation of the original semigroup, but it is not clear what is the generator of the semigroup. In this direction we have the following.

Proposition 8.12

If there exists a Green's formula (8.20) with $B = C^*$, then V_t is a quasi evolution operator with quasi generator $\tilde{A}$ on $D(\tilde{A}) \cap \text{kernel}(F-D) \cap \text{kernel}(E) = \mathscr{D}$ (see Definition 2.35).

Proof

We need to show

$$\int_0^t V_\rho \tilde{A} z_o \, d\rho = V_t z_o - z_o \tag{8.28}$$

for $z_o \in \mathcal{D}$. Let $z_o \in \mathcal{D}$ and $x \in X$, then

$$<x,\int_0^t V_{t-\rho}\tilde{A}z_o d\rho>_{X,Z} = <x,\int_0^t T_{t-\rho}\tilde{A}z_o d\rho>_{X,Z} + <x,\int_0^t\int_\rho^t T_{t-s}BFV_{s-\rho}\tilde{A}z_o ds\, d\rho>_{X,Z}$$

$$= <\int_0^t S_{t-\rho}x\, d\rho,\tilde{A}z_o>_{X,Z} + <x,\int_0^t\int_0^s T_{t-s}BFV_{s-\rho}\tilde{A}z_o d\rho\, ds>_{X,Z}$$

But $\int_0^t S_{t-\rho}x\, d\rho \in D(\mathcal{a})$, $\forall\, x \in X$, and $\mathcal{a}\int_0^t S_{t-\rho}x\, d\rho = S_t x - x$

Hence using the Green's formula (8.20), we have

$$<x,\int_0^t V_{t-\rho}\tilde{A}z_o d\rho>_{X,Z} = <S_t x-x,z_o>_{X,Z} + <C\int_0^t S_{t-\rho}x\, d\rho,Dz_o>_{Y,U}$$

$$+ <x,\int_0^t T_{t-s}BF\int_0^s V_{s-\rho}\tilde{A}z_o d\rho\, ds>_{X,Z}$$

$$= <x,T_t z_o-z_o>_{X,Z} + <x,\int_0^t T_{t-\rho}BFz_o d\rho>_{X,Z}$$

$$+ <x,\int_0^t T_{t-s}BF\int_0^s V_{s-\rho}\tilde{A}z_o d\rho\, ds>_{X,Z}$$

since $Dz_o = Fz_o$.

Thus

$$<x,\int_0^t V_{t-\rho}\tilde{A}z_o d\rho+z_o>_{X,Z} = <x,T_t z_o+\int_0^t T_{t-s}BF[\int_0^s V_{s-\rho}\tilde{A}z_o d\rho+z_o]ds$$

for all $x \in X$. So for $z_o \in \mathcal{D}$ $\int_0^t V_{t-\rho}\tilde{A}z_o d\rho + z_o$ satisfies (8.24), and hence

$$\int_0^t V_{t-\rho}\tilde{A}z_o d\rho = V_t z_o - z_o \quad \text{for } z_o \in \mathcal{D}$$

that is $\tilde{A}$ is the quasi generator of V_t (see Definition 2.35).

Now let $\mathcal{A}$ be the generator of V_t (in the sense of Definition 2.7), then clearly $D(\mathcal{A}) \supset \mathcal{D}$, and

$$\mathcal{A}z_o = \tilde{A}z_o \text{ for } z_o \in \mathcal{D} \tag{8.29}$$

Hence the generator of V_t is a closed extension of $\tilde{A}$.

Example 8.13

Consider the controlled diffusion equation

$$z_t = z_{\xi\xi}$$

(8.30) $$z(0,t) = 0, \quad z_\xi(1,t) = u, \quad z(\xi,0) = z_0(\xi)$$

If we denote by T_t the semigroup generated by the operator A, where

$$Az = z_{\xi\xi}$$

and $D(A) = \{z \in L^2[0,1] : z(0) = z_\xi(1) = 0\} \cap H^2(0,1)$,

we have the following Green's formula

$$<\phi,\tilde{A}\psi>_{L^2[0,1]} = <\mathcal{A}\phi,\psi>_{L^2[0,1]} + \phi(1)\psi_\xi(1)$$

where $\mathcal{A} = A^* = A$, $C\phi = \phi(1)$, and

$$\tilde{A}\psi = \psi_{\xi\xi}$$

$$D(\tilde{A}) = \{\psi \in L^2[0,1]; \ \psi(0) = 0\} \cap H^2(0,1)$$

Thus $$z(t) = T_t z_0 + \int_0^t T_{t-s} Bu(s)ds$$

is a weak solution of (8.30) where $B = \delta(1-\xi)$. The term $z_\xi(1,t) = u$, being interpreted as $-[z_\xi(\xi,t)]_1 = u(t)$.

We take as feedback control $u = \alpha z(\xi_1,t)$, $0 < \xi_1 < 1$, so $(Fz)(\xi,t) = \alpha z(\xi_1,t)$. F satisfies the conditions (8.23), so we are able to define a semigroup V_t such that

$$V_t z = T_t z + \int_0^t T_{t-s} BFV_s z \, ds$$

Its generator being an extension of the operator $\tilde{A}$ with domain $\mathcal{D}$, where

$$\tilde{A}z = z_{\xi\xi}$$

and $\mathcal{D} = \{z \in L^2[0,1]: z(0) = 0, \ z_\xi(1) = \alpha z(\xi_1)\} \cap H^2(0,1)$

In order to examine the linear quadratic control and filtering problems with unbounded control and sensing we will need to consider time dependent feedback operators F. However, in general they will not be unbounded but will satisfy the following conditions

(8.31)
(a) $F(t) \in \mathcal{L}(Z,U)$ for almost all $t \in [0,t_1]$

(b) $\|F(t)\|_{\mathcal{L}(Z,U)} \leq \underline{g}(t)$, where $\underline{g} \in L^p[0,t_1]$

Moreover we will show in §8.5 that (8.31)(b) may be replaced by

$$\|F(t)\|_{\mathcal{L}(Z,U)} \leq \bar{M}\, \underline{g}(\alpha-t) \text{ for } t_1 \geq \alpha > t$$

where $\bar{M}$ is a constant.

Clearly we would not expect to generate a semigroup from these time dependent feedback operators. However, by a straightforward extension of Theorem 8.9 , it is possible to prove

Proposition 8.14

Under the conditions (8.31) on the feedback operator and conditions (8.17) on B there exists a mild evolution operator U(t,s) satisfying

$$U(t,s)z = T_{t-s}z + \int_s^t T_{t-\rho}BF(\rho)U(\rho,s)z \, d\rho \tag{8.32}$$

Moreover the evolution operator is quasi in the sense that

$$\int_s^t U(t,\rho)\left[A + BF(\rho)\right]z_o \, d\rho = U(t,s)z_o - z_o \tag{8.33}$$

for $z_o \in D(A)$. Or equivalently

$$\int_s^t U(t,\rho)\tilde{A}z_o \, d\rho = U(t,s)z_o - z_o \tag{8.34}$$

for $z_o \in D(\tilde{A}) \cap \ker[D - F(\rho)] \cap \text{kernel } E$ for almost all $\rho \in [0,t_1]$.

8.4 Controllability, observability and stabilizability

In the preceding sections we have set up a structure by which problems of unbounded sensing and control can be examined. This framework ensures that all the definitions in Chapter 3 make sense, and Theorems 3.7, 3.11, 3.25 are still valid. We will now consider a number of specific applications to problems of controllability, observability and stabilizability.

---

* When there is no confusion we will drop the subscript from $\|\cdot\|$

Example 8.15

Consider the system

$$x_t = x_{\xi\xi}$$

$$x_\xi(0,t) = x_\xi(1,t) = 0, \; x(\xi,0) = x_o(\xi)$$

with observation map given by

$$y(t) = Cx(t) = x(\xi_1,t)$$

We seek sufficient conditions on ξ_1, t_1 for the system to be finally continuously observable on $[0,t_1]$; that is the map

$$R: x(\xi_1,\cdot) \to x(\cdot,t_1) \text{ from } L^q[0,t_1] \to X = L^2[0,1]$$

is well defined and continuous. In §8.1 we have already seen that $Cx \in L^q[0,t_1]$ for all $q < 4$. Now

$$x(\xi,t) = \sum_{n=o}^{\infty} C_n e^{-n^2\pi^2 t}\psi_n(\xi)$$

where

$$\psi_n(\xi) = \begin{cases} \sqrt{2}\cos n\pi\xi & n \neq 0 \\ 1 & n = 0 \end{cases}$$

and

$$C_n = \langle x_o, \psi_n \rangle_X$$

The first requirement we make is that $|\psi_n(\xi_1)| > 0$, which means that ξ_1 is an irrational number. Then by a result of Luxemburg and Korevaar[17]

$$|C_n| \leq (d_n|\psi_n(\xi_1)|)^{-1}\|x(\xi_1,\cdot)\|_{L^q[0,t_1]}$$

$$d_n^{-1} \leq \exp(2\varepsilon n^2\pi^2) \text{ as } n \to \infty \text{ for any } \varepsilon > 0.$$

where d_n is the distance between $x^{n^2\pi^2}$ and the closed linear hull of $\{x^{m^2\pi^2}\}_{m\neq n}$ in L^q norm spaces.

Thus

$$\|x(\cdot,t_1)\|_X \leq \sum_{n=0}^{\infty} |c_n| \, \|\psi_n\| e^{-n^2\pi^2 t_1}$$

$$\leq \sum_{n=0}^{\infty} \frac{e^{-n^2\pi^2 t_1}}{d_n|\psi_n(\xi_1)|} \|x(\xi_1,\cdot)\|_{L^q[0,t_1]}$$

$$\leq \sum_{n=0}^{\infty} \frac{e^{-n^2\pi^2(t_1-2\varepsilon)}}{|\psi_n(\xi_1)|} \|x(\xi_1,\cdot)\|_{L^q[0,t_1]}$$

So the map R will be well defined and continuous if the series

$$\sum_{n=0}^{\infty} \frac{e^{-n^2\pi^2(t_1-2\varepsilon)}}{|\psi_n(\xi_1)|}$$

is convergent, and this is so for any irrational ξ_1, and any $t_1 > 2\varepsilon$. That is, the system is finally continuously observable on $[0,t_1]$ for any $t_1 > 0$.

By the duality Theorem 3.7 we are able to conclude that the dual system

$$z_t = z_{\xi\xi}$$

$$z_\xi(0,t) = z_\xi(1,t) = 0, \; z(\xi,0) = z_0(\xi)$$

$$-\; [z_\xi(\xi,t)]_{\xi_1} = u(t)$$

with $u \in L^p[0,t_1]$ and $p > \frac{4}{3}$ is exactly initially controllable on $[0,t_1]$ for any $t_1 > 0$ if ξ_1 is an irrational point.

In Chapter 3 we introduced the concept of stabilizability which we now extend to allow for unbounded control action and unbounded sensing.

Definition 8.16

We say that the system (8.1) is exponentially stabilizable for T_t and B satisfying (8.17) if there exists a feedback control law $u = Fz$ satisfying (8.23) such that the semigroup V_t generated by

(8.35) $$V_t z = T_t z + \int_0^t T_{t-s} BFV_s z \, ds$$

satisfies

$$\|V_t\| \leq Me^{-\omega t} \qquad \text{for some } \omega > 0.$$

If we now assume that Assumption 3.2 holds so that we can decompose the dynamical system 8.1 into components

$$z_u(t) = T_t^u z_{ou} + \int_o^t T_{t-\rho}^u Bu(\rho)d\rho$$

$$z_s(t) = T_t^s z_{os} + \int_o^t T_{t-\rho}^s Bu(\rho)d$$

then we are able to prove the following generalization of Theorem 3.32.

Theorem 8.17

If

(a) (8.17) holds for T_t and B, and Assumption 3.1 holds for T_t^s

(b) the projection onto Z_u is exponentially stabilizable by a feedback control, $F \in \mathcal{L}(Z_u,U)$

then (A,B) is exponentially stabilizable.

Proof

If P is the projection of Z onto Z_u, we have

$$T_t^s = (I-P)T_t$$

and by (a) there exists K,δ, such that

$$\|(I-P)T_t\|_{\mathcal{L}(Z_s)} \leq Ke^{-(\delta-\varepsilon)t} \quad t \geq 0, \ \varepsilon > 0.$$

Thus

$$\|(I-P)T_{2t}\|_{\mathcal{L}(\tilde{W},Z_s)} \leq \|(I-P)T_t\|_{\mathcal{L}(Z_s)}\|T_t\|_{\mathcal{L}(\tilde{W},Z)}$$

$$\leq Ke^{-(\delta-\varepsilon)t}g(t) \quad g \in L^q[0,t_1]$$

or

$$\|(I-P)T_t\|_{\mathcal{L}(\tilde{W},Z_s)} \leq Ke^{-\frac{\delta-\varepsilon}{2}t}g'(t) \quad g' \in L^q[0,t_1]$$

From Assumption (b) there exists a feedback control $u = Fz_u$ with

$$z_u(t) = T_t^u z_o + \int_o^t T_{t-s}^u BFz_u(s)ds$$

and

$$\|z_u(t)\| \leq Ce^{-\rho t}\|z_{ou}\|$$

for some C and $\rho > 0$.

The application of this control on Z_s yields

$$\|z_s(t)\| \le Ke^{-(\delta-\varepsilon)t}\|z_{os}\| + \int_0^t e^{\frac{-\delta-\varepsilon}{2}(t-\sigma)} g'(t-\sigma)e^{-\rho\sigma}\|B\|_{\mathcal{L}(U,\tilde{W})}\|F\|KC\|z_{ou}\|d\sigma$$

$$\le Ke^{-(\delta-\varepsilon)t}\|z_{os}\| + \|g'\|_{L^q[0,t_1]}\|B\|_{\mathcal{L}(U,\tilde{W})}\|F\|KC\frac{e^{-\frac{\delta-\varepsilon}{2}t}-e^{-\rho t}}{[p(\frac{\delta-\varepsilon}{2}-\rho)]^{1/p}}\|z_{ou}\|$$

where $\frac{1}{p} + \frac{1}{q} = 1.$

Thus the response of the whole system is given by

$$\|z(t)\| = \|z_s(t) + z_u(t)\|$$

$$\le \left(K\|I-P\|e^{-(\delta-\varepsilon)t} + \|P\|\|g'\|_{L^q}\|B\|_{\mathcal{L}(U,\tilde{W})}\|F\|KC\left[\frac{e^{-\frac{(\delta-\varepsilon)}{2}t}-e^{-\rho t}}{[p(\frac{\delta-\varepsilon}{2}-\rho)]^{1/p}}\right] + Ce^{-\rho t}\|P\|\right)\|z_o\|$$

and this completes the proof.

Corollary 8.18

If the conditions of Theorem 8.3 hold except (b) is replaced by

(a) The space Z_u is finite dimensional

(b) The projection onto Z_u is controllable

then the same conclusion of the theorem is valid.

Example 8.19

Consider the system

$$z_t = z_{\xi\xi} + 4\pi^2 z \text{ on } (0,1)$$

$$[z_\xi]_0 = u,\ z_\xi(1,t) = 0,\ z(\xi,0) = z_o(\xi)$$

The semigroup T_t on $L^2[0,1]$ is given by

$$T_t z_o = e^{4\pi^2 t}\int_0^1 z_o(\xi)d\xi + \sum_{n=1}^{\infty} 2e^{\pi^2(4-n^2 t)}\cos n\pi\xi \int_0^1 \cos n\pi\eta\, z_o(\eta)d\eta$$

Hence Z_u is the three dimensional space spanned by

$$\{\cos n\pi\xi;\ n = 0,1,2\}$$

We have

$$\|T_t^s\| \leq e^{-5\pi^2 t}$$

As in Example 8.2 it is possible to check that $T_t:(H^{\frac{1}{2}+\varepsilon}(0,1))^* \to L^2[0,1]$ with

$$\|T_t\|_{\mathcal{L}((H^{\frac{1}{2}+\varepsilon})^*,H^0)} \leq g(t) \quad g \in L^q,\ q < 4$$

The projection of Z_u is exactly controllable, in the case

$$B^* T_t^{u*} P z_u = 0 \ \forall\ t \geq 0 \text{ implies } P z_u = 0.$$

But

$$B^* T_t^{u*} P z_u = e^{4\pi^2 t} z_1 + 2e^{3\pi^2 t} z_2 + 2z_3$$

Hence the system is controllable on the finite dimensional space Z_u and so the overall system is stabilizable by Corollary (8.2).

8.5 The quadratic cost control problem

In this section we consider the linear quadratic control problem and develop the Riccati equation for the control problem on a Hilbert space H

$$(8.36) \qquad z(t) = T_{t-t_o} z_o + \int_{t_o}^{t} T_{t-s} Bu(s)ds$$

where T_t and B are assumed to satisfy (8.17) with $p = 2$, $u \in L^2[t_o,t_1;U]$ and U is a Hilbert space. The performance index is taken to be

$$(8.37) \quad J(u;t_o,z_o) = \langle z(t_1),Gz(t_1)\rangle_H + \int_{t_o}^{t_1} [\langle z(t),Mz(t)\rangle_H + \langle u(t),Ru(t)\rangle_U]dt$$

with the conditions that M and $G \in \mathcal{L}(H)$ are self adjoint and non-negative and $R^{-1}, R \in \mathcal{L}(U)$ is self adjoint and strictly positive.

The optimal control will be determined by the same method as in Chapter 4, that is we consider the following sequence of feedback controls for $k = 0,1,2,\ldots$

$$(8.38) \qquad u_k(t) = -F_k(t)z(t)$$

$$(8.39) \qquad F_k(t) = R^* B^* Q_{k-1}(t),\ F_o(t) = 0$$

$$(8.40) \qquad M_k(t) = M + F_k^*(t)RF_k(t)$$

$$(8.41)\qquad Q_k(t)h = U_k^*(t_1,t)GU_k(t_1,t)h + \int_t^{t_1} U_k^*(s,t)M_k(s)U_k(s,t)h\,ds$$

where $U_k(t,s)$ is the perturbation of T_t by $-BF_k(t)$, that is

$$(8.42)\qquad U_k(t,s)h = T_{t-s}h - \int_s^t T_{t-\rho}BF_k(\rho)U_k(\rho,s)h\,d\rho$$

First we need to verify that the iterative scheme is well defined.
For $k = 1$, we have

$$F_1(t) = R^{-1}B^*Q_o(t)$$

where

$$Q_o(t)h = T^*_{t_1-t}GT_{t_1-t}h + \int_t^{t_1} T^*_{s-t}MT_{s-t}h\,ds$$

Now from (8.17)

$$\|T_t\|_{\mathcal{L}(\tilde{W},H)} \leq g(t), \quad g \in L^2[t_o,t_1]$$

and from Theorem 2.5 there exists a constant $\bar{M}$ such that

$$\|T_t\|_{\mathcal{L}(H)} \leq \bar{M} \text{ for } t \in [t_o,t_1], \text{ so}$$

$$(8.43)\qquad \|Q(t)\|_{\mathcal{L}(\tilde{W},H)} \leq \bar{M}\|G\|g(t_1-t) + \int_t^{t_1} \bar{M}\|M\|g(s-t)ds$$

where we do not specify $\|\ \|$ if it is the norm in $\mathcal{L}(H)$ or $\mathcal{L}(U)$.
Thus

$$(8.44)\qquad \|F_1(t)\|_{\mathcal{L}(H,U)} = \|F_1^*(t)\|_{\mathcal{L}(U,H)} \leq \|R^{-1}\|\|B\|_{\mathcal{L}(U,\tilde{W})}\|Q_o(t)\|_{\mathcal{L}(\tilde{W},H)}$$

$$= \underline{g}_1(t)$$

where

$$g_1(t) = \|R^{-1}\|_{\mathcal{L}(U)}\|B\|_{\mathcal{L}(U,\tilde{W})}\left[\bar{M}\|G\|g(t_1-t) + \int_o^{t_1-t} \bar{M}\|M\|g(s)ds\right]$$

and $g \in L^2[t_o,t_1]$.
Note also that since $T_t = T_{t-s}T_s$ for $t \geq s$, we have

$$\|T_t\|_{\mathcal{L}(\tilde{W},H)} \leq \bar{M}g(t-s) \text{ for } t > s.$$

Then substituting in (8.43) we obtain

$$\|Q_o(t)\|_{\mathcal{L}(\widetilde{W},H)} \leq \overline{M}^2\|G\|g(\alpha-t) + \int_t^{t_1} \overline{M}\|M\|g(s-t)ds$$

for any $t_1 \geq \alpha > t$. Hence since $\overline{M} \geq 1$

(8.45) $$\|F_1(t)\|_{\mathcal{L}(H,U)} \leq \overline{M}\underline{g}_1(\alpha-t) \text{ for any } t_1 \geq \alpha > t.$$

So (8.44) and (8.45) allow us to appeal to Proposition (8.14) which says that $U_1(t,s)$ is well defined by (8.42). Furthermore, from (8.45) we have

$$\|U_1(t,s)\|_{\mathcal{L}(\widetilde{W},H)} \leq g(t-s) + M\int_s^t g(t-\rho)\|B\|_{\mathcal{L}(U,\widetilde{W})}g_1(t-\rho)\|U_1(\rho,s)\|_{\mathcal{L}(\widetilde{W},H)}d\rho$$

Now $g\ \underline{g}_1 \in L^1[t_o,t_1]$, hence using the generalized Gronwall's inequality (Corollary 8.1) we have

$$\|U_1(t,s)\|_{\mathcal{L}(\widetilde{W},H)} \leq g_1(t-s) \text{ where } g_1 \in L^2[t_o,t_1].$$

From (8.40)

$$\|M_1(t)\| \leq \|M\| + \|R\|\ \|F_1(t)\|^2_{\mathcal{L}(H,U)} \leq \|M\| + \|R\|\underline{g}_1^2(t)$$

Thus (8.41) is well defined, for $k = 1$, moreover using (8.45) and $\|U_1(t,s)\| \leq \overline{M}_1$ for some $\overline{M}_1 > 0$, $t_1 \geq s \geq t_o$.

$$\|Q_1(t)\|_{\mathcal{L}(\widetilde{W},H)} \leq \overline{M}_1\|G\|g_1(t_1-t) + \int_t^{t_1} \overline{M}_1\left[\|M\| + \|R\|\underline{g}_1^2(t_1-s)\right]g_1(s-t)ds$$

Hence

$$\|F_2(t)\|_{\mathcal{L}(H,U)} \leq \underline{g}_2(t) \text{ for some } \underline{g}_2 \in L^2[t_o,t_1]$$

and by the same argument used to show (8.45) we can show that

$$\|F_2(t)\|_{\mathcal{L}(H,U)} \leq \overline{M}_1\underline{g}_2(\alpha-t) \text{ for } t_1 \geq \alpha > t$$

So the iterative scheme is well defined for $k = 1$, and the estimates on $U_1(t,s)$ and $F_2(t)$ are similar to those assumed for T_{t-s} and $F_1(t)$. A simple induction argument can now be used to extend the argument for all k.

It is now straightforward to prove the extensions of Lemmas 4.1 and 4.2 for this unbounded case, and so we are able to show that $Q_k(t)$ converges strongly to a self adjoint operator $Q(t)$ as $k \to \infty$. However, before we can derive an integral expression for $Q(t)$ it is necessary to show that the estimates are uniform on k.

Lemma 8.20

F_k, U_k are uniformly bounded in the sense that there exist functions $g_\infty, g_\infty \in L^2[t_o, t_1]$ and a constant $\beta > 0$, such that

$$\|U_k(t,s)\|_{\mathcal{L}(H)} \le \beta \quad t_1 \ge t \ge s \ge t_o \quad \forall\, k = 0,1,\ldots$$

$$\|F_k(t)\|_{\mathcal{L}(H,U)} \le \underline{g}_\infty(t) \quad \forall\, k = 0,1,\ldots$$

$$\|U_k(t,s)\|_{\mathcal{L}(W,H)} \le g_\infty(t) \quad \forall\, k = 0,1,\ldots$$

Proof

As in the proof of Lemma 4.3 there exists a constant β such that

$$\sup_{t \in T} \|Q_k(t)\| \le \beta \quad \forall\, k = 0,1,\ldots$$

Now

$$\langle h, Q_k(t)h\rangle = \langle U_k^*(t_1,t)h, GU_k(t_1,t)h\rangle + \int_t^{t_1} \langle h, U_k^*(s,t)\left[M+F_k^*(s)RF_k(s)\right]U_k(s,t)h\rangle\, ds$$

Hence

$$\int_t^{t_1} \|R^{\frac{1}{2}}F_k(s)U_k(s,t)h\|^2\, ds \le \beta\|h\|^2$$

But R, R^{-1} are positive operators, so

$$\int_t^{t_1} \|F_k(s)U_k(s,t)h\|^2\, ds \le \beta\|h\|^2\|R^{-1}\| \tag{8.47}$$

From (8.42)

$$\|U_k(t,s)h\| \le \|T_{t-s}h\| + \int_s^t \|T_{t-\rho}\|_{\mathcal{L}(\tilde{W},H)}\|B\|_{\mathcal{L}(U,\tilde{W})}\|F_k(\rho)U_k(\rho,s)h\|\, d\rho$$

Therefore

$$\|U_k(t,s)\|_{\mathcal{L}(H)} \le M + \|B\|_{\mathcal{L}(U,W)}\|g\|_{L^2[t_o,t_1]}\beta^{\frac{1}{2}}\|R^{-1}\|^{\frac{1}{2}} = \alpha$$

For any $h \in H$, we have

$$\langle h, Q_k(t)h\rangle = \langle U_k(t_1,t)h, GU_k(t_1,t)h\rangle_H + \int_t^{t_1} \langle U_k(s,t)h, M_k(s)U_k(s,t)h\rangle_H\, ds$$

Now $U_k(t,s) \in \mathcal{L}(\widetilde{W},H)$ for almost all $t > s$, so the right hand side may be extended to $\widetilde{W}$, and since $Q_k(t)$ is a decreasing sequence, we have for $w \in \widetilde{W}$

$$<U_k(t_1,t)w, GU_k(t_1,t)w>_H + \int_t^{t_1} <U_k(s,t)w, M_k U_k(s,t)w>_H \, ds$$

$$\leq <T_{t_1-t}w, GT_{t_1-t}w>_H + \int_t^{t_1} <T_{s-t}w, MT_{s-t}w>_H \, ds$$

for almost all t and all k = 1,... But from (8.17) there exists $\gamma \in L^1[t_o,t_1]$ such that

$$<T_{t_1-t}w, GT_{t_1-t}w>_H + \int_t^{t_1} <T_{s-t}w, MT_{s-t}w>_H ds \leq \gamma(t_1-t)\|w\|^2_{\widetilde{W}}$$

$$\int_t^{t_1} \|F_k(s)U_k(s,t)w\|_U^2 \leq \gamma(t_1-t)\|w\|^2_{\widetilde{W}}\|R^{-1}\| \tag{8.48}$$

for all k = 1,2,... and all $w \in \widetilde{W}$. Then from (8.42) we have for $w \in \widetilde{W}$

$$\|U_k(t,s)w\|_H \leq \|T_{t-s}w\|_H + \int_s^t g(t-\rho)\|B\|_{\mathcal{L}(U,\widetilde{W})}\|F_k(\rho)U_k(\rho,s)w\|_U \, d\rho$$

Hence

$$\|U_k(t,s)\|_{\mathcal{L}(\widetilde{W},H)} \leq g(t-s) + \|B\|_{\mathcal{L}(U,\widetilde{W})}\|g\|_{L^2[t_o,t_1]}\|\gamma(t-s)\|^{\frac{1}{2}} \|R^{-1}\|^{\frac{1}{2}} \tag{8.49}$$

$$= g_\infty(t-s)$$

Finally

$$\|F_k(t)\|_{\mathcal{L}(U,H)} = \|F_k^*(t)\|_{\mathcal{L}(H,U)} \leq \|R^{-1}\| \, \|B\|_{\mathcal{L}(U,\widetilde{W})}\|Q_k(t)\|_{\mathcal{L}(\widetilde{W},H)}$$

But from (8.47)(8.48)(8.49)

$$\|Q_k(t)\|_{\mathcal{L}(\widetilde{W},H)} \leq \alpha\|G\|_{\mathcal{L}(H)}g_\infty(t_1-t) + \int_t^{t_1} \alpha\|M\|g_\infty(s-t)$$

$$+ \beta^{\frac{1}{2}}\|R\|[\gamma(t_1-t)]^{\frac{1}{2}}\|R^{-1}\|$$

Hence

$$\|F_k(t)\| \leq \underline{g}_\infty(t) \qquad \text{for all } k$$

where

$$\underline{g}_\infty(t) = \|R^{-1}\|\|B\|_{\mathcal{L}(U,\tilde{W})}\Big[\alpha\|G\|_{\mathcal{L}(H)}g(t_1-t) + \alpha\|M\|_{\mathcal{L}(H)}\int_t^{t_1} g_\infty(s-t) + \beta^{\frac{1}{2}}\|R\|^{\frac{1}{2}}[\gamma(t_1-t)]^{\frac{1}{2}}\|R^{-1}\|^{\frac{1}{2}}\Big]$$

and clearly $\underline{g}_\infty \in L^2[t_o,t_1]$.

<u>Theorem 8.21</u>

The optimal control which minimizes $J(u,t_o,z_o)$ is the feedback control

$$u^*(t) = -R^{-1}B^*Q(t)z(t) \tag{8.50}$$

where $Q(t)$ is the unique solution of

$$Q(t)h = U^*(t_1,t)GU(t_1,t)h + \int_t^{t_1} U^*(s,t)\left[M+Q(s)BR^{-1}B^*Q(s)\right]U(s,t)h\,ds \tag{8.51}$$

and the evolution operator $U(t,s)$ is given by

$$U(t,s)h = T_{t-s}h - \int_s^t T_{t-\rho}BR^{-1}B^*Q(\rho)U(\rho,s)h\,d\rho \tag{8.52}$$

Moreover $Q(t) \in \mathcal{L}(\tilde{W},H)$, $U(t,s) \in \mathcal{L}(\tilde{W},H)$ for almost all t,s.

<u>Proof</u>

Since $Q_k(t)$ converges strongly to $Q(t)$ it follows that $F_k(t)$ and $M_k(t)$ both converge strongly to $R^{-1}B^*Q(t)$ in $\mathcal{L}(C[t_o,t_1;H],\ L^2[t_o,t_1;U]) \cap \mathcal{L}(L^2[t_o,t_1;H],\ L^1[t_o,t_1;U])$ and $M + Q(t)BR^{-1}B^*Q(t)$ in $\mathcal{L}(C[t_o,t_1;H],\ L_1[t_o,t_1;H])$ respectively. Then using the same argument as that in Lemma 4.3, and the uniform bounds of Lemma 8.20 we are able to establish that $U_k(t,s) \to U(t,s)$ strongly. Using the Lebesgue dominated convergence theorem and Lemma 8.20 we see that $Q(t)$ satisfies (8.51). The uniqueness of $Q(t)$ and the fact that $u^*(t)$ is the optimal control are proved in the same way as in Lemmas (4.5) and (4.4) respectively.

It is also possible to obtain an alternative version of (8.51).

<u>Theorem 8.22</u>

The solution $Q(t)$ of the integral Riccati equation (8.51) is also given by

(8.53) $$Q(t)h = U^*(t_1,t)GT_{t_1-t}h + \int_t^{t_1} U^*(s,t)MT_{s-t}h\, ds$$

where U(t,s) is the evolution operator determined by (8.52).

Proof

Substituting for U(t,s) from (8.52) into (8.51) we obtain

$$Q(t)h = U^*(t_1,t)GT_{t_1-t}h - U^*(t_1,t)G\int_t^{t_1} T_{t_1-\rho}BR^{-1}B^*Q(\rho)U(\rho,t)h\, d\rho$$
$$+ \int_t^{t_1} U^*(s,t)MT_{s-t}h ds - \int_t^{t_1} U^*(s,t)M\int_t^s T_{s-\rho}BR^{-1}B^*Q(\rho)U(\rho,t)h\, d\rho\, ds$$
$$+ \int_t^{t_1} U^*(s,t)Q(s)BR^{-1}B^*Q(s)U(s,t)h\, ds$$

Therefore

$$Q(t)h - U^*(t_1,t)GT_{t_1-t}h - \int_t^{t_1} U^*(s,t)MT_{s-t}h\, ds$$
$$= \int_t^{t_1} U^*(s,t)\left[Q(s)-U^*(t_1,s)GT_{t_1-s}-\int_s^{t_1} U^*(\rho,s)MT_{\rho-s}\right]BR^{-1}B^*Q(s)U(s,t)h\, d\rho\, ds$$

From which the result follows by Gronwall's inequality.

Since by Proposition 8.3 we know that U(t,s) is a quasi-evolution operator, it is possible to differentiate the integral Riccati equation as in Lemma 4.6. However, we will obtain two different expressions depending on whether we use the expression (8.33), that is

(8.54) $$\int_s^t U(t,\rho)\left[A-BR^{-1}B^*Q(\rho)\right]h\, d\rho = U(t,s)h - h\ , \quad h \in D(A)$$

or the expression (8.34), that is

(8.55) $$\int_s^t U(t,\rho)\tilde{A}h\, d\rho = U(t,s)h - h$$

for $h \in D(\tilde{A}) \cap \ker[D-R^{-1}B^*Q(\rho)] \cap \ker E$ for almost all $\rho \in [t_o,t_1]$.

Using (8.54) we obtain an analogous expression to (4.18), namely

(8.56) $$\frac{d}{dt}\langle Q(t)h,k\rangle + \langle Q(t)h,Ak\rangle + \langle Ah,Q(t)k\rangle$$
$$= \langle Q(t)BR^{-1}B^*Q(t)h,k\rangle - \langle Mh,k\rangle$$

$Q(t_1) = G$ where $h,k \in D(A)$.

Alternatively using (8.55) and assuming we have a Green's formula, we obtain

(8.57) $$\frac{d}{dt}\langle Q(t)h,k\rangle + \langle Q(t)h,\tilde{A}k\rangle + \langle\tilde{A}h,Q(t)k\rangle$$
$$= -\langle Q(t)BR^{-1}B^{*}Q(t)h,k\rangle - \langle Mh,k\rangle$$

$Q(t_1) = G$ where $h,k \in D(\tilde{A}) \cap \ker[D-R^{-1}B^{*}Q(\rho)]$.

The uniqueness of the solution of (8.56) follows the same argument as in the bounded case up to equation (4.22), that is we obtain

$$\langle F(t)h,k\rangle = -\int_t^{t_1} \langle[Q_1(\rho)BR^{-1}B^{*}F(\rho) + F(\rho)BR^{-1}B^{*}Q_1(\rho)]T_{\rho-t}h,T_{\rho-t}k\rangle$$

Hence, since $\overline{D(A)} = H$

$$\|B^{*}F(t)h\| \leq 2\int_t^{t_1} \|Q_1(\rho)\|_{\mathcal{L}(\tilde{W},H)}\|B\|^2_{\mathcal{L}(U,\tilde{W})}\|R^{-1}\|\,\|T_{\rho-t}\|_{\mathcal{L}(\tilde{W},H)}\|B^{*}F(\rho)h\|d\rho$$

So by Gronwall's inequality we have $\|B^{*}F(t)\| = 0$, and thus $\|F(t)\| = 0$. In a similar manner we can prove the uniqueness of the solution of (8.57) if $D(\tilde{A}) \cap \ker[D-R^{-1}B^{*}Q(\rho)]$ is dense in H.

We illustrate these results with the following example.

<u>Example 8.23</u>

Consider the boundary control system

$$z_t = z_{\xi\xi}$$

$$[z_\xi]_0 = u,\ z_\xi(1,t) = 0,\ z(\xi,0) = z_0(\xi)$$

with cost

$$J(u,0,z_0) = \int_0^1 z^2(\xi,t_1)d\xi + \int_0^{t_1}\left[\int_0^1 z^2(\xi,t)d\xi + u^2(t)\right]dt$$

Then if we take $H = L^2[0,1]$, $u \in L^2[0,t_1]$, it is easy to show that $(Bu)(\xi) = -\delta(\xi)u$ and

(8.58) $$T_t z_0 = \langle z_0,1\rangle + \sum_{n=1}^{\infty} 2e^{-n^2\pi^2 t}\cos n\pi\xi\langle z_0(\cdot),\cos n\pi\cdot\rangle$$

The conditions (8.17) are verified if we take

$$\tilde{W} = \left(H^{\frac{1}{2}+\varepsilon}(0,1)\right)^{*},\ \varepsilon > 0,\ g(t) = \frac{M}{t^{1/4+\varepsilon/2}} \in L^2[0,t_1].$$

Setting $(Q(t)z)(\xi) = \int_0^1 K(\xi,\eta,t)z(\eta)d\eta$, then (8.56) becomes

$$\begin{aligned}&\int_0^1\int_0^1 [K_t(\xi,\eta,t) + k_{\xi\xi}(\xi,\eta,t) + K_{\eta\eta}(\xi,\eta,t) + \delta(\xi-\eta)\\ &- K(\eta,0,t)K(0,\xi,t)]h(\xi)k(\eta)d\xi d\eta + \int_0^1 K_\xi(0,\eta,t)h(\eta)k(0)d\eta\\ &- \int_0^1 K_\xi(1,\eta,t)h(\eta)k(1)d\eta + \int_0^1 K_\eta(\xi,0,t)h(0)k(\xi)d\xi\\ &- \int_0^1 K_\eta(\xi,1,t)h(1)k(\xi)d\xi = 0\end{aligned} \tag{8.59}$$

with

$$\int_0^1 K(\xi,\eta,t_1)h(\eta)d\eta \Rightarrow h(\xi) \text{ or } K(\xi,\eta,t_1) = \delta(\xi-\eta)$$

Alternatively, if we use (8.57) we obtain

$$\begin{aligned}&\int_0^1\int_0^1 [K_t(\xi,\eta,t) + K_{\xi\xi}(\xi,\eta,t) + K_{\eta\eta}(\xi,\eta,t) + \delta(\xi-\eta)\\ &+ K(\eta,0,t)K(0,\xi,t)]h(\xi)k(\eta)d\xi d\eta + \int_0^1 K_\xi(0,\eta,t)h(\eta)k(0)d\eta\\ &- \int_0^1 K_\xi(1,\eta,t)h(\eta)k(1)d\eta + \int_0^1 K_\eta(\xi,0,t)h(0)k(\xi)d\xi\\ &- \int_0^1 K_\eta(\xi,1,t)h(1)k(\xi)d\xi - \int_0^1 K(0,\eta,t)h_\xi(0)k(\eta)d\eta\\ &- \int_0^1 K(\xi,0,t)h(\xi)k_\eta(0)d\xi = 0\end{aligned} \tag{8.60}$$

But now $h_\xi(0) = \int_0^1 K(0,\eta,t)h_\xi(\eta)d\eta$ and substitution in (8.60), using $K(\xi,\eta,t) = K(\eta,\xi,t)$ yields (8.59). If we choose K to satisfy

$$\begin{aligned}K_t + K_{\xi\xi} + K_{\eta\eta} + \delta(\xi-\eta) - K(\eta,0,t)K(0,\xi,t) &= 0\\ K(\xi,\eta,t_1) &= \delta(\xi-\eta)\end{aligned} \tag{8.61}$$

with $K_\xi = 0$ on $\xi = 0,1$ $\forall$ $\eta \in (0,1)$, and $K_\eta = 0$ on $\eta = 0,1$ $\forall$ $\xi \in (0,1)$ then (8.59) is satisfied, and the optimal control is given by

$$u^*(t) = -\int_0^1 K(0,\eta,t)z(\eta,t)d\eta$$

In fact it is natural to seek a solution of (8.61) in terms of the basis which generates the semigroup T_t, that is

$$K(\xi,\eta,t) = 2 \sum_{m=o}^{\infty} \sum_{n=o}^{\infty} a_{mn}(t)\cos m\pi\xi \cos n\pi\eta$$

Substitution in (8.61) yields

$$\dot{a}_{mn} - (m^2\pi^2+n^2\pi^2)a_{mn} + \delta_n^m - 2\sum_{i=o}^{\infty} a_{im} \sum_{j=o}^{\infty} a_{jn} = 0 \quad m,n > 0$$

(8.62)

$$a_{mn}(t_1) = \delta_n^m$$

where $\delta_n^m = 0 \quad m \neq n, \; \delta_n^m = 1 \quad m = n$

$$\dot{a}_{on} - n^2\pi^2 a_{on} + \delta_n^o - 2\sqrt{2} \sum_{i=o}^{\infty} a_{io} \sum_{j=o}^{\infty} a_{jn} = 0, \; n > 0$$

$$\dot{a}_{oo} + 1 - 4\sum_{i=o}^{\infty} a_{io} \sum_{j=o}^{\infty} a_{jo} = 0$$

Example 8.24

Consider

$$z_t = z_{\xi\xi}$$

(8.63)

$$z(0,t) = u, \; z(1,t) = 0, \; z(\xi,0) = z_o(\xi)$$

with the same cost functional as in Example 8.23. We find that for $H = L^2[0,1]$ $(Bu)(\xi) = -\delta'(\xi)u$ and this does not yield a value for $g \in L^2[0,t_1]$. So we are not able to conclude that $z \in L^2[0,1]$ for all controls $u \in L^2[0,t_1]$. So the optimal control may not exist. If we relax our concept of a mild solution from $z \in C[0,t_1;Z]$ to $z \in L^2[0,t_1;Z]$ then it is possible to show that the mild solution of (8.63) is well defined and $z \in L^2[0,t_1,L^2[0,1]]$. Then it is possible to prove that the optimal control is well defined via a Riccati equation in the special case of a pure integral cost functional.

8.6 The estimation problem

At the beginning of this chapter we motivated the extension of our analysis to a class of unbounded B and C, by pointing out that in practice one can usually only sense or observe at limited regions of the system region Ω and this leads naturally to such unbounded B and C. In the estimation problem we are already restricted to a finite dimensional observation space and so we are interested in extending the estimation theory of Chapter 6 to allow for point observations. Examples of such operators C have already been considered in Examples 8.1 and 8.8 and the abstract framework for treating these observation maps has already been set up in §8.2.

We take our general abstract signal and observation process to be

$$x(t) = S_t x_o + \int_o^t S_{t-s} D\, dw(s) \quad 0 \leq t \leq t_1 \tag{8.64}$$

$$y(t) = \int_o^t Cx(s)ds + Fv(t) \tag{8.65}$$

where all operators are as previously specified for (6.1) and (6.2) in Chapter 6, with the exception of C, which satisfies conditions analagous to (8.14), namely

There exists a Banach space W dense in H with respect to the H norm, such that

$$\text{(8.66)} \quad \begin{aligned} &\text{(a) } H \supset D(C) \supset \underset{\sim}{W} \\ &\text{(b) } C \in \mathcal{L}(\underset{\sim}{W}, R^k) \\ &\text{(c) } S_t \in \mathcal{L}(H, \underset{\sim}{W}) \quad t > 0 \\ &\text{(d) } \|S_t h\|_{\underset{\sim}{W}} \leq g(t)\|h\|_H \text{ for all } h \in H \text{ where } g \in L^2[0,t_1] \end{aligned}$$

From (8.16) we deduce that

$$C \int_o^t S_{t-s} f(s)ds = \int_o^t CS_{t-s} f(s)ds \tag{8.67}$$

for all $f \in L^2[0,t_1;H]$.

So $\int_o^t Cx(s)ds$ in (8.64) is indeed well-defined and we can extend the arguments of §6.1 to this unbounded C situation to prove the existence of the best primal linear estimate

$$\hat{x}(t) = \int_o^t K(t,s)dy(s) \tag{8.68}$$

where $K(t,\cdot) \in \mathcal{B}^2(0,t_1; \mathcal{L}(R^k,H))$ is the unique solution of the generalized Wiener Hopf equation

$$\int_o^t K(t,s)C\Lambda(s,\sigma)C^* y\, ds + K(t,\sigma)F V F^* y = \Lambda(t,\sigma)C^* y, \quad y \in R^k \tag{8.69}$$

where $\Lambda(t,s)$ is defined as before by (6.4).

The existence and uniqueness of solutions of (8.69) can be proved as in Lemma 6.7 using estimates like

$$\|C\Lambda(s,\sigma)\|_{\mathcal{L}(H,R^K)} \leq \text{const } g(t) \tag{8.70}$$

which follows from the expression (6.4) for $\Lambda(t,s)$ and (8.66). Continuing the same development as in Chapter 6, the next step is to show that $K(t,s)$ of (8.68) is actually given by

$$K(t,s) = Y(t,s)P(s)C^*(FVF^*)^{-1} \tag{8.71}$$

where $P(t)$ is the solution of an appropriate Riccati equation and $Y(t,s)$ is some perturbation of S_t. Again this can be done by establishing a duality with a control problem with unbounded B operator and using the results of §8.5.

The dual Riccati equation whose existence and uniqueness is proved in §8.5 is

$$Q(t)h = U^*(t_1,t)GT_{t_1-t}h + \int_0^{t_1} U^*(s,t)MT_{s-t}h\, ds \tag{8.72}$$

where $U(t,s)$ is the unique solution of

$$U(t,s)h = T_{t-s}h - \int_s^t T_{t-\rho}BR^{-1}B^*Q(\rho)U(\rho,s)h\, d\rho \tag{8.73}$$

and it has been assumed that T_t and B satisfy conditions (8.17) with $q = 2$. We make the following dual identifications

$$T_t^* = S_t,\ B = C^*,\ M = DWD^*,\ Y(t,s) = U^*(t_1-s,t_1-t)$$

$$G = P_o,\ P(t) = Q(t_1-t)$$

Then with $U = R^k$, $Z = H$ and $\widetilde{W} = \underset{\sim}{W}^*$, (8.17) is implied by (8.66) and $P(t)$ is the unique solution of

$$P(t)h = Y(t,o)P_oS_t^*h + \int_o^t Y(t,s)DWD^*S_{t-s}^*h\, ds; \quad h \in H \tag{8.74}$$

and $Y(t,s)$ is the perturbation of S_t given by

$$Y(t,s)h = S_{t-s}h - \int_s^t S_{t-\alpha}P(\alpha)C^*(FVF^*)^{-1}CY(\alpha,s)h\, d\alpha \tag{8.75}$$

using the duality with (8.56)(or (8.57)), we can also express $P(t)$ in differential form, namely

$$(8.76)\qquad \frac{d}{dt}\langle P(t)h,k\rangle - \langle P(t)h,\mathcal{A}^*k\rangle - \langle \mathcal{A}^*h,P(t)k\rangle$$

$$= \langle DWD^*h,k\rangle + \langle P(t)C^*(FVF^*)^{-1}CP(t)h,k\rangle$$

$$P(0) = P_o \ ; \ h,k \in D(\mathcal{A}^*)$$

and a similar expression from (8.57).

That (8.68) is in fact the best global filter follows as in Theorem 6.10, and P(t) again has the physical interpretation as the covariance operator of the error process.

From Theorem 8.21 and the duality, we see that $P(s) \in \mathcal{L}(\underset{\sim}{W},H)$ and $Y(t,s) \in \mathcal{L}(H,\underset{\sim}{W})$ and consequently $K(t,s) \in \mathcal{L}(R^k,\underset{\sim}{W})$ and we can define the innovations process $\rho(t)$ by (6.7) as before. With the interpretation that $C \in \mathcal{L}(\underset{\sim}{W},R^k)$, $P(t) \in \mathcal{L}(\underset{\sim}{W}^*,H) \cap \mathcal{L}(H,\underset{\sim}{W})$ and $Y(t,s) \in \mathcal{L}(H,\underset{\sim}{W})$, the results on smoothing aid prediction estimators in §6.3 can be proved in exactly the same way.

Example 8.25

Consider the stochastic system described formally by

$$dx = x_{\xi\xi}dt + dw(t,\xi)$$

$$(8.77)\qquad x_\xi(0,t) = 0 = x_\xi(1,t)$$

$$x(\xi,0) = x_o(\xi)$$

$$y(t) = x(\xi_o,t) + v(t) \ ; \ 0 < \xi_o < 1$$

where w,v and x_o are as in Example 6.23.

The semigroup S_t is just T_t of Example 5.39 if we take $H = L_2(0,1)$ and $\underset{\sim}{W} = H^{\frac{1}{2}+\varepsilon}(0,1)$ for small $\varepsilon > 0$, then C defined by

$$Ch = h(\xi_o)$$

is in $\mathcal{L}(\underset{\sim}{W},R)$ and it is readily verifiable that $S_t \in \mathcal{L}(H,\underset{\sim}{W})$ with the estimate

$$\|S_t h\|_{\underset{\sim}{W}} \le \frac{M}{t^{1/4+\varepsilon/2}}\|h\|_H$$

and assumptions (8.66) are satisfied. Hence there exist a unique optimal estimator for (8.77) and we can obtain explicit equations for the error covariance operator P(t) analagously to Example 8.23 by letting

(8.78)
$$\begin{cases} P(t)h(\xi) = \int_0^1 K(\xi,\eta,t)h(\eta)d\eta \\ P_o h(\xi) = \int_0^1 \alpha(\xi,\eta)h(\eta)d\eta;\ Wh(\xi) = \int_0^1 r(\xi,\eta)h(\eta)d\eta \end{cases}$$

and substituting in (8.76) to obtain

$$\int_0^1\int_0^1 \Big[K_t(\xi,\eta,t) + K_{\xi\xi}(\xi,\eta,t) + K_{\eta\eta}(\xi,\eta,t)$$

$$- r(\xi,\eta) + K(\xi,\eta,t)K(\xi_o,\xi,t)\Big| h(\xi)k(\eta)d\xi\, d\eta$$

$$= \int_0^1 \big[K_\xi(1,\eta,t)k(1) - K_\xi(0,\eta,t)k(0)\big]h(\eta)d\eta$$

$$- \int_0^1 \big[K_\eta(\xi,1,t)h(1) - K_\eta(\xi,0,t)h(0)\big]k(\eta)d\eta$$

with $K(\xi,\eta,0) = \alpha(\xi,\eta)$.

The symmetry of P(t) implies that $K(\xi,\eta,t) = K(\eta,\xi,t)$ and (8.78) simplifies to

(8.80)
$$K_t(\xi,\eta,t) + K_{\xi\xi}(\xi,\eta,t) + K_{\eta\eta}(\xi,\eta,t) - r(\xi,\eta)$$
$$+ K(\xi_o,\eta,t)K(\xi,\xi_o,t) = 0$$

with $K_\xi(0,\eta,t) = K_\xi(1,\eta,t) = K_\eta(\xi,0,t) = K_\eta(\xi,1,t) = 0$ and $K(\xi,\eta,0) = \alpha(\xi,\eta)$.

We now seek a solution for $K(\xi,\eta,t)$ in terms of an eigenfunction expansion in terms of the eigenfunctions of $\mathcal{A}$, namely

(8.81)
$$K(\xi,\eta,t) = \sum_{m,n=o}^{\infty} a_{mn}(t)\cos m\xi\pi \cos n\pi\eta$$

We assume

$$W \cos n\pi\xi = \lambda_n \cos n\pi\xi\ ;\ n \geq 0$$

and

$$P_o \cos n\pi\xi = \alpha_n \cos n\pi\xi\ ;\ n \geq 0$$

upon substitution in (8.78), we obtain the following system of equations for a_{mn}; $m,n \geq 0$

$$\dot{a}_{mn} - (\pi^2)(m^2+n^2)a_{mn} = 2\delta_m^n \lambda_n + \sum_{k=o}^{\infty} a_{km}\cos k\pi\xi_o \sum_{k=o}^{\infty} a_{kn}\cos k\pi$$

$$a_{mn}(0) = 2\alpha_m\delta_m^n$$

References

[1] Balakrishnan, A.V. Applied functional analysis, Springer Verlag, 1976.

[2] Balakrishnan, A.V. Identification and control of a distributed system with boundary noise, Proc. Symp. on Control Theory, Numerical Methods and Computer System Modelling, Paris, (Lecture Notes in Computer Science, Springer Verlag, 1975.)

[3] Chewning, W.C. and Seidman, T.I. A convergent scheme for boundary control of the heat equation, SIAM J. Control, 15 (1977), pp.64-72.

[4] Curtain, R.F. and Pritchard, A.J. An abstract theory for unbounded control action for distributed parameter systems, SIAM J. Control, 15 (1977), pp.566-611.

[5] Curtain, R.F. Linear stochastic control for distributed systems with boundary control, boundary noise and point observations, to appear in Appl. Math. and Optimisation.

[6] Curtain, R.F., Ichikawa, A. and Ryan, E.P. Optimal location of point sensors, Proc. IFIP Conference on Modelling and Identification of Distributed Parameter Systems, Rome, 1976.

[7] Curtain, R.F., Ichikawa, A. and Ryan, E.P. Modelling and control of river pollution, Proc. IFAC Symp. on Environmental Systems, Planning and Control, Kyoto, 1977.

[8] Datko, R. Some linear nonautonomous control problems with quadratic cost, J. Diff. Eqns., 21 (1976), pp.231-262.

[9] Dolecki, S. Observability for the one dimensional heat equation, Studia Mathematica, 48 (1973), pp.291-305.

[10] Erzberger, H. and Kim, M. Optimum boundary control of distributed parameter systems, Int. J. Control, 9 (1966), pp.265-278.

[11] Fattorini, H.O. Boundary control systems, SIAM J. Control, 6

[12] Fattorini, H.O. Boundary control of temperature distributions in a parallelopipedon, SIAM J. Control, 13 (1975), pp.1-13.

[13] Glashoff, K. and Weck, N. Boundary control of parabolic differential equations in arbitrary dimensions: supremum norm problems, SIAM J. Control, 14 (1976), pp. 662-681.

[14] Graham, K. and Russell, D.L. Boundary value control of the wave equation in a spherical region, SIAM J. Control, 13 (1975), pp.174-196.

[15] Kim, M. and Erzberger, H. On the design of optimum distributed parameter systems with boundary control function, IEEE Trans. Auto. Control, 12 (1967), pp.22-28.

[16] Lions, J.L. and Magenes, E. Non-homogeneous boundary value problems, I, II, III, Springer Verlag, 1972.

[17] Luxemburg, W. and Korevaar, J. Entire functions and Muntz Szasz type approximations, Trans. Amer. Math. Soc., 157 (1971), pp.23-37.

[18] MacCamy, R.C., Mizel, V.J. and Seidman, T.I. Approximate boundary controllability of the heat equation I, J. Math. Anal. Appl., 23 (1969), pp.699-703; II, J. Math. Anal. Appl., 28 (1969), pp.482-492.

[19] Mizel, V.J. and Seidman, T.I. Observation and prediction for the heat equation, J. Math. Anal. Appl., 28 (1969), pp.303-312; 38 (1972), pp.149-166.

[20] Ouvrard, J.Y. Projection of martingales and linear filtering in Hilbert space, Proc. European Congress of Statisticians, Grenoble, 1976.

[21] Pritchard, A.J. and Wirth, A. Unbounded control and observation systems and their duality, to be published in SIAM J. Control.

[22] Pritchard, A.J. and Zabczyk, J. Stability and stabilizability of infinite dimensional systems, Control Theory Centre Report No.70, University of Warwick, 1977.

[23] Russell, D.L. On boundary value controllability of linear symmetric hyperbolic systems, Mathematical Theory of Control, Ed. Balakrishnan, A.V. and Neustadt, L.W., Academic Press, 1967.

[24] Russell, D.L. Quadratic performance criteria in boundary control of linear symmetric hyperbolic systems, SIAM J. Control, 2 (1973), pp.475-509.

[25] Russell, D.L. A unified boundary controllability theory for hyperbolic and parabolic partial differential equations, Stud. App. Math., LII, 3 (1973), pp.189-211.

[26] Russell, D.L. Boundary value control of the higher dimensional wave equation I, SIAM J. Control, 9 (1971), pp.29-42; II, SIAM J. Control, 9 (1971), pp.401-419.

[27] Seidman, T.I. Exact boundary control for some evolution equations, Mathematics Research Report No.77-4, University of Maryland, 1977.

[28] Seidman, T.I. Problems of boundary control and observation for diffusion processes, Math. Research Report No.73-10, UMBC, 1973.

[29] Seidman, T.I. Observation and prediction for the heat equation III, J. Diff. Eqns., 20 (1976), pp.18-27.

[30] Vinter, R.B. Semigroups on product spaces and applications to initial value problems with non-local boundary conditions, Proc. 2nd IFAC Symposium on the Control of Distributed Parameter Systems, Warwick 1977.

[31] Washburn, D.C. A semigroup theoretic approach to modelling of boundary input problems, Proc. IFIP Conference on Modelling and Identification of Distributed Parameter Systems, Rome 1976.

[32] Zabczyk, J. A semigroup approach to boundary value control, Proc. 2nd IFAC Symposium on the Control of Distributed Parameter Systems, Warwick 1977.

[33] Zabczyk, J. On decomposition of generators, to appear in SIAM J. Control & Opt. .

[34] Zabczyk, J. On semigroups corresponding to non-local boundary conditions with applications to systems theory, Control Theory Centre Report No.49, University of Warwick, 1976.

CHAPTER 9

TIME DEPENDENT SYSTEMS

Up to now we have considered systems of the general type

$$(9.1) \qquad z(t) = T_{t_o} z_o + \int_{t_o}^{t} T_{t-s} Bu(s)ds + \int_{t_o}^{t} T_{t-s} Ddw(s) + \int_{t_o}^{t} T_{t-s} g(s)ds$$

which were motivated by autonomous stochastic differential equations

$$(9.2) \qquad \begin{aligned} dz(t) &= Az(t)dt + Bu(t)dt + Ddw(t) + g(t)dt \\ z(t_o) &= z_o \end{aligned}$$

If we wish to consider time dependent stochastic systems motivated by stochastic differential equations like

$$(9.3) \qquad \begin{aligned} dz(t) &= A(t)z(t)dt + B(t)u(t)dt + D(t)dw(t) + g(t)dt \\ z(t_o) &= z_o \end{aligned}$$

we are led to consider the corresponding mild form

$$(9.4) \qquad z(t) = U(t,t_o)z_o + \int_{t_o}^{t} U(t,s)B(s)u(s)ds + \int_{t_o}^{t} U(t,s)D(s)dw(s) + \int_{t_o}^{t} U(t,s)g(s)ds$$

where $U(t,s)$ is the mild evolution operator associated with $A(t)$. For example, if $A = A + A_1(t)$ where $A_1 \varepsilon \mathcal{B}^{\infty}(t_o,t_1; \mathcal{L}(H))$, then from Theorem 2.33 we know that $A + A_1(t)$ generates a quasi-evolution operator. (Definition 2.35).

We now define a very general type of mild evolution operator on a Hilbert space and consider systems defined by (9.4), where $U(t,s)$ is this mild evolution operator and $D \varepsilon \mathcal{B}^{\infty}(t_o,t_1; \mathcal{L}(H))$ and $B \varepsilon \mathcal{B}^{\infty}(t_o,t_1; \mathcal{L}(K,H))$.

<u>Definition 9.1</u> <u>Mild evolution operator</u>

Let H be a Hilbert space and $[0,t_1]$ a real time interval and let $\Delta(t_1) = \{(t,s): 0 \leq s \leq t \leq t_1\}$, then $U(t,s): \Delta(t_1) \to \mathcal{L}(H)$ is a mild evolution operator if

(a) $U(t,t) = I,\ t \in [0,t_1]$

(b) $U(t,r)U(r,s) = U(t,s)$ for $0 \leq s \leq r \leq t \leq t_1$

(c) $U(t,s)$ is weakly continuous in s on $[0,t]$ and in t on $[s,t_1]$

(d) $\sup_{\Delta(t_1)} \|U(t,s)\| \leq M < \infty$

We remark that in contrast to Definition 2.32 we restrict ourselves to Hilbert spaces as we are only concerned here with the quadratic cost control problem and stochastic differential equations. Moreover, due to our weaker assumption (c), we now need the additional assumption (d). The motivation for this generalization is that the 'dual' evolution operator

$$Y(t,s) = U^*(t_1-s,t_1-t)$$

also satisfies the requirements of Definition 9.1 and this 'dual' evolution operator is important in the filtering problem. From Theorem 2.33, we have already met a wide class of mild evolution operators, namely those with quasi generator $A + A_1(t)$, where $A_1 \in \mathcal{B}^\infty(0,t_1;\mathcal{L}(H))$. We now prove that mild evolution operators are stable under such bounded perturbations.

9.1 Perturbation theory of mild evolution operators

Theorem 9.2

If $U(\cdot,\cdot)$ is a mild evolution operator on $\Delta(t_1)$ and $D \in \mathcal{B}^\infty(0,t_1;\mathcal{L}(H))$, then the following integral equation has a unique solution $U_D(\cdot,\cdot)$ on $\Delta(t_1)$ in the class of weakly continuous bounded linear operators on H.

$$U_D(t,s)h = U(t,s)h + \int_s^t U(t,r)D(r)U_D(r,s)h\,dr \tag{9.5}$$

Moreover, $U_D(\cdot,\cdot)$ is a mild evolution operator and we call it the perturbed mild evolution operator corresponding to the perturbation D.

Proof

(a) Existence

Suppose that $\operatorname{ess}\sup_{[0,t_1]} \|D(t)\| < M_1$ and $\sup_{\Delta(t_1)} \|U(t,s)\| < M_2$, and let

$$U_o(t,s)h = U(t,s)h \qquad \text{for all } h \in H$$

$$U_1(t,s)h = \int_s^t U(t,r)D(r)U(r,s)h\, dr$$

$$U_n(t,s)h = \int_s^t U(t,r)D(r)U_{n-1}(r,s)h\, dr$$

where the integrals are well-defined Bochner integrals.

By induction we have

$$\|U_n(t,s)h\| \leq M_2(M_1M_2)^n \frac{(t-s)^n}{n!}\|h\|$$

Hence

$$\|U_n(t,s)\| \leq M_2(M_1M_2)^n \frac{(t-s)^n}{n!}$$

and

$$\|\sum_{n=1}^{N} U_n(t,s)\| \leq M_2 \exp(M_1M_2(t-s)) \text{ for all } N.$$

Therefore $\sum_{n=1}^{\infty} U_n(t,s)$ is convergent on $\Delta(t_1)$ in the uniform topology and

$$\sup_{\Delta(t_1)}\|\sum_{n=1}^{\infty} U_n(t,s)\| \leq M_2\exp(M_1M_2t_1)$$

But

$$\sum_{n=o}^{\infty} U_n(t,s)h = U(t,s)h + \sum_{n=1}^{\infty} U_n(t,s)h$$

$$= U(t,s)h + \sum_{n=1}^{\infty} \int_s^t U(t,r)D(r)U_{n-1}(r,s)h\, dr$$

$$= U(t,s)h + \int_s^t \sum_{n=1}^{\infty} U(t,r)D(r)U_{n-1}(r,s)h\, dr$$

Therefore $U_D(t,s) = \sum_{n=o}^{\infty} U_n(t,s)$ satisfies (9.5)

and $U_D(t,t) = I$; $\sup_{\Delta(t_1)} \|U_D(t,s)\| \leq M_2\exp(M_1M_2t_1)$

(b) Uniqueness

Suppose there is another solution $U_1(t,s)$ and let

$$R(t,s) = U_1(t,s) - U_D(t,s)$$

Then

$$R(t,s)h = \int_s^t U(t,r)D(r)R(r,s)h\ ds$$

$$\|R(t,s)h\| \le M_1M_2 \int_s^t \|R(r,s)h\|\ ds$$

So $R(t,s)h = 0$ for all $h \in H$, by Gronwall's inequality.

(c) Semigroup property

$$U_D(t,r)U_D(r,s)h = U(t,r)U(r,s)h + \int_s^r U(t,r)U(r,\beta)D(\beta)U_D(\beta,s)h\ d\beta$$
$$+ \int_r^t U(t,\beta)D(\beta)U_D(\beta,r)U_D(r,s)h\ d\beta$$

Therefore

$$U_D(t,r)U_D(r,s)h - U_D(t,s)h = \int_r^t U(t,\beta)D(\beta)(U_D(\beta,r)U_D(r,s) - U_D(\beta,s))h\ d\beta$$

Let

$$R(\beta,r,s) = U_D(\beta,r)U_D(r,s) - U_D(\beta,s)$$

$$\|R(t,r,s)h\| \le M_1M_2 \int_r^t \|R(\beta,r,s)h\|\ d\beta$$

Since $U_D(t,t) = I$, Gronwall's inequality implies $R(t,r,s)h = 0\ \forall\ h \in H$ and $s \le r \le t$.

Hence $U_D(t,r)U_D(r,s) = U_D(t,s)$ for $s \le r \le t$.

(d) Continuity

We now show that $U_D(t,\cdot)$ is weakly continuous on $[0,t]$ and $U_D(\cdot,s)$ is weakly continuous on $[s,t_1]$.

Consider

$$\phi(t,s)h = \int_s^t U(t,r)D(r)U_D(r,s)h\ dr$$

Take $\delta > 0$, $s_1 \in [s,t_1)$, $s_2 \in (s,t_1]$, then we have

$$\phi(s_1+\delta,s)h - \phi(s_1,s)h = \int_s^{s_1} (U(s_1+\delta,r) - U(t,r))D(r)U_D(r,s)h\ dr$$
$$+ \int_{s_1}^{s_1+\delta} U(s_1+\delta,r)D(r)U_D(r,s)h\ dr$$

and

$$\phi(s_2,s)h - \phi(s_2-\delta,s)h = \int_s^{s_2-\delta} (U(s_2,r) - U(s_2-\delta,r))D(r)U_D(r,s)h\,dr + \int_{s_2-\delta}^{s_2} U(s_2,r)D(r)U_D(r,s)h\,dr$$

Therefore

$$|\langle k,\phi(s_1+\delta,s)h - \phi(s_1,s)h\rangle| \le \int_s^{s_1} |\langle k,U(s_1+\delta,r) - U(s_1,r)D(r)U_D(r,s)h\rangle|dr + \int_{s_1}^{s_1+\delta} M_1M_2^2\exp(M_1M_2(r-s))\|h\|\|k\|dr$$

Using the Lebesgue dominated convergence theorem and the weak continuity of $U(\cdot,r)$ on $[s,t_1)$, we have

$$|\langle k,\phi(s_1+\delta,s)h - \phi(s_1,s)h\rangle| \to 0 \quad \text{as } \delta \to 0$$

Similarly,

$$|\langle k,\phi(s_2,s)h - \phi(s_2-\delta,s)h\rangle| \le \int_s^{s_2-\delta} |\langle k,(U(s_2,r) - U(s_2-\delta,r))D(r)U_D(r,s)h\rangle|\,dr + \int_{s_2-\delta}^{s_2} M_1M_2^2\exp(M_1M_2(r-s))\|h\|\|k\|dr$$

so $\phi(\cdot,s)$ is weakly continuous on $[s,t_1]$.

To prove continuity with respect to the second variable, we use the fact that $U_D(\cdot,\cdot)$ is also the unique solution of

(9.6) $$U_D(t,s)h = U(t,s)h + \int_s^t U_D(t,r)D(r)U(r,s)h\,dr$$

(this is proved in Corollary 9.4).

Consider

$$\Psi(t,s)h = \int_s^t U_D(t,r)D(r)U(r,s)h\,dr,$$

we take $\delta > 0$, $s_1 \in [0,t)$ and $s_2 \in (0,t]$, then

$$\Psi(t,s_1+\delta)h - \Psi(t,s_1)h = \int_{s_1+\delta}^t U_D(t,r)D(r)(U(r,s_1+\delta) - U(r,s_1))h\,dr - \int_{s_1}^{s_1+\delta} U_D(t,r)D(r)U(r,s_1)h\,dr$$

and

$$\Psi(t,s_2-\delta)h - \Psi(t,s_2)h = \int_{s_2}^{t} U_D(t,r)D(r)(U(r,s_2-\delta) - U(r,s_2))h\,dr + \int_{s_2-\delta}^{s_2} U_D(t,r)D(r)U(r,s_2-\delta)h\,dr$$

therefore

$$|\langle k,\Psi(t,s_1+\delta)h - \Psi(t,s_1)h\rangle| \le \int_{s_1+\delta}^{t} |\langle D^*(r)U_D^*(t,r)k,(U(r,s_1+\delta) - U(r,s_1))h\rangle|\,dr + \int_{s_1}^{s_1+\delta} M_1M_2^2\exp(M_1M_2T)\|h\|\|k\|\,dr$$

$$\to 0 \text{ as } \delta \to 0$$

by the Lebesgue dominated convergence theorem, since U is weakly continuous and since $\|D^*(r)\| \le M_1$, $\|U^*(t,r)\| \le M_2$.

Similarly,

$$|\langle k,\Psi(t,s_2-\delta)h - \Psi(t,s_2)h\rangle| \le \int_{s_2}^{t} |\langle D^*(r)U_D^*(t,r)k, [U(r,s_2-\delta)-U(r,s_2)]h\rangle|\,dr + \int_{s_2-\delta}^{s_2} M_1M_2^2\exp(M_1M_2T)\,dr\|h\|\|k\|$$

$$\to 0 \text{ as } \delta \to 0.$$

Corollary 9.3

If $\operatorname{ess\,sup}_{[0,t_1]}\|D(t)\| < M_1$ and $\sup_{\Delta(t_1)}\|U(t,s)\| < M_2$, then on $\Delta(t_1)$,

$$\|U_D(t,s)\| \le M_1\exp M_1M_2(t-s)$$

Corollary 9.4

The unique solution of (9.5), $U_D(t,s)$, is also the unique solution of

$$(9.6)\qquad U_D(t,s)h = U(t,s)h + \int_s^t U_D(t,r)D(r)U(r,s)h\,dr\,, \qquad h \in H$$

in the class of weakly continuous bounded operators on H.

Proof

As in the proof of Theorem 9.2(a), we define

$$U_n'(t,s)h = \int_s^t U_{n-1}'(t,r)D(r)U(r,s)h\,dr\ ; \qquad U_o'(t,s) = U(t,s).$$

Then $U_D'(t,s)h = \sum^{\infty} U_n'(t,s)h$ is the unique solution of (9.8).

We show $U_n'(t,s)h = U_n(t,s)h$ for all n.

Suppose the assertion is true for $n = k-1, k-2$; then

$$U_k'(t,s)h = \int_s^t U_{k-1}'(t,r)D(r)U(r,s)h\,dr$$

$$= \int_s^t U_{k-1}(t,r)D(r)U(r,s)h\,dr$$

$$= \int_s^t \left[\int_r^t U(t,\alpha)D(\alpha)U_{k-2}(\alpha,r)D(r)U(r,s)h\,d\alpha\right]dr$$

$$= \int_s^t \left[\int_s^\alpha U(t,\alpha)D(\alpha)U_{k-2}(\alpha,r)D(r)U(r,s)h\,dr\right]d\alpha$$

changing the order of integration

$$= \int_s^t U(t,\alpha)D(\alpha)U_{k-1}'(\alpha,s)h\,d\alpha$$

$$= \int_s^t U(t,\alpha)D(\alpha)U_{k-1}(\alpha,s)h\,d\alpha$$

$$= U_k(t,s)h$$

And $\quad U_o'(t,s) = U_o(t,s); \quad U_1'(t,s) = U_1(t,s)$

So $\quad U_D'(t,s) = U_D(t,s)$

In Theorem 2.34, we proved that if $U(t,s) = T_{t-s}$, where T_t is a strongly continuous semigroup, then its perturbation $U_D(t,s)$ by $D \in \mathcal{B}^\infty(0,t_1; \mathcal{L}(H))$ has the property of differentiability in the second variable. This property is important in the study of the Riccati equation for time dependent systems and so we generalize this concept of a quasi evolution operator.

Definition 9.5 Quasi-evolution operator

A quasi evolution operator is a mild evolution operator $U: \Delta(t_1) \to H$ such that there exists a nonzero $h \in H$ and a closed linear operator $A(s)$ on H for almost all $s \in [0,t_1]$, satisfying

(9.7) $$\langle k, U(t,s)h - h\rangle = \int_s^t \langle k, U(t,\rho)A(\rho)h\rangle d\rho \quad \text{for all } k \in H.$$

We denote the set of $h \in H$ for which (9.7) is valid as D_A, and we call $A(\cdot)$ the quasi generator of $U(\cdot,\cdot)$.

An immediate consequence of the definition is

(9.8) $$\frac{\partial}{\partial s}\langle k,U(t,s)h\rangle = -\langle k,U(t,s)A(s)h\rangle \text{ a.e. for } h \in D_A,\ k \in H \quad .$$

This class of evolution operators is also stable under 'bounded' perturbations.

Theorem 9.6

If U is a quasi evolution operator with generator A and $D \in \mathcal{B}^{\infty}(0,t_1;\mathcal{L}(H))$, then the perturbed mild evolution operator corresponding to D is also a quasi evolution operator with quasi generator A+D.

Proof

(a) From Theorem 9.2 and Corollary 9.4, U_D is uniquely defined by

$$U_D(t,\rho)h = U(t,\rho)h + \int_\rho^t U_D(t,r)D(r)U(r,\rho)h\,dr$$

Therefore

$$\langle k,U_D(t,\rho)A(\rho)h\rangle = \langle k,U(t,\rho)A(\rho)h\rangle + \langle k,\int_\rho^t U_D(t,r)D(r)U(r,\rho)A(\rho)h\,dr\rangle$$
for $h \in D_A$, $k \in H$.
$$= \langle k,U(t,\rho)A(\rho)h\rangle + \int_\rho^t \langle D^*(r)U_D^*(t,r)k,U(r,\rho)A(\rho)h\rangle\,dr$$

Both terms on the right side are integrable with respect to ρ on $(0,t)$ by (9.7) and so

$$\int_s^t \langle k,U_D(t,\rho)A(\rho)h\rangle d\rho = \int_s^t \langle k,U(t,\rho)A(\rho)h\rangle d\rho + \int_s^t\int_\rho^t \langle D^*(r)U_D^*(t,r)k,U(r,\rho)A(\rho)h\rangle\,dr\,d\rho$$
for all $h \in D_A$, $k \in H$.

$$= \int_s^t \langle k,U(t,\rho)A(\rho)h\rangle d\rho + \int_s^t\int_s^r \langle D^*(r)U_D^*(t,r)k,U(r,\rho)A(\rho)h\rangle\,d\rho\,dr$$

by (9.7) and changing the order of integration

$$= \langle k,U(t,s)h - h\rangle + \int_s^t \langle D^*(r)U_D^*(t,r)k,U(r,s)h - h\rangle dr$$ by (9.7)

Therefore

$$\int_s^t \langle k, U_D(t,\rho)(A(\rho)+D(\rho))h\rangle d\rho = \langle k, U_D(t,s)h - h\rangle \text{ for } h \in D_A,\ k \in H$$

by Corollary 9.3.

So $U_D(t,s)$ is a quasi evolution operator with quasi generator A+D.

We again define an almost strong evolution operator as in Definition 2.36, and we define the related concept of strong evolution operator, in both cases using Definition 2.32 for mild evolution operator.

Definition 9.7

A strong evolution operator on a Banach space Z is a mild evolution operator on Z, for which there exists an associated closed, linear operator A(t) on Z for all $t \in [0,t_1]$ such that

$$(9.9) \qquad U(t,s) : D(A(s)) \to D(A(t)) \text{ for all } (t,s) \in A(t_1)$$

$$(9.10) \qquad \frac{\partial}{\partial t} U(t,s)z_o = A(t)U(t,s)z_o \text{ for } z_o \in D(A(s))$$

In applications the difference between strong and almost strong evolution operators is that the latter need only have t-measurable coefficients, whereas the former need continuity in t. For the Hilbert space case we can examine the relationship between quasi and strong evolution operators.

Theorem 9.8

If U(t,s) is a strong evolution operator with $D_A = \bigcap_{r \in [s,t]} D(A(r)) \neq \emptyset$ for $0 \leq s \leq t \leq t_1$ and for all $h \in D_A$, $k \in H$, $\langle U(t,r)A(r)h,k\rangle$ is integrable in r for $0 \leq r \leq t$, then U(t,s) is a quasi evolution operator with quasi-generator A(t) and D_A defined above.

Proof

For $\delta > 0$,

$$\frac{1}{\delta}\langle U(t,r+\delta)h - U(t,r)h,k\rangle = \frac{1}{\delta}\langle U(t,r+\delta)(I-U(r+\delta,r))h,k\rangle$$

$$\to -\langle U(t,r)A(r)h,k\rangle$$

for $h \in D(A(r))$ by (9.10).

Thus

$$\frac{\partial^+}{\partial r}\langle U(t,r)h,k\rangle = -\langle U(t,r)A(r)h,k\rangle \text{ for } h \in D(A(r)),\ k \in H.$$

Since $\langle U(t,r)h,k\rangle$ is continuous, right differentiable everywhere and its derivative is integrable, it is absolutely continuous and

$$\int_s^t \langle U(t,r)A(r)h,k\rangle \, dr = \langle U(t,r)h-h,k\rangle$$

for $h \in \bigcap_{s\leq r\leq t} D(A(r))$.

That is, $U(t,s)$ is a quasi evolution operator with quasi generator $A(t)$ and $D_A = \bigcap_{s\leq r\leq t} D(A(r))$.

There is also an interesting relationship between an almost strong evolution operator and the dual operator. We are also able to prove the following.

Theorem 9.9

If $U(t,s)$ is an almost strong evolution operator on H whose generator $A(t)$ has dense domain for all t, then the dual evolution operator $Y(t,s) = U^*(t_1-s,t_1-t)$ is a quasi evolution operator on $\Delta(t_1)$ with quasi generator $A^*(t_1-s)$ provided $D_{A*} = \bigcap_{o\leq r\leq t_1} D(A^*(t_1-r)) \neq \emptyset$.

Proof

Since $U(t,s)$ is an almost strong evolution operator on H

$$\int_s^t \langle A(r)U(r,s)h,k\rangle \, dr = \langle U(t,s)h-h,k\rangle \qquad ;h \in D(A(s))$$

Thus

$$\int_{t_1-t}^{t_1-s} \langle A(r)U(r,t_1-t)h,k\rangle \, dr = \langle U(t_1-s,t_1-t)h-h,k\rangle \quad ;h \in D(A(t_1-t))$$

$$= \langle h,Y(t,s)k-k\rangle$$

So

$$\int_s^t \langle A(t_1-\rho)U(t_1-\rho,t_1-t)h,k\rangle \, d\rho = \langle h,Y(t,s)k-k\rangle$$

and

$$\int_s^t \langle h,Y(t,\rho)A^*(t_1-\rho)k\rangle \, d\rho = \langle h,Y(t,s)k-k\rangle \tag{9.11}$$

for $h \in D(A(t_1-t))$, $k \in D_{A*}$

Since $D(A(t_1-t))$ is dense in H, $Y(t,s)$ is a quasi evolution operator, with quasi generator $A^*(t_1-\cdot)$.

Corollary 9.10

If any perturbation $D \in \mathcal{B}^\infty(0,t_1; \mathcal{L}(H))$ of a mild evolution operator $U(t,s)$ satisfies Theorem 9.8, then the dual operator $Y(t,s)=U^*(t_1-s,t_1-t)$ is a quasi evolution operator.
(Similarly for Theorem 9.11).

Unfortunately almost strong evolution operators are not stable under bounded perturbations in general, although in Lemma 2.37 we did present some particular perturbation results giving conditions for $A+D(\cdot)$ to generate an almost strong evolution operator.
The following generalization of Lemma 2.37 can be proved in exactly the same way.

Theorem 9.11

Suppose $U(t,s)$ is an almost strong evolution operator on $\Delta(t_1)$ and $D \in \mathcal{B}^\infty(0,t_1;\mathcal{L}(H))$ satisfies

$$U(t,s)D(s) : H \to D(A(t)) \text{ for all } t > s \in [0,t_1] \tag{9.12}$$
$$A(t)U(t,s)D(s)h \in L_1(0,t;H) \text{ for all } h \in H$$

then the mild evolution operator $U_D(t,s)$ generated by $A(t)+D(t)$ is an almost strong evolution operator.

9.2 Examples

Of course evolution operators were motivated by the study of linear partial differential equations and for justification that a given evolution operator is mild, quasi, strong or almost strong, we shall appeal to known results on linear differential equations.

Example 9.12 Parabolic partial differential equations

In [18] Lions considers parabolic partial differential equations of the form

$$\dot{z} = A(t)z(t) \; ; \; z(0) = z_0 \tag{9.13}$$

where $A(t)$ is a partial differential operator on a Hilbert space H, and is defined via a bilinear form $a(t,\rho,\phi)$ on another Hilbert space V, where

$$V \subset H \subset V^*$$

and the injections are continuous and dense.

He assumes that the family of bilinear forms on V are such that

(9.14) $a(t;\phi,\psi)$ is measurable on $(0,t_1)$ for all $\phi,\psi \in V$

(9.15) $$|a(t;\phi,\psi)| \leq c\|\phi\|_V\|\psi\|_V$$

(9.16) there exists λ,α such that $\alpha > 0$ and

$$a(t;\phi,\psi) + \lambda\|\phi\|_H^2 \geq \alpha\|\phi\|_V^2, \text{ for all } \phi \in V,\ t \in (0,t_1).$$

Then for each t it is possible to write

$$a(t;\phi,\psi) = -\langle A(t)\phi,\psi\rangle_{V^*V}$$

where $\langle\cdot,\cdot\rangle_{V^*V}$ denotes the duality between V^* and V. He then shows that there is a unique solution in $W(0,t_1)$ of (9.13), where the equation is to be interpreted in the sense of distributions, and $W(0,t_1)$ is the Hilbert space

$$W(0,t_1) = \{h : h \in L^2(0,t_1;V),\ \frac{dh}{dt} \in L^2(0,t_1;V^*)\}$$

with norm

$$\|h\|^2_{W(0,t_1)} = \|h\|^2_{L^2(0,t_1;V)} + \|\frac{dh}{dt}\|^2_{L^2(0,t_1;V^*)}$$

Moreover, the solution depends continuously on the initial data, in the sense that the map $h_0 \to h(\cdot)$ from $H \to W(0,t_1)$ is continuous. By considering the equation

$$\begin{cases} \dfrac{dz}{dt} = A(t)z & \text{on } (0,t_1) \\ z(s) = z_0 \in H & \end{cases}$$

it is easy to see that the solution can be written in the form

(9.17) $$z(t) = U(t,s)z_0$$

where
$U(t,s) \in \mathcal{L}(H)$, and satisfies properties (a) and (b) of Definition 9.1. Using the continuous dependence on the initial data it is easy to show that $U(t,s)$ is strongly continuous in s and uniformly bounded on $\Delta(t_1)$.

Since all $h \in W(0,t_1)$ are with modification on a set on measure zero, continuous from $[0,t_1] \to H$, it follows that $U(t,s)$ is strongly continuous in t. Thus $U(t,s)$ is certainly a mild evolution operator.

Moreover, it follows easily that the solution of (9.17) must also satisfy

$$\int_s^t a(\rho;z(\rho),v)d\rho = -\langle z(t),v\rangle + \langle z(s),v\rangle$$

where $\langle\ ,\ \rangle$ denotes the inner product on H, and $v \in V$.

Now

$$a(\rho;z(\rho),v) = \langle A(\rho)z(\rho),v\rangle_{V^*V}$$

$$= -\langle z(\rho),A^*(\rho)v\rangle_{VV^*}$$

But $\langle\ ,\ \rangle_{VV^*}$ is an extension of the inner product on H, so if we define D_{A^*} by

$$D_{A^*} = \{v \in V : A^*(t)v \in H\}$$

then for $v \in D_{A^*}$, we have

$$a(\rho;z(\rho),v) = -\langle z(\rho),A^*(\rho)v\rangle$$

Thus

$$-\int_s^t \langle U(\rho,s)z_o,A^*(\rho)v\rangle d\rho = -\langle U(t,s)h_o,v\rangle + \langle z_o,v\rangle$$

Setting $\rho = t_1-\gamma$, $t = t_1-s$ and $Y(t,s) = U^*(t_1-s,t_1-t)$ gives

$$\int_s^t \langle z_o,Y(t,\gamma)A^*(t_1-\gamma)v\rangle d\gamma = \langle z_o,Y(t,s)v\rangle - \langle z_o,v\rangle \text{ for } v \in D_{A^*}$$

So $Y(t,s) = U^*(t_1-s,t_1-t)$ is a quasi evolution operator.

In a similar manner, using the unique solution of the adjoint equation, it is possible to show that $U(t,s)$ is also a quasi evolution operator, with quasi generator $A(t)$, where

$$D_A = \{v \in V : A(t)v \in H\}$$

However $U(t,s)$ and $Y(t,s)$ are not in general almost strong evolution operators.

In [7],[16],[17] various abstract sufficient conditions are given for $A(t)$ to generate a strong evolution operator. The approach is more direct and the assumptions on $A(t)$ are that it generates an analytic semigroup for $t > 0$, some restrictions on $D(A(t))$ and smoothness of $A(t)$ in t. Roughly speaking, these are applicable to parabolic partial differential equations with smooth coefficients of the type studied by Kato in [16],[17].

Example 9.13 Non symmetric hyperbolic partial differential equations

Consider the hyperbolic system studied by Rauch in [19]

$$(9.18)\qquad \begin{cases} \dfrac{\partial y}{\partial t} = \displaystyle\sum_{i=1}^{m} A_i \frac{\partial y}{\partial x_i} + Ky \\ My|_{\partial\Omega} = 0 \\ y(0) = y_0 \end{cases}$$

on the spatial domain $\Omega = \{x \in R^m;\ x_1 > 0\}$; $0 \le t \le t_1$, where A_i, K, M are C^∞ matrix valued functions on $Q = [0,t_1]\times\Omega$ and $\Sigma = [0, t_1]\times\partial\Omega$ respectively. Denote by $C^\infty_{(0)}(Q;R^k)$ the restriction of $C^\infty_0(R^{m+1};R^k)$ to the closure of $[0,t_1)\times\Omega$. Then we define a strong solution $y \in L^2(Q;R^n)$ to (9.18), if given $y_0 \in L^2(\Omega;R^n)$, there exists a sequence $\{y_n\}$ with $y_n \in C^\infty_{(0)}(Q;R^n)$ such that

$$\|y_n - y\|_{L^2(Q;R^n)} \to 0$$

$$\|y_n - y\|_{L^2(\Sigma;R^n)} \to 0$$

$$\left\|\frac{\partial}{\partial t} y_n - \sum_{i=1}^{m} A_i \frac{\partial y_n}{\partial x_i} - Ky_n\right\|_{L^2(Q;R^n)} \to 0$$

$$\|My^n\|_{L^2(\Sigma;R^k)} \to 0$$

$$\|y_n(0) - y_0\|_{L^2(\Omega;R^n)} \to 0$$

Then under technical assumptions on A_i, which ensure that the system is strictly hyperbolic with non-characteristic boundary and determinate boundary values, from [19] we know that, given $y_0 \in L^2(\Omega;R^n)$, (9.18) has a unique strong solution $y \in L^2(Q;R^n)$. Furthermore, the map $t \to y(t)$ from $(0,t_1) \to L^2(\Omega;R^n)$ is strongly continuous, and we have the estimate

$$(9.19)\qquad \|y(t)\|_{L^2(\Omega;R^n)} \le C\|y_0\|_{L^2(\Omega;R^n)} \text{ for all } t \in [0,t_1]$$

and C is a constant independent of t.

Similarly the following adjoint system has a unique strong solution

$p \in L^2(Q;R^n)$ with $p(t)$ well defined and strongly continuous in t as an element of $L^2(\Omega;R^n)$.

$$(9.20) \quad \begin{cases} -\frac{\partial p}{\partial t} = \sum_{i=1}^{m} A_j' \frac{\partial p}{\partial x_j} + K'p - \sum_{j=1}^{m} \frac{\partial A_j}{\partial A_j} p \\ M'p|_{\partial\Omega} = 0 \\ p(t_1) = 0 \end{cases}$$

Moreover we have a similar estimate to (9.19).

It is easy to show that (9.18) and (9.20) are equivalent to (9.21), (9.22), which are a more appropriate formulation for our purposes.

$$(9.21) \quad \begin{cases} \dot{z}(t) = A(t)z(t) \\ z(0) = z_0 \end{cases}$$

$$(9.22) \quad \begin{cases} \dot{p}(t) = -A^*(t)p(t) \\ p(t_1) = p_1 \end{cases}$$

where $z_0, p_1, z(t), p(t) \in H = L^2(\Omega;R^n)$ for each $t \in [0,t_1]$, and $A(t)$ is a linear operator on H given by

$$(A(t)h)(x) = \sum_{i=1}^{m} A_i(t,x)\frac{\partial h}{\partial x_i} + K(t,x)h$$

with domain $D(A(t)) = \left\{ \begin{matrix} h \in H : A(t)h \in H \text{ and} \\ Mh|_{\partial\Omega} = 0 \end{matrix} \right\}$

$A^*(t)$ is then the H-adjoint of $A(t)$ for each $t \in t_1$. Since the map $z_0 \to z(t)$ is continuous from H to H, we may write $z(t) = U(t,s)z(s)$ for $0 \leq s \leq t \leq t_1$. Then using the estimate (9.17) and the continuity of $z(t)$ in t, we can show in a manner similar to the previous example (9.12) that $U(t,s)$ is a mild evolution operator on $\Delta(t_1)$. We can also show it is quasi, as follows:

First we show that the solution of (9.22) is

$$p(t) = U^*(t_1,t)p_1$$

To see this we use a result of [19] where it is shown that

$$\langle z(t_o),p(t_o)\rangle = \langle z(s_1),p(s_1)\rangle \text{ for } 0 \le t_o \le s_1 \le t_1$$

But $z(s_1) = U(s_1,t_o)z(t_o)$, hence

$$\langle z(t_o),p(t_o) - U^*(s_1,t_o)p(s_1)\rangle = 0 \text{ for all } z_o \in H.$$

Hence $p(t_o) = U^*(s_1,t_o)p(t_1)$.

Now let $\{p_1^n\}$ be an approximating sequence in $C^\infty_{(o)}(Q;R^n)$ to p_1, then it is known [19] that the strong solution $p^{(n)}$ such that $p^n(t) = p_1^n$, belongs to $C_o^\infty(Q;R^n)$. Thus for any $h \in L^2(\Omega;R^n)$, we have

$$\int_s^t \langle \dot{p}^n(\rho) + A^*(\rho)p^n(\rho),h\rangle d\rho = 0$$

or

$$\int_s^t \langle A^*(\rho)p^n(\rho),h\rangle d\rho + \langle p_1^n,h\rangle - \langle p^n(s),h\rangle = 0$$

Now if $h \in D_A$, we obtain

$$\int_s^t \langle p^n(\rho),A(\rho)h\rangle d\rho + \langle p_1^n,h\rangle - \langle p^n(s),h\rangle = 0$$

Applying the Lebesgue dominated convergence theorem and using

$$p(\rho) = U^*(t,\rho)p_1, \quad p_1 \in H$$

gives

$$\int_s^t \langle p_1,U(t,\rho)A(\rho)h\rangle d\rho = \langle p_1,U(t,s)h\rangle - \langle p_1,h\rangle$$

Thus $U(t,\rho)$ is a quasi evolution operator. Similarly it can be shown that $U^*(t_1-\rho,t_1-t)$ is also quasi, but neither has the almost strong or strong property.

Example 9.14 Differential delay equations

Consider the following class of linear differential delay systems on $[0,t_1]$

$$\frac{dx(t)}{dt} = A_{oo}(t)x(t) + \sum_{i=1}^{N} A_i(t)\begin{cases} x(t+\theta_i) & ; t+\theta_i \ge 0 \\ h(t+\theta_i) & ; t+\theta_i < 0 \end{cases}$$

(9.23)

$$+ \int_{-b}^{o} A_{o1}(t,\theta)\begin{cases} x(t+\theta) & ; t+\theta \ge 0 \\ h(t+\theta) & ; t+\theta < 0 \end{cases} d\theta$$

$$x(0) = h(0)$$

where H is a real separable Hilbert space, $A_{00} \in L^{\infty}(0,t_1;\mathcal{L}(H))$, $A_i \in L^{\infty}(\mathcal{L}(H))$, $A_{01} \in L^{\infty}((0,t_1)\times(-b,0);\mathcal{L}(H))$ and $-b < -\theta_N < \ldots < -\theta_0 = 0$.

As in Example 2.42 we introduce $\mathcal{M}^2(-b,0;H)$ and consider the following abstract evolution equation on $\mathcal{M}^2(-b,0;H)$

$$(9.24) \quad \begin{cases} \dfrac{dz}{dt} = A(t)z(t) \\ z(s) = h \; ; \; h \in D \end{cases}$$

where A(t) is a closed linear operator on $\mathcal{M}^2$ with domain D defined in Example 2.42 and for $h \in D$.

$$(9.25) \quad (A(t)h)(\theta) = \begin{cases} A_{00}(t)h(\theta) + \sum_{i=1}^{N} A_i(t)h(\theta_i) + \int_{-b}^{0} A_{01}(t,\theta)h(\theta)d\theta; & \theta = 0 \\ \dfrac{dh(\theta)}{d\theta} & ; \theta \neq 0 \end{cases}$$

In [8] it is proved that (9.24) has the unique solution $z(t) = U(t,s)h$, where $U(t,s)$ is a mild evolution operator on $\mathcal{M}^2$ and moreover,

$$U(t,s) : D \to D \text{ and}$$

$$\frac{\partial}{\partial t}U(t,s)h = A(t)U(t,s)h \text{ a.e for } t > s \in [0,t_1] \quad \forall\, h \in D$$

From the boundedness assumptions on the $\mathcal{L}(H)$ operators $A_{00}(t)$, $A_i(t)$ and $A_{01}(t,\theta)$, we see that for $h \in D$, $A(t)U(t,s)h$ is Bochner integrable in t and hence $U(t,s)$ is an almost strong evolution operator with generator A(t). If the coefficients are continuous in t, A(t) generates a strong evolution operator. In both cases $(U(t,0)h)(\theta = 0)$ corresponds to the unique solution of the original equation (9.23). From Theorem 9.9, we know that the dual evolution operator is quasi, but whether or not it is a strong or almost strong evolution operator is an open question.

9.3 Abstract evolution equations

Although evolution operators were motivated by evolution equations of the form (9.3), in general (9.4) need not be a strong solution of (9.3) even for the homogeneous case. Again we shall call (9.4) the mild solution of (9.3), whenever it is well-defined.

Consider the homogeneous equation

$$(9.26)\qquad \begin{cases} \dot{z}(t) = A(t)z(t) \\ z(0) = z_0 \in D(A(0)). \end{cases}$$

If $U(t,s)$ is an almost strong evolution operator, then (9.26) has the unique solution $z(t) = U(t,0)z_0$ which satisfies (9.26) everywhere on $[0,t_1]$.

It is natural to ask whether the quasi evolution operator has any connection with weak solutions of partial differential equations and in this direction we prove the following result.

Lemma 9.15

Let $U(t,s)$ be a quasi evolution operator on $\Delta(t_1)$ and consider the dual equation

$$(9.27)\qquad \dot{z}(t) = A^*(t_1-t)z(t) \qquad s \le t \le t_1$$

Then $z(t) = U^*(t_1-s,t_1-t)z(s)$ is a weak solution of (9.27) in the sense that

(a) $z(t)$ is weakly continuous on $[s,t_1]$.

(b) $z(t)$ satisfies

$$\int_s^{t_1} \langle z(t), \dot{\psi}(t) + A(t_1-t)\psi(t)\rangle dt = \langle z(t_1),\psi(t_1)\rangle - \langle z(s),\psi(s)\rangle$$

for all D_A-valued $\psi(t)$ functions such that ψ, $\dot{\psi}$ and $A(t_1-t)\psi(t)$ are weakly continuous on (s,t_1).

Proof

$$\int_s^{t_1} \langle U^*(t_1-s,t_1-t)z(s),\ \dot{\psi}(t)+ A(t_1-t)\psi(t)\rangle dt$$

$$= \int_s^{t_1} \langle z(s),U(t_1-s,t_1-t)\dot{\psi}(t)+ U(t_1-s,t_1-t)A(t_1-t)\psi(t)\rangle dt$$

$$= \int_s^{t_1} \frac{\partial}{\partial t}\langle z(s),U(t_1-s,t_1-t)\psi(t)\rangle dt$$

since U is a quasi evolution operator and $\langle z(s),U(t_1-s,t_1-t)\psi(t)\rangle$ is absolutely continuous

$$= \langle z(t_1),\psi(t_1)\rangle - \langle z(s),\psi(s)\rangle$$

Thus z(t) is a weak solution.

For the inhomogeneous evolution equation

$$\text{(9.28)} \qquad \begin{aligned} \dot{z}(t) &= A(t)z(t) + f(t) \\ z(t_o) &= z_o \ \varepsilon\ D(A(t_o)) \end{aligned}$$

we can prove the following generalizations of Theorem 2.38 and Corollary 2.39 in an analogous fashion using property (2.47)' for almost strong evolution operators.

Theorem 9.16

If A(t) generates an almost strong evolution operator U(t,s), then (9.28) has the unique solution

$$\text{(9.29)} \qquad z(t) = U(t,t_o)z_o + \int_{t_o}^{t} U(t,s)f(s)ds$$

provided either one of the following conditions holds:

(a) $z_o \ \varepsilon\ D(A(t_o))$ and $f(\cdot)$ is strongly continuously differentiable on $[t_o,t_1]$.

(b) $U(s,t_o)z_o$ and $U(t,s)f(s) \ \varepsilon\ D(A(t))$ for almost all $s \ \varepsilon\ [t_o,t_1]$ and $A(t)U(t,\cdot)f(\cdot)$ is integrable on $[t_o,t_1]$.

Finally we consider the stochastic evolution equation

$$\text{(9.30)} \qquad \begin{cases} dz(t) = A(t)z(t)dt + D(t)dw(t) + g(t)dt \\ z(t_o) = z_o \end{cases}$$

where H,K are separable Hilbert spaces, $w(t)$ is a K-valued Wiener process, $D \in \mathcal{B}^{\infty}(0,t_1;\mathcal{L}(K,H))$, $g \in L^1((t_0,t_1);H)$ w.p.1 and z_0 an H-valued random variable. Then the mild solution of (9.30)

$$z(t) = U(t,t_0)z_0 + \int_{t_0}^{t} U(t,s)D(s)dw(s) + \int_{t_0}^{t} U(t,s)g(s)ds \tag{9.31}$$

is a well-defined stochastic process.

The following theorem is a generalization of Theorem 5.35 and is proved analagously.

Theorem 9.17

If $A(t)$ generates an almost strong evolution operator $U(t,s)$ then (9.31) is the unique strong solution of (9.30) under the following assumptions

$$\begin{aligned} &U(t,s)D(s)e_i \in D(A(t)) \text{ w.p.1 for almost all } t > s \in [t_0,t_1] \\ &\text{and } \sum_{i=0}^{\infty} \lambda_i \int_{t_0}^{t} \|A(t)U(t,s)D(s)e_i\|^2 ds < \infty \end{aligned} \tag{9.32}$$

$$U(t,t_0)z_0 \in D(A(t)) \text{ w.p.1} \tag{9.33}$$

$$\begin{aligned} &U(t,s)g(s) \in D(A(t)) \text{ w.p.1 for almost all } t > s \in [t_0,t_1] \\ &\text{and } \int_{t_0}^{t} \|A(t)U(t,s)g(s)\| ds < \infty \text{ w.p.1} \end{aligned} \tag{9.34}$$

((λ_i,e_i) are the eigenvalue,eigenvector pairs associated with $w(t)$ as in Lemma 5.23).

9.4 The quadratic cost control problem

We consider the following time dependent controlled system

$$z(t) = U(t,t_0)z_0 + \int_{t_0}^{t} U(t,s)B(s)u(s)ds \tag{9.35}$$

where U and H are real Hilbert spaces, $U(t,s)$ is a mild evolution operator on H, $B \in \mathcal{B}^{\infty}(t_0,t_1;\mathcal{L}(U,H))$, $z_0 \in H$, and we seek $u \in L^2(t_0,t_1;U)$ which minimizes the cost functional

$$\begin{aligned} C(u,t_0,z_0) &= \langle z(t_1)-r(t_1), G(z(t_1)-r(t_1))\rangle \\ &+ \int_{t_0}^{t_1} \{\langle z(s)-r(s), M(s)(z(s)-r(s))\rangle + \langle u(s), R(s)u(s)\rangle\} ds \end{aligned} \tag{9.36}$$

where $M \in \mathcal{B}^{\infty}(t_o,t_1;\mathcal{L}(H))$, $R \in \mathcal{B}^{\infty}(t_o,t_1;\mathcal{L}(U))$, $G \in \mathcal{L}(H)$, $M(s)$ and $R(s)$ are self adjoint and positive with $\langle R(s)v,v\rangle \geq \alpha\|v\|^2$ for all $v \in U$ and some $\alpha > 0$.
$r(t)$ is a given continuous H-valued function on $[t_o,t_1]$.

Then using a time dependent analogue of the approach in Chapter 4 we are able to establish:

Theorem 9.18

There exists an optimal control u^* given by

$$u^*(t) = -R^{-1}(t)B^*(t)(Q(t)z(t)+s(t)) \tag{9.37}$$

where $Q(t)$ is the unique solution of the integral Riccati equation

$$Q(t)h=U^*_{\infty}(t_1,t)GU_{\infty}(t_1,t)h+\int_t^{t_1} U^*_{\infty}(s,t)\left[M(s)+Q(s)B(s)R(s)^{-1}B^*(s)Q(s)\right] U_{\infty}(s,t)h\,ds\ , \tag{9.38}$$

$U_{\infty}(t,s)$ is the perturbation of $U(t,s)$ by $-B(t)R^{-1}(t)B^*(t)Q(t)$ and

$$s(t) = U^*_{\infty}(t_1,t)Gr(t_1) - \int_t^{t_1} U^*_{\infty}(s,t)M(s)r(s)ds \tag{9.39}$$

The optimal cost is given by

$$\begin{aligned} C(u_o;t_o,z_o) &= \langle z_o,Q(t_o)z_o\rangle + \langle r(t_1),Gr(t_1)\rangle + \int_{t_o}^{t_1} \langle r(s),M(s)r(s)\rangle ds \\ &\quad + 2\langle z_o,s(t_o)\rangle - \int_{t_o}^{t_1} \langle s(s),B(s)R^{-1}(s)B^*(s)s(s)\rangle\, ds \end{aligned} \tag{9.40}$$

The obvious analogue of Corollary 4.7 giving alternative integral expressions for $Q(t)$ also holds. Differences arise when it comes to expressing $Q(t)$ in a differential form analagous to (4.18) of Lemma 4.6.

Theorem 9.19

(a) If $U(t,s)$ is a quasi evolution operator with quasi generator $A(t)$, then $Q(t)$ satisfies the following differential Riccati equation

$$\begin{aligned} &\frac{d}{dt}\langle Q(t)h,k\rangle + \langle Q(t)h,A(t)k\rangle + \langle A(t)h,Q(t)k\rangle \\ &- \langle Q(t)B(t)R^{-1}(t)B^*(t)Q(t)h,k\rangle + \langle M(t)h,k\rangle = 0 \end{aligned} \tag{9.41}$$

$Q(t_1) = G$ for $h,k \in D_A$.

(b) If $U(t,s)$ is a quasi and a strong evolution operator with generator $A(t)$ and $\overline{D_A} = H$, then $Q(t)$ is the unique solution of (9.41) in the class of self adjoint weakly continuous operators P such that $\langle h,P(\cdot)k\rangle$ is absolutely continuous for all $h,k \in D_A$. Furthermore, $s(t)$ satisfies the differential equation

$$(9.42)\quad \begin{cases} \frac{d}{dt}\langle s(t),h\rangle = -\langle s(t),(A(t)-B(t)R^{-1}(t)B^*(t)Q(t))h\rangle + \langle M(t)r(t),h\rangle \\ s(t_1) = Gr(t_1) \end{cases}$$

(c) If $U(t,s)$ is quasi and the dual evolution operator $Y(t,s) = U^*(t_1-s, t_1-t)$ is an almost strong evolution operator and

$$(9.43)\qquad U^*(t_1,t)G \text{ and } U^*(s,t)M(s) : H \to D(A^*(t))$$

$$(9.44)\quad \left.\begin{aligned} &\int_t^{t_1} \|A^*(t)U^*(s,t)M(s)h\|ds < \infty \\ &\int_t^{t_1} \|A^*(t)U^*(t_1,s)Gh\|ds < \infty \end{aligned}\right\} \quad \text{for all } h \in H$$

then $s(t)$ is the unique solution of the evolution equation

$$(9.45)\quad \begin{cases} \dot{s}(t) = -(A^*(t)-Q(t)B(t)R^{-1}(t)B^*(t))s(t) + M(t)r(t) \\ s(t_1) = Gr(t_1) \end{cases}$$

Proof

(a) If we formally differentiate $\langle Q(t)h,k\rangle$ with respect to t, where $Q(t)$ is defined by (9.38), then we obtain (9.41) using the quasi evolution operator property (9.8) of $U_\infty(t,s)$. We justify this formal differentiation for a typical term.

Let

$$g(t) = \langle\int_t^{t_1} U_\infty^*(s,t)M(s)U_\infty(s,t)h\,ds,k\rangle \text{ for } h,k \in D_A$$

$$= \int_t^{t_1} \langle M(s)U_\infty(s,t)h,U_\infty(s,t)k\rangle ds$$

Hence

$$\frac{dg(t)}{dt} = -\langle M(t)h,k\rangle + \int_t^{t_1} \frac{\partial}{\partial t}\langle M(s)U_\infty(s,t)h,U_\infty(s,t)k\rangle ds$$

assuming for the moment that differentiation under the integral is justified

$$= -\langle M(t)h,k\rangle - \int_t^{t_1} \langle M(s)U_\infty(s,t)(A(t)-B(t)R^{-1}B^*(t)Q(s))h,U_\infty(s,t)h\rangle ds$$

$$- \int_t^{t_1} \langle M(s)U_\infty(s,t),U_\infty(s,t)(A(t)-B(t)R^{-1}(t)B^*(t)Q(t))k\rangle\, ds$$

using Property (9.8) and Theorem 9.6

$$= -\langle M(t)h,k\rangle - \langle (A(t)-B(t)R^{-1}(t)B^*(t)Q(t))h, \int_t^{t_1} U^*(s,t)M(s)U(s,t)k\, ds\rangle$$

$$-\langle \int_t^{t_1} U_\infty^*(s,t)M(s)U_\infty(s,t)h\, ds,(A(t)-B(t)R^{-1}(t)B^*(t)Q(t))k\rangle$$

taking $A(t)$ outside the integral since it is a closed operator.

Finally, differentiation under the integrand is justified since

$$f(s,t) = \langle M(s)U_\infty(s,t)h,U_\infty(s,t)h\rangle$$

satisfies

$$\int_s^{t_1} \left| \frac{\partial}{\partial t} f(s,t)\right| dt \leq \int_s^{t_1} |\langle U_\infty(s,t)A_\infty(t)h,M(s)U_\infty(s,t)k\rangle| ds$$

$$+ \int_s^{t_1} |\langle M(s)U_\infty(s,t)h,U_\infty(s,t)A_\infty(t)y\rangle|\, ds$$

$$< \infty$$

by Property (9.7) for the quasi evolution operator $U_\infty(s,t)$ with quasi generator $A_\infty(t)$.

(b) Let P_1, P_2 be solutions of (9.41) and write $Q(t) = P_1(t) - P_2(t)$. Then it is readily verified that for $h,k \in D_A$,

$$(9.46)\quad \frac{d}{dt}\langle Q(t)h,k\rangle = -\langle (A(t)-C(t)P_1(t))h,Q(t)k\rangle$$

$$- \langle Q(t)h,(A(t)-C(t)P_1(t))k\rangle - \langle Q(t)C(t)Q(t)h,k\rangle \text{ a.e.}$$

and

$$(9.47)\quad \frac{d}{dt}\langle Q(t)h,k\rangle = -\langle (A(t)-C(t)P_2(t))h,Q(t)k\rangle$$

$$- \langle Q(t)h,(A(t)-C(t)P_2(t))k\rangle + \langle Q(t)C(t)Q(t)h,k\rangle \text{ a.e.}$$

where $C(t) = B(t)R^{-1}(t)B^*(t)$.

Let

$$F(t)h = \int_t^{t_1} U_1^*(s,t)Q(s)C(s)Q(s)U_1(s,t)h\,ds$$

where $U_1(t,s)$ is the quasi perturbed operator generated by $A(t)-C(t)P_1(t)$. Then for $h,k \in D_A$ by Theorem 9.6 and (9.8), we may differentiate to obtain

$$\frac{d}{dt}\langle F(t)h,k\rangle = -\langle Q(t)C(t)Q(t)h,k\rangle - \langle F(t)h,(A(t)-C(t)P_1(t))k\rangle$$
$$-\langle (A(t)-C(t)P_1(t))h,F(t)k\rangle \text{ a.e.}$$

and subtracting from (9.46), we have

$$(9.48)\quad \frac{d}{dt}\langle (Q(t)-F(t))h,k\rangle = -\langle (Q(t)-F(t))h,(A(t)-C(t)P_1(t))k\rangle$$
$$-\langle (A(t)-C(t)P_1(t))h,(Q(t)-F(t))k\rangle$$

$$Q(t_1) = F(t_1) = 0$$

Assuming for the moment that (9.48) has a unique solution, we have

$$Q(t) = F(t)$$

and

$$\langle Q(t)h,h\rangle = \int_t^{t_1} \langle U_1^*(s,t)Q(s)C(s)Q^*(s)U_1(s,t)h,h\rangle ds \geq 0 \quad \forall\, h \in H.$$

Similarly, using (9.47) with P_2 perturbations, we find

$$\langle Q(t)h,h\rangle \leq 0 \quad \forall\, h \in H$$

Consequently, $Q(t) = 0$ on $[0,t_1]$.

It remains to show that (9.48) has a unique solution. Consider equivalently

$$(9.49)\quad \frac{d}{dt}\langle P(t)h,k\rangle = -\langle P(t)h,(A(t)-D(t))k\rangle - \langle (A(t)-D(t))h,P(t)k\rangle \text{ a.e.}$$

$$P(t_1) = 0$$

where $D \in \mathcal{B}_\infty(0,t_1;\mathcal{L}(H))$.

Let $Q(t) = U^*(t,s)P(t)U(t,s)$, where $U(t,s)$ is a strong evolution operator and so $U(t,s)h$ is strongly differentiable in t for $h \in D_A$, and hence $\langle P(t)U(t,s)h,U(t,s)k\rangle$ is absolutely continuous with

$$\frac{d}{dt}\langle h,Q(t)k\rangle = \langle P(t)A(t)U(t,s)h,U(t,s)k\rangle + \langle P(t)U(t,s)h,A(t)U(t,s)k\rangle$$

$$- \langle P(t)U(t,s)h,(A(t)-D(t))U(t,s)k\rangle - \langle (A(t)-D(t))U(t,s)h, P(t)U(t,s)k\rangle$$

$$= \langle P(t)U(t,s)h,D(t)U(t,s)k\rangle + \langle D(t)U(t,s)h,P(t)U(t,s)k\rangle$$

and

$$\langle U^*(t,s)P(t)U(t,s)h,k\rangle = -\int_t^{t_1} \langle (D^*(r)P(r)+P(r)D(r))U(r,s)h,U(r,s)h\rangle dr$$

for all $h \in H$, since $\overline{D_A} = H$.

Letting $s \to t$, we obtain

$$\langle P(t)h,h\rangle = -\int_t^{t_1} \langle (D^*(r)P(r)+P(r)D(r))U(r,t)h,U(r,t)h\rangle dr \quad \forall\, h \in H.$$

Now $P(t)$ is self adjoint and so

$$\|P(t)\| = \sup_{\|h\|=1} \|\langle P(t)h,h\rangle\| \le \sup_{\|h\|=1} \int_t^{t_1} C\|P(r)\|\,\|h\|^2 dr$$

Therefore

$$\|P(t)\| \le C \int_t^{t_1} \|P(r)\| dr$$

Then by Gronwall's inequality, $\|P(t)\| = 0$ on H, i.e.(9.49) has the unique solution zero on H.

To establish (9.42), we first obtain from (9.39) that

$$(9.50)\quad \langle s(t),h\rangle = -\langle Gr(t_1),U_\infty(t_1,t)h\rangle - \int_t^{t_1} \langle M(s)r(s),U_\infty(s,t)h\rangle ds$$

Now since $U(t,s)$ is a quasi evolution operator, by Theorem 9.6 its perturbation $U_\infty(t,s)$ is also quasi. Thus for $h \in D(A(t))$ we can diff- (9.50) with respect to t to obtain (9.42).

(c) (9.42) is not in the usual form for evolution equations; however, if we write $\bar{A}(t) = A^*(t_1-t)$, $\bar{s}(t) = s(t_1-t)$, $\bar{Q}(t) = Q(t_1-t)$, and so on, (9.42) is equivalent to

$$(9.51)\quad \begin{cases} \frac{d}{dt}\bar{s}(t) = (\bar{A}(t)-\bar{Q}(t)\bar{B}(t)\bar{R}^{-1}(t)\bar{B}^*(t))\bar{s}(t) - \bar{M}(t)\bar{r}(t) \\ \bar{s}(0) = G\bar{r}(0) = Gr(t_1) \end{cases}$$

and assumptions (9.43) and (9.44) can be rewritten

$$(9.52)\qquad Y(t,0)G \text{ and } Y(t,s)\bar{M}(s): H \to D(\bar{A}(t))$$

$$(9.53)\quad \begin{cases} \int_0^t \|\bar{A}(t)Y(t,s)\bar{M}(s)h\|ds < \infty \\ \int_0^t \|\bar{A}(t)Y(t,0)Gh\|ds < \infty \end{cases} \quad \text{for all } h \in H.$$

First we show that $\bar{A}(t) - \bar{Q}(t)\bar{B}(t)\bar{R}^{-1}(t)\bar{B}^*(t)$ generates an almost strong evolution operator.

By the time dependent analogue of Corollary 4.7 and the semigroup property of $U(t,s)$, we deduce that

$$(9.54)\quad U^*(s,t)Q(s)h = U^*(t_1,t)GU_\infty(t_1,s)h + \int_s^{t_1} U^*(\rho,t)M(\rho)U_\infty(\rho,s)h\, d\rho$$

and writing $Y_\infty(t,s) = U_\infty^*(t_1-s,t_1-t)$, this is equivalent to

$$Y(t,s)\bar{Q}(s)h = Y(t,0)GY_\infty^*(s,0)h + \int_0^s Y(t,\rho)\bar{M}(\rho)Y_\infty^*(s,\rho)h\, d\rho$$

So by (9.52) and (9.53) and since $\bar{A}(t)$ is closed, $Y(t,s)\bar{Q}(s):H \to D(\bar{A}(t))$ and

$$\bar{A}(t)Y(t,s)\bar{Q}(s)h = \bar{A}(t)Y(t,0)GY_\infty^*(s,0)h + \int_0^s \bar{A}(t)Y(t,\rho)\bar{M}(\rho)Y_\infty^*(s,\rho)h\, d\rho$$

and again by (9.53), it is integrable on $(0,t_1)$. Hence, by Theorem 9.11, $\bar{A}(t) - \bar{Q}(t)\bar{B}(t)\bar{R}^{-1}(t)\bar{B}^*(t)$ generates the almost strong evolution operator, $Y_\infty(t,s)$, which is the unique solution of

$$Y_\infty(t,s)h = Y(t,s)h - \int_s^t Y(t,\rho)\bar{Q}(\rho)\bar{B}(\rho)\bar{R}^{-1}(\rho)\bar{B}^*(\rho)Y_\infty(\rho,s)h\, d\rho$$

This, together with (9.52) and (9.53), implies that $Y_\infty(t,s)$ satisfies

$$Y_\infty(t,0)G \text{ and } Y_\infty(t,s)\bar{M}(s) : H \to D(\bar{A}(t)) \text{ with}$$

$$\int_0^t \|\bar{A}(t)Y_\infty(t,s)\bar{M}(s)h\|ds < \infty$$

By Theorem 9.16 this ensures that (9.51) has the unique solution

$$\bar{s}(t) = Y_\infty(t,0)G\bar{r}(0) - \int_0^t Y_\infty(t,s)\bar{M}(s)\bar{r}(s)ds$$

or equivalently,

$$s(t) = U_\infty^*(t_1,t)Gr(t_1) - \int_t^{t_1} U_\infty^*(s,t)M(s)r(s)ds$$

is the unique solution of (9.45).

9.5 State estimation

We consider the following time dependent stochastic state and observation process

$$(9.55)\qquad z(t) = U(t,0)z_o + \int_0^t U(t,s)D(s)dw(s) + \int_0^t U(t,s)g(s)\, ds$$

$$(9.56)\qquad y(t) = \int_0^t C(s)z(s)ds + \int_0^t F(s)dv(s)$$

where H,K are separable Hilbert spaces, $D \in \mathcal{B}^\infty(0,t_1;\mathcal{L}(K,H))$, $C \in \mathcal{B}^\infty(0,t_1;\mathcal{L}(H,R^k))$, $F \in L^\infty(0,t_1;\mathcal{L}(R^k))$, $g \in L^2(0,t_1;H)$, $U(t,s)$ is a mild evolution operator on H, $w(t)$ is an H-valued Wiener process with incremental covariance W, $v(t)$ is an R^k-valued Wiener process with incremental covariance V, $z_o \in L^2(\Omega,p;H)$ is Gaussian with zero mean and covariance matrix P_o. v,w and z_o are mutually independent. The estimation problem is to find the best unbiased estimate $\hat{z}(t|t_o)$ of the state $z(t)$ at time t_1 based on y_{t_1}.

Then using a time dependent analogue of the proofs in Chapter 6, we are able to establish:

Theorem 9.20

There is a unique optimal filter given by

$$(9.57)\qquad \hat{z}(t) = E_{y_t}\{z_t\} = \int_0^t Y(t,s)g(s)ds + \int_0^t Y(t,s)P(s)C^*(s)(F(s)VF^*(s))^{-1} dy(s)$$

where $Y(t,s)$ is the perturbation of $U(t,s)$ by $-P(t)C^*(t)(F(t)VF^*(t))^{-1}C(t)$ and $P(t)$ is the unique solution of the equivalent integral Riccati equations

$$(9.58)\qquad P(t)h = Y(t,0)RY^*(t,0)h + \int_0^t Y(t,s)\big[D(s)WD^*(s) + P(s)C^*(s)(F(s)VF^*(s))^{-1}C(s)P(s)\big]Y^*(t,s)h\, ds$$

$$(9.59)\qquad P(t)h = U(t,0)P_oY^*(t,0)h + \int_0^t U(t,s)D(s)WD^*(s)Y^*(t,s)h\, ds$$

Furthermore, $P(t)$ is the covariance of the error process $\tilde{z}(t)=z(t)-\hat{z}(t)$

$$P(t) = E\{\tilde{z}(t)\circ\tilde{z}(t)\}$$

Introducing the innovations process $\rho(t)$ for (9.55)(9.56)

$$(9.60) \qquad \rho(t) = y(t) - \int_0^t C(s)\hat{z}(s)ds$$

we are able to express the filter in terms of this innovations process.

Corollary 9.21

$$(9.61) \qquad \hat{z}(t) = \int_0^t U(t,s)g(s)ds + \int_0^t U(t,s)P(s)C^*(s)(F(s)VF^*(s))^{-1}\, d\rho(s)$$

As before, $\rho(t)$ is a martingale relative to the sigma field generated by y_t and can be represented by

$$(9.62) \qquad \rho(t) = \int_0^t F(\alpha)dv_o(\alpha)$$

where $v_o(\alpha)$ is a k dimensional Wiener process with incremental covariance matrix V.

Moreover, using this property of the innovations process allows us to obtain equations for the optimal smoother and predictor analagous to those of Chapter 6.

Theorem 9.22

The best smoothed estimate of $z(t)$ based on y_{t_o} is given by

$$(9.63) \qquad \hat{z}(t|t_o) = E_{y_{t_o}}\{z(t)\} = \hat{z}(t) + P(t)\int_t^{t_o} Y^*(s,t)C^*(s)(F(s)VF^*(s))^{-1}d\rho(s); \quad t_o > t$$

and the optimal predictor of $z(t)$ based on y_{t_o} is given by

$$(9.64) \qquad \hat{z}(t|t_o) = U(t,t_o)\hat{z}(t_o) + \int_0^t U(t,\alpha)g(\alpha)d\alpha \quad ; \quad t > t_o$$

The differences between the time invariant and the time dependent cases again manifest themselves when differential forms for the estimates are sought. Using the duality between the control and filtering problems, we can deduce the following from Theorems 9.19 and 9.9.

Theorem 9.23

If $U(t,s)$ is an almost strong evolution operator with

$$\overline{D(A(t))} = H$$

and

$$D_{A^*} = \bigcap_{t\epsilon[0,t_1]} D(A^*(t)) \neq \emptyset$$

then P(t) satisfies the following differential Riccati equation

$$(9.65)\quad \frac{d}{dt}\langle P(t)h,k\rangle - \langle P(t)h,A^*(t)k\rangle - \langle A^*(t)h,P(t)k\rangle$$
$$+ \langle P(t)C^*(t)(F(t)VF^*(t))^{-1}C(t)P(t)h,k\rangle = \langle D(t)WD^*(t)h,k\rangle$$
$$P(0) = P_o \qquad \text{for } h,k \in D_{A^*}$$

If furthermore, $U^*(t_1-s,t_1-t)$ is a strong evolution operator, and quasi with $\overline{D}_{A^*} = H$, then P(t) is the unique solution of (9.65) in the class of weakly continuous operators such that $\langle P(t)h,k\rangle$ is absolutely continuous for all $h,k \in D_{A^*}$.

For $\hat{z}(t)$ and $\hat{z}(t|t_o)$ to be expressed in differential form as in Theorem 6.21, we need stronger assumptions on the noise covariances.

<u>Theorem 9.24</u>

Suppose U(t,s) is an almost strong evolution operator, then the optimal predictor $\hat{z}(t|t_o)$ is the unique solution of

$$(9.66)\qquad d\hat{z}(t|t_o) = A(t)\hat{z}(t)dt \ ; \ \hat{z}(t|t_o) = \hat{z}(t_o)$$

If furthermore, $U(t,s)g(s)$, $U(t,s)D(s)e_i$, $U(t,0)P_oe_i \in D(A(t))$ for all i and almost all $t > s$ and

$$(9.67)\qquad \int_0^t \|A(t)U(t,s)g(s)\|ds < \infty$$

$$(9.68)\qquad \sum_{i=0}^{\infty} \lambda_i \int_0^t \|A(t)U(t,s)D(s)e_i\|^2 ds < \infty$$

$$(9.69)\qquad \int_0^{t_1} \|A(t)U(t,0)P_oh\|dt < \infty$$

then $\hat{z}(t)$ is the unique solution of the following stochastic evolution equation

$$(9.70)\quad \begin{cases} d\hat{z}(t) = A(t)\hat{z}(t)dt + g(t)dt + P(t)C^*(t)(F(t)VF^*(t))^{-1}d\rho(t) \\ \hat{z}(0) = 0 \end{cases}$$

and the optimal smoother $\hat{z}(t|t_o)$ is the unique solution of

$$(9.71)\qquad \begin{cases} d\hat{z}(t|t_o) = A(t)\hat{z}(t|t_o)dt + D(t)WD^*(t)\lambda(t)dt \\ \hat{z}(t_o|t_o) = \hat{z}(t_o) \end{cases}$$

where
$$\lambda(t) = \int_t^{t_o} Y^*(s,t)C^*(s)(F(s)VF^*(s))^{-1}\, d\rho(s)$$

Proof

(a) (9.66) is trivial.

(b) Consider (9.70) noting that from (9.62)

$$P(t)C^*(t)(F(t)VF^*(t))^{-1}\, d\rho(t) = P(t)C^*(t)(F^*(t))^{-1}V^{-1}\, dv_o(t)$$

where $v_o(t)$ is a k-dimensional Wiener process.
From (9.59)

$$(9.72)\qquad P(t)h = U(t,0)P_oY^*(t,0)h + \int_0^t U(t,s)D(s)WD^*(s)Y(t,s)h\, ds$$

and so arguing as in the proof of Theorem 6.21 we can show that

$$P(t)\colon H \to D(A(t))$$

and

$$(9.73)\qquad \int_0^t \|A(t)U(t,s)P(s)C^*(s)y\|^2 ds < \infty \quad \text{for all } y \in R^k$$

which, together with (9.67), shows that (9.70) has a unique solution by Theorem 9.17.

Consider now (9.71), where there is no 'dw(t)' term, but a stochastic forcing term of the form g(t)dt. We note that our assumptions ensure that $U(t,t_o)\hat{z}(t_o)$ and $U(t,s)D(s)WD^*(s)\lambda(s) \in D(A(t))$ w.p.1. and so by Theorem 6.16, (9.71) has a unique solution provided that

$$\int_0^t \|A(t)U(t,s)D(s)WD^*(s)\lambda(s)\|\, ds < \infty \quad \text{w.p.1.}$$

Arguing as in Theorem 6.21, we establish this via the following estimate

$$E\{\int_0^{t_1} \|A(t)U(t,s)D(s)WD^*(s)\lambda(s)\|^2 ds$$

$$\leq \int_0^{t_1} E\{\|D^*(s)\lambda(s)\|^2\} \sum_{i=0}^{\infty} \lambda_i{}^2 \|A(t)U(t,s)D(s)e_i\|^2 ds$$

$$\leq \text{const} \sup_{0\leq s\leq t_1} E\{\|\lambda(s)\|^2\} \int_0^{t_1} \sum_{i=0}^{\infty} \lambda_i^2 \|A(t)U(t,s)D(s)e_i\|^2 ds$$

$$< \infty \text{ from (9.68)}$$

and since $\lambda \in C(0,t_1;L^2(\Omega;H))$ by Lemma 5.31.

9.6 Stochastic optimal control

Consider the following time dependent stochastic control problem

$$\text{(9.74)} \quad \begin{aligned} z(t) &= U(t,0)z_0 + \int_0^t U(t,s)D(s)dw(s) + \int_0^t U(t,s)B(s)u(s)ds \\ &\quad + \int_0^t U(t,s)g(s)ds \end{aligned}$$

$$\text{(9.75)} \quad y(t) = \int_0^t C(s)z(s)ds + \int_0^t F(s)dv(s)$$

with the cost functional given by

$$\text{(9.76)} \quad \begin{aligned} C(u) &= E\{\langle z(t_1)-r(t_1),\ G(z(t_1)-r(t_1))\rangle \\ &\quad + \int_0^{t_1} \langle z(s)-r(s), M(s)(z(s)-r(s))\rangle + \langle u(s), R(s)u(s)\rangle ds\} \end{aligned}$$

where $H,K,U(t,s),D,g,z_0,C,v,F$ are defined as in §9.4 and r,U,B,G,M and R as in §9.3.

For our class of admissible controls as in Chapter 7, we take

$$U_{ad} = \int^{\oplus} U_{\eta_t} dt \cap \int^{\oplus} U_{y_t} dt$$

where $U = L^2(\Omega,p;U)$, and

$$\text{(9.77)} \quad \begin{cases} \xi(t) = U(t,0)z_0 + \int_0^t U(t,s)D(s)dw(s) + \int_0^t U(t,s)g(s)ds \\ \eta(t) = \int_0^t C(s)\xi(s)ds + \int_0^t F(s)dv(s) \end{cases}$$

Using the same approach as in Chapter 7, we can prove the time dependent analogue of Theorem 7.8.

Theorem 9.25

There exists a unique optimal control $u_* \in U_{ad}$ minimizing (9.78), which is given by

$$(9.78) \qquad u_*(t) = -R^{-1}(t)B^*(t)(Q(t)\hat{z}_*(t)+s(t))$$

$$(9.79) \qquad \hat{z}_*(t) = \int_0^t U_\infty(t,s)g(s)ds + \int_0^t U_\infty(t,s)P(s)C^*(s)(F(s)VF^*(s))^{-1}d\rho(s)$$

$$(9.80) \qquad s(t) = -U_\infty^*(t_1,t)Gr(t_1) + \int_t^{t_1} U_\infty^*(s,t)(Q(s)g(s)-M(s)r(s))ds$$

where P and Q are the unique solutions of (9.58) and (9.38) respectively, U_∞ is the perturbation of U(t,s) by $-B(t)R^{-1}(t)B^*(t)Q(t)$ and $\rho(t)$ is the innovations process of (9.74),(9.75) given by

$$(9.81) \qquad \rho(t) = y_*(t) - \int_0^t C(s)\hat{z}_*(s)ds.$$

Furthermore, $\hat{z}_*(t) = E_{Y_t}\{z(t)\}$, and $\hat{z}_*(t)$ can also be expressed by

$$(9.82) \qquad \hat{z}_*(t) = \int_0^t U_{PQ}(t,s)g(s)ds + \int_0^t U_{PQ}(t,s)P(s)C^*(s)(F(s)VF^*(s))^{-1}dy(s)$$

where U_{PQ} is the perturbation of U(t,s) by $-B(t)R^{-1}(t)B^*(t)Q(t) - P(t)C^*(t)(F(t)VF^*(t))^{-1}C(t)$.

9.7 Concluding remarks

In §9.4 to §9.6 we have indicated how one can solve the quadratic cost control problem, the linear estimation problems and the linear stochastic control problems for time varying systems, whose dynamics are described by evolution operators. In particular, we can consider systems of the types considered in Examples 9.12, 9.13 and 9.14 where the control and stochastic inputs are the time varying analogues of those in Examples 4.9, 4.10, 4.11, 6.23, 6.24, 6.25, 7.12, 7.13 and 7.14. For all these examples one can obtain a unique optimal control and/or state estimator in terms of operators Q(t) and P(t) which are unique solutions of integral Riccati equations of the type (9.38) and (9.58) respectively. Furthermore, as the evolution operators and their duals in Examples 9.12 - 9.14 are all quasi, both Q(t) and P(t) also satisfy a differential Riccati equation of the type (9.41) and (9.65) respectively. Differences occur when we consider uniqueness of these differential operator equations and differential versions of the estimators.

We can say nothing further about hyperbolic systems of the type considered in Example 9.13, but for parabolic systems of the type considered in Example 9.12, Q(t) and P(t) will be unique solutions of the differential Riccati equations provided the coefficients of A(t) are sufficiently smooth in t and the estimators are unique solutions of stochastic evolution equations if in addition we make assumptions on the noise parameters (cf Example 6.23). For the delay systems considered in Example 9.14 the situation is no longer symmetric, because A(t) and $A^*(t)$ turn out to be rather different in character. If the coefficients are continuous, A(t) generates a strong evolution operator and so Q(t) is the unique solution of a differential Riccati equation, and it is possible to obtain a decomposition analagous to that in Example 4.11. But as $A^*(t)$ is in general only quasi, for the filtering problem P(t) need not be the unique solution of the differential Riccati equation and as we indicated in Example 5.41, it is not even meaningful to talk of strong M^2 solutions for the estimates. The important point is to show that the solution of the original stochastic delay equation can be identified with the projection of the $\mathcal{M}^2$ mild solution and this can be done analagously as in Example 6.25. For a more detailed analysis of time dependent systems using this approach we refer the reader to [3]-[12].

References

[1] Bensoussan, A. Filtrage optimal des systemes lineaires, Dunod, 1971.

[2] Curtain, R.F. and Falb, P.L. Stochastic differential equations in Hilbert space, J. Diff. Eqns., 10 (1971), pp.412-430.

[3] Curtain, R.F. and Pritchard, A.J. The infinite dimensional Riccati equation, J. Math. Anal. Appl., 47 (1974), pp.43-57.

[4] Curtain, R.F. Infinite dimensional filtering, SIAM J. Control, 13 (1975), pp.89-104.

[5] Curtain, R.F. The infinite dimensional Riccati equation with applications to affine hereditary differential systems,

SIAM J. Control, 14 (1975), pp.951-983.

[6] Curtain, R.F. A Kalman-Bucy filtering theory for affine hereditary differential equations, Int. Symp. on Control Theory, Numerical Methods and Computer System Modelling, June 1974, (Springer Verlag: Lecture Notes in Economics and Math. Systems, 107, 1974.)

[7] Curtain, R.F. The infinite dimensional Riccati equation for systems defined by evolution operators, SIAM J. Control, 14 (1975) pp.951-983.

[8] Curtain, R.F. Estimation theory for abstract evolution equations exited by general white noise processes, SIAM J. Control, 6 (1977), pp.1124-1150.

[9] Curtain, R.F. Stochastic evolution equations with general white noise disturbance, J. Math. Anal. Appl., 60 (1977), pp.570-595.

[10] Curtain, R.F. and Ichikawa, A. The separation principle for stochastic evolution equations, SIAM J. Control, 15 (1977), p.367.

[11] Curtain, R.F. and Pritchard, A.J. An abstract theory for unbounded control action for distributed parameter systems, SIAM J. Control, 15 (1977), pp.566-611.

[12] Curtain, R.F. Linear stochastic control for distributed systems with boundary control, boundary noise and point observations, J. Appl. Math. and Opt., to appear.

[13] Datko, R. Unconstrained control problems with quadratic cost, SIAM J. Control, 2 (1973), pp.32-52.

[14] Delfour, M.C. and Mitter, S.K. Hereditary differential systems with constant delays II: A class of affine systems and the adjoint problem, J. Diff. Eqns., 18 (1975), pp.18-28.

[15] Delfour, M.C. and Mitter, S.K. Controllability, observability and optimal feedback control of affine hereditary differential systems, SIAM J. Control, 10 (1972), pp. 298-328.

[16] Kato, T. Abstract evolution equations of parabolic type in Banach and Hilbert spaces, Nagoya Math. J., 19 (1961), pp.93-125.

[17] Kato, T. and Tanabe, H. On the abstract evolution equation, Osaka Math. J., 14 (1962), pp.107-133.

[18] Lions, J.L. Optimal control of systems governed by partial differential equations, Springer Verlag, 1971.

[19] Rauch, J. L^2 is a continuable initial condition for Kreiss' mixed problems, Comm. Pure Appl. Math., 25 (1972), pp. 265-285.

[20] Vinter, R.B. and Johnson, T.L. Optimal control of non symmetric hyperbolic systems in n variables on the half space, SIAM J. Control, 15 (1977), pp.129-133.

ADDITIONAL REFERENCES

The following is by no means a complete list of papers on infinite dimensional systems theory, and more references may be found in the survey articles [17],[84],[89],[103],[115],[116],[140], books [23],[136] and conference proceedings [111],[112],[113],[114].

[1] Ahmed, N.U. and Theo, K. Necessary conditions for optimality of Cauchy problems for parabolic partial differential equations, SIAM J. Control, 13 (1975), pp.981-998.

[2] Ahmed, N.U. Optimal control of a class of strongly nonlinear parabolic systems, J. Math. Anal. Appl., 61 (1977), pp.188-209.

[3] Aggarwal, J.K. Feedback control of linear systems with distributed delay, Automatica, 9 (1973), pp.367-379.

[4] Aidarous, S.E. On a direct method for optimisation of stochastic distributed parameter systems, Int. J. Control, 21 (1975), pp.929-944.

[5] Aidarous, S.E., Gevers, M.R. and Installé, M.J. Optimal pointwise discrete control and controller's allocation for stochastic distributed systems, Int. J. Control, 24 (1976), pp.493-508.

[6] Ajinka, M.B., Köhnes, M., Müder, H.F. and Ray, W.H. The experimental implementation of a distributed parameter filter, Automatica, 2 (1975), pp.571-577.

[7] Ajinka, M.B., Ray, W.H., Yu, T.K. and Seinfeld, J.H. The application of an approximate filter to systems governed by coupled ordinary and partial differential equations, Int. J. Systems Sci., 6 (1975), pp.313-332.

[8] Amouroux, M., Babary, J.P. and El Jai, A. Adaptive open loop control for a class of distributed parameter systems, Proc. IFAC Symp. on Control of Distributed Parameter Systems, Warwick, 1977.

[9] Amouroux, M. and Babary, J.P. Optimal pointwise control for a class of distributed parameter systems, Proc. IFAC Congress, Boston, 1975.

[10] Asatani, K. Near optimum control of distributed parameter systems via singular perturbation theory, J. Math. Anal. Appl., 54 (1976), pp.719-818.

[11] Asner, B. and Halanay, A. Delay feedback using derivatives for minimal time linear control problems, J. Math. Anal. Appl., 48 (1974), pp.257-263.

[12] Athans, M. Towards a practical theory for distributed parameter systems, IEEE Trans. AC 15 (1970), pp.245-247.

[13] Bagchi, A. A martingale approach to state estimation in delay differential equations, J. Math. Anal. Appl., 56 (1976), pp.195-210.

[14] Balakrishnan, A.V. Optimal control in Banach spaces, SIAM J. Control, 3 (1965), pp.152-180.

[15] Balakrishnan, A.V. and Lions, J.L. State estimation for infinite dimensional systems, J. Comput. Systems Sci., (1967), pp.391-403.

[16] Balas, M. Active control of flexible systems, AIAA Symp. Dynamics and Control of Large Flexible Spacecraft, Blacksburg, 1977.

[17] Banks, H.T. and Manitius, A. Application of abstract variational theory to hereditary systems - a survey, IEEE Trans., AC 19 (1974), pp.524-533.

[18] Banks, S.P. Stability of nonlinear distributed parameter systems, Proc. 2nd IFAC Symp. on Control of Distributed Parameter Systems, Warwick, 1977.

[19] Banks, S.P. Perturbation of linear accretive operators by nonlinear nonaccretive operators, Control Theory Centre Report No.56, University of Warwick, 1976.

[20] Banks, S.P. On the generation of nonlinear multivalued semigroups, Control Theory Centre Report No.62, University of Warwick, 1976.

[21] Banks, S.P. Nonlinear discontinuous perturbations of m-accretive operators, Control Theory Centre Report No.64, University of Warwick, 1977.

[22] Baras, J., Brockett, R. and Fuhrmann, P. State space models for infinite dimensional systems, IEEE Trans., AC 19 (1974), pp.693-700.

[23] Barbu, V. Nonlinear semigroups and differential equations in Banach space, Noordhoff, 1976.

[24] Barbu, V. Convex control problems of Bolza in Hilbert spaces, SIAM J. Control, 13 (1975), pp.754-770.

[25] Barbu, V. Constrained control problems with convex cost in Hilbert space, J. Math. Anal. Appl., 56 (1976), pp.502-528.

[26] Barnes, E.R. Necessary and sufficient optimality conditions for a class of distributed parameter control systems,

SIAM J. Control, 9 (1971), pp.62-82.

[27] Bensoussan, A. and Temam, R. Equations aux derivées partielles stochastiques nonlinéaires, Israel J. Math., 2 (1972).

[28] Bhatker, V. and Rao, B. Variational embedding and application to distributed systems control, Int. J. Control, 23 (1976), pp.805-820.

[29] Blakeley, W.T. and Pritchard, A.J. Perturbation results and stability for linear and nonlinear evolution equations with applications to structural dynamics, Proc. IUTAM Conference on Applications of Functional Analysis in Theoretical Mechanics, Marseilles, 1975.

[30] Blakeley, W.T. and Pritchard, A.J. Stability of abstract evolution equations, Proc. 2nd IFAC Symp. on Control of Distributed Parameter Systems, Warwick, 1977.

[31] Bradshaw, A. Modal control of distributed parameter vibratory systems, Int. J. Control, 19 (1974), pp.957-968.

[32] Butkovskii, A.G. and Lerner, A.Ya. Optimal control of systems with distributed parameters, Avtomat. i Telemek., 21 (1960), pp.682-691.

[33] Butkovskii, A.G. The maximum principle for optimum systems with distributed parameters, Avtomat. i Telemek., 22 (1961), pp.1288-1301.

[34] Butkovskii, A.G., Egorov, A.I. and Lurie, K.A. Optimal control of distributed parameter systems, SIAM J. Control, 6 (1968), pp.437-476.

[35] Carmichael, D. and Goh, B.S. Optimal vibrating plates and a distributed parameter singular control problem, Int. J. Control, 26 (1977), pp.19-32.

[36] Casti, J. and Rao, H.S. An initial value method for a class of distributed control processes, IEEE Trans., AC 16 (1971), pp.513-515.

[37] Chavent, G. Identification de la non linearité d'une equation parabolique que quasi-lineaire, Report IRIA Laboria Rocquencourt, France, 1973.

[38] Chewning, W.C. Controllability of the nonlinear wave equation in several space variables, SIAM J. Control, 14 (1976), pp.19-25.

[39] Chewning, W.C. Control of nonlinear parabolic equations to meet finitely many terminal conditions, J. Math. Anal. Appl., 56 (1976), pp.185-194.

[40] Chojnowska-Michalik, M. Stochastic differential equations in Hilbert spaces and some of their applications, Thesis, Banach Centre, Warsaw, 1977.

[41] Colonius, F. and Hinrichsen, D. Optimal control of hereditary differential systems, Part I, II, Univ. Bremen, Arbeitspapiere Mathematik, Nos.2 & 8, 1976, 1977.

[42] Curtain, R.F. and Pritchard, A.J. Functional analysis in modern applied mathematics, Academic Press, 1977.

[43] Desalu, A., Gould, L. and Schweppe, Dynamic estimation of air pollution, IEEE Trans., AC 19 (1974), pp.904-910.

[44] Dolecki, S. Observability for regular processes, J. Math. Anal. Appl., 58 (1977), pp.178-188.

[45] Egorov, Yn.V. Certain problems in the theory of optimum control, Dokl. Akad. Nauk. USSR, 145 (1962), pp.720-723.

[46] Egorov, Yn.V. On optimal control of processes in distributed objects, Prikl. Mat. Mech., 27 (1963), pp.688-696.

[47] Egorov, Yn.V. Optimal control in Banach space, Soviet Math. Dokl. 4 (1963), pp.630-633.

[48] Egorov, Yn.V. Necessary conditions for optimality in Banach space, Mat. Sbornik, 764(106)(1964), pp.79-101.

[49] Egorov, A.I. Necessary optimality conditions for distributed parameter systems, SIAM J. Control, 5 (1967), pp.352-408.

[50] Egorov, A.I. Optimal control in Banach space, Math. Systems Theory, 1 (1968), pp.347-352.

[51] Fattorini, H.O. Time optimal control of solutions of operational differential equations, SIAM J. Control, 2 (1964), pp.54-59.

[52] Fattorini, H.O. Local controllability of a nonlinear wave equation, Math. System Theory, 9 (1976), pp.30-45.

[53] Friedman, A. Optimum control for parabolic equations, J. Math. Anal. Appl., 18 (1967), pp.479-491.

[54] Friedman, A. Optimum control in Banach space, J. Math. Anal. Appl., 19 (1967), pp.35-55.

[55] Friedman, A. Optimum control in Banach space with fixed end points, J. Math. Anal. Appl., 24 (1968), pp.161-181.

[56] Friedman, A. Differential games of pursuit in Banach space, J. Math. Anal. Appl., 25 (1969), pp.93-113.

[57] Fuhrmann, P.A. On realisation of linear systems and applications to some questions of stability, Math. Systems Theory, 9 (1976), pp.132-141.

[58] Fuhrmann, P.A. Exact controllability and observability and realization theory in Hilbert space, J. Math. Anal. Appl., 53 (1970), pp.377-392.

[59] Fuhrmann, P.A. On series and parallel coupling of a class of discrete time infinite dimensional systems, SIAM J. Control, 14 (1976), pp.339-358.

[60] Gilai, D. and Tabak, D. An alternative formulation of a distributed parameter optimal control problem applied to nuclear shielding, IEEE Trans., AC 21 (1976), pp.668-676.

[61] Giurgiu, M. A feedback solution of a linear quadratic problem for boundary control of the heat equation, Rev. Roum. Pures et Appl., 20 (1975), pp.383-403.

[62] Goldwyn, R.M., Sriram, K.P. and Graham, M. Time optimal control of a linear diffusion process, SIAM J. Control, 5 (1967), pp.295-308.

[63] Goodson, R. and Klein, R. A definition and some results for distributed system observability, IEEE Trans. AC 15 (1970), pp.165-174.

[64] Hamza, M.H. and Rasmy, M.E. Optimal control of distributed parameter systems with discrete constrained inputs, Int. J. Control, 20 (1974), pp.159-168.

[65] Halanay, A. Optimal control for systems with time lag, SIAM J. Control, 6 (1968), pp.215-234.

[66] Hemming, F. and Vandelirde, V.D. An optimal control problem in Banach space, J. Math. Anal. Appl., 39 (1972), pp.647-654.

[67] Ichikawa, A. Linear quadratic games in Hilbert space, SIAM J. Control, 14 (1976), pp.120-136.

[68] Ichikawa, A. Optimal control of a linear stochastic evolution equation with state and control dependent noise, Proc. IMA Conference on Recent Theoretical Developments in Control, Leicester, 1976.

[69] Ichikawa, A. Evolution equations with delay, Control Theory Centre Report No.52, University of Warwick, 1976.

[70] Ichikawa, A. Quadratic control and filtering for evolution equations with delay in control and observation, Control Theory Centre Report No.53, University of Warwick, 1976.

[71] Ichikawa, A. Linear stochastic evolution equations in Hilbert space, Control Theory Centre Report No.51, University of Warwick, 1976 to be published in J. Diff. Eqns.

[72] Ichikawa, A. Dynamic programming approach to stochastic evolution equations, Control Theory Centre Report No.60, University of Warwick, 1977.

[73] Ichikawa, A. and Pritchard, A.J. Existence, uniqueness and stability of nonlinear evolution equations, Control Theory Centre Report No.65, University of Warwick, 1977.

[74] Jacobs, M.Q. and Langenhop, C.E. Criteria for function space controllability of linear neutral systems, SIAM J. Control, 14 (1976), pp.1009-1048.

[75] Jacobs, M.Q. and Kao, T. An optimum settling problem for time lag systems, J. Math. Anal. Appl., 40 (1972), pp687-707.

[76] Johnson, T.L. Minimum-energy terminal state control of first order hyperbolic systems in one spatial variable using the method of characteristics, SIAM J. Control, 2 (1973), pp.11-19.

[77] Johnson, T.L. and Athans, M. A minimum principle for smooth first order systems, IEEE Trans. AC 19 (1974), pp.136-139.

[78] Klamka, J. Absolute controllability of linear systems with time variable delays in control, Int. J. Control, 26 (1977), pp.57-64.

[79] Klamka, J. Relative and absolute controllability of discrete systems with delays in the control, Int. J. Control, 26 (1977), pp.65-74.

[80] Klamka, J. Minimum energy control of discrete systems with delays in the control, Int. J. Control, 26 (1977), pp.737-744.

[81] Klamka, J. On the controllability of linear systems with delays in the control, Int. J. Control, 25 (1977), pp.875-884.

[82] Koivo, H.N. and Lee, E.B. Controller synthesis for linear systems with retarded state and control variables and quadratic cost, Automatica, 8 (1972), pp.203-208.

[83] Knowles, G. The time optimal control of infinite dimensions SIAM J. Control, 14 (1976), pp.919-933.

[84] Kubrusly, C.S. Distributed parameter system identification - a survey, Int. J. Control, 26 (1977), pp.509-536.

[85] Kusic, G. Finite differences to implement the solution for optimal control of distributed parameter systems, IEEE Trans. AC-15 (1970), pp.397-400.

[86] Lamont, G.B. and Kumar, K.S.P. State estimation in distributed parameter systems via least squares and invariant embedding, J. Math. Anal. Appl., 38 (1972), pp.588-606.

[87] Lee, K.Y., Chow, S., and Barr, R. On the control of discrete time distributed parameter systems, SIAM J. Control, 10 (1972), pp.361-376.

[88] Liang, D.F. and Christensen, G.S. New filtering and smoothing algorithms for discrete non-linear delayed systems with coloured noise, Int. J. Control, 25 (1977), pp.821-826.

[89] Manitius, A. Optimal control of hereditary systems, Control Theory and Topics in Functional Analysis, Vol.III, Int. Atomic Energy Agency, Vienna, 1976, pp.43-178.

[90] Mayhew, M.J.E. Discrete time control of distributed parameter systems, Proc. IMA Conference on Recent Theoretical Developments in Control, Bath, 1972.

[91] Mayhew, M.J.E., and Pritchard, A.J. Feedback from discrete points for distributed parameter systems, Int. J. Control, 14 (1971), pp.619-630.

[92] Mayhew, M.J.E., and Pritchard, A.J. A reduction of the Riccati equation for distributed parameter systems, Elec. Letters, 17 (1971).

[93] McGlothin, G.E. A modal control model for distributed systems with application to boundary controllability, Int. J. Control, 20 (1974), pp.417-432.

[94] McGlothin, G.E. Optimal control of one dimensional distributed parameter systems with mixed boundary conditions, Int. J. Control, 20 (1974), pp.945-954.

[95] McGlothin, G.E. Optimal control of distributed parameter systems with penalties on spatial derivatives of the state, Int. J. Control, 24 (1976), pp.445-466.

[96] Métivier, M. and Pistone, G. Une formule d'isométrie l'integrale stochastique hilbertienne et équations d'evolution lineaires stochastiques, Z. Warh., 33 (1975), pp.1-18.

[97] Meyer, G.H. On fixed time control problems in a Banach space, SIAM J. Control, 8 (1970), pp.41-54.

[98] Michel, P. Generalized controls: a necessary condition for optimality in a Banach space, J. Math. Anal. Appl., 50 (1975), pp.20-41.

[99] Minamide, N. and Nakamura, N. A minimum cost control problem in a Banach space, J. Math. Anal. Appl., 36 (1971), pp.73-85.

[100] Mossino, J. An application of duality to distributed optimal control problems with constraints on the control and state, J. Math. Anal. Appl., 50 (1975), pp.223-242.

[101] Nieva, R., Christensen, G.S., and El Haivary, M.E. Suboptimal control of a nuclear reactor using functional analysis, Int. J. Control, 26 (1977), pp.145-156.

[102] Pardoux, E. Equations aux derivées partielles stochastiques nonlineaires monotone, Thèse l'Université Paris Sud, France, 1975.

[103] Polis, M.P. and Goodson, R.E. Parameter identification in distributed systems: a synthesizing overview, Proc. IEEE, 64 (1976), pp.45-60.

[104] Porter, W. On the optimal control of distributed systems, SIAM J. Control, 4 (1966), pp.466-472.

[105] Prabhu, S.S. and McCausland, I. Method of moments and controllability of certain distributed parameter systems, Int. J. Control, 23 (1976), pp.89-96.

[106] Pritchard, A.J. and Parker, K.T. Simplified Liapunov matrix equation with application to the control of distributed parameter systems, Elec. Letters, 7 (1971), pp.398-399.

[107] Pritchard, A.J. and Ryan, E.P. Control and identification of distributed parameter systems, Proc. IFIP Conference on Distributed Parameter System Modelling and Identification, Rome, 1976.

[108] Pritchard, A.J. and Crouch, P.E. Modelling and control of distributed parameter systems, Proc. IFIP Conference on Modelling and Optimization, Nice, 1975.

[109] Pritchard, A.J. and Parker, K.T. A lower bound for the cost functional for control problems in Hilbert space, J. Inst. Math. Appl., 13 (1974), pp.97-110.

[110] Pritchard, A.J. Sensitivity analysis for evolution equations in Hilbert space, Proc. 3rd. IFAC Symposium on Sensitivity, Adaptivity, Optimality, Ischia, 1973.

[111] Proc. 1st. IFAC Symposium on the Control of Distributed Parameter Systems, Banff, 1971.

[112] Proc. IMA Conference on Control of Systems described by Partial Differential Equations, Control Theory Centre Report No.3, Warwick, 1971.

[113] Proc. IFIP Conference on Modelling and Identification of Distributed Parameter Systems, Rome, 1976.

[114] Proc. 2nd. IFAC Symposium on the Control of Distributed Parameter Systems, Warwick, 1977.

[115] Ray, W.H. Distributed parameter state estimation algorithms and applications - a survey, Proc. 6th. IFAC Congress, Boston, 1975.

[116] Robinson, A.C. A survey of optimal control of distributed parameter systems, Automatica, 7 (1971), pp.371-388.

[117] Rogak, E.D., Kazannoff, N.D., and Scott-Thomas, J.F. Sufficient conditions for bang-bang control in Hilbert space, J. Opt. Th. Appl., 5 (1970), pp.1-11.

[118] Rogak, E.D. and Scott-Thomas, J.F. On necessary conditions for optimality in Banach spcae, J. Math. Anal. Appl., 41 (1973), pp.44-53.

[119] Russell, D.L. The Kuhn Tucker conditions in Banach space with an application to control theory, J. Math. Anal. Appl., 15 (1966), pp.200-212.

[120] Russell, D.L. Control theory of hyperbolic equations related to certain questions in harmonic analysis and spectral theory, J. Math. Anal. Appl., 40 (1972), pp.336-368.

[121] Sakawa, Y. and Matsushita, T. Feedback stabilization of a class of distributed systems and construction of a state estimator, IEEE Trans. AC-20 (1975), pp.748-753.

[122] Schmaedeke, V. Mathematical theory of optimal control for semilinear hyperbolic systems in two independent variables, SIAM J. Control, 5 (1967), pp.138-152.

[123] Seinfeld, J.H., Gavales, G.R., and Hwang, M. Nonlinear filtering in distributed parameter systems, J. Dyn. Sys. Meas. Control, 936 (1971), pp.157-163.

[124] Seinfeld, J.H. Nonlinear estimation for partial differential equations, Chem. Eng. Sci. (1969), pp.75-83.

[125] Sheirah, M.A. and Hamza, M.H. Optimal control of distributed parameter systems, Int. J. Control, 19 (1974), pp. 891-902.

[126] Shelar, M.S. and Wiberg, D.M. Canonical equations for boundary feedback control of stochastic distributed parameter systems, Automatica, 8 (1972), pp.287-298.

[127] Shuckla, V. and Srinath, M.D. Optimal filtering in linear distributed systems with multiple time delays, Int. J. Control, 16 (1972), pp.673-687.

[128] Simionescu, C. Optimal control problems in Sobolev spaces with weights, SIAM J. Control, 14 (1976), pp.137-143

[129] Slemrod, M. An application of maximal dissipative sets in control theory, J. Math. Anal. Appl., 46 (1974), pp.369-387.

[130] Suryanarayana, M.B. Necessary conditions for optimisation problems with hyperbolic partial differential equations, SIAM J. Control, 2 (1973), pp.130-147.

[131] Viand, D. Control problems with time lags, J. Math. Anal. Appl., 50 (1975), pp.1-19.

[132] Vinkurov, V.R. Optimal control of processes described by integral equations I - III, SIAM J. Control, 7 (1969), pp. 324-355.

[133] Vinter, R. Some remarks concerning perturbed evolution operators with applications to delay equations, Dept. of Computing and Control Report, Imperial College, 1975.

[134] Viot, M. Solution faibles d'equations aux derivées partielles stochastiques nonlineaires, Thèse, IRIA, Rocquencourt, 1976.

[135] Viswanathan, J. Estimation problems in affine hereditary differential systems, Thesis, School of Automation, Indian Institute of Science, Bangalore, 1975.

[136] Wang, P.K.C. Control of distributed parameter systems, Advances in Control Systems, 1 (1964), Academic Press.

[137] Wang, P.K.C. Optimum control of distributed parameter systems with time delay, IEEE Trans. AC-9 (1964), pp.13-22.

[138] Wang, P.K.C. Optimal confinement of collisionless plasmas by localized time varying electric fields, Int. J. Control, 19 (1974), pp.449-472.

[139] Wang, P.K.C. Optimal control of a class of linear symmetric hyperbolic systems with applications to plasma confinements, J. Math. Anal. Appl., 28 (1969), pp. 594-608.

[140] Wang, P.K.C. Bibliography of distributed parameter systems, Int. J. Control, 7 (1968), pp.101-116.

[141] Wang, P.K.C. Time optimal control of time lag systems with time lag controls, J. Math. Anal. Appl., 52 (1975), pp. 366-378.

[142] Wang, P.K.C. Optimal control of parabolic systems with boundary conditions involving time delays, SIAM J. Control, 13 (1975), pp.274-293.

[143] Webb, G.F. Autonomous nonlinear functional differential equations and nonlinear semigroups, J. Math. Anal. Appl., 46 (1974), pp.1-12.

[144] Wong, J.K. and Sondack, A. Stochastic optimum pointwise regulation control for linear discrete time distributed parameter systems, Int. J. Control, 21 (1975), pp. 593-610.

[145] Wong, J.K. and Sondack, A. Stochastic suboptimal pointwise regulator control for linear discrete time distributed parameter systems, Int. J. Control, 21 (1975), pp. 611-626,

[146] Yakowitz, S. and Nosen, P. On the identification of inhomogeneous parameter in dynamic linear partial differential equations, J. Math. Anal. Appl., 53 (1976), pp.521-538.

[147] Yu, T.K. and Seinfeld, J.H. Observability of a class of hyperbolic distributed systems, IEEE Trans. AC-16 (1971), pp.495-497.

[148] Yu, T.K., Seinfeld, J.H., and Ray, W.H. Filtering in nonlinear time delay systems, IEEE Trans. AC-19 (1974), pp. 324-333.

[149] Zabczyk, J. On optimal control of discrete time systems in Hilbert space, SIAM J. Control, 13 (1975), pp.1217-1234.

[150] Zabczyk, J. On the stability of infinite dimensional stochastic systems, Banach Centre, Warsaw, 1976.

Lecture Notes in Economics and Mathematical Systems

For information about Vols. 1–99 please contact your bookseller or Springer-Verlag

Vol. 100: B. S. Duran and P. L. Odell, Cluster Analysis. A Survey. VI, 137 pages. 1974.

Vol. 101: W. M. Wonham, Linear Multivariable Control. A Geometric Approach. X, 344 pages. 1974.

Vol. 102: Analyse Convexe et Ses Applications. Comptes Rendus, Janvier 1974. Edited by J.-P. Aubin. IV, 244 pages. 1974.

Vol. 103: D. E. Boyce, A. Farhi, R. Weischedel, Optimal Subset Selection. Multiple Regression, Interdependence and Optimal Network Algorithms. XIII, 187 pages. 1974.

Vol. 104: S. Fujino, A Neo-Keynesian Theory of Inflation and Economic Growth. V, 96 pages. 1974.

Vol. 105: Optimal Control Theory and its Applications. Part I. Proceedings 1973. Edited by B. J. Kirby. VI, 425 pages. 1974.

Vol. 106: Optimal Control Theory and its Applications. Part II. Proceedings 1973. Edited by B. J. Kirby. VI, 403 pages. 1974.

Vol. 107: Control Theory, Numerical Methods and Computer Systems Modeling. International Symposium, Rocquencourt, June 17–21, 1974. Edited by A. Bensoussan and J. L. Lions. VIII, 757 pages. 1975.

Vol. 108: F. Bauer et al., Supercritical Wing Sections II. A Handbook. V, 296 pages. 1975.

Vol. 109: R. von Randow, Introduction to the Theory of Matroids. IX, 102 pages. 1975.

Vol. 110: C. Striebel, Optimal Control of Discrete Time Stochastic Systems. III. 208 pages. 1975.

Vol. 111: Variable Structure Systems with Application to Economics and Biology. Proceedings 1974. Edited by A. Ruberti and R. R. Mohler. VI, 321 pages. 1975.

Vol. 112: J. Wilhlem, Objectives and Multi-Objective Decision Making Under Uncertainty. IV, 111 pages. 1975.

Vol. 113: G. A. Aschinger, Stabilitätsaussagen über Klassen von Matrizen mit verschwindenden Zeilensummen. V, 102 Seiten. 1975.

Vol. 114: G. Uebe, Produktionstheorie. XVII, 301 Seiten. 1976.

Vol. 115: Anderson et al., Foundations of System Theory: Finitary and Infinitary Conditions. VII, 93 pages. 1976

Vol. 116: K. Miyazawa, Input-Output Analysis and the Structure of Income Distribution. IX, 135 pages. 1976.

Vol. 117: Optimization and Operations Research. Proceedings 1975. Edited by W. Oettli and K. Ritter. IV, 316 pages. 1976.

Vol. 118: Traffic Equilibrium Methods, Proceedings 1974. Edited by M. A. Florian. XXIII, 432 pages. 1976.

Vol. 119: Inflation in Small Countries. Proceedings 1974. Edited by H. Frisch. VI, 356 pages. 1976.

Vol. 120: G. Hasenkamp, Specification and Estimation of Multiple-Output Production Functions. VII, 151 pages. 1976.

Vol. 121: J. W. Cohen, On Regenerative Processes in Queueing Theory. IX, 93 pages. 1976.

Vol. 122: M. S. Bazaraa, and C. M. Shetty, Foundations of Optimization VI. 193 pages. 1976

Vol. 123: Multiple Criteria Decision Making. Kyoto 1975. Edited by M. Zeleny. XXVII, 345 pages. 1976.

Vol. 124: M. J. Todd. The Computation of Fixed Points and Applications. VII, 129 pages. 1976.

Vol. 125: Karl C. Mosler. Optimale Transportnetze. Zur Bestimmung ihres kostengünstigsten Standorts bei gegebener Nachfrage. VI, 142 Seiten. 1976.

Vol. 126: Energy, Regional Science and Public Policy. Energy and Environment I. Proceedings 1975. Edited by M. Chatterji and P. Van Rompuy. VIII, 316 pages. 1976.

Vol. 127: Environment, Regional Science and Interregional Modeling. Energy and Environment II. Proceedings 1975. Edited by M. Chatterji and P. Van Rompuy. IX, 211 pages. 1976.

Vol. 128: Integer Programming and Related Areas. A Classified Bibliography. Edited by C. Kastning. XII, 495 pages. 1976.

Vol. 129: H.-J. Lüthi, Komplementaritäts- und Fixpunktalgorithmen in der mathematischen Programmierung. Spieltheorie und Ökonomie. VII, 145 Seiten. 1976.

Vol. 130: Multiple Criteria Decision Making, Jouy-en-Josas, France. Proceedings 1975. Edited by H. Thiriez and S. Zionts. VI, 409 pages. 1976.

Vol. 131: Mathematical Systems Theory. Proccedings 1975. Edited by G. Marchesini and S. K. Mitter. X, 408 pages. 1976.

Vol. 132: U. H. Funke, Mathematical Models in Marketing. A Collection of Abstracts. XX, 514 pages. 1976.

Vol. 133: Warsaw Fall Seminars in Mathematical Economics 1975. Edited by M. W. Loś, J. Loś, and A. Wieczorek. V. 159 pages. 1976.

Vol. 134: Computing Methods in Applied Sciences and Engineering. Proceedings 1975. VIII, 390 pages. 1976.

Vol. 135: H. Haga, A Disequilibrium – Equilibrium Model with Money and Bonds. A Keynesian – Walrasian Synthesis. VI, 119 pages. 1976.

Vol. 136: E. Kofler und G. Menges, Entscheidungen bei unvollständiger Information. XII, 357 Seiten. 1976.

Vol. 137: R. Wets, Grundlagen Konvexer Optimierung. VI, 146 Seiten. 1976.

Vol. 138: K. Okuguchi, Expectations and Stability in Oligopoly Models. VI, 103 pages. 1976.

Vol. 139: Production Theory and Its Applications. Proceedings. Edited by H. Albach and G. Bergendahl. VIII, 193 pages. 1977.

Vol. 140: W. Eichhorn and J. Voeller, Theory of the Price Index. Fisher's Test Approach and Generalizations. VII, 95 pages. 1976.

Vol. 141: Mathematical Economics and Game Theory. Essays in Honor of Oskar Morgenstern. Edited by R. Henn and O. Moeschlin. XIV, 703 pages. 1977.

Vol. 142: J. S. Lane, On Optimal Population Paths. V, 123 pages. 1977.

Vol. 143: B. Näslund, An Analysis of Economic Size Distributions. XV, 100 pages. 1977.

Vol. 144: Convex Analysis and Its Applications. Proceedings 1976. Edited by A. Auslender. VI, 219 pages. 1977.

Vol. 145: J. Rosenmüller, Extreme Games and Their Solutions. IV, 126 pages. 1977

Vol. 146: In Search of Economic Indicators. Edited by W. H. Strigel. XVI, 198 pages. 1977.

Vol. 147: Resource Allocation and Division of Space. Proceedings. Edited by T. Fujii and R. Sato. VIII, 184 pages. 1977.

Vol. 148: C. E. Mandl, Simulationstechnik und Simulationsmodelle in den Sozial- und Wirtschaftswissenschaften. IX, 173 Seiten. 1977.

Vol. 149: Stationäre und schrumpfende Bevölkerungen: Demographisches Null- und Negativwachstum in Österreich. Herausgegeben von G. Feichtinger. VI, 262 Seiten. 1977.

Vol. 150: Bauer et al., Supercritical Wing Sections III. VI, 179 pages. 1977.

Vol. 151: C. A. Schneeweiß, Inventory-Production Theory. VI, 116 pages. 1977.

Vol. 152: Kirsch et al., Notwendige Optimalitätsbedingungen und ihre Anwendung. VI, 157 Seiten. 1978.

Vol. 153: Kombinatorische Entscheidungsprobleme: Methoden und Anwendungen. Herausgegeben von T. M. Liebling und M. Rössler. VIII, 206 Seiten. 1978.

Vol. 154: Problems and Instruments of Business Cycle Analysis. Proceedings 1977. Edited by W. H. Strigel. VI, 442 pages. 1978.

Vol. 155: Multiple Criteria Problem Solving. Proceedings 1977. Edited by S. Zionts. VIII, 567 pages. 1978.

Vol. 156: B. Näslund and B. Sellstedt, Neo-Ricardian Theory. With Applications to Some Current Economic Problems. VI, 165 pages. 1978.